The Political Economy of European Security

What is the relationship between private actors and international institutions in global governance, as institutions such as the EU develop aspects of political authority once in the sole domain of nation states? Important areas of recent EU development have been immigration, security, and defense policies. Are these EU policies the result of strategic imperatives, or are they also driven by the political economy of markets? Kaija Schilde argues that answers require evaluating the EU in the comparative tradition of the political development of authority. Drawing on industry documents, interviews, interest group data, an original survey, and comparative political theory, *The Political Economy of European Security* demonstrates that interest groups can change the outcomes of developing political institutions because they provide sources of external capacity, which in turn can produce authority over time. In this way, the EU is like a developing state in its relationship with interest groups.

KAIJA SCHILDE is an assistant professor of international relations at the Boston University Pardee School of Global Studies.

The Political Economy of European Security

Kaija Schilde

Boston University

CAMBRIDGE
UNIVERSITY PRESS

University Printing House, Cambridge CB2 8BS, United Kingdom

One Liberty Plaza, 20th Floor, New York, NY 10006, USA

477 Williamstown Road, Port Melbourne, VIC 3207, Australia

4843/24, 2nd Floor, Ansari Road, Daryaganj, Delhi - 110002, India

79 Anson Road, #06-04/06, Singapore 079906

Cambridge University Press is part of the University of Cambridge.

It furthers the University's mission by disseminating knowledge in the pursuit of education, learning and research at the highest international levels of excellence.

www.cambridge.org
Information on this title: www.cambridge.org/9781107198432
DOI: 10.1017/9781108182492

© Kaija Schilde 2017

First published 2017

Printed in the United Kingdom by Clays, St Ives plc

A catalogue record for this publication is available from the British Library

ISBN 978-1-107-19843-2 Hardback

Contents

Figures

Tables

Preface

This book touches on three areas of interest for scholars of politics and government. It is about the foundations of political authority in the twenty-first century, how bottom-up interest groups influence the development of political institutions, and the origins of defense and security organizations. It argues that interest groups change the outcomes of developing political institutions such as the European Union because they are sources of external capacity. It compares the European Union to developing states: a framework in which interest groups are sometimes older, more organized, and better resourced than new public institutions. For interest groups, the European Union provides an opportunity structure for projecting interests and agendas. For the EU, interest groups provide the expertise, resources, and ideas that legitimize involvement in public policies that were previously the exclusive domain of European nation states.

I began this project with the aim of demonstrating the significance of state–society relationships in the political development of the EU. As the project developed, I observed that this interaction was intensifying in a policy area where interest groups traditionally are less mobilized and influential: the high politics of defense. What made this particularly puzzling was that it was happening in an international organization with no defense mandate. Only a few years into the project did the EU begin to develop institutions for defense cooperation.

On the other hand, this was not the pattern of political development across all EU policy areas. In the case of asylum and immigration, the opposite phenomenon was happening: the EU had increasing authority for making European policies, but no interest groups took notice, and the EU made little progress in the area for over a decade. This began to change when defense interest groups mobilized to define European security markets, resulting in immigration, asylum, and border policies becoming more security oriented. After immigration and internal security policies merged, the political development of EU institutions accelerated.

Although I did not originally intend to study the cases of internal security and external defense, they were both outliers in patterns of EU state–society relations. Over the course of my research, internal security and external defense both became increasingly mainstream in the EU project. This inquiry took on added significance with the growing migration and refugee crisis on the borders of Europe. And external developments such as terror attacks, instability in the EU's southern and eastern neighborhoods, and political shocks in the United States and to the NATO alliance have elevated the likelihood of defense cooperation from impossible to probable.

After I completed the initial research, a new phenomenon took hold in EU affairs: EU internal security and external defense agendas have been effectively combined into a single policy area. French and Belgian nationals committed the November 2015 Paris attacks that killed 130. It was a domestic attack committed by European nationals, a matter involving criminal movement across the internal borders of the EU. In response to the attacks, France invoked the EU Article 42(7) mutual defense clause. This is an example of what had been internal security blurring into external defense. The blurring has also gone in the other direction: in response to the refugee crisis, the EU announced a Common Security and Defense Policy (CSDP) mission to the Mediterranean to fight human trafficking to Europe. The mission – Operation EUNAV-FOR MED – was designed to cooperate with internal security organizations such as Frontex (now the European Border and Coast Guard Agency) and Europol. This came after the increasing "securitization" of border security over the previous decade. In this case, external defense blurred into internal security. Border security and migration were previously an internal security matter.

These anecdotes are not outliers. Erasing the boundaries between internal and external has become a central feature of EU policymaking. The 2013 EU Comprehensive Approach to external conflict and crises and the 2016 EU Global Strategy on Foreign and Security Policy both emphasized the close link between internal and external security policies. This link goes beyond agenda setting. The 2009–15 Stockholm Programme proposed fighting transnational crime through integrated CSDP missions and EU internal security. Multiple internal security and external defense agencies interact through an FSJ (Freedom, Security, and Justice)–CSDP roadmap, which coordinates joint committees, agreements, and policy design.

The conventional wisdom about this blurring is that it is driven by twenty-first century events, primarily the transnational, internal, and external threat of asymmetrical terror attacks after September 11, 2001.

In 2009, an EU directive on defense procurement stated that the EU's "overall approach to security ... responds to changes in the strategic environment. The emergence of asymmetrical transnational threats has increasingly blurred the boundary between external and internal and military and non-military security."[1] This book, however, proposes that this kind of reasoning is insufficient for explaining the European Union in the beginning of the twenty-first century. An important and often forgotten part of how foreign policy agendas are created has to do with the political economy of defense interests and institutions. The merging of first immigration and security policy, and later security and defense policy, although driven by strategic changes, also has origins in the imperatives of security and defense markets.

---

[1] Defence Procurement Directive, EU Directive 2009/81/EC. http://eur-lex.europa.eu/legal-content/EN/TXT/?uri=celex:32009L0081

Acknowledgments

In the decade I have been researching and writing this book, I have accumulated more debts than I can acknowledge here. My greatest debt is to Ian Lustick, my advisor at the University of Pennsylvania. I still recall the day I attended a Rand workshop in DC on complex systems, and heard from another attendee that Ian Lustick was studying the evolution of political institutions and identities. This news, and meeting Ian, changed the direction of my life. While the journey started with complexity theory and agent-based modeling, it morphed into the more traditional but broader study of state-building and political authority. His fearless intellectual curiosity, boundless energy, and democratic pedagogy continue to inspire me. I am grateful for his support, his willingness to discuss all aspects of the mind and the human condition, and his devotion to his family and friends. I am also deeply grateful to his wife Terri for her kindness and wisdom.

I am likewise indebted to the professors and advisors who advised my research and academic development: Mark Pollack, Tom Callaghy, Rudy Sil, Tulia Falleti, Ed Mansfield, Avery Goldstein, Bob Vitalis, Don Kettl, Heiner Schulz, Brendan O'Leary, Eileen Doherty-Sil, Vincent Price, Diana Mutz, and Rogers Smith. My graduate student cohort at UPenn continues to be like family: Dani Miodownik and Lilach Nir, Darren Schreiber, Sarah Salwen, Keren Yarhi-Milo, Matthew Tubin, Ryan Grauer, Allison Evans, Jenny Stepp Breen, Wendy Ginsburg, David Faris, Barbara Elias, Meredith Wooten, Murad Idris, Meral Uğur Çınar, Max Prilutsky, Tim and Joanna Weaver, Britt Cartrite, Ian Hartshorn, David Bateman, and Alan Bell (www.alanslegacy.org).

I could not have written this book without the support of many individuals and institutions. The University of Pennsylvania and the Christopher H. Browne Center at the University of Pennsylvania generously supported my research and allowed me to attend conferences and workshops at the early stages of the project. John Haslam of Cambridge University Press and three anonymous book reviewers contributed detailed and invaluable comments, which inspired significant changes and improvements to the book. Critical insights from Noora Lori, Manjari Miller, Cornel Ban, Mark Blyth, Peter Katzenstein, Andrew James, Jonathan Caverley, Sidney Tarrow, Alex Cooley, and Jonas Tallberg all changed the book for the better. I want to particularly thank Pablo Yanguas and Jeremy Menchik for reading the penultimate version of the manuscript. They all have my gratitude for their kindness and insights.

I also thank the individuals whom I do not name in order to preserve their anonymity amongst a small policy community in sensitive policy areas. I am indebted to the officials, politicians, civil servants, and industry representatives who provided insights and analyses. For important background information on European defense cooperation at the earliest stages of my research, I am especially grateful to Robert Bell, Frank Boland, Daniel Keohane, Robert Draper, Robert Cooper, Constanze Stelzenmüller, Antonio Missiroli, Brooks Tigner, Burkard Schmitt, Andrew James, Aude Fleurant, and Jolyon Howorth. And for my education on the intricacies of the world of EU lobbying, I thank Louise Harvey, Sara Tesorieri, and Richard Hudson.

I could not have written the original dissertation without the daily companionship, grace, and humor of my writing partner Aida Gureghian. We were the daily visitors to the Burke Library at the Union Theological Seminary for over 7 months of nonstop writing. When writing at the seminary got too quiet, we would write at the Ace Hotel lobby or other NYC coffee shops until the evening hours, when the dissonance of academic writing was too much in contrast with the revelers around us.

This book argues that the EU should be studied like a normal polity. While the claim is new, the territory it covers is not. It builds upon established ideas about political institutions, mostly from outside EU studies. It owes much to research in comparative politics, sociology, and new institutional economics. While the citations in the book reflect the breadth of this intellectual tradition and debt, I am indebted to Susan Strange, Linda Weiss, Peter Evans, and Paul Verkuil for providing powerful intellectual inspiration.

Since 2010, I have been an assistant professor of international relations at the Pardee School of Global Studies at Boston University, where I am lucky to have a supportive department, progressive leadership, and an extraordinary group of colleagues. Henrik Selin, Thomas Berger, Cathie Jo Martin, Joe Fewsmith, Jessica Stern, Susan Eckstein, Betty Anderson, and Kevin Gallagher have been wonderful mentors. I owe my deepest gratitude to my mentor Vivien Schmidt, who has been central to the completion and revisions of the book. I am also grateful for the leadership of Richard Norton, Erik Goldstein, William Grimes,

Andy Bacevich, and Adil Najam, who have built a culture of collegiality and academic excellence. I am also lucky to have a wonderful junior faculty cohort: Manjari Miller, Jeremy Menchik, Cornel Ban, Renata Keller, Julie Klinger, Noora Lori, Michael Woldemariam, and Min Ye. And Rosella Cappella Zielinski is a threefer: graduate school confidant and friend, junior faculty colleague, and inspirational collaborator and co-author. Working with Rosella has changed my life for the better.

At BU, I have had the pleasure of working with a number of talented individuals who have supported the research and writing of this book: Florian Bodamer, Elizabeth Amrien, Claire Coffey, Lenka Wieluns, Matthew Kolasa, Kate Skow, and Alexander Falco. I am also grateful for the administrative support and friendship of Vicky Kelberer-McKee, Noorjehan Khan, Victoria Puyat, Christian Estrella, and Allison Patenaude.

I acknowledge the support of many individuals and institutions to justify any merits of the book. For errors in research, analysis, or conclusions, only I am responsible.

I want to thank all of my friends for their patience, friendship, and understanding. My debts go beyond this list, but I want to acknowledge friends who supported me at critical stages of the project. To Sara Tesorieri for sharing her Brussels apartment for extended periods of time. For the support of Colleen O'Brien Cherry, Ethan and Sunday Howe, Greer Boyle Thornton and Christian Thornton, Claire and Dick Laton-Taylor, Krista Coombs and Andy Schlatter, Stephanie Anderson, Trudy Pendergraft, Bree Richey and Scott Pressler, Paula Lytle and Michael Segal.

I could not have finished this book without the trusted support of my children's caregivers: Mary Carmen Tello, Maggie Rosenthal, Jonathan Shepherd, Becky Shepherd, Janete Domingos, Libby Meehan, Gwyndolyn Jones, Lavonne Bishop, Peejay Clarke, and Sara Rytivaara.

I owe particular thanks to my friends and family. My brother Martin is my intellectual guide through life, with a wit and a diligence to truth and social justice. My childhood was shaped by strong women who persisted: my aunt Margarete and my grandmothers Gwen and Ruth. My parents gave me a happy childhood filled with travel, books, ideas, and ethics. My mother Karen has been my inspiration. I am thankful for the paths she opened and for her unconditional love and support. My father Klaus has been a source of wisdom and grace. I am also grateful for the patience and generosity of my in-laws, Amy and Joe Langhirt.

I dedicate this book to my husband Matt, who has supported me with confidence, patience, and humor. He parented our young children alone during the countless days, nights, and weekends when I had to work. And I dedicate the book to our joyful daughters Sylvie and Naomi. I hope that someday they will know how much happiness they have brought us, and how lucky we are to be on this adventure together.

Introduction

On December 1, 2009, the Lisbon Treaty of the European Union ushered in the Common Security and Defense Policy. The Lisbon Treaty formalized more structured cooperation in EU defense matters and created a European Defence Agency (EDA) for coordinating and streamlining European defense markets. That said, the Lisbon Treaty changed little about EU defense policy. It was politically developed well before the treaty was implemented. The EDA was founded in 2004, a full five years before the Lisbon Treaty gave it legal recognition and formal EU legal authority. During those five years, the EDA had developed policy agendas on defense cooperation, defense industry consolidation, joint European defense investment programs, and other defense and security market reforms. In other words, it developed a political agenda for transforming the political economy of European defense long before it had the legal foundation to do so.

At the same time that defense cooperation was formalized, the EU's internal security domain of Justice and Home Affairs (JHA) was mired in paralysis despite having a legal basis in EU treaty for over a decade. JHA comprises police cooperation, border security, and immigration policy – or internal security. Before 1997, JHA was under the sole authority of EU member states. After 1997, the Amsterdam Treaty supranationalized parts of it, including illegal immigration, visas, asylum, and civil security cooperation. Amsterdam gave the EU legal authority to set policy agendas and legislate over these areas, but there has been little EU policy output, policy success, or implementation until very recently, a "delay" of nearly 15 years. Similarly, while the European Agency for the Management of Operational Cooperation at the External Borders, Frontex, was founded in 2004, it was not until 2011 that its operational authority, budget, and resources increased dramatically, granting it effective operational capacity for the first time. In JHA, the EU possessed the legal foundations for regulating, legislating, and agenda setting but initially failed to do so.

These defense and security policy domains share a common background yet divergent paths of political development. Internal security is increasingly supranational, while external defense remains intergovernmental. Until very recently, JHA has lagged in both policy output and agenda setting, while defense has had accelerated political development. What explains this variation? What do these processes reveal about the fundamentals of the European security project and how political authority over defense or security is created in an emerging political institution? And how does this inform our understanding of the relationship between private actors and international institutions in global governance more generally, as international institutions take on aspects of statehood once in the sole domain of nation states?

I argue that mobilized transnational interest groups created informal European policy institutions that, in turn, shaped the timing and development of formal EU institutions. In the case of defense, industry groups mobilized to Brussels as early as 1990 and created informal European institutions for developing EU policy solutions. In contrast, interest groups were initially absent from the EU JHA agenda. They did not mobilize in response to EU authority or create informal institutions.

A shift in the security domain occurred in the late 2000s, when defense interest groups re-organized themselves into informal security institutions in civilian, homeland, and border security. Because of this shift in interest-group interests and informal institutions, the patterns of political development in defense and security have converged over time. Immediately prior to the 2003 creation of the EDA and the 2011 expansion of Frontex's authority and resources, interest groups mobilized and created informal institutions in the domains of both external and internal security.

International institutions such as the EU are supposed to derive power from the authority delegated to them by member states. But the amount of formal authority European member states give to the EU does not always explain how the EU governs. In some policy areas, the EU is an ineffective political authority and agenda setter vis-à-vis powerful member states and economic or social actors. In other policy areas, the EU develops innovative policy agendas and effective legislation. The difference in these outcomes depends on the EU's relative governing capacity: the ability of a political authority to achieve its chosen outcomes. Features of bureaucracy such as expertise, recruitment, and organizational culture are sources of governing capacity.[1] The presence, mobilization,

---

[1] Michael Barnett and Martha Finnemore, *Rules for the World: International Organizations in Global Politics* (Ithaca, NY: Cornell University Press, 2004); Michael N. Barnett and

and density of organized interest groups are also sources of governing capacity. In the EU "state," "the capacity of the state to govern society depends on the configuration of society as much as the configuration of the state."[2]

The very presence of interest groups changes the structure of EU governance. Interest groups change political domains by their very presence – even if they disagree with the public authorities over specific policy agendas – and their choice to engage one political authority strengthens it vis-à-vis other political authorities.[3]

How do interest groups change EU governance? The first mechanism through which interest groups change EU governing capacity is through the development of informal institutions at the EU level. Mobilized interest groups within a particular policy domain often create informal institutions that can precede, coexist, or compete with formal institutions and public bureaucracies. When the informal and formal agendas align, formal and informal institutions effectively merge, enhancing the governing capacity of the EU. This is the mechanism through which the authority of EU institutions can be deepened, outside of formal intergovernmental or supranational treaties. It can also explain how formal EU institutions and organizations emerge where there were none before, outside of normal EU processes.

The second mechanism linking interest groups to EU governing capacity is the provision of external sources of capacity. Expertise and resources are particularly important to new bureaucracies but also enhance the capacity of stable institutions such as the U.S. Congress.[4] U.S. executive agencies developed power and legitimacy through intimate networks between powerful interest groups and new bureaucracies.[5] Increasing power and legitimacy produced more bureaucratic autonomy: autonomy not of the state from society but of the executive branch from the legislature.

Martha Finnemore, "The Politics, Power, and Pathologies of International Organizations," *International Organization* 53, no. 4 (1999): 699–732.

[2] Peter A. Hall, *Governing the Economy: The Politics of State Intervention in Britain and France* (Oxford: Oxford University Press, 1986), 17.

[3] Susan Strange, *The Retreat of the State: The Diffusion of Power in the World Economy* (Cambridge, UK: Cambridge University Press, 1996).

[4] Tim LaPira and Herschel F. Thomas, "Congressional Analytic Capacity, Party Polarization, and the Political Economy of Revolving Door Lobbying," paper presented at the American Political Science Association meeting, August 9, 2016, Philadelphia, PA.

[5] Daniel P. Carpenter, *The Forging of Bureaucratic Autonomy: Reputations, Networks, and Policy Innovation in Executive Agencies, 1862–1928* (Princeton, NJ: Princeton University Press, 2001).

Similarly, in the contemporary EU, interest groups often have more market knowledge, policy history, and legitimacy than EU bureaucracies. State–society interactions also produce bureaucratic autonomy at the EU level: the autonomy of EU bureaucracies vis-à-vis other political authorities and states. This has implications for the direction and content of EU political development, as autonomy gained through powerful interest groups comes with a cost, such as private influence on EU policy agendas. In the case of European security and defense, this private influence framed the blurring of the two policy domains.

Indeed, the European Commission released its first-ever report on political corruption within EU member states on February 3, 2014. The ongoing study originally attempted but failed to also measure corruption within EU institutions themselves. The Commission concluded it could not evaluate EU corruption because there are no existing frameworks or measures for evaluating international or supranational corruption.[6] Corruption is one form of state–society interaction at the EU level. To theorize contemporary EU political development, one must look to other processes of state formation. The EU is a supranational entity, created by advanced industrialized nation states, but its new institutions appear to have many of the characteristics of developing states. In the EU state–society relationship, society is sometimes more powerful and better organized than European political authority.

Nearly sixty years ago, Ernst Haas (1958) proposed interest groups would drive European integration. Their bottom-up demands for supranational governance would lead to the functional creation of EU institutions and authority. He predicted interest groups and associations would begin to see European political institutions as the best venue through which to pursue their material and private interests, and would shift their allegiances away from the national arena. However, Haas's neofunctionalism did not unfold as he said it would: the process has not been linear and continuous but uneven, punctuated, and uncertain. The history of the EU–society relationship is not one driven by waves of mobilized actors activated by forces such as spillover[7] or globalization pressures.[8] Although neofunctionalism did not reflect the reality of European political development, we now see the same antecedent and outcome conditions in contemporary EU governance: there are increasing degrees

---

[6] "EU-Wide Corruption Report Drops Chapter on EU Institutions," *EU Observer*, 2014, accessed February 6, 2014. http://euobserver.com/justice/122955.

[7] E. B. Haas, *The Uniting of Europe: Political, Social, and Economic Forces, 1950–1957* (Stanford, CA: Stanford University Press, 1958).

[8] W. Sandholtz and A. Stone Sweet, *European Integration and Supranational Governance* (Oxford, UK: Oxford University Press, 1998).

of interest-group mobilization toward directly lobbying EU institutions, and there have been large changes in the degree and creation of EU supranational authority in the last two decades.

Indeed, the contemporary political environment in Brussels looks eerily similar to Haas' predicted end-point. Second only to Washington, DC, Brussels has the highest concentration of lobbying activity in the world. Although interest groups in DC spend about 50 percent more money toward lobbying, there are greater numbers of them in Brussels. While they are there to advise, influence, and understand the EU policy process, there is also an increasing amount of advocacy, outsourcing, privatization, and revolving doors between public and private actors. The types of interest groups are also proliferating rapidly: there has been dramatic growth in consultancies, law firms, think tanks, industry associations, and many other forms of interest groups.

In this book, I analytically link two phenomena to understand the relationship between EU political authority and transnational European society. These two phenomena are (1) the mobilization of transnational interest groups and their formation of informal institutions and (2) extralegal changes in EU political development – including the creation, deepening, or stagnation of EU agencies, bureaucracies, and policy agendas. In short, I argue they are interdependent: that Ernst Haas was more correct than not in proposing the emerging connection between bottom-up mobilization and EU political development. The story, however, is more complicated, path dependent, and counterintuitive than Haas originally proposed. The mechanism linking the bottom-up to the top-down is the EU's relative governing capacity. There is, therefore, no direct causal link between interest groups and EU authority, as Haas proposed. Interest-group mobilization is neither predetermined by the internal pressures of European integration nor determined by uniform exogenous forces such as globalization pressures.[9] But interest-group mobilization is one factor that fundamentally alters the governing capacity of EU institutions. Changes in EU governing capacity can lead to changes in the formal authority of the EU, including the creation and deepening of EU institutional authority.

Framework

I build this analysis of the structure of EU state–society relations from both the macro and micro levels of analysis. I first establish different mobilization patterns of interest groups in Brussels and link them

[9] Ibid.

broadly to EU political outcomes. Drawing on original research from interest-group directories, surveys, archives, and personal interviews, I also address the relationship between organized interests and EU agenda setting in a political environment where the institutions and actors are coevolving. I first establish whether the relationship between the EU state and society is purely functional, as in whether the twin phenomena of the mobilization of European interest groups and EU governing capacity outcomes can be explained by more straightforward logic such as changes in formal EU authority. I establish that a change in formal, treaty-based authority is not an adequate explanation for EU governance outcomes, and there is a great deal of variation among all of these elements. I then evaluate the parts of the puzzle: are there links between the presence or absence of interest groups and EU governing capacity? Using original data to document interest-group mobilization within a policy domain over time, I find a possible structural relationship between interest groups and governing capacity outcomes without establishing why this relationship exists.

Next I focus on the micro level of relations between state and society in EU governance, establishing the factors that lead to high or low EU governing capacity. I trace these relationships over time and define concepts and measures for the subjective and relational elements of the interactions between public and private actors in EU policy domains. Then, in two case studies – EU defense policy and EU security policy – I trace interest-group mobilization and EU political development. The cases demonstrate that mobilization, density, and messaging of interest groups and civil society can be directly linked to EU governing capacity and legislation. The cases also document the emergence over time of bottom-up informal institutions among key interest groups within the policy domains. The coordination of the policy agenda among interest groups through the emergence of informal institutions sometimes precedes the definition and crafting of the EU policy agenda. It also precedes changes in the creation or deepening of EU authority within policy domains. These findings are tested in a survey instrument measuring the relative governance quality and public–private interactions of an international institution, adapted from the survey instruments international institutions themselves use to evaluate the developing world.

Formal Authority: Insufficient for Explaining European Political Development

Within the study of political systems, particularly advanced industrial democracies, authority and capacity are often used interchangeably.

Indeed, fundamental theories of power, such as Max Weber's idea of authority and legitimacy, bind the concepts interchangeably, where capacity is a product of legitimate authority.[10] There is no space, then, for the two concepts to exist independently of each other. Outside the study of advanced industrial democracies, however, these concepts are often sharply distinguished from each other and can vary over time and across domestic institutions in inverse directions. The authority to conduct policy might not translate into a capacity to conduct that policy, and actors might also possess a capacity to conduct policy without the concomitant authority to do so. What conditions cause these concepts to diverge? Authority varies independently of capacity because of two conditions: (1) uncertainty over the allocation of formal authority and rapidly changing interpretations over rules of the game (for example, treaties, constitutions, and institutional formation) and (2) state–society relations. State–society relations can influence capacity in both directions: dense relations between public and private actors can facilitate policy outcomes because of close coordination and implementation, or they can create suboptimal policy outcomes because of private interests, capture, and increasing constraints on public policy.

Governing capacity is the link between organized European society and EU outcomes: it is what some EU bureaucracies lack, and interest groups are often willing sources of resources and expertise. Ideally, capacity allows EU agencies and institutions to set effective public agendas. However, capacity varies independently of authority: a bureaucracy can have ample legal authority but lack capacity, or it can lack legal authority but cobble together the capacity to frame agendas and promote policy outcomes. One of the main ways bureaucracies supplement their capacity in the absence of legal authority is through creative linkages with external resources.

The EU sometimes gets authority not from its member states but through its organizational effectiveness, which is enhanced by external interest groups. Effectiveness increases legitimacy, which in turn can transform informal relations between state and society into formal institutions. Informal institutions become formal based on the degree to which interest groups enhance the governing capacity of EU bureaucracies and public–private policy agendas align. Governing capacity comes from the internal structure of bureaucracies but also the interaction between interest groups and public authorities.

---

[10] M. Weber, *Economy and Society*, edited by Guenther Roth and Claus Wittich (New York, NY: Bedminster, 1968).

This book questions two theoretical propositions: that the only source of formal EU authority comes from member states, and that bottom-up functional demand from interest groups has prompted the political development of the EU. How much governing capacity the EU has within each policy domain has also driven its political development. This capacity is neither an automatic product of treaty-based authority, nor a result of simple policy instruments and organizational innovations from within EU bureaucracies. When the EU has greater governing capacity, it happens because strong EU bureaucracies harness the resources provided by mobilized interest groups, allowing for them to access external sources of capacity at the European and transnational level from interest groups. When governing capacity is high, EU bureaucracies enjoy increased legitimacy. When formal institutions have increased legitimacy and also have a parallel informal institutional network of interest groups enhancing their governing capacity in a particular policy domain, conditions exist for the endogenous creation of more EU authority, even when this does not derive from the preferences of sovereign member states.

I do not theorize why interest groups mobilized to Brussels. From a state–society perspective, understanding why they are there is less crucial than their presence. These private actors are often interested in more EU power and governance in a particular area. They are not lobbying for or against a particular policy or influence outcome: often one of their lobbying purposes is the creation or strengthening of EU institutions themselves. One could call this a "heresthetic" lobbying, in the rational choice institutionalism of William Riker,[11] where actors see the opportunity to "manipulate the dimensions" of institutions, and mobilized interest groups therefore lobby for different rules of the game, in this case, more EU institutional authority.

The governing capacity of the EU in particular policy areas depends on the strength of its institutions. This strength, however, cannot be reduced to formal authority or even material measures of resources such as budgets. It requires the combination of the organizational capabilities of EU bureaucracies with the external resources of mobilized interest groups. The important question this framing raises is why EU capacity is robust in certain policy areas at certain times and weak in other policies or at other times. Why does the EU sometimes manage the pressures of social and market actors more effectively or weakly? Also, why do EU policy agendas sometimes produce few results, when policy solutions are mandated by states, while at other times EU policy agendas seem to

---

[11] William H. Riker, *The Art of Political Manipulation*, Vol. 587 (New Haven, CT: Yale University Press, 1986), 147–8.

come out of nowhere and are not effectively predicted by the interests of European states? Answers to these questions can only be understood by looking at the interaction of interests within EU policy domains.

Implications

There are multiple configurations of supply and demand for EU governance and structures of state–society relations, with differing implications for EU political development. The most significant involve agenda setting and changes in formal institutions and authority. There are also unintended consequences of interest-group activity in EU policymaking. Under certain conditions, the attempt to preserve member state sovereignty by limiting the resources of EU institutions can risk the unintended consequence of accidental privatization of policy agenda setting.

Governing Capacity Implication I: Agenda Setting

This book links governing capacity to EU political development. Governing capacity is the ability to effectively set and implement policy agendas, and I propose that it is strongly influenced by informal factors such as interest-group mobilization. Interest groups impact EU governing capacity, but they have private interests. When they alter EU governing capacity, they also leave their mark on the EU policy agenda. Interest groups influence public governing agendas along multiple dimensions. These include (1) the timing of the policy agenda; (2) the parameters and boundaries of the policy issue agenda; and (3) the direction and trajectory of the policy agenda, whether it gets moved from high to low politics, or low to high politics, as in shifting the policy framework from an economic to a security focus.

Policy Agenda Setting in the European Union Agenda setting is how some issues become major policy platforms while other issues do not receive governmental attention.[12] It involves political actors formulating, framing, packaging, and prioritizing issues within a

---

[12] See F. Baumgartner and B. Jones, *Agendas and Instability in American Politics* (Chicago, IL: Chicago University Press, 1993); David Lowery and Virginia Gray, "How Some Rules Just Don't Matter: The Regulation of Lobbyists," *Public Choice* 91, no. 2 (1997): 139–47; R. W. Cobb and C. D. Elder, *Participation in American Politics. The Dynamics of Agenda-Building* (Baltimore, MD: The Johns Hopkins University Press, 1972); E. E. Schattschneider, *The Semi-Sovereign People* (New York, NY: Harcourt Brace College Publishers, 1960/1975); J. W. Kingdon, *Agendas, Alternatives, and Public Policies*, 2nd ed. (New York, NY: HarperCollins, 1995).

political system.[13] Agenda-setting dynamics can be contentious, competitive, and politically charged or cooperative and consensual. Agenda dynamics often occur prior to actual formal decision procedures, before an issue is officially promoted or launched by the executive authority. Sometimes the most critical stage of an agenda's life cycle is in its prehistory, when actors debate whether and how to package the issue. In some political systems, such as the United States, the most important stage of agenda setting is formal, when a policy is debated through legislative channels. In other political systems, such as the EU, important agenda decisions are set at the informal stage. Interest-group activity is highest at the beginning of EU agenda setting because actors attempt to shape the contents of policy directives at the stage when the Commission bureaucracy is crafting policy agendas.[14] It is "the *informalities* of the policy process ... [including] informal exchange and backroom bargaining" that are as central to policy formation as the "formal, parliamentary institutions of government."[15]

The dynamic of the EU agenda-setting process are far more interesting at the beginning than at the end of the policy life cycle. There is little lobbying during the legislative phase of policymaking because agendas rarely change then. In fact, the EU regulatory process often produces a successful policy outcome, even if it takes some time.[16] In contrast, the most common outcome of U.S. formal policy proposals is policy failure. In the United States, the agenda content and survival is still being negotiated as it passes through formal decision-making channels, whereas in the EU, the formal policy agendas have already crystallized at early, informal policy stages, and they are more likely than not to become European legislation.[17] EU agenda setting happens

---

[13] Cobb and Elder, 86; Kingdon, 3. The agenda-setting literature distinguishes between the public agenda – in which media has a large agenda-setting role – and the political agenda, which is the result of the dynamic between elites and decision makers.

[14] A. Dür, "Measuring Interest Group Influence in the EU: A Note on Methodology," *European Union Politics* 9, no. 4 (2008): 559.

[15] B. Rosamond, *Theories of European Integration* (New York, NY: St. Martin's Press, 2000), p. 123. Emphasis in original.

[16] C. Mahoney, "Networking vs. Allying: The Decision of Interest Groups to Join Coalitions in the US and the EU," *Journal of European Public Policy* 14, no. 3 (2007): 366–83.

[17] The EU literature on agenda setting is limited, with a few exceptions. Pollack has produced a research agenda on factors influencing EU agenda setting, using principal-agent analysis to explain intergovernmental power dynamics ("Representing Diffuse Interests in EC Policy-Making," *Journal of European Public Policy* 4, no. 4 [1997]: 572–90; *Delegation, Agency, and Agenda Setting in the European Community* [Cambridge, UK: Cambridge University Press, 2003]). The emphasis, however, is often on national or EU power dynamics between governmental institutions. Within the context of the EU, this is logical, given that the European Commission is the institution that officially sets the agenda for supranational policies in the EU, setting into motion a legislative and

primarily at the European Commission, and the most important stage is the informal bureaucratic discussion with experts. Private actors have a critical agenda-setting role in this process.

Interest Groups and Agenda-Setting Dynamics over Time Interest groups are often key agenda-setting actors. This is particularly true in the case of the United States. In the U.S., different issue areas have different mobilization patterns.[18] Policy systems develop over time, with great variation among different issue areas. There is a continuum of interest-group density: some are unified, powerful, and autonomous,[19] while others are adversarial, less autonomous, and less able to bring their issues to the agenda.[20] Some policy communities are well established, while others are new. Some are well organized into professional associations or consortia, while others are not. Some issue areas are adversarial, while others are not. Interest groups are less able to influence government institutions and agendas when there is conflict. When there is no conflict, issues reach the policy agenda based on how much effort the first mover puts into lobbying. With less competition, the group mobilizing first often defines the policy issue, and this message successfully defines the parameters and direction of the policy agenda.

These interest-group dynamics are evident in the study of the U.S. political system. In the mid-twentieth century, for-profit interests dominated the scene until more civil society or nonprofit groups mobilized to

intergovernmental political process. Tension of control over the political agenda exists between European member states and between the Commission and member states. There are also process-tracing case studies of policy domains (J. M. Dostal, "Campaigning on Expertise: How the OECD Framed EU Welfare and Labour Market Policies – and Why Success Could Trigger Failure," *Journal of European Public Policy* 11, no. 3 [2004]: 440–60; M. G. Green Cowles, "Setting the Agenda for a New Europe: The ERT and EC 1992," *Journal of Common Market Studies* 33, no. 4 [1995, December]: 501–26; Sonia Mazey, "The European Union and Women's Rights: From the Europeanization of National Agendas to the Nationalization of a European Agenda?," *Journal of European Public Policy* 5, no. 1 [1998]: 131–52; Irina Michalowitz, "What Determines Influence? Assessing Conditions for Decision-Making Influence of Interest Groups in the EU 1," *Journal of European Public Policy* 14, no. 1 [2007]: 132–51) and EU institutions (C. Burns, "Codecision and the European Commission: A Study of Declining Influence?" *Journal of European Public Policy* 11, no. 1 [2004]: 1–18; M. E. Smyrl, "When (and How) Do the Commission's Preferences Matter?," *JCMS: Journal of Common Market Studies* 36, no. 1 [1998]: 79–100; J. Tallberg, "The Agenda-Shaping Powers of EU Council Presidency," *Journal of European Public Policy* 10, no. 1 [2003]: 1–19). These have proposed multiple sources of power and influence over the EU political agenda.

[18] Baumgartner and Jones.

[19] K. J. Meier, *Regulation: Politics, Bureaucracy, and Economics* (London, UK: Palgrave Macmillan, 1985); J. A. Thurber, "Representation, Accountability, and Efficiency in Divided Party Control of Government," *PS: Political Science and Politics* (1991): 653–7.

[20] Schattschneider.

Washington in the 1960s and 1970s. Relative business and consumer or nonprofit group bias varies across issues.[21] Usually, businesses mobilize first, then citizen or nonprofit groups follow much later. Business interests often dominate new policy areas. Some policy domains are more permeable to this phenomenon than others – those where "quiet politics" dominates – where interest groups are able to set policy agendas outside public scrutiny.[22] As the policy domain ages, more nonprofit interests mobilize. This plurality of interests makes informal institutions and quiet politics less sustainable.

Issue salience also conditions interest group influence on agenda outcomes. The more public exposure to a policy domain, the less agenda-setting room concentrated interest groups have for influencing policymakers.[23] In a less publicized and more technocratic policy domain, there is greater opportunity for interest groups to influence policymakers. Business and industry interests often mobilize early in the life of a policy domain, whereas nonprofit and civil society groups are diffuse, less organized, and late to the game of lobbying. When generalized, this model implies that new, technocratic, or "quiet" policy agendas are most susceptible to business and industry influence.[24] When policy agendas are established, highly political, and publicly salient, there is less public–private intimacy and less concentrated business or industry influence.

These insights from the comparative life cycles of interest-group mobilization generate conflicting research hypotheses about agenda influence. Are policy agendas framed as low politics (such as regulatory or economic policy) more open to influence and capture than high politics domains because they are technocratic in nature? Or are policy agendas framed as high politics (such as finance or security) more susceptible to external agenda-setting dynamics because they reflect quiet, densely organized, and consensus-based interest groups?

I harness this tension between high and low politics policy agendas in my predicted implications of mobilized interest groups in the EU. When powerful interests mobilize early in a policy domain, they are able to provide capacity to EU bureaucracies, helping set the policy agenda. Agenda-setting influence is greatest at the earliest, most informal stages

---

[21] D. Vogel, *Fluctuating Fortunes: The Political Power of Business in America* (New York, NY: Basic Books, 1989).

[22] Pepper D. Culpepper, *Quiet Politics and Business Power: Corporate Control in Europe and Japan* (New York, NY: Cambridge University Press, 2010).

[23] R. D. Arnold, *The Logic of Congressional Action* (New Haven, CT: Yale University Press, 1990), 19.

[24] Culpepper.

of policymaking. As a policy domain ages, the ability of interest groups to maintain influence diminishes because increasing EU governing capacity draws more interest-group mobilization to the policy domain.

As EU policy domains develop, they become less influenced by outside interests. The possible exception to this decreasing reliance is when interest groups manage to shift the parameters and boundaries of the policy agenda to expand or diversify the policy environment. Then they regain influence in the new policy domain. An example of this is in Chapter 6, where defense interest groups successfully shifted the immigration policy agenda toward a more securitized border security agenda.

Any interest-group window of influence is limited over time. As time goes on, business over nonprofit advantages dissolve, at least in terms of agenda setting. Policy domains become so pluralistic over time that it is often difficult to attribute outcomes in a mature policy system to the resources of interest organizations at all. Although this conclusion arises from observations of U.S. politics, there is evidence that this is also the case in the EU: in established policy domains, the financial resources of interest groups are not a predictor of policy success in Brussels, and businesses may have only a slight advantage over nonprofit groups.[25] As there are more relatively new policy domains in the EU than the United States, this structural business advantage may also disappear over time as policy domains become more established. Most evidence points to this being the case: for example, in 1980, U.S. business interests outnumbered nonprofit interests by two to one. Today, there are still more business interests than nonprofits, but the margins are much smaller.

Interest-Group Impact on Agenda Setting Agenda setting is not limited to agenda content: it can also mean agenda direction. Topics can be introduced on the EU agenda "from above," or from high politics and diplomacy, or they can emerge "from below," or through low politics and bureaucratic or technocratic decisions.[26] There are three distinct types of agenda dynamics. An issue can (1) come from the outside public and move to the political elites and the formal agenda;[27] (2) mobilize

---

[25] Baumgartner et al., *Lobbying and Policy Change: Who Wins, Who Loses, and Why* (Chicago, IL: University of Chicago Press, 2009).

[26] S. Princen, "Agenda-Setting in the European Union: A Theoretical Exploration and Agenda for Research," *Journal of European Public Policy* 14, no. 1 (2007): 21–38; S. Princen and M. Rhinard, "Crashing and Creeping: Agenda-Setting Dynamics in the European Union," *Journal of European Public Policy* 13, no. 7 (2006): 1119–32.

[27] Princen and Rhinard ("Agenda-Setting in the European Union") dismiss Cobb et al.'s first agenda-setting path: *that in which the policy initiative comes from outside of government*. They explicitly state "[i]n the context of the EU, the distinction between public and political agendas is less likely to be relevant...public involvement in EU

from government elites "inside-out" to the public; or (3) arise "inside" government and high politics quarters and stay there. Each path has different dynamics determining its challenges and prospects.[28] I argue that the direction of an agenda can also be influenced: from high to low politics or from low to high politics. In the case of CSDP, what started as high politics of defense cooperation has become the low, technocratic politics of joint acquisition and research and technology cooperation. In the domain of immigration and border security, what was initially low, legal politics of citizenship, social benefits, and family immigration law has become high politics of border security, monitoring, and extradition.

Governing Capacity Implication II: Authority and Institutional Change

Under certain conditions, interest-group mobilization and state–society dynamics that affect governing capacity can have far-reaching impacts. These effects can go beyond just changes in policy agendas and governing effectiveness to changes in the political institutions and the sources of their authority. State–society interactions and mobilized private interests sometimes create informal institutions within a policy domain, which

decision-making is very limited" (Princen and Rhinard, 1121). By "public" they mean open, mobilized, and explicit political protest ("conflict expansion" in the U.S. literature). This is justified because of evidence that social movements and social protests have had limited success in the EU political "opportunity structure" (D. Imig and S. Tarrow, "The Europeanisation of Movements? A New Approach to Transnational Contention," in *Social Movements in a Globalizing World*, edited by D. della Porta, H. Kriesi, & D. Rucht, 112–33. London, UK: Macmillan, 1999). Indeed, there is no "public" in Brussels: no common media, no newspaper of record, and no common media language. Nonprofit interest groups have arrived late on the policy scene in Brussels, possibly impacting their success vis-à-vis for-profit interest groups. However, there are significant interest-group constituencies in Brussels with empirically demonstrated influence over agenda setting. It is theoretically and empirically limiting to confine agenda-setting dynamics purely to governmental actors. In order to strengthen the heuristics of agenda-setting dynamics in the EU, I return to the core U.S. theories to include the role of outside interests in policy agenda outcomes.

28 In Princen's 2007 review article, he noted that identifying the precise origin of an idea is not a fruitful path of research, in that there are so many multiple infinite regress sources and origins of ideas floating around policy communities as latent at any given point in time (Princen, 23). He proposed a more effective approach to look at the conditions for agenda setting, or the "set of (political or other) factors that account for the rise and fall of issues on the political agenda" (ibid.). Princen and Rhinard put two EU policies to the test, an anti-smoking policy agenda developed by epistemic/technocratic expertise and a bioterrorism policy agenda developed by high diplomatic efforts. The key differences found in these two paths corresponded to the "inside out" and "inside" agenda dynamics, where the anti-smoking policy agenda was well specified and incremental, whereas the bioterrorism policy agenda was loosely specified and subject to wide public and bureaucratic interpretation.

can lead to the deepening of formal authority or even endogenous institutional change.[29]

Interest groups promoting policy change create informal institutions alongside or in place of formal political institutions. Informal institutions emerge from configurations of bottom-up or top-down social, political, and economic networks. These networks can have equal or unequal distributions of resources and power and can be subject to competition involving winners and losers. Informal institutions emerge because formal institutions are incomplete, ineffective, uncertain, or do not reflect political reality. They may also emerge because the political domain has shifted rapidly, and this provokes venue shopping on the part of actors and organizations to try to address this institutional uncertainty. They are also created in pursuit of goals not internationally acceptable (in a domestic political arena) or alternatively not domestically acceptable (in an international or intergovernmental arena).

Whether informal institutions undermine or enhance formal institutions – or endogenously create new formal institutions – depends on the degree to which their policy agendas match. Their influence on governing capacity and the creation of formal authority can go in both directions. Formal–informal institutional relationships can have multiple paths and outcomes.[30] Informal institutions can be functional, where they provide solutions to political, economic, or social coordination problems, and where their capacity enhances the performance of formal institutions. This is because their agenda goals match public agenda goals. This enhanced governing capacity reinforces the existing authority of formal institutions and does not change institutional or authority boundaries.

Informal institutions can also undermine governing capacity, where the agendas of informal institutions do not match formal institutions. This results in more dysfunctional outcomes such as clientelism, corruption, or patrimonialism.[31] In these scenarios, formal institutions retain their formal authority, but their governing capacity suffers because of these dysfunctional dynamics and disconnects between public and private goals. In still other scenarios, informal institutions reinforce or substitute for the formal institutions they appear to undermine.

When informal institutions emerge in EU policy domains, they are sometimes a source of EU political development. This can explain why

[29] Kellee S. Tsai, "Adaptive Informal Institutions and Endogenous Institutional Change in China," *World Politics* 59, no. 1 (2006): 116–41.

[30] Gretchen Helmke and Steven Levitsky, "Informal Institutions and Comparative Politics: A Research Agenda," *Perspectives on Politics* 2, no. 4 (2004): 725–40.

[31] Ibid.

Europeanization sometimes outpaces the interests of sovereign member states and how some EU institutions, agencies, or policy agendas can gather momentum without (or against) the preferences of member states. In Chapter 4, I document how defense industry interest groups created informal institutions to promote European defense markets and civilian-military research integration at least a decade before formal EU efforts. In this case, interest groups created informal institutions because formal EU institutions did not yet exist to absorb their interests. Informal agendas aligned with emerging EU formal agendas (Chapter 5), both addressing how to expand the EU Common Market into civilian security research and dual-use technology. The alignment of public and private agendas resulted in informal institutions enhancing rather than undermining EU governing capacity in defense. It also accelerated the political development of EU defense policy, including the creation of the European Defence Agency. Formal EU defense institutions have simultaneously increased EU governing capacity over defense matters but weakened the informal defense institutions that led the effort for over a decade. This "substitutive" informal institution in European defense accelerated the timing of EU formal defense authority, enhanced the governing capacity of EU bureaucracies, and generated policy agendas when EU bureaucracies were too new to do so on their own. Their success, however, leads to a lessened importance over time of the role of private interests and their informal institutions. In Chapter 2, this is shown to be evident in a number of policy domains – including defense – where interest-group activity peaks prior to the creation of more formal EU authority, and then subsides.

Governing Capacity Implication III: Unintentional Privatization

The last implication of the book is the most counterintuitive and troubling. Interest-group agenda-setting influence is often peaks at the beginning of a policy issue area. Private actors acting through informal institutions often supplement new bureaucracies with external capacity because of weaknesses in the structure or resources of those new organizations. EU member states – out of concern for their sovereignty – deliberately underfund and understaff EU bureaucracies to control them and limit their power. This occurs even when there is a consensus that there must be a European solution to a public policy problem. This is an institutional design with an unstable equilibrium. Either EU bureaucracies will remain weak until member states give them more resources or authority, or mobilized interest groups will fill the governing capacity gaps with external expertise, agenda setting, and resources.

However, if there is a societal and market need for EU governance in a particular policy domain, but EU member states hesitate to create a robust EU institution for addressing the policy – or they create an institution but intentionally weaken and hamper its organizational capacity, resources, or expertise – then the chances of private capture of the EU policy agenda are highest. The implications for this scenario are counterintuitive but important: European member states confronting sovereignty-sensitive policy challenges, when underfunding or designing EU organizations to fail, may end up simultaneously Europeanizing and privatizing the policy agenda, when trying to prevent more supranational authority.

Structure of Chapters

Chapter 1 proposes an original political economy theory explaining EU governing capacity within a comparative institutionalist framework for European political development. The key feature of this framework is the relationship between interest groups and emerging public institutions adapted from theories of the political development of developing states. A key state–society concept is "embeddedness," describing closely managed relations between public and private actors that can enhance developing governing capacity and transformational policy outcomes.

Chapters 2 and 3 evaluate sources of EU governing capacity. The focus in Chapter 2 is the structure of organized European interest groups and society. It links European interest-group mobilization to EU political outcomes, demonstrating variation in transnational mobilization and density over time and across policy domains. It establishes that interest-group mobilization varies independently of treaty authority. Chapter 3 evaluates the microfoundations of this link between state–society relations and governing capacity.

Chapters 4, 5, and 6 trace the political economy and political development of European defense, immigration, and security policies. Chapter 4 introduces the bottom-up mobilization of industry actors in EU defense policy. Defense and aerospace industry groups established Brussels lobbying offices in the late 1980s and early 1990s, ten years before the first CSDP developments. Chapter 5 traces the political development of EU defense institutions, including the timing and direction of institutional developments. Defense industry actors and organizations created informal institutions that precede CSDP developments. This has given CSDP institutions a governing capacity that has outpaced EU treaty authority granted by member states, and had implications for defense agenda setting.

Chapter 6 introduces organized interests in the Immigration and Border Security Policy domain and the development of JHA political institutions. The case takes a different path, with little mobilization or lobbying prior to the increase in EU asylum authority in 1997,[32] and instead an almost decade-long lag in private interests (immigration and human rights nongovernmental organizations [NGOs], employers and unions, and the homeland security industry) with a stake in EU policy outcomes. The initial lack of public–private interaction on the part of key constituencies and the persistent unevenness of representation of private interests initially resulted in EU institutions with weak governing capacity and relatively ineffective policy agendas. A critical juncture changes this pattern: because of changing incentive structures designed by the European Commission in civilian security research, defense industry interest groups began to laterally reorganize toward influencing EU internal and border security. The creation of informal European security institutions preceded a rapid increase in JHA resources, authority, and governing capacity. This culminates in developments in 2009–11 that fundamentally changed the operational authority of the EU border security agency Frontex, giving it the authority to make treaty agreements with non-EU member states to source, purchase, and maintain their own operational equipment.

[32] EU cooperation in the field of JHA was not part of the original 1957 Treaty of Rome but was launched as an intergovernmental domain in the 1992 Maastricht treaty. In 1997, the Treaty of Amsterdam emphasized the need to abolish obstacles to the free movement of persons while making internal security an objective of the EU. Under the Amsterdam Treaty, a large part of JHA was subsumed under the community (supranational) method of decision making and governance. These competencies include areas such as border security, immigration and visa policy, asylum procedures, and rules for judicial cooperation in civil matters.

1 The Governing Capacity of the European Union

The Political Economy of Institutions: Rule Making and Market Making

The EU is an increasingly centralized political authority. It faces governing challenges similar to states attempting transformational policy developments: both are tasked with managing informal relationships with interest groups. This alliance between the EU "state" and organized society reinforces EU authority, promotes EU policy agendas, and creates bureaucratic autonomy layered over other political authorities, including European nation states. In its political authority, the EU is not a Weberian state, a "compulsory association which organizes domination" and "claims the monopoly of the legitimate use of physical force within a given territory."[1] However, contemporary political authority derives as much from economic as Weberian security logic: the roles of market making, wealth distribution or redistribution, and welfare have been state features for the past century, with statecraft responsible for the rules governing markets and socioeconomic stability. Political authorities have also been increasingly responsible for economic transformation, where public institutions broker between market actors, identify growth opportunities and entrepreneurs, and promote new modes of political economy. Whereas the classical nation state reflected an ideal Weberian definition of control of power over a particular territory, taxation, military development, and industrialization, contemporary states rule as much through infrastructural as through despotic power.[2] Politics, markets, and organized interests interact in institutional settings that include states but also other forms of political authority outside the state, such as the EU.

[1] M. Weber, *Economy and Society*, translated by Guenther Roth and Claus Wittich (New York, NY: Bedminster Press, [Originally published 1922] 1968), 82.
[2] M. Mann, *The Sources of Social Power* (Cambridge, UK: Cambridge University Press, 1984).

Institutional accounts attempt to explain how rules and other social orders arise from the nexus among markets, politics, and organizations.[3] The heart of this relationship is between political authority and markets[4] and between political authority and organized interests.[5] Political authority provides the boundaries, rules, and property rights forming the institutional structure of markets and societies – the stability of these rules is what allows for the functioning of markets and societies. Institutional change comes in many forms: through crisis, punctuation, top-down initiatives, or accreting demands from the bottom up. From the bottom-up perspective of market and social actors, when their interests outgrow the existing rules, they lobby the political authorities to create new rules or adapt the old ones. This logic usually translates into a constant demand from society in the form of lobbying of political authorities for changes to the rules, especially when economic or social realities are outpacing the institutional structure. Once the bottom-up demands are stabilized, following the introduction of new rules, economic and social activity usually expands beyond where it had stalled before. This increased bottom-up activity puts new pressures on the institutional structure, and the equilibrium is unbalanced again.[6]

---

[3] See Peter A. Hall and R. C. R. Taylor, "Political Science and the Three New Institutionalisms," *Political Studies* 44, no. 5 (1996): 936–57; D. C. North, *Institutions, Institutional Change, and Economic Performance* (Cambridge, UK: Cambridge University Press, 1990); D. C. North, *Understanding the Process of Economic Change* (Princeton, NJ: Princeton University Press, 2005).

[4] See P. B. Evans, *Embedded Autonomy: States and Industrial Transformation* (Princeton, NJ: Princeton University Press, 1995); P. B. Evans and J. E. Rauch, "Bureaucracy and Growth: A Cross-National Analysis of the Effects of 'Weberian' State Structures on Economic Growth," *American Sociological Review* (1999): 748–65; N. Fligstein, "Markets as Politics: A Political Cultural Approach to Market Institutions," *American Sociological Review* 61 (1996): 656–73; North, *Institutions, Institutional Change, and Economic Performance*; North, *Understanding the Process of Economic Change* (Princeton, NJ: Princeton University Press, 2005); K. Polanyi, *The Great Transformation: The Political and Economic Origins of our Time* (Boston, MA: Beacon Press, 1944).

[5] See Evans, *Embedded Autonomy*; P. J. Katzenstein, *Small States in World Markets: Industrial Policy in Europe* (Ithaca, NY: Cornell University Press, 1985); L. Weiss, *The Myth of the Powerless State* (Ithaca, NY: Cornell University Press, 1998).

[6] There has been increased interest for almost twenty years across the social sciences in explaining how social institutions, defined as rules that produce social interaction, come into existence, remain stable, and are transformed. Despite their differences, all new institutional theories contain a set of agreements (Hall and Taylor). They focus on the construction of local social orders, what could also be called fields, arenas, or games. New institutionalist theories are social constructionist in the sense that they view the creation of institutions as an outcome of social interaction between actors confronting one another in fields or arenas. Most important, preexisting rules of interaction and resource distributions operate as sources of power and, when combined with a model of actors, serve as the basis on which institutions are constructed and reproduced. Once in existence, institutions both enable and constrain social actors. Privileged actors can use

Market actors and organized interest groups often have a preference for fewer rules and a less constraining institutional structure. However, when society and the market outpace older rules and regulations, market actors sometimes have a mutual interest in increasing the institutional depth and breadth of the relevant political authority.[7] In settings with multiple, overlapping authorities and rule structures, market or social actors can choose to pressure more than one political authority at a time or venue shop their interests and agendas. Their interest in one political authority over another might strengthen its legitimacy, capacity, or authority, even indirectly. As Susan Strange argued, the presence or absence of interest groups changes structural power dynamics, insofar as the choice of one political authority over another for interest representation strengthens it vis-à-vis other institutions, even if interest groups are mobilized to lobby against the policies of the political authority rather than in support of it.[8] The literature on informal endogenous institutions[9] also provides a framework for how formal authority can deepen through informal or extralegal processes. When interest groups form informal institutions with agendas that align with the public goals of a political authority, this can accelerate the institutionalization of one political authority over another. However, micro-level decisions to lobby and venue shop are costly and often constrained by the paths of the actors and their original institutional environments.

In most institutional accounts of stability and change, at least one element is stable: either the political authority or the demands of society are fixed and do not change. In historical institutionalist accounts, political authority is fixed; in rational choice institutionalism, the demands of society are stable. How do we account for moments when both the institutional rules of the game and the bottom-up demands from market actors are coevolving, such as in the contemporary EU? While the EU's authority structure shapes the market and society, the market and society also shape the uncertain path of the authority structure and, in turn, the future rules of the institution. EU institutions are a "set of organizations to produce, interpret, apply, and enforce market rules in order

institutions to reproduce their position. Actors can use existing institutions to found new arenas of action. Actors without resources are most often constrained by institutions but, under certain circumstances, can use existing rules in unintended ways to create new institutions. New institutional theory is located at the meso level of analysis, as it focuses on the construction of local social orders that can be applied to a wide variety of research settings.

[7] See N. Fligstein, *The Transformation of Corporate Control* (Cambridge, MA: Harvard University Press, 1990); J. W. Meyer and W. R. Scott. *Organizational Environments: Ritual and Rationality* (Beverly Hills, CA: Sage, 1983).
[8] Strange.   [9] Helmke and Levitsky; Tsai.

to promote, among other things, economic exchange across national borders."[10] The political development of the EU has been an exercise in the simultaneous construction of a political authority and a market, with the accompanying social forces intertwining the two. Indeed, the EU is a real-time laboratory in which to study the emergence of an institutional structure and the politics of states and markets, where both are coevolving in simultaneous or successive movements.

Understanding the EU as a political authority requires a framework beyond seeing the EU as (1) an international institution, (2) comparable to modern European states and their state–society relations, or (3) a unique political entity with novel paradigms of power sharing between state and society. The nexus of interaction among the EU, markets, and society finds an analogy in developing states: in many developing countries, centralizing bureaucracies have had intimate, varying interactions with powerful private interests. These bureaucrats often temporarily shelve concerns about public–private boundaries in their desire to promote policy at their level of government, vis-à-vis powerful existing political authorities at lower levels of government. The EU should be analyzed as a political institution, but one facing governing challenges similar to those of developing states attempting transformational policy developments beyond their resources, which have innovated their state–society relationships and institutions through an accretion of existing social or political authorities.

The EU as a Developing Political Institution

Looking at the EU through an institutional lens elevates the interactions between political elites within and across different public and private organizations.[11] Within an emerging institutional framework, EU officials face high uncertainty, as their organizations are relatively new political institutions with a democratic legitimacy problem. To reduce this uncertainty, EU elites such as Commission officials strategically recruit allies from among organized interests vying for attention and

---

[10] N. Fligstein and A. Stone Sweet, "Constructing Polities and Markets: An Institutionalist Account of European Integration," *American Journal of Sociology* 107 (2002): 1208.

[11] The EU institutional framework is the emerging institution while many organizations vie to position themselves and their entrepreneurs to push the future of this institution. There are a number of organizations: (1) organized groups of European civil society and market actors; (2) EU member states; (3) territorial interest groups representing subnational states, regions, and cities; and (4) the bureaucracies and agencies of the EU itself.

support.[12] This is a common bureaucratic uncertainty reduction strategy, as "external support is particularly crucial for a new bureau."[13] Maintaining external support includes continually demonstrating the relevance and usefulness of a bureaucracy to influential groups with sufficient resources.[14]

The relationship between public bureaucracy and organized private interests with a stake in political outcomes can be one of policy adversaries or allies. Organized private interests can sometimes be stronger and better resourced than public bureaucracies, but private interests can also provide important bases for outside policy support and implementation. Alternatively, organized interests in new policy domains may be "weak, scattered and not accustomed to relations with the bureau... [and have to] rapidly organize so that their services become very valuable to the users."[15] Once a bureaucracy successfully mobilizes or creates a bottom-up network of outside constituents, it can then rely on inertia to maintain ongoing external support.[16]

This maintenance of external support has been critical to the development of EU institutions. The EU has a classic resource–dependence relationship between its bureaucracies and organized interests.[17] EU bureaucracies act rationally as "purposeful opportunists"[18] in expanding policy domains and creating new ones. EU officials have also practiced the art of "strategic group politics" when they "regulate their interactions with outside constituencies in a way that fulfils their strategic objectives."[19] Even before the Maastricht Treaty (1992), the Commission actively sought out or created external partners: "[its] interactions... with associations or other corporate economic actors seem to be of crucial importance in linking macro- and meso-levels and result in the emergence of network configurations" which eventually

---

[12] Mitchell P. Smith, "How Adaptable is the European Commission? The Case of State Aid Regulation." *Journal of Public Policy* 21, no. 3 (2001): 219–38.

[13] A. Downs, *Inside Bureaucracy* (Boston, MA: Little, Brown, 1967), 2.

[14] Ibid., 7.

[15] Ibid., 7–8, quoted in S. Mazey and J. Richardson, "Interest Groups and EU Policy-Making: Organizational Logic and Venue Shopping," In *European Union: Power and Policy-Making*, edited by J. Richardson, 247–65 (London, UK: Routledge, 1996/2001/2006).

[16] Downs, 8.

[17] See S. Mazey and Richardson, J., eds., Lobbying in the European Community (Oxford University Press, 1993); A. Butt Philip. *Directory of Pressure Groups in the European Community* (London, UK: Longman, 1991).

[18] Mazey and Richardson, *Lobbying in the European Community*.

[19] John Peterson, "The European Union: Pooled Sovereignty, Divided Accountability," *Political Studies* 45, no. 3 (1997): 512.

become institutionalized.[20] I propose that this political development of EU authority resembles a larger comparative phenomenon in which public–private linkages through informal institutions can endogenously deepen formal institutions. What creates this process is the governing capacity produced by the linkages between public and private actors in these informal networks.

Framing the EU bureaucracies in this context – as rational, purposeful organizations with entrepreneurial actors attempting to maximize their positions by reducing uncertainty – is key to understanding the EU through an institutional lens. Bureaucracies have unique institutional and social histories and face novel problems, but they share more commonalities than differences. All bureaucracies (and the entrepreneurial actors within them) attempt to minimize uncertainty, all find interest groups and outside resources useful, and many have attempted to institutionalize these relationships. While all public bureaucracies share similar challenges and motivations, some bureaucracies have greater responsibilities and burdens than others. These bureaucracies are tasked with changing the status quo – with transforming the political economy of their policy environment – in addition to policy regulation and implementation. Because their task is so complex and burdens their existing capacity, they have greater incentives to seek the resources of outside actors and organizations. This dynamic of seeking outside resources and allies may be even more pronounced in political environments where there is resource scarcity and agenda competition among different levels of political authority, such as in the EU. Member states may delegate limited authority and resources to EU institutions to address particular policy issues, but these public resources may often be too limited for resolving difficult European policy issues involving changing the status quo.

We know how interest groups and bureaucracies usually interact within states, particularly within the United States and other advanced industrialized democracies. Much of the literature on interest groups, however, assumes a relatively powerful bureaucracy or state apparatus. Bureaucracy interest-group modes of interaction range in their relative power dynamics, depending on different paths of political development. In early stages of political development, public bureaucracies are often more dependent on the resources, legitimacy, and ideas of private organized interests. If public bureaucracies remain weak beyond their inception, powerful interest groups may create parallel informal institutions that can gain enough legitimacy and capacity to replace or

---

[20] Lehmbruch quoted in Mazey and Richardson, *Lobbying in the European Community*, 21.

enhance formal institutions. Even when public bureaucracies are strong and autonomous, their strategies for enacting major, transformational policy changes necessitate the involvement of powerful interest groups for agenda setting and implementation. This latter model is the developmental state, coined in 1982 by Chalmers Johnson to describe the structure of state–society relations in Japan during a time of economic transformation, and later used to describe the domestic patterns of South Korea and Taiwan.

Models of Institutional Development

A significant debate within EU studies has been the search for a model through which to understand EU politics. The EU used to be regarded as a unique supranational organization not comparable to any contemporary national or international political order. EU scholars have been highly innovative in developing unique concepts and categories for classifying the political system of the EU but have recently shifted toward comparing the EU to other federal and other state political systems. Governance scholars have also subsumed the study of the EU under their frameworks of multilevel, network, or regulatory institutions that have variable geometries, state and nonstate actors, or multiple decision points.[21]

Many analytical frameworks, however, assume the EU is unique in its form of governance when in many ways it is not. As a political authority, the EU has had relative openness to organized interests, elaborate public–private networks, a massive public–private resource imbalance (with 80,000 to 100,000 lobbyists and only 30,000 civil servants), and elaborate "governance networks with the involvement of public and private actors [as] the real core of the political system."[22] States in the developing world are also characterized as having weak central bureaucracies with limited mandates, heavy regulatory responsibilities, powerful competing political authorities at lower levels of government, and a motivated base of organized interests. When developing states – such as Taiwan and South Korea – successfully transformed their economies or societies, scholars differentiated them as developmental states and located

---

[21] Simon Hix, "The Study of the European Union II: The 'New Governance' Agenda and its Rival," *Journal of European Public Policy* 5, no. 1 (1998): 38–65; Beate Kohler-Koch, "Catching up with Change: The Transformation of Governance in the European Union," *Journal of European Public Policy* 3, no. 3 (1996): 359–80.

[22] T. R. Burns and M. Carson, "Actors, Paradigms, and Institutional Dynamics: The Theory of Social Rule Systems Applied to Radical Reforms," in *Advancing Socio-Economics: An Institutionalist Perspective*, edited by J. Rogers Hollingsworth, Karl H. Mueller, and Ellen Jane Hollingsworth (Oxford: Rowman & Littlefield, 2002), 144.

the basis of this transformation in a strong public bureaucracy and a nexus of informal institutions with powerful private organized interests. Coined in the 1980s[23] to describe the structure of public–private relations of transformational Asian states, developmental state models assume bureaucratic structure translates into state capacity to construct markets (like Weber), but truly transformational policy outcomes are dependent on the relationships between public authorities and private elites.[24]

By the 1990s, the developmental state became an alternative conception of comparative "stateness": a category of political economy mirroring empirical changes in the possible "ways of being" a state, outside the modern European redistributive state.[25] This paralleled the analytical return of the state in the market and society, after years of neglect and exclusive focus on features of minimalist neoliberal or pluralist ideas of state behavior. Institutionalist ideas about the role of state action and state–society interaction are core to the study of comparative politics, including Polanyi's claim that states are prior to markets, Weber's formulas for how the internal organization of bureaucracies provide state capacity for constructing markets, and Gerschenkron and Hirschman's theories relating the political–economic transformation of states to the structures of their relationships with entrepreneurial elites. In these comparative institutionalisms, variations in the structures of state institutions determine political outcomes, in the way variations in state bureaucratic structures explain differences in development.

In a minimalist sense, once can view the developmental state as a description of a certain kind of authority structure at particular place (Asia) at a particular point in time (end of the twentieth century). In fact, it has been characterized as an ideal type created from unique historical accidents more than the structure of the state and its relations with society. Chalmers Johnson emphasized the role of state intervention in the market in the Japanese case, in contrast to the capitalist economies of the United States and Britain. Peter Evans and others positioned the developmental state as the conceptual opposite of the predatory state – such as Zaire – where the state extracts resources from its population and impedes economic development. A developmental state intervenes

---

[23] C. A. Johnson, *MITI and the Japanese Miracle: The Growth of Industrial Policy, 1925–1975* (Stanford, CA: Stanford University Press, 1982); Evans, *Embedded Autonomy*.

[24] Alexander Gerschenkron, *Economic Backwardness in Historical Perspective: A Book of Essays*, No. HC335 G386 (Cambridge, MA: Belknap Press of Harvard University Press, 1962); A. O. Hirschman, *Shifting Involvements: Private Interest and Public Action* (Princeton, NJ: Princeton University Press, 2002).

[25] Johnson.

in its society but only to "foster long-term entrepreneurial perspectives among private elites by increasing incentives to engage in transformative investments and lowering the risks."[26] These scholars questioned the underlying assumption that a necessary condition of predatory states was an excess of bureaucracy. A comparative institutional perspective – building from Weber's hypothesis that bureaucracy and capitalism are compatible and necessary elements – implies that predatory states can actually lack sufficient bureaucracy, whereas developmental and transformational states are associated with a surplus of bureaucracy.

The original inspiration for the idea that bureaucracy and state–society relations changed political and economic outcomes was postwar Japan, where public institutions directed an economic miracle with the intensive assistance of industry actors. This was in contrast to the conventional wisdom that greater state involvement in market reforms and porousness between state and society boundaries would produce suboptimal political and economic outcomes. The Japanese Ministry of International Trade and Industry (MITI) led the economic transformation, essentially as an archetypal Weberian bureaucracy.[27] It had (1) a small but elite meritocratic bureaucracy formulating economic policy, and was internally insular and informal; (2) a political system allowing the bureaucracy the autonomy to set the agenda; and (3) a mutually beneficial relationship between interest groups and bureaucrats. Interactions resembling borderline corruption were fostered for the larger benefit of developing the policy agenda. The state encouraged a revolving door between industry and public agencies, championed key industries as leaders in transforming the economy, and created nongovernmental "deliberation councils" for public–private information sharing and policy formulation without boundaries.

This last point is the most crucial element for political authorities in uncertain policy environments. Indeed, structured ties between bureaucracies and external civil society can be a source of Weberian effectiveness. Developing political authorities do not have "their own inherent capacity" and their policy outcomes come "from the complexity and

---

[26] Evans, *Embedded Autonomy*, 44.

[27] Johnson intended for the term "developmental state" to be descriptive and not an analytical category because he only focused on Japan's state–society relations. However, he asserted that a developmental state as a concept would not just mean the kind of state that intervened in its economy, as the opposite of a neoliberal state. Economic development and transformation of the economy is part of a developmental state, but the concept also refers to a specific institutional setup in which the role of society and market actors is crucial to successful policy outcomes.

stability of [their] interactions with market players."[28] This was true in the early United States, where autonomy (vis-à-vis other government actors such as Congress) was an outcome of the legitimacy bureaucracies gained via close relations with powerful interest groups.[29] In practice, there is often nothing inherently contradictory about the internal coherence of states and bureaucracies and their integration with private external networks. Bureaucracies must have some internal coherence, competence, and autonomy to participate in external networks at all, because this interaction requires the capacity for offering incentives to the private sector, managing expertise from external networks, and addressing collective action problems among external constituencies. Bureaucracies often face tasks even greater than these. The more difficult tasks – such as managing transformational change, policy reform, or authority change – result not just from internal Weberian bureaucratic capacity but also from the structure of a bureaucracy's interaction with external actors.

What Peter Evans calls "embedded autonomy," then, is an ideal type representing the structure of state–society outcomes in developmental states leading to transformative outcomes. It implies that the core of political authority is coherent and somewhat insulated and does not need to be overly isolated to preserve capacity and prevent capture. Governing capacity is enhanced through connections to external actors, and the resources of the interest groups are channeled through joint projects, while their risk is reduced under a rapidly changing environment. Ideally, the autonomy of the bureaucracy allows it to manage this risk while formulating its own goals, avoiding capture of the public agenda by private interests.

State Capacity and Political Development

In the political science subfield of comparative politics, there has been a resurgent interest in theorizing and measuring the dimensions of the "state" as an actor since the 1985 publication of Evans, Rueschemeyer, and Skocpol's influential text *Bringing the State Back In*.[30] A major element of states is their capacity, not just their authority. State capacity is a difficult and slippery concept, but it is distinguishable from concepts of

---

[28] R. J. Samuels, *The Business of the Japanese State: Energy Markets in Comparative and Historical Perspective* (Ithaca, NY: Cornell University Press, 1987), 262, cited in Evans, *Embedded Autonomy*, 50.

[29] Carpenter.

[30] Peter B. Evans, Dietrich Rueschemeyer, and Theda Skocpol, editors, *Bringing the State Back In* (New York, NY: Cambridge University Press, 1985).

authority and power. In the broadest sense, state capacity reflects a government's ability to harness social and economic support and maintain order and consent for public policy goals.[31] It is often created through other mechanisms such as the capacity for taxation or military action, or to enforce property rights. It is also a relational concept, based on the interactions and balances of power and resources between a state and its society. This goes in two directions, from the bottom-up mobilization of society in support of a state to the top-down influence over or control of a society by the state. It is also a structural concept, meaning it is about raw inputs of the configuration of social groups and the state, and does not – by itself – predict governing outcomes. It is separate from – and conceptually larger than – the real-world sum of a state's policy outcomes, effectiveness, and administrative resources.[32]

Social scientists have historically neglected the concept of a state's capacity for structuring social relations. This may be an Anglo-American phenomenon, because these states are relatively weak vis-à-vis their societies and therefore have a weak capacity for governing domestic adjustment. However, the return of the state as an important variable has restored the idea of capacity as a critical comparative dimension of institutions. Differences among states have more to do with the degree and type of institutional depth (insulation) and breadth (embeddedness) than with the presence or absence of institutions.[33] Institutional depth is the degree to which the boundaries of the state and the orientation of the state actors define a public sphere distinguishable from the larger society, whereas institutional breadth is the density of the links between state activities and those of other social entities. Together, depth and breadth bring measures of insulation and embeddedness to the complex of organizations constituting all modern states.

It is difficult to actually measure "state capacity," because states are institutions with many different organizations and bureaucracies within them. Michael Mann defines the modern state as "polymorphous and factionalized in its structure."[34] Different policy domains such as military or economic affairs "mobilize differing, if overlapping and intersecting, power networks, and their solutions have consequences, some unintended for each other."[35] This creates variations in

---

[31] Martin Painter and Jon Pierre, "Unpacking Policy Capacity: Issues and Themes." In *Challenges to State Policy Capacity*, edited by Martin Painter and Jon Pierre (London, UK: Palgrave Macmillan UK, 2005), 2.

[32] Ibid., 3.

[33] Stephen D. Krasner, "Sovereignty an Institutional Perspective," *Comparative Political Studies* 21, no. 1 (1988): 66–94.

[34] Mann, 796.   [35] Ibid.

capacities not just between states but also between various bureaucracies in different policy domains. There is often less value in theorizing the overall capacity of a state or governance organization; there is more explanatory power inside its constituent parts, organizations, or policy domains.[36]

Capacity also varies over space and time because it depends not only on raw governing resources (including internal resources, institutional arrangements, and formal authority) but also on how those resources are effectively used.[37] Capacity to make political decisions can vary independently of the ability of a state to implement the same policies.[38] The type of policy domain is relevant because different tasks impose qualitatively different policymaking demands on government.[39] Financial deregulation and trade or investment liberalization require governments to stop or reduce activity: to stop providing financial subsidies, for example, or to end restrictions on foreign investment. These policies may be politically difficult to adopt but, once adopted, remain in effect until rescinded by new policy. In contrast, policies such as capital account monitoring need continuous enforcement. These are regulatory or active policies: they demand the involvement of government authorities for as long as they are to remain operative. Still other domains require both: defense politics requires the executive bureaucracy to be simultaneously the regulator and the monopsonistic buyer.

---

[36] See Barbara Hobson, "Feminist Strategies and Gendered Discourses in Welfare States: Married Women's Right to Work in the United States and Sweden." In *Mothers of a New World: Maternalist Politics and the Origins of Welfare States*, edited by Seth Koven and Sonya Michel, 396–429 (London, UK: Routledge, 1993) (examining the role of women's agency in the "the politics of social policy and the origins of welfare states"); see generally Robert W. Jackman, *Power without Force: The Political Capacity of Nation-States* (Ann Arbor: University of Michigan Press, 1993) (examining political capacity through a behavioral approach, which examined "informal patterns of observed behavior" rather than "formal descriptions . . . of particular institutions").

[37] See Stephen D. Krasner, *Defending the National Interest: Raw Materials, Investments and U.S. Foreign Policy* (Princeton, NJ: Princeton University Press, 1978), 329 (explaining that the state is not a "unified rational actor" but rather a "complex set of bureaucratic institutions and roles").

[38] Hillel Soifer and Matthias vom Hau, "Unpacking the Strength of the State: The Utility of State Infrastructural Power," *Studies in Comparative International Development* 43 (2008): 219, 227 (explaining that the "line between control and provision" is often overlooked).

[39] See Merilee S. Grindle, "Policy Content and Context in Implementation," in *Politics and Policy Implementation in the Third World*, edited by Merilee S. Grindle, 3–39 (Princeton, NJ: Princeton University Press, 1980).

Disaggregating State Capacities

As states have multiple – not singular – capacities,[40] it is an empirical task to identify and predict these "differences in the way states are organized and then connect those differences to variations in [political] outcomes."[41] Any attempt to capture how state capacity varies over time or across domestic institutions "requires differentiating among the features of the state in order to assess their relative importance; [so] the state becomes less than the sum of its parts."[42] Following Skocpol, there are three "general underpinnings of state capacities": plentiful resources, administrative–military control of a territory, and loyal and skilled officials.[43] These features generally correspond with the two necessary dimensions of state capacity: extractive/coercive capacity and bureaucratic capacity. Extractive/coercive capacity involves the power sources of the state–society relationship, while bureaucratic capacity reflects the quality and autonomy of public institutions.

There are also variations in a state's infrastructural and despotic power: the degree to which states are capable of implementing policies is analytically separate from how policy priorities are chosen and the extent of citizen control over elites.[44] Both types of power involve policy implementation but differ in where the sources of capacity come from. Despotic power allows leaders to act autonomously from social or market actors: they can thus make unpopular decisions about force or unpopular legislation, particularly over the "high politics" of security policy.[45] The despotic capacity for coercion is central to the powers of a modern Weberian state, which possesses a monopoly on the legitimate use of force within its territory.[46] This is the element that allows a state to protect against internal and external threats, control borders, and enforce compliance over policies controlling and harnessing violence. Tied to coercive capacity is the despotic capacity to raise and maintain revenue for the security apparatus of the state. States are defined by their ability to tax constituents,[47] and a state's extractive capacity directly determines its

---

[40] Weiss.   [41] Evans, *Embedded Autonomy*, 40–1.

[42] Margaret Levi, "The State of the Study of the State." In *Political Science: The State of the Discipline*, edited by Ira Katznelson & Helen V. Milner (New York, NY: W. W. Norton, 2002), 33, 34.

[43] Theda Skocpol, "Bringing the State Back In: Strategies and Analysis of Current Research," in Evans, *Bringing the State Back In*, 16.

[44] M. Mann, *The Sources of Social Power* (Cambridge, UK: Cambridge University Press, 1984), 59.

[45] Ibid.   [46] Ibid.

[47] See Douglass Cecil North, *Structure and Change in Economic History* (New York, NY: W. W. Norton, 1981), 17, 21.

ability to extend its power, sovereignty, and security.[48] States must have enough extractive capacity to reach their entire population for the collection of rent and enough legitimacy to manage compliance and personnel for taxation.[49] The literature on despotic power is centrally concerned with policy implementation, evident most clearly when states overcome societal resistance.

In contrast, infrastructural power concerns how much a state can penetrate its society to implement policy.[50] A state with more infrastructural capacity is able to implement policy and enforce laws because of its effective interaction with society. This capacity requires dense linkages with social and market actors.[51] Infrastructural power reflects institutional quality: bureaucratic or administrative capacity relates to the ability of a state to formulate impartial and effective policy agendas and legislation in the national interest, deliver public goods and services, and regulate commercial activity.[52] Bureaucratic capacity requires autonomous, meritocratic, and professional bureaucracies and personnel with high expertise, legitimacy, enforced coordination, limited corruption and capture by private actors, and effective reach across state institutions and throughout a state's society.[53]

The relative quality and autonomy of bureaucracy varies and is a feature of effective governance. In the developing world, it is "the scarcity rather than the surfeit of bureaucracy that impedes development" and transformative policymaking; and "[i]f transformation demands an effective bureaucracy, there is no guarantee that supply will match demand."[54] Good bureaucratic institutions do not simply materialize because of legal authority or resources. Bureaucratic capacity is both crafted and dependent on linkages at many stages in the institutional process. The supply of high-quality, independent bureaucracies varies across states and political authorities, and also varies within states

---

[48] See Margaret Levi, *Of Rule and Revenue* (Berkeley: University of California Press, 1988), 2 ("The greater the revenue of the state, the more possible it is to extend rule."); Charles Tilly, *Coercion, Capital, and European states, AD 990–1992* (Hoboken, NJ: Wiley-Blackwell, 1992), 90–1 (using the Dutch as an example of a "capital-intensive state[]" that used "heavy-handed taxation" to extract military resources).

[49] See Levi, *Of Rule and Revenue*, 29–3 (explaining the importance of extracting capacity and managing the collection of and compliance with taxation).

[50] Mann, *The Sources of Social Power*, 59.   [51] Skocpol, 57.

[52] See generally Helena Olofsdotter Stensöta, "Impartiality and the Need for a Public Ethics of Care," in *Good Government: The Relevance of Political Science*, edited by Sören Holmberg & Bo Rothstein, 87–149 (Cheltenham, UK: Edward Elgar, 2012).

[53] Max Weber, *Vol. II: Economy and Society: An Outline of Interpretive Sociology*, Guenther Roth & Claus Wittich eds., Ephraim Fischoff et al. trans. (New York, NY: Bedminster Press, 1968/1978).

[54] Evans, *Embedded Autonomy*, 40.

themselves. All of these state capacities are interrelated: coercive capacity relies on the generation of revenues and high-quality bureaucracies. High-quality bureaucracies rely on revenue and the legitimacy of successful control of a population. The Weberian factors enhancing capacity include stable finances, authority, organizational coherence, and loyal and skilled officials. In an ideal type, the core public political authority is coherent and insulated but does not need to be so isolated as to preserve capacity and prevent capture. Capacity is enhanced through connections to external actors, and through joint projects, the resources of the private actors are channeled, while their risk is reduced under a rapidly changing environment. Ideally, the autonomy of the bureaucracy allows it to manage this risk while formulating its own goals, avoiding capture of the public agenda by private interests.

Governing Capacity

State capacity is a structural concept reflecting the latent and relative power of a state in its environment. It is based on the relative internal strength of its bureaucracies and its relations (infrastructural or coercive/despotic) with society. It reflects material inputs, not governing outputs. Governing capacity, on the other hand, captures actual policy agenda outcomes, or the "capacity of the state to effectively achieve its chosen policy outcomes."[55] A more descriptive definition of governing capacity is "the ability to marshal the necessary resources to make intelligent collective choices about and *set strategic directions* for the allocation of scarce resources to public ends."[56]

Governing capacity is enhanced by internal bureaucratic capacities, but good internal resources alone do not dictate policy outcomes. It is an analytical concept separate from the others. Governing capacity is also not coterminous with state authority but is interrelated with it, as it lies at the heart of agenda-setting governance, the exercise of power, and the translation of authority and resources into outcomes. Capacity – particularly governing capacity – has to be evaluated by looking at both "the quality and quantity of institutional resources and from the success of specific outputs and outcomes."[57] This can be done by looking at the whole of government but is most effective by looking at particular sectors or policy domains.

---

[55] Felicity Matthews, "Governance and State Capacity," *The Oxford Handbook of Governance* (2012): 291.
[56] Painter and Pierre, 2. Italics added.   [57] Ibid.

Sources of Capacity: Inside Out or Outside In?

State capacity is the structural, latent ability of the state to formulate and implement strategies to achieve economic and social goals. Whereas state capacity is latent, governing capacity reflects actual outcomes. Governing capacity is the relative effectiveness and governing skill involved in making public policy. The central premise of this book is that relative governing capacity explains other important EU outcomes such as agenda change and endogenous institutional authority. Another premise is that there are multiple sources of governing capacity: bureaucracy, society, and state–society interaction. From an institutional perspective, there are two competing or complementary sources of governing capacity. The first is the quality of the governing institutions, specifically the bureaucracy. These are the "inside" features of the political institutions. As Max Weber was the first to characterize the ideal features of a bureaucracy – such as expertise, meritocracy, material resources, and personnel continuity – we can think of this as the relative "Weberianness" of institutions. The other sources of capacity are external and come from factors such as the structure of society; the mobilization, density, and character of the interest group population; or the relational structure of the state–society relationship – its relative embeddedness.

Different kinds of states have different kinds of capacities. Different kinds of political challenges also require different kinds of capacities. An authoritarian or colonial state would require extractive capacity, a welfare state would require distributive capacity, and a state attempting to innovate the relationship between its society and market might require transformative – or a high governing – capacity.[58] It is more difficult to identify and to measure the outcome of governing capacity than extractive capacity.[59] In the past, scholars have assumed that state governing capacity is the product of insulated powerful bureaucracies, innovative policy instruments, or relative societal weaknesses. Four general approaches explain where capacity comes from, what causes capacity to increase or decrease, and why there are variations across states and time in capacity: (1) corporatism, or organized social interests, (2) statism, or strong states coercing organized social interests, (3) state bureaucracies insulated from interest group capture, or (4) embedded autonomy, where capacity is the result of positive interactions between state bureaucracies and organized social interests.

---

[58] Weiss.
[59] J. Kugler and W. Domke, "Comparing the Strength of Nations," *Comparative Political Studies* 19, no. 1 (1986): 39–69.

From a corporatist perspective, governing capacity comes exclusively from external industry groups. Organized social and market interest groups are able to powerfully negotiate with government actors and also deliver policy implementation outcomes because of densely reinforced linkages within the private actors.[60] Measuring corporatist capacity entails measuring the structure of society and variations in these bottom-up interests.

From a statist perspective, governing capacity comes from inside the state institutions; the stronger and more insulated it is, the better it can withstand any private social influence.[61] Government performance is therefore predicted by the internal resources of a bureaucracy: Weberian factors including stable finances, authority, organizational coherence, and loyal and skilled officials. Variation is explained by weak states having fragmented institutions and strong states having centralized or insulated institutions.[62] This internal capacity allows states to "implement official goals, especially over the actual or potential opposition of powerful social groups or in the face of recalcitrant socioeconomic circumstances."[63] A strong state is defined by the organizational quality of its executive branch and bureaucracy, which produces the capacities to formulate policy agendas and implement them without any concerns of interest-group capture, to coerce powerful private actors in opposition to go along with the policy agenda[64] or implementation,[65] to ignore the best-organized social interests within a policy domain,[66] and to restructure the content and boundaries of a policy environment, including laws, regulations, and rights.[67]

A third bureaucratic autonomy perspective delinks state autonomy in its ability to formulate policy agendas in the public interest from its ability to implement those policy agendas.[68] The heart of state capacity, then, is bureaucratic insulation from powerful interest groups during the

---

[60] For example, see Katzenstein, *Small States in World Markets*; J. H. Goldthorpe, *Order and Conflict in Contemporary Capitalism* (Oxford: Clarendon Press, 1984).

[61] J. Zysman, *Governments, Markets, and Growth: Financial Systems and the Politics of Industrial Change* (Ithaca, NY: Cornell University Press, 1983), 269.

[62] P. J. Katzenstein, *Between Power and Plenty: Foreign Economic Policies of Advanced Industrial States* (Madison: University of Wisconsin Press, 1978); Zysman; Krasner, *Defending the National Interest*; Peter Gourevitch, "The Second Image Reversed: The International Sources of Domestic Politics," *International Organization* 32, no. 4 (1978): 881–912; G. John Ikenberry, *Reasons of State: Oil Politics and the Capacities of American Government* (Ithaca, NY: Cornell University Press, 1988).

[63] Skocpol, 9.   [64] Gourevitch, 902.   [65] Skocpol, 9.

[66] Amanda R. Tillotson, "Open States and Open Economies: Denmark's Contribution to a Statist Theory of Development," *Comparative Politics* 21, no. 3 (1989): 341.

[67] Krasner, *Defending the National Interest*.

[68] Evans, *Bringing the State Back In*; Zysman.

agenda setting stage of policymaking.[69] The factors that insulate a state from society are Weberian in nature: bureaucratic meritocracy and the political insulation and centralization of the bureaucracy.

Perspectives locating state capacity in either the relative organization of state or society have limitations, however. Corporatism narrowly focuses on outcomes of state economic policy (because of its focus on unions and industry) and on the relationships among private actors, rather than the state–society or government–industry relationships. It overemphasizes the organization and structure of society and underemphasizes the organization and structure of the state. Statist perspectives emphasize the important variations in the organization of state bureaucracies and administrative structures but underemphasize the organization and structure of society and the state–society relationship. Additionally, state strength is often not uniform across policy domains: a state can have a strong foreign policy but weak industrial policy. There is no one idea of state capacity: it is a relational concept that varies along different "arenas" or state institutions and policy domains. In fact, the unevenness of state capacity might be the factor with the most explanatory power over state behavior and capabilities.[70]

Additionally, state strength might produce successful policy outcomes (policy agenda formulation and implementation), but it does not explain the content of policy agendas. A state might achieve limited policy goals, but this should not mark it as having high capacity, per se. The difficulty of those goals should also be taken into account, to understand where capacity comes from in complex and challenging policy environments. Similarly, state autonomy is not the same as effectiveness. A state can be highly autonomous in formulating and implementing profoundly ineffective policy agendas. The bureaucratic autonomy perspective produces a refined organizational conceptualization of why state capacity varies, but it also overemphasizes bureaucratic structures and underemphasizes social organization and state–society linkages.

Embedded Autonomy and Governed Interdependence

The fourth framework for understanding sources of capacity is the idea of embedded autonomy. It reverses the assumption that any state capacity to formulate and implement policy depends on the weakness of social or industry actors, either their lack of mobilization or fragmentation. It

[69] Stephan Haggard and Chung-In Moon, "Institutions and economic policy: Theory and a Korean case study," *World Politics* 42, no. 2 (1990): 210–37.
[70] Skocpol.

comes from observations of newly industrializing countries and historical European states. Peter Evans recognized the capacity of developing states as both a product of both strong institutions insulating public bureaucracies from capture and policy networks crafted between state and society. Capacity explains why some states were able to transform their socioeconomic environments; it is highest in institutions simultaneously insulating the economic bureaucracy from special interests and establishing coordinated links between bureaucrats and organized business.[71] High-capacity, effective bureaucracies are autonomous in their policymaking but are sufficiently embedded in particular industrial networks to implement policy. Bureaucratic structure, authority, or autonomy do not provide sufficient raw governing material for effective and transformational public policy because when the state is too insulated, it cannot interact with society for the sake of implementing policy.[72] This balancing act – embedded autonomy – is an ideal type reflecting a delicate state–society relationship where the state is autonomous enough to avoid policy capture while being embedded enough to implement policy agendas. Embeddedness does not just help with decentralized implementation: it also provides bureaucrats with intelligence and expertise for formulating effective and relevant policy agendas.

This embeddedness perspective shifts the idea of capacity away from an exclusive focus on formal state institutions. Autonomy by itself does not lead to governing capacity in complex or challenging policy environments. Autonomy and Weberian bureaucratic insulation are important, but these must be intensely "embedded in a concrete set of social ties which bind the state to society and provide institutionalized channels for the continual negotiation and renegotiation of goals and policies."[73] The embeddedness perspective is Weberian in that it has a strong corporate identity and is meritocratic. It also has dense links to private elites in a shared project around a particular policy agenda. The variable is not just state or society but their interaction. Instead, good policy outcomes reflect the chemistry of combining "Weberian bureaucratic insulation" with "intense immersion in the surrounding social structure."[74] For Evans, the

---

[71] Peter B. Evans, "Predatory, Developmental, and Other Apparatuses: A Comparative Political Economy Perspective on the Third World State," *Sociological Forum* 4, no. 4 (1989): 561–87.

[72] Mann, *The Sources of Social Power*, chapter 3.

[73] Peter Evans, "The State as Problem and Solution: Predation, Embedded Autonomy and Structural Change," in *The Politics of Economic Adjustment: International Constraints, Distributive Conflicts, and the State*, edited by Stephan Haggard and Robert R. Kaufman (Princeton, NJ: Princeton University Press, 1992), 162.

[74] Evans, "Predatory, Developmental, and Other Apparatuses," 561.

efficacy of the developmental state depends on a meritocratic bureaucracy with a strong sense of corporate identity and a dense set of institutionalized links to private elites... it depends on the existence of a project shared by a highly developed bureaucratic apparatus with capacity built on historical experience and a relatively organized set of private actors who can provide useful intelligence and a possibility of decentralized implementation.[75]

The idea of embedded autonomy does not only apply to late industrializing developing countries with successful outcomes. Most modern political systems have elements combining an insulation of bureaucracies (such as lobbying transparency laws and revolving-door policies) and embeddedness (such as public–private partnerships, epistemic policy communities, or advisory boards). The postwar development of Japanese capacity was driven by this combination of Weberian bureaucracies and linkages between bureaucrats and interest groups.[76] In a European context, Peter Hall explained variation in British and French capacity by adding the relational study of the state–society relationship to the structure of the state and society.[77] Many states and societies face transformational policy challenges (political, economic, or social) requiring effective governing power, albeit different forms of power.[78]

Variations in Embedded Autonomy

How does a state–society outcome like embedded autonomy emerge? Is it by accident, by design, or both? Explaining why embedded autonomy drives capacity outcomes in some states more than others, Linda Weiss (1998) developed the idea that when bureaucracies face particularly challenging policy environments, they consciously develop tight but selective linkages with private actors, actively structuring access points for some groups and excluding others. The result of this strategic but balanced network, when successfully led by state bureaucracies, is high governing (Weiss calls it transformational) capacity. This governing capacity outperforms policy expectations for major social, political, economic, or industrial reforms. Embeddedness is not serendipitous; it is strategic on both the state and society sides of the network. It is inherently about politics and power, not the product of a neutral, interest- or cleavage-free epistemic community.

Embeddedness is tightly circumscribed and delicate, involving two highly strategic groups of actors: bureaucrats seeking to include some groups and exclude others, and interest groups seeking access points.

---

[75] Ibid., 575.   [76] Johnson.   [77] Hall, "Governing the Economy."
[78] See Weiss, 66–8 on different kinds of economic transformations.

It is tightly circumscribed because it usually happens only in the early stages of a policy domain, before an explosion of pluralist interests overwhelms any form of gatekeeping (on the part of bureaucrats) and venue shopping (on the part of entrepreneurial private actors). It is delicate because it requires some prior internal bureaucratic capacity: to manage this interaction, to extract intelligence and expertise, and to direct decentralized policy implementation, all while preventing or minimizing private capture of the public policy agenda. The ideal of embedded autonomy exists in a narrow window of time: the state–society interactions of embeddedness create the kind of governing capacity that outperforms policy expectations, but its balance of state–society power may be inherently too delicate to last.[79] The relative strength of society is a special kind of "infrastructural power"[80] when it is tapped by Weberian bureaucrats for policy collaboration. This interaction also requires skilled bureaucrats to manage this infrastructural power so it does not overwhelm state power.

The embedded autonomy framework is analytically powerful for understanding cross-national differences in institutional arrangements and policy outcomes. However, there are missing elements. The first is how the balance of embeddedness changes over time. If informal networks between bureaucrats and private actors evolve over time, there must be multiple possible paths for this state–society interaction. Society could overwhelm the state, the state could suppress society, or the nature of the policy agenda could shift and reorganize interests and power. The conditions under which embeddedness evolves could also either deepen or undermine formal public institutions and authority through the emergence of informal institutions.

The embedded autonomy framework assumes an ideal scenario where there is consensus and coordination between interested public and private actors, rather than conflict or competition among different interests. There might not just be consensus between embedded public and private elites; there might also be gaps in interest representation, socioeconomic cleavages, and political economy dynamics of winners and losers that produce less than ideal outcomes such as capture or corruption. Over time, embedded networks between public and private actors often also become informal institutions. Only some networks between

---

[79] Evans acknowledged this himself (by making capital strong, they become their own gravediggers; Evans, *Embedded Autonomy*, endnote 22 on page 37). Linda Weiss, however, does not agree, as she considered the increasing strength of social actors to be possible new and reinvigorated sources for state capacity "in line with the changing nature of transformative tasks in industrial society" (Weiss, 38).

[80] Weiss, 39.

public and private actors are made formal, such as the EU phenomenon of "expert groups" advising the European Commission on policymaking. Over time, these informal institutions might alternately undermine or reinforce formal institutions and authority, depending on their sources of power and authority. Last, the embedded autonomy framework is not only an ideal type; it reflects a stable political environment. Formal institutions and roles are set, authority is clear, and Weberian bureaucratic capacity has had time to mature. In a new, nascent, or shifting political area, this delicate balance between insulation and embeddedness may not be so clear. There may be an important prehistory to how public bureaucracies became autonomous – or not – in the first place. There may even be no formal authority at all within a policy domain, just emerging informal institutions. This is often the case in "limited statehood," but it could also be analytically relevant to international, regional, and supranational institutions, who also govern under conditions of "limited statehood."[81]

The Demand for and Supply of EU Authority?

So how do organized private interests affect the governing capacity of EU institutions within a policy domain? Do they strengthen the EU's organizational resources through acquiring private expertise and market knowledge? Do they enhance the ability of EU institutions to craft better policy agendas, know their social or market constituencies, or more effectively implement policy? Do interactions with interest groups allow EU institutions to promote broader and deeper policy agendas? Or do interactions with interest groups constrain EU institutions by way of more pluralism, more voices and demands, and even the possible imprint of powerful private interests on EU public policy agendas? Under what conditions do organized private interests create alternative, competing, complementary, or substitutive informal institutions that change EU authority over time?

Research linking interest groups and EU governing capacity has been brought up once before. The neofunctionalists Sandholtz and Stone Sweet observed that "the capacity of supranational organizations to make rules in a given policy domain appears to vary as a function of the level of transnational activity."[82] They proposed this association goes beyond

---

[81] For a discussion of the idea of "limited statehood" see T. A. Börzel and T. Risse, "Governance Without a State: Can It Work?," *Regulation & Governance* 4 (2010): 113–34.

[82] Sandholtz and Stone Sweet, 14.

mere correlation to a causal linkage: when there are more transactions occurring from the bottom up in a particular domain, there may be greater EU authority to take initiative and make policy than where there are fewer transactions.[83] If there is transnational demand for a Europeanized policy but no treaty-based EU authority, "the relevant actors will create one."[84] They also proposed the opposite: when there are no transnational, bottom-up interest groups demanding more integration and no costs to a lack of EU cooperation, the EU policy domain will not develop. This is why, they argue, as of the mid-1990s, there was no EU Common Foreign and Security Policy (CFSP).

Sandholtz and Stone Sweet's framework has a functional logic predicting the emergence of policy domains based on bottom-up transnational demand. In addition to institutional emergence, they proposed that interest-group activity predicts the success or failure of EU institutions. When the EC/EU project stalled or slowed, the culprit was not sovereignty problems or intergovernmental bargaining but the creation of policy domains without sufficient transnational social or market demands for those institutions. The opposite logic is also at work: transnational demand for international regimes can surge ahead of the rate at which they are constructed by national and European elites. While "the treaty revisions of the 1980s took place in the context of a demand for more cooperation," the EU institutional crisis that followed was "partially precipitated by the limits of the institutions and organizations of the EC to deal with these activities."[85]

---

[83] Rather than transcend these questions, the authors attempted to provide a much-needed taxonomy of policy domains in the European Union. It has been one of the core debates in EU analysis to evaluate whether the EU should be thought of as an intergovernmental organization representing the preferences and limitations of the member states or as a supranational governance organization with agency, preferences, and ability to shape outcomes. In Sandholtz and Stone Sweet's contribution to this debate, they subsumed the argument by constructing a continuum where some policy domains are more intergovernmental in nature (such as defense policy), whereas others are more supranational (such as the single market or monetary policy).

[84] Sandholtz and Stone Sweet, 17. The example they give for supranational governance in a policy domain in lieu of an intergovernmental treaty authorizing it is the telecommunications sector. It was not in the founding Treaty of Rome, and subsequent provisions specifically exempted it from EU competition regulations. This exemption was undermined by a succession of European Court of Justice (ECJ) rulings, which the European Commission used to reinterpret and refine its role in the domain. The commission then issued clarifying directives, supported by transnational lobbies, which generated an informal body of rules that had the effect of liberalizing the sector beyond any of the member states' preferences (Sandholtz and Stone Sweet, 18, see chapters 5, 11).

[85] Sandholtz and Stone Sweet, 14.

The Demand for European Governance?

The idea that bottom-up demand might overwhelm insufficient public institutions is familiar but one not normally associated with the European Union or international institutions. It is also not part of the contemporary logic of Western European states, as they are advanced industrial social democracies that generally have an institutional surfeit rather than an institutional deficit. Students of comparative politics – particularly in the developing world – would recognize this phenomenon immediately, however. In developing states with rapidly changing social or economic conditions, there are often suboptimal outcomes when there is a bottom-up demand for institutions, but the (often young) public institutions are not sufficiently developed in order to absorb and redirect this demand.[86] This logic of institutional supply and demand can also apply to international regimes. With the increasing phenomenon of social or market interests directing their interest toward regional or international institutions, there may also be a mismatch between supply of governing institutions and the demand for those institutions. This could take a number of different forms (in the EU context): (1) if there is bottom-up demand but no existing intergovernmental treaty, interest groups may mobilize to create the policy domain; (2) if there is bottom-up demand but weak intergovernmental treaty authority or resources, the international institution such as the EU may not have the capacity to deal with the volume of demand and activities, leading to institutional decay and policy stagnation; and (3) if there is no transnational demand, there should be no emergence of a European treaty, regime, or institution[87] in that policy domain.

---

[86] Samuel P. Huntington, *Political Order in Changing Societies* (New Haven, CT: Yale University Press, 1968).

[87] In assessing how policy domains are constructed in the EU, Fligstein and McNichol establish three necessary theoretical features (N. Fligstein and J. McNichol, "The Institutional Terrain of the EU," in *European Integration and Supranational Governance*, edited by A. Stone Sweet and H. Sandholtz, 59–91 [Oxford: Oxford University Press, 1998]). Adapted from the organizational state literature (E. O. Laumann and D. Knoke, *The Organizational State: Social Choice in National Policy Domains* [Madison: University of Wisconsin Press, 1987]), mature policy domains require an eventual constitutional/legal agreement to create legislation; a collective definition of what the issues are, who has power and why; a set of organized governmental actors responsible for policy in the domain (their "turf"); and "organizational capacity and procedures to mobilize the production of new rules in the domain (i.e. legislation)" (Fligstein and McNichol, 60). The actors constituting the domain are government organizations but often also include nongovernmental actors and outside interest groups, which can also be other governmental organizations. All of the domain actors are "organized to participate in a collective debate with the goal affecting the content of legislation or agreements" (ibid., 61).

Neofunctionalists have proposed that interest-group mobilization is linked to EU political development. But in order to explain and understand this possible structural relationship between the EU "state" and its society, I have incorporated this logic into a larger institutional and comparative framework. This has come with a few major changes regarding the assumptions and dynamics at work. First, I have relaxed the functional logic predicting the demand for European institutions as driven by rational or universal processes. In neofunctionalist theory, the rational logic of spillover made interest groups demand European integration for their domain after having observed success in other domains. This never happened empirically, and it proved to be the (premature) downfall of the theoretical framework. Later neofunctionalists such as Sandholtz and Stone Sweet (1998) theorized the cause of interest-group bottom-up mobilization to be the threats and opportunities of globalization, creating pressures on markets and societies, leading to a demand for the EU to provide an institutional bulwark against these forces. This very well may be true, under certain conditions, but globalization is too blunt a driver for predicting all bottom-up mobilization. There is too much variation across policy domains and over time – as I discuss in Chapter 2 – for this to be the case.

There have to be other institutional or political economy mechanisms at work between the bottom-up demand and top-down supply of EU institutions, where supply and demand might not always be neatly matched. If bottom-up demand (fueled by globalization pressures) were the source of all EU institutionalization, we would not see significant variation in both demand mobilization and quality of EU institutions and agendas. There would be almost uniform mobilization from all parts of society and the market, not irregular mobilization. In the next section, I review the possible mismatching of supply and demand for EU institutions. There are multiple paths and outcomes of the state–society relationship: ones taking into account the uncertain and multivariate roles that play out between public institutions and private interest groups, particularly in developing political environments.

This leads to my third major departure from the neofunctional framework: the introduction of disaggregated concepts and mechanisms for understanding the multiple causes and consequences of different state–society configurations of supply and demand. This has taken two forms. The first was to theorize and measure the role of capacity in EU governance. Capacity is a difficult and slippery concept, with multilayered causes and effects. It is also a chicken–egg problem: governing capacity is the outcome of interest for this study, but governing capacity often comes from some form of previously existing capacity, making for confusing causal relationships. These causal dynamics, however, are clearer when disaggregated, separated by different policy domains, and traced over time periods and institutional sequences. Organized interests can provide one source of external capacity for EU bureaucracies, but there are other internal structural factors involved in this process, including the degree to which the EU bureaucracy possesses sufficient resources for its policy tasks, the timing of mobilization, and, most importantly, the trade-offs balanced by EU bureaucrats between the additional capacity provided by external groups and their public interest autonomy.[88]

In order to deal with the complexity of capacity, it has to be disaggregated into multiple separable but interrelated concepts. There are at least three different kinds of capacity. There is the outcome variable of governing capacity, also called policy capacity in certain literatures. It is a measure of governing effectiveness. It may emerge from the bottom-up sources of the mobilization of society or the structure of society. As theorized by neofunctionalists, the structure of society is based on the overall mobilization of social or economic interests. It can also reflect the density[89] or "configuration of bias"[90] within mobilized private interests. Density reflects how many actors are involved in the policy process (whether the policy domain is quiet or cacophonous, intimate or diverse). The structure of bias reflects the degree to which for-profit or nonprofit interests dominate policy domains, and the degree to which this is in flux or stable. The structure of society – meaning mobilized interest groups – has varying degrees of "infrastructural power,"[91] based on its second-order concepts: mobilization, density, and bias. It is an open question, however, to what degree society directly impacts public governing capacity, or whether other factors are also at work. Under many conditions, the sources of governing capacity may also be an outcome of other elements, such as internal bureaucratic capacity and state–society embeddedness.

The concept of embeddedness is the most complex of all state capacities because it varies as a product of the right kind of public interactions with the private sector, rather than simply by internal resources or authority. In many historical or ideal forms of bureaucracy, there was little room for direct interactions between bureaucrats and civil society,

---

[88] For Sandholtz and Stone Sweet, the dependent variable is degree of institutionalization. For this study, the dependent variables are the amount of legislation and the content of the policy agenda emanating from EU institutions.

[89] D. Knoke and J. H Kuklinski, *Network Analysis* (Sage, 1982).

[90] Baumgartner and Jones.   [91] Weiss, 39.

and public policy research focused solely on the delegation and interaction between the politicians and administrators. However, this ideal type has little to do to with the effectiveness of public administrations in many countries, as delegation is often not the sole product of power relations between branches of government.[92] The mode, scope, and character of relations between agencies of the state and organizations in society – in particular major economic actors – are equally important to political outcomes.

Internal Capacity: Bureaucratic Autonomy and Governing Capacity

State capacity reflects all of the possible (latent and active) structural resources a state can harness for governance, both within its institutions and from its society and state–society interactions. The internal source of capacity for a state is its bureaucratic capacity (sometimes called organizational capacity or bureaucratic autonomy), reflecting the variation in the internal characteristics of public governing institutions. Bureaucratic capacity is the ability of the state to "manage efficiently the human and physical resources required for delivering the outputs of government."[93] It is the sum of the internal resources and structure of state institutions. It does not, however, reflect governance outcomes, such as policymaking, agenda setting, or implementation.

The idea that bureaucracy matters comes from Max Weber's original hypotheses on the taxonomy of ideal administrative forms. The quality and capacity of bureaucracy is a feature of effective governance. A well-organized, meritocratous bureaucracy with a commonly understood purpose can set quality agendas, craft effective policies, and implement political solutions. In contrast to the idea that states and bureaucracies get in the way of good policy, it is "the scarcity rather than the surfeit of bureaucracy that impedes development" and governing capacity, and "if [policy] transformation demands an effective bureaucracy, there is no guarantee that supply will match demand."[94] Good bureaucratic institutions do not simply materialize because of legal authority or bottom-up functional demand. Bureaucratic capacity is crafted at many

---

[92] See Myung-Jae Moon and Patricia Ingraham, "Shaping Administrative Reform and Governance: An Examination of the Political Nexus Triads in Three Asian Countries," *Governance* 11, no. 1 (1998): 77, 79 (explaining that in Korea the bureaucratic apparatus "gradually became more politically empowered in the course of continuing political democratization and bureaucratic institutionalization" despite relatively even political power split among the branches of government).

[93] Evans, *Embedded Autonomy*, 40.   [94] Ibid.

stages in the institutional process. The supply of high-quality, independent bureaucracies varies across states and political authorities, and it also varies within states themselves. States have multiple – not singular – capacities,[95] and it is an empirical task to identify and predict these "differences in the way states are organized and then connect those differences to variations in [political] outcomes."[96]

Bureaucratic capacity is a necessary condition for producing governing capacity and governing effectiveness, but it does not exist in a vacuum. Even the strongest public institutions have relied to a certain degree on their interactions with relevant sectors of the society or market they are tasked with transforming. This is particularly true when a governing institution has weak or new sources of authority or legitimacy. In Gerschenkron's 1962 study of late industrializing states in Europe, the developing state possesses few entrepreneurial capacities on its own: it requires interaction with society to transform the political economy. Rather than regulate or redistribute, its primary role is to manage risk. It is a topic of research at the level of the nation state but not normally applied to international, regional, or supranational organizations such as the EU. Although nearly two decades have passed since Barnett and Finnemore (1999) called for the greater study of the "organization" of international organizations, there are few systematic studies of the structure of international bureaucracies.

State capacity – the broadest and most structural concept – is interrelated with both bureaucratic and governing capacity but is relational, reflecting public–private dependence and alliances. For reasons I explain in the next section, I refer to state capacity in this context as "embeddedness." High embeddedness (state capacity) ends up impacting both bureaucratic and governing capacity, but may not be even across policy areas of government. It can even have inverse effects across state policies, where high embeddedness (state capacity) in one policy domain means low embeddedness (state capacity) in another.

Governing Capacity Processes and Outcomes

A state's embeddedness can vary based on its interaction with interest groups, but the causal impact on governing capacity is not clear: interest groups sometimes enhance governing capacity and sometimes detract from it. Interest groups can detract from governing capacity when their preferences overwhelm the public interest on legislation or policy or when state functions are hollowed out from the outside in when too many

---

[95] Weiss.   [96] Evans, *Embedded Autonomy*, 40.

aspects of public policy are outsourced or based on private power. This process is driven by the interaction over time of key factors such as the prior existence of a certain level of bureaucratic capacity and the relative agreement between public and private interests over the policy agenda.

This translates into unintended consequences for embeddedness increasing or decreasing EU governing capacity, particularly when it comes to policy agendas. When organized interests anticipate EU authority and mobilize early, EU institutions will enjoy increased governing capacity, but their bureaucratic capacity and autonomy for setting policy agendas without private influence can be constrained. If EU institutions have sufficient authority and public resources, however, this embeddedness translates not into agenda capture, but into more effective implementation, as the EU can craft policies more relevant and legitimate to social and market actors.

Enhanced EU governing capacity as a result of these interactions is not a predetermined outcome. Outcomes – particularly for agenda setting and institutionalization – can vary greatly in the configuration of mobilized interest groups and EU institutions. One result is zombie policy,[97] where the policy domain remains somewhat "ungoverned." Another result is increasing endogenous EU political authority but accompanied by private-interest capture of the policy agenda. Yet another result looks like "governed interdependence"[98] or "embedded autonomy," where a strong and mobilized bureaucracy is able to effectively harness the interests of mobilized interest groups to use their external capacity and resources, all while avoiding complete policy agenda capture.

Alternately, when there is a surfeit of organized interests in a policy domain, EU institutions may have sufficient legal authority but will not have the benefit of access to embedded transnational social and market actors. They may have bureaucratic capacity, but no embeddedness, or state capacity. This negatively impacts the governing capacity of EU organizations. There is also no risk of agenda capture, cronyism, or corruption because bureaucrats have a great deal of autonomy from private influence. But the success of the policy agenda (governing capacity) will suffer from a lack of social partners to provide expertise or assist with implementation.

These premises translate into a window of opportunity early on in the life of an EU policy domain. There is a temporal story to the structure of EU–society relations, as there is in other developing and established

---

[97] Clifford Bob, *The Global Right Wing and the Clash of World Politics* (New York, NY: Cambridge University Press, 2012).
[98] Weiss.

polities. This window allows for partnerships between nascent public and strong private actors. If interest groups are not mobilized at this time, the public bureaucracy will have a reduced bureaucratic capacity. Even when more authority is delegated to the EU and more groups eventually mobilize, there may be too much pluralism to produce partnerships. Policymaking then happens in a vacuum or in a cacophonous and weak pluralist network.

There are differential paths in the demand and supply for EU institutions and state–society relations. This interaction can take different forms and will have different opportunities and constraints. For example, interest groups may well enhance EU governing capacity, but they may do so at a cost to bureaucratic autonomy. There are differential implications for agenda setting and policy capture. The neofunctionalist framework may well be correct that interest groups are a key driver of EU governing capacity, but this association may have important, real-life implications for policy agendas and institutionalization. This is straightforward: if interest groups have an interest in the creation of EU institutions and authority, they may likely leave their preference imprint on EU agendas.

Changes in European Union Institutions and Authority

In a last major departure from the neofunctional framework, I introduce additional mechanisms into this uncertain institutional process to better understand the paths and outcomes. These mechanisms include informal institutions – the "rules of the game" that coordinate aspects of politics outside of official public authority structures. They are created by public and private actors as competing, substituting, or complementary to formal institutions and can often end up replacing or advancing them. This is the final theoretical innovation, which fills a gap in our understanding of how interest groups could enhance the EU's governing capacity, leading to outcomes where capacity could create or enhance authority. The classic political theories of institutions, derived from Weberian notions, posit that formal authority leads to capacity. The mechanisms explaining how informal institutions can create formal institutions provides a pathway for explaining how the opposite can also hold: interest groups creating informal institutions, which have so much legitimacy they may enhance the (state and bureaucratic) capacity of formal public institutions, leading to changes in formal authority.

Informal institutions can be created from a number of bottom-up or top-down social, political, and economic networks. These networks can have more or less even distribution of resources and power[99] and can be subject to phenomena where there are winners and losers. This concept is equivalent – in the study of U.S. institutions and agenda setting – to the idea that there are varying structures of society, or "configurations of bias," that change by policy domain and directly impact policy outcomes.[100] Informal institutions emerge because formal institutions are incomplete, ineffective, uncertain, or do not reflect political reality. When they become regular practices reinforced over time, they are analogous to the concept of "subgovernments" in the study of U.S. politics.[101]

Informal institutions may also be created in pursuit of goals that are not internationally acceptable. In the case of the EU, informal institutions may be created at the EU level in pursuit of goals that may not be domestically acceptable back in European capitals. They may also emerge because the political domain has shifted rapidly, and this provokes venue shopping on the part of actors and organizations to try to address this institutional uncertainty.

Informal and Formal Institutions

What is the relationship between informal and formal institutions? Is there a way informal institutions can endogenously become formal? Helmke and Levitsky (2004) developed a typology of the degree to which the policy agenda goals of informal institutions and formal institutions are in conflict or consensus and possible outcomes where informal institutions undermine, reinforce, or substitute for formal institutions. This goes beyond static frameworks characterizing formal–informal institutional relationships as inherently cooperative (for example, epistemic communities, where all actors are working toward the same goals) or dysfunctional (for example, where all public–private interactions are considered clientelism or corruption). There are two dimensions: the first is the degree to which formal and informal institutional outcomes converge or diverge. The second is the relative effectiveness of extant formal institutions or the degree to which they constrain or enable the choices of political actors. These dimensions create four patterns of informal institutions. Two reflect the traditional questions of whether state–society

---

[99] Precisely because of these differences, scholars should take seriously the process of making informal rules by identifying the actors, coalitions, and interests behind the creation of such rules. To the extent that these rules are created in a context in which power and resources are unevenly distributed, they can be expected to produce winners and losers.

[100] Baumgartner and Jones.   [101] Ibid.

interactions are competing or complementary, but there are two other patterns to address: accommodating and substitutive. Competing informal institutions result in informal institutions that violate formal rules, with familiar outcomes such as corruption. Complementary informal institutions result in informal institutions that converge with and complement already effective formal institutions. These scenarios resemble arrangements such as corporatist bargaining in advanced industrial democracies.

In the two analytically novel outcomes, accommodating informal institutions complement and legitimate formal institutions but simply serve as an extra channel or outlet for divergent social or market interests. An example of this is a consociational state, where ethnic or religious interests organize along informal institutional rules but do not challenge the core governing rules of the state. Substitutive informal institutions are the most interesting for explaining institutional change: bottom-up rules are compatible with formal, top-down public institutions, and eventually the informal institution successfully achieves the goals formal institutions were designed to achieve. These informal institutions typically emerge where state institutions are weak or lack authority. Although examples of substitutive informal institutions proliferate in less developed states, they may also have explanatory power for understanding institutional change in international or supranational political systems such as the EU.

This typology reflects the idea that informal institutions do not always undermine formal institutions and public agendas. This is analytically similar to the concepts surrounding embedded autonomy. Sometimes they can achieve public agenda results that public institutions could not achieve alone or have failed to achieve altogether. It is an open question, however, to what degree informal institutions over time continue to exist alongside formal institutions, or whether they eventually endogenously become formal institutions with political authority. In the language of institutional sequencing and historical institutionalism, path dependence sometimes reinforces the trajectory of institutions, but some paths are "self-reinforcing" while others are "non-reinforcing."[102] Some informal institutions may reinforce formal institutions; others may undermine them or trigger institutional change that replaces or competes with existing formal institutions.[103]

---

[102] Paul Pierson, "Increasing Returns, Path Dependence, and the Study of Politics," *American Political Science Review* 94, no. 2 (2000): 77.

[103] Avner Greif and David D. Laitin, "A Theory of Endogenous Institutional Change," *American Political Science Review* 98, no. 4 (2004): 633–52.

Explaining Endogenous Institutional Change

Typologies of informal institutions reveal the conditions under which institutional change might occur and the linkages between informal and formal arrangements. Typologies do not explain, however, the processes through which informal institutions become formal. Formal institutions are often created by a legal demand for authority or coordination, but can also endogenously emerge out of the "repetition and diffusion" of informal strategies and interactions among economic, social, and political actors.[104] This bottom-up diffusion of informal practices can create "both the impetus and the legitimizing basis for... key reforms."[105]

The opposite can also happen, where changes in formal institutions impact the basis for informal institutions. Informal institutions may change because of changes in formal institutions, including legal or administrative reforms or changes in allocation of resources or authority. Changes in formal institutions may also impact the capacity and effectiveness of public bureaucracies. Depending on the type of relationship between formal and informal institutions, these formal changes may either weaken or strengthen informal institutions.

When public and private actors interact to create informal institutions with mutual benefits for all, this is the threshold that can trigger endogenous institutional change.[106] Whether or not adaptive informal institutions replace formal institutions depends on the relative capacity, effectiveness, and legitimacy of the existing formal and emerging informal institutions. Importantly, these adaptive institutions and formal changes can emerge even in the absence of interest group demand.[107] Any organized interests creating institutional practices through cumulative informal interactions have a powerful yet indirect structural effect on the endogenous creation of formal institutions or the deepening of their authority. Understanding how this happens, however, is an empirical question requiring the process tracing of reaction sequences between top-down and bottom-up state and society movements over a policy agenda over time. Indeed, "[d]etermining when and whether adaptive informal institutions will have such catalytic effects is politically contingent and requires empirical study of both the high politics and the apparently apolitical low politics of grassroots adaptations to formal institutions."[108]

This logic of informal endogenous adaptive institutions comes from an observation of formal and informal practices in the Chinese political system. It can also explain the political development of a political system

---

[104] Tsai, 118.   [105] Ibid.   [106] Ibid., 126.   [107] Ibid., 140.   [108] Ibid., 141.

such as the EU. The Tsai (2006) informal adaptive institutions framework helps us understand how interest groups can indirectly (and even accidentally) create external capacity (through informal institutions with increasing legitimacy) that serves to advance a policy agenda at the EU political level. When the policy agenda goals of this informal institution align with the goals of formal EU institutions, this can lead to the conditions under which EU authority endogenously emerges or significantly deepens. This endogenous institutional change can occur, even in the absence of external shocks, functional demands, direct bottom-up lobbying of interest groups, and the preferences of powerful member states.

The indirect mechanism of how informal institutions with external, bottom-up capacity can lead to more political development fills an analytical gap in the original neofunctional theory of the European Union. The causes (bottom-up interest-group activity) and consequences (more EU authority and deeper formal institutions) are the same in the neofunctional framework and in my emergent, adaptive institutional framework. What differs are the paths taken in how the process unfolds and the mechanisms at work for how interest groups with Europeanized goals and interests can lead to the emergence of formal EU institutional outcomes. Interest groups fuel political development in structural and unintended ways: they may not even want more EU authority or regulation, but the accumulation of their practices and interactions creates informal institutions promoting EU legitimacy and capacity, which can lead to more EU authority and formal institutional change. Political development can then follow the same logic as neofunctionalism, as it can happen without (or against) the preferences of powerful EU member states. The phenomenon of endogenous institutionalization also provides an alternative to the conventional wisdom about the theoretical relationship between authority and capacity. The conventional wisdom is that formal authority is prior to governing capacity and that formal authority creates governing capacity. This informal adaptive institutional logic also allows for the reverse phenomenon: capacity that emerges out of the interactions between bottom-up actors and the legitimacy of their informal institutions can lead to changes in formal authority and, consequently, in state and bureaucratic capacity.

2 Mr. Smith Goes to Brussels

The EU provides a rare contemporary opportunity to study the coevolution of political institutions, markets, and society. The "rules" of the EU originate in the 1957 Treaty of Rome, which expanded the common market and created functional issue areas.[1] In the context of EU policy and EU studies, these issue areas are known as policy domains. Environment is one policy domain, for example, and Energy is another. The European Economic Community (EEC) and European Atomic Energy Community (Euratom) were created in 1958. The Treaty on the European Union (TEU) – the Maastricht Treaty – was signed in 1992, creating the EU out of the foundations of the EEC.

The Treaty of Rome established an institutional structure with four branches: the Council of Ministers, the European Commission, the European Court of Justice (ECJ), and the European Parliament. The Council is an intergovernmental body of foreign ministers from each member state, voting on legislation proposed by the Commission based on qualified majority rules, whose decisions national legislatures are legally bound to follow. As a diplomatic body, it is the least accessible institution for transnational European society and interest groups.

The European Commission is supranational, meaning it is not bound by intergovernmental input or diplomatic bargaining between European

---

[1] The 1957 Treaty of Rome that established the European Economic Community created an institutional structure divided by policy fields (or policy domains). Additional treaties have added more policy domains to the EU's institutional structure, but member states established most EU policy domains in 1957. However, changes in legislation have altered the voting rules in many policy domains, from unanimous to qualified majority voting, or from intergovernmental to transfer to the supranational authority of the European Commission. These changes in domains have significantly altered the boundaries and content of the EU's agenda in a given issue area. Subsequent intergovernmental treaties such as Maastricht (1992) added domains such as education, culture, public health, and consumer protection. Newer domains, such as information policy and immigration and border security, have been even more recent. Only one area of policy activity was not the product of a formal intergovernmental treaty until the Lisbon Treaty implemented in December 2009: military and security cooperation.

member states. It is the executive branch of the EU, generating legislative proposals for the Council and parliament and overseeing policy implementation. It offers the greatest access to lobbyists, experts, and interest groups through its twenty-eight Directorate-Generals (DGs), distinct departments organized by policy areas. Indeed, the Commission is reliant on outside advice and expertise, as it has a broad regulatory burden and limited resources. The DGs are each led by a Commissioner, individuals appointed by their member states for long tenures with no term limits. The Commission is supported by a long-term EU civil service with meritocratic recruitment.

The judicial branch of the EU is the ECJ. It enforces the treaties and secondary legislation pursuant to litigation brought by private organizations, individuals, and states. These decisions are binding on all parties involved, including nation states. In the 1960s, the ECJ established the principle that EC/EU rules could overrule national law in situations in which the two came into conflict, in what is called the doctrine of supremacy. The ECJ also decided, under certain conditions, that EC/EU law confers judicially enforceable rights and duties on all subjects of EC/EU law, including firms and individuals. National laws and courts are obliged to protect these rights, in the doctrine of direct effect. Taken together, these decisions have transformed the Treaty of Rome and the EC/EU over time from an international organization to a quasi-federal hybrid political system.[2]

The European Parliament is a directly elected body co-legislating with the Council, which sets the EU budget and advises the Commission. When founded, it served as an advisory body, but after the Maastricht treaty, the Parliament gained greater agenda-setting powers and some veto authority.[3] It gained even greater powers with the 2009 Lisbon Treaty. The Parliament has intensive contacts with organized society and lobbyists, and it monitors them through a mandatory register. In exchange for registering, lobbyists are accredited and receive special passes to access Members of the European Parliament (MEPs). MEPs have been elected every five years since 1979.

[2] R. D. Kelemen, "Built to Last? The Durability of EU Federalism," in *Making History: European Integration and Institutional Change at Fifty*, edited by S. Meunier and K. R. McNamara, 51–66 (New York, NY: Oxford University Press, 2007); A. M. Slaughter, A. Stone Sweet, and J. Weiler, *The European Court and National Courts-Doctrine and Jurisprudence: Legal Change in Its Social Context* (New York, NY: Bloomsbury Press, 1998).

[3] G. Tsebelis, "The Power of the European Parliament as a Conditional Agenda Setter," *American Political Science Review* 88, no. 1 (1994): 128–42.

In addition to these primary EU institutions, there is a plethora of independent EU agencies and executive bodies.[4] The function of the agencies is similar in nature to the European Commission, which acts as an independent executive body. The European Commission used to be viewed as an independent, neutral "superagency," but over the past few decades, member states have viewed the Commission with increasing suspicion over its federalist motives.[5] Indeed, as member states have become more sensitive to the transfer of additional authority to the Commission, there has been a political conflict between the necessity of expanding the regulatory capacity of the EU without adding to the supranational authority of the Commission. As a solution to this impasse and to limits on expanding its own capacity, the Commission proposed the creation of independent agencies.

Member states often created institutional structures for these agencies that were designed to fail, or which were at least weak by design, in order to limit any further bureaucratic or political drift of power toward Brussels.[6] Agencies have been established in areas where the Commission is weakest and where it has the least control over intergovernmental policies. In areas where the EU already had broad supranational authority and competencies, the Commission has been more reluctant to establish agencies and delegate power or outsource capacity to another political entity. This logic is similar to the dynamic noted in other federal or multilevel polities such as the United States or developing states, where the greatest administrative challenge for the federal bureaucracy is posed by the preexisting institutional authorities at another level of government.[7]

Two agencies studied in this book are the EDA and Frontex, the EU's border control agency. Established in 2004, the EDA operates in a political environment where the EU has had little to no supranational authority over policy, reports directly to the European Council, and is controlled by a board of member states. Established in 2005, Frontex reports directly to the Commission, has had increasing resources and

---

[4] There are currently more than forty independent executive agencies, including the European Food Safety Authority, the European Space Agency, and the Office for Harmonisation in the Internal Market.

[5] G. Majone, "The European Commission: The Limits of Centralization and the Perils of Parliamentarization," *Governance* 15, no. 3 (2002): 330.

[6] R. D. Keleman, "The Politics of 'Eurocratic' Structure and the New European Agencies," *West European Politics* 25, no. 4 (2002): 93–118.

[7] S. Skowronek, *Building a New American State: The Expansion of National Administrative Capacities, 1877–1920* (New York, NY: Cambridge University Press, 1982); T. M. Callaghy, *The State–Society Struggle: Zaire in Comparative Perspective* (New York, NY: Columbia University Press, 1984).

legal authority since its founding, but has had mixed policy outcomes in a high-profile domain of immigration, asylum, and border security.

This complex mix of organizational competences, decision rules, and legislative procedures can be confusing to participants and analysts. National governments often seek to maintain power through their control of the Council and through the activities of their permanent representatives in processes otherwise managed by the Commission. But, with qualified majority voting in many policy domains and the enhanced role of the EP, member states often find themselves having to accept legislation they voted against. Monitoring and controlling the Commission are costly and difficult propositions, especially when the Commission has a more activist agenda. Finally, national governments do not control the interpretation or enforcement of EU law; they have to contend with the possibility that the Commission or a private party may win a court case for (government) noncompliance with EC rules.[8]

The fragmented nature of EU institutional structures provides multiple channels or venues through which advocacy groups seek to influence policymaking in multiple areas. Although many groups lobby through their national representatives in intergovernmental forums such as the Council or their national legislatures, the most important institutional targets are the Commission, the European Parliament, and increasingly, independent agencies. The Commission is an interest group target because it sets the agenda and legislative initiative in areas covered by EU community law, while the European Parliament attracts attention from lobbyists who target legislative committees. In addition to these established, more formal methods of influence, there are myriad cooperative formats for influence and lobbying, such as the expert groups the Commission relies on for policy expertise, "groups of personalities" in advisory roles, and public–private forums set up by European bureaucrats for access to key market and social actors.

In addition to these informal institutions, there is an unknown element of informal influence and consultation going on at the day-to-day level, where lunches, conferences, policy briefings, informal meetings, and telephone conversations link public and private actors. Academics and other observers have described these relations, noting the rise of groups and the increasing interaction between the EU and organized European society. Some have attempted to characterize the variation in interest groups by policy domain, arguing that there might be more groups in

---

[8] A. Stone Sweet and T. L. Brunell, "Constructing a Supranational Constitution: Dispute Resolution and Governance in the European Community," *American Political Science Review* 92, no. 1 (1998): 63–81.

supranational domains than in intergovernmental domains, or more in redistributive domains than regulatory domains.[9] There have been few efforts, however, to assess how variations in these relations across different policy areas and over time affect governance at the EU, particularly the content and direction of agendas.

Interest Groups and Lobbying in Brussels

Brussels has become an active and dynamic center of political activity. The EU has grown in size and scope since its establishment in 1992 and its history as the EEC: within a decade "approximately 80 percent of all social, economic, and environmental regulation applicable in the Member States [was] adopted through the EU policy process."[10] European capitals still control key areas of national policy such as education and taxation, but in other policy areas, they have delegated significant amounts of governing and regulatory responsibility to the EU. Even more visible has been the explosion of interest and advocacy groups in the EU political arena. It is not a mystery why the lobbyists are interested in EU public affairs: "all the [regulatory] decisions are made here . . . telecom, health care, and if you think of any other industry, then regulation that is going to impact your business is going to come out of here."[11] EU officials' interactions are over "80 percent [with] lobbyists . . . they phone me, they pick me up downstairs, they write me a hundred letters a day . . . it is not possible to get from here to the entrance and not see any lobbyists."[12] Lobbying is not just about influencing legislation: "monitoring" – the insider term for surveillance of EU institutions, including reviewing draft legislative material for informal industry feedback – accounts for up to 70 percent of professional lobbying in Brussels.[13] Lobbying comes in all shapes and sizes: even the Vatican lobbied EU institutions at one point to include more explicit mentions of Christianity in the EU's Draft Constitutional Treaty,[14] and delegations representing regions of Ukraine have lobbied for accession to the EU.[15]

---

[9] See, for example, Fligstein and McNichol.

[10] S. Hix, *The Political System of the European Union* (New York, NY: St. Martin's Press, 1999), 211.

[11] G. Bowley, "As the EU's Influence Grows, So Does an Army of Lobbyists," *The International Herald Tribune*, November 19, 2004.

[12] Ibid.

[13] A. Rettman, "Multi-Million Market for Inside EU Knowledge," *EU Observer*, March 10, 2012.

[14] Bowley, "As the EU's Influence Grows, So Does an Army of Lobbyists."

[15] G. Gotev, "Special Report: Ukraine Region Tests EU Lobbying Water," *EurActiv*, September 16, 2011.

This interest-group activity is intensifying, but it is not new. Ever since the 1950s and the formation of the European Coal and Steel Community (ECSC), European society has been mobilizing to lobby European institutions. Industry interests, European Federalists, and some national interest groups advocating for including more sectors in what would become the EEC in 1958 were among the first organized actors. Even Jean Monnet – the federalist founder of the ECSC – used a powerful, private lobby group made up of national party and trade union leaders (the "Action Committee for the United States of Europe") to push for more supranational authority and to implement federalist goals for the EC.[16] Business interests mobilized first, because the EEC regulated industry. Big business formed the first transnational industry associations, such as the European Roundtable of Industrialists (ERT), which pushed for greater breadth and depth of market integration across Europe.[17] Formed in 1983, the ERT lobbied national governments and the commission for deeper market integration across Europe, allowing them to operate in a larger scale market than their fragmented national markets. With exclusive access to leaders and deeper resources than public bureaucracies, the advocacy of the ERT is what pushed the single-market project to the top of the European agenda and imprinted business preferences on the agenda.[18] A few years later, European member states passed the Single European Act of 1986, the precursor to the Maastricht Treaty of 1992.

Until the 1970s, interest groups were few in number. A handful of business associations lobbied the EC, mostly through informal diplomatic channels. This changed with the first direct election of the European Parliament (EP) in 1979. Across Europe, firms, associations, and civil society mobilized to investigate the policy process in Brussels. The 1986 Single European Act was another impetus for mobilization, as it eliminated unanimity voting in the European Council and enhanced the role of the European Commission and Parliament. These changes made EU legislation more complex and advocacy more attractive to social and market actors across Europe.

Large degrees of influence over EU policy outcomes have been attributed to EU interest groups. Officials have recounted how EU standards and market reforms were outsourced to industry associations in areas of electronics, telecom, and services. Indeed, industry groups seem to enjoy a certain honeymoon phase in EU policymaking – for a period

---

[16] D. Dinan, *Ever Closer Union: An Introduction to European Integration* (Boulder, CO: Lynne Rienner, 1999), 30.

[17] Hix, *The Political System of the European Union and How to Fix It*, 234.

[18] Green Cowles, "Setting the Agenda for a New Europe."

of time, they have often been the only outside interests involved in policy domains. For example, organized farming interests advocated for policy reforms in the Common Agricultural Policy (CAP). Until the 1980s, rural and agribusiness interests were alone at the table with the EC and "had a firm grip on the CAP and could successfully resist major reform. Farmers maximized political support for the CAP by lobbying effectively and by portraying themselves as a disadvantaged and beleaguered group providing a vital service to society."[19] In the CAP policy domain, other interests organized later in the 1980s, resulting in more interest pluralism, including "consumer and environmental groups, several Member States governments and a number of foreign governments."[20] The greatest acceleration in interest-group mobilization occurred after 1992 and the Maastricht Treaty establishing the EU. This trend increased throughout the 1990s, when the executive role of the European Commission bureaucracy expanded and many independent policy and regulatory agencies were created to deal with the growing EU agenda.

But how do EU officials and organized European society interact? Initial academic inquiries into the topic of EU interest groups asked why groups were in Brussels in the first place. Nonstate actors taking interest in the affairs of an international institution created by states, for states is a novel phenomenon. In recent decades, the intensifying political role of the EU has muted this question. Other research agendas focused on identifying the identity and numbers of actors and groups. There is no clear answer, however, to how the presence of European interest groups changes EU political outcomes. Many observers have applauded the increase in advocacy and lobbying in Brussels because such input might make the EU more transparent, legitimate, and democratic. Others are concerned about this explosion of unregulated and undocumented lobbying interacting with an international institution designed for member-state interests.

By 2005 an estimated 20,000 individual lobbyists and more than 2,600 interest groups had established offices in Brussels, operating with more than 60 to 90 million euros of revenue.[21] In comparison, the European Commission and Parliament employed around 20,000 total European civil servants. Some lobbyists themselves say 20,000 is a low estimate: a more maximalist definition estimates 50,000 to

---

[19] Dinan, 339.
[20] Hix, *The Political System of the European Union and How to Fix It*, 252.
[21] Kallas, S. "The Need for a European Transparency Initiative." Speech at the The European Foundation for Management, Nottingham Business School, March 3, 2005, Nottingham, England.

100,000 lobbyists.[22] In comparison, there were 13,167 registered lobbyists in Washington, DC, the same year.[23] Ten years later, EU lobbying increased by upward of 50 percent,[24] while U.S. numbers actually decreased to 11,162. Estimates put 70 percent of EU interest groups as for-profit and 20 percent nonprofit; less than 10 percent represent other levels of government, such as subnational regions, cities, and other international institutions.[25] These are estimates because there is no consistent reporting of how many interest groups, firms, associations, NGOs, and other actors are active in Brussels. Nor are they required to report their existence, contacts, or budgets to the EU or European states; since 2011 there has been a voluntary lobby register with limited participation, although it is set to become mandatory in 2017,[26] due to a lack of compliance on the part of major firms and industries.[27]

This concentration of lobbying makes Brussels the second largest point of public–private interaction in the world, behind Washington, DC. Large multinational firms and small- to medium-size businesses lobby on their own behalf, but they also contract out to professional lobbying consultancies. Political and management consultants have flourished, as have law firms crossing over into the business of professional lobbying. U.S. lobbying firms have proliferated in Brussels, seeing the EU as a "regulatory superpower" allowing easier access to power than Washington, with fewer constraints and weaker ethics rules than in the United States.[28]

Interactions between the EU and European society are far broader and more complex than the activities of professional lobbyists. Experts, EU-funded "expert groups," academics, NGOs, European interest associations, national interest associations, and other private and public actors advocate through both formal and informal channels. This is done formally through "consultation,"[29] where any advocacy group may register a formal response to EU policymaking. A brief glance at the consultation database reveals little private-sector activity on record, meaning that

[22] Bowley, "As the EU's Influence Grows, So Does an Army of Lobbyists."

[23] OpenSecrets Website. https://www.opensecrets.org/lobby/

[24] Euractiv News, "EU Lobbyist Register to Become Mandatory by 2017," *EurActiv*, April 16, 2014.

[25] S. Bianchi, "EU Confronts the 'Murky World' of Corporate Lobbying," *Inter Press Service*, December 22, 2004.

[26] L. Philips, "EU Lobbyists Shun European Commission Register," *EU Observer*, 2004. http://EUObserver/9/26695/?rk=1.

[27] N. Nielsen, "EU Lobbyist Register Gives Incomplete Picture," *EU Observer*, June 25, 2012.

[28] E. Lipton and D. Hakim, "Lobbying Bonanza as Firms Try to Influence European Union," *The New York Times*, October 18, 2013.

[29] See http://ec.europa.eu/yourvoice/consultations/index_en.html

70 percent of interest groups lobby via other means. Informal interactions are the norm, as policymaking is "more discreet and informal than in Washington,"[30] where "important work happens on the telephone, or a lunch or coffee get-together."[31]

Expertise in European-level policy is at a premium in Brussels. EU policy institutes and think tanks are on the rise, driven in part by retiring EU officials and other policymakers capitalizing on their EU-specific expertise. Privatization and outsourcing practices are also increasing. In fact, one of the inaugural decisions of the European External Action Service (EEAS) upon its creation in 2010 was to hire private security firms rather than public servants to guard its new foreign embassies and diplomats.[32]

The extent to which interest groups have influenced the content of EU legislation is unknown. But anecdotes of influence abound. MEPs have been accused of writing an amendment weakening an EU terrorism and money laundering directive "borrowed word-for-word from the European Banking Industry Committee [EBIC],"[33] and without identifying "which [words] came from EBIC and which came from other sources."[34] An American lobbyist with Verizon recalled she "even sat at a keyboard in the Commission and the [European] Parliament and typed in language" into legislation and had relatively easy access to directly influencing legislative content: "because they have such a shortage of staff, the Commissioners are relatively easy to see."[35]

So far there have been several high-profile impropriety exposures of blurred public–private boundaries.[36] Watchdogs are concerned about how easy it is to move from the public to the private sector, with limited and lagging revolving-door policies for EU officials. After a recent scandal, the Commission suggested a voluntary code of conduct with a one-year "cooling off" period for commissioners before accepting private sector jobs.[37] The code of conduct was further clarified in 2010 after a number of Commissioners immediately joined the

---

[30] W. Bland, "Le Lobbying, forgotten victim of a revolution," *European Voice*, September 22–28, 2005, 27.
[31] Lipton and Hakim, "Lobbying Bonanza as Firms Try to Influence European Union."
[32] A. Rettman, "Ashton to Spend €15mn on Private Security Firms," *EU Observer*, March 3, 2012.
[33] G. Simpson, "Lobby in Europe Helps Sway Law on Terror Funding," *Wall Street Journal*, May 24, 2005, sec. News.
[34] Ibid.
[35] C. Matlack, "Why Brussels Is Abuzz with Lobbyists," *Business Week*, October 29, 2007.
[36] M. Saltmarsh, "EU: Lobbying, European style," *International Herald Tribune*, October 27, 2006.
[37] "The Revolving Door Temptation," *Corporate Europe Observatory*, 2007. http://archive.corporateeurope.org/revolvingdoors.html

industries they formerly supervised.[38] An influence scandal in 2012 prompted further review of the evolving ethics codes and a promise of future reform, including strengthening the investigative role of the EU ombudsman.[39] Commissioners have not helped matters by "blank[ing] out, CIA-style, the names of lobbyists when releasing records of meetings."[40]

In addition to hiring former civil servants, some lobbyists have imported techniques from the United States such as front groups, where a corporation threatened with regulation hires a public relations or lobbying firm to produce its own scientific arguments. For example, the Bromine Science and Environmental Forum and the Alliance for Consumer Fire Safety in Europe were created by and share office space in Brussels with the international public relations firm Burson-Marsteller, working on behalf of a consortium of manufacturers of the chemical bromine, a substance the EU had been trying to limit.[41] In 2005, a grassroots effort called Campaign for Creativity featured artists and musicians in favor of a patent directive to protect their "creative genius" that – "like a butterfly" – is "fragile and needs to be nurtured,"[42] but the campaign was backed by Microsoft and other software multinationals and organized by a London public relations firm (using a technique originating in the United States known as "astroturfing").[43]

A growing watchdog community has raised alarm about the role of interest groups in EU policymaking. Groups such as Corporate European Observatory, ALTER-EU, Lobbycontrol, and Spinwatch have been framing EU politics as a smoky backroom of corporate influence over public policy. They actively investigate corporate activities and lobbying, including nominating corporations and EU bureaucrats for "Worst EU Lobbying" and "EU Conflict of Interest" awards each year.[44] According to the watchdogs, the EU is ripe for corruption due to a lack of mandated transparency. They highlight the voluntary lobby register as an

[38] L. Philips, "Commission Rules to Be 'Improved' in Light of Revolving Doors Cases," *EU Observer*, September 9, 2010.
[39] J. Fleming, "Commission Probed over 'Revolving Door' Lobbying Allegations," *EurActiv*, February 14, 2013.
[40] A. Bounds, "Shielding Lobbyists' Identities Keeps Lid Firmly on 'Black Box' of Brussels," *Financial Times*, July 25, 2007.
[41] M. Saltmarsh, "EU: Lobbying, European style," *International Herald Tribune*, October 27, 2006.
[42] See the campaign's website at http://web.archive.org/web/20050305124006/campaignforcreativity.org/camp4creativity/
[43] An example of astroturfing in Europe: http://www.spectrezine.org/content/europesworst-lobby-campaign-creativity-wins-coveted-award
[44] L. Philips, "Biofuel Worst Lobbying Award," *EU Observer*, December 9, 2008.

example of this.[45] After intense media coverage of transparency failure, the biggest lobbying firms promised to sign up for the register, but many firms and interest groups still have not done so.[46]

In 2008, the transparency advocacy alliance ALTER-EU (made up of 160 smaller organizations of environmental, labor, and academic groups) published a report called "Secrecy and Corporate Dominance," accusing the European Commission of excessive reliance on experts from business and industry groups. The specific charge centers on "expert groups," a system of more than 1,200 panels of individuals advising the Commission on policy areas such as biotechnology, clean coal, and car emissions.[47] The groups have increased by over 40 percent since 2000, with more than 50,000 individuals as members. The memberships and agendas of expert groups are not public information, but ALTER-EU requested access and received the records for about a third of the Commission's groups.[48] The records document corporate representatives making up the majority of the membership of more than two thirds of the groups, while only one third of the groups had a "more balanced allocation of stakeholders" and one expert group was unbalanced in favor of NGOs.[49] Under pressure, the Commission promised to release its information on expert groups, but eventually stalled because of experts' privacy concerns.[50]

Specific cases highlighted by the transparency campaigners include the EU chemical legislation known as REACH – "Registration, Evaluation, and Authorization of Chemicals" – an eight-year campaign by EU officials to increase consumer protection from environmental chemicals and pollutants. REACH generated an intense lobbying campaign pitting corporations against NGOs and resulted in a significantly reduced

---

[45] L. Philips, "Major Lobby Firms Set to Join EU Register," *EU Observer*, September 9, 2008.

[46] Media articles cited lobbying firms' fears of client confidentiality and financial disclosure in not signing up for the register. PR firms such as Hill & Knowlton are also absent because of concerns over journalists uncovering "how much (the) Russian firm Gazprom pays for advocacy in the EU capital, or if the government of Ukraine has hired a consultancy company to help out its diplomats." In Philips, "Major Lobby Firms Set to Join EU register."

[47] H. Mahony, "EU Accused of Heavy Reliance on Industry Lobbyists," *EU Observer*, March 25, 2008.

[48] Ibid. The Commission cited privacy concerns over commerce or security in refusing to disclose information on 34 percent of the groups and released only partial information on another 34 percent.

[49] "Secrecy and Corporate Dominance: A Study on the Composition and Transparency of European Commission Expert Groups," *ALTER-EU*, 2008. http://www.alter-eu.org/documents/reports-studies/2008/03/25/secrecy-and-corporate-dominance

[50] H. Mahony, "EU under Pressure to Shed Light on Expert Panels," *EU Observer*, August 11, 2008.

final legislation. EU Commissioners were so inundated with faxes, meetings, and calls from the chemicals industry that they "just didn't have the resources to respond" with alternative policy proposals to the corporate interests.[51] Similarly, Statewatch highlighted the EU homeland security sector, specifically the €1.4 billion European Security Research Programme (ERSP), as one vulnerable to private influence.[52]

Beyond exposés over alleged influence or high-profile incidents, it is difficult to capture the everyday lobbying[53] dynamic in Brussels. In contrast to Washington, there are no mandatory registries, nor are there concrete regulations for the interaction of public and private actors. Of all the EU institutions, only the European Parliament has an accreditation registry and a mandatory code of conduct for interest groups. In other branches of EU government, there is little accounting for the real degree of interaction between EU and interest groups. The paucity of data in this area undermines our ability to understand EU policymaking: relations between interest groups and non-elected bureaucrats or public servants are critical axes of power and interest.

A lack of facts has not stopped a normative policy debate over private influence. In the corridors of Brussels, the question is not the degree to which the EU is influenced but whether lobbying is normatively good or bad. The Commission promoted transparency measures to protect policymakers from "listen[ing] to the inner voice of evil . . . it is always better to install a set of tangible guarantees to prevent human weaknesses to prevail. Sometimes political institutions are on the slippery slope before they are aware of it."[54] Reformers felt the EU was particularly vulnerable to outside influence because its policymakers acutely need lobbyists and policy advocates for their experience, resources, and information. Siim

---

[51] M. Saltmarsh, "EU: Lobbying, European Style," *International Herald Tribune*, October 27, 2006.

[52] L. Philips, "EU 'Homeland Security' Lacks Democratic Oversight, Says Watchdog," *EU Observer*, February 10, 2009.

[53] There is some debate over which terms to use for the concept of lobbying (Mahoney, "Networking vs. Allying."). There are a number of different groups involved, from professional consultancies and lobbying firms to interest groups, advocacy, and organized civil society. Other terms, such as *private actor activity* or *organized bias*, also imply the same activity. However, not all actors are private: they represent other levels of government or public affairs. Some actors involved in lobbying are not as organized, however, as individual firms and associations lobby, as well. I use the terms "interest groups" or "organized interests" when I want to characterize all actors and groups, as they are all entities attempting to influence the EU political process, regardless of their size, affiliation, or profit status. Somewhat confusingly, official EU documents equate the term "interest group" with nongovernmental, nonprofit groups, but I use the term more broadly, in the American context, to mean groups that are nongovernmental, both nonprofit and for profit.

[54] Kallas, "The Need for a European Transparency Initiative."

Kallas, who led the transparency initiative on behalf of the Commission, penned an editorial entitled "Mr. Smith Goes to Brussels," where he argued that although Brussels has less corporate involvement in elections and more moderate sums of money spent on advocacy, it should not ignore the moral quandary of public–private boundaries and fall prey to "excessive naivety," hoping Abramoff-scale affairs would not happen in Brussels.[55]

Indeed, the European Commission released its first-ever report on political corruption within EU member states on February 3, 2014. The study originally attempted but failed to also measure corruption within EU institutions themselves. The Commission concluded it could not evaluate EU corruption because there are no existing academic studies or objective metrics on international or supranational corruption and therefore could not further pursue the topic.[56] Transparency International followed up with an external 250-page report on EU institutions, concluding that they are vulnerable to corruption due to loopholes and poor enforcement of rules on ethics, transparency, and financial control.[57]

In contrast, many in Brussels argue that true violations of the public interest or detrimental private capture are impossible. Even though the EU lacks transparency, there are fewer material temptations than in Washington for impropriety: less money and pork and fewer personnel revolving between the public and private sectors. Advocacy and lobbying may change EU outcomes, but everyone in Brussels has the "best intentions," is "on good behavior,"[58] and are a "bunch of gentlemen compared to the U.S."[59] EU lobbyists claim U.S. lobbyists woo public officials for distributing funds, while in the EU, these interactions are legitimately based on the regulatory expertise of interest groups. They argue the €90+ million in lobbying spending in Brussels is dwarfed by the over €2.4 billion U.S. firms spent (in 2004). Although these distinctions are important, they only serve to compare elected legislative branches of government and their public–private relations, not the interactions of unelected bureaucrats with organized interests.

Others argue there is little difference between lobbying approaches or tactics in the two capitals, only differences between issue characteristics

[55] S. Kallas, "Mr. Smith Goes to Brussels," *Wall Street Journal*, February 6, 2006.
[56] N. Nielsen, "EU-Wide Corruption Report Drops Chapter on EU Institutions," *EU Observer*, January 31, 2014.
[57] J. Kanter, "Anti-Corruption Group Finds Fault With European Union," *The New York Times*, April 24, 2014.
[58] W. Underhill, "Real Wheeling and Dealing in Brussels; Has the Lobbying Industry Grown out of Control?" *Newsweek*, March 6, 2006.
[59] A. Bounds, "Secret Lobbying of Brussels Condemned," *Financial Times*, December 18, 2007.

and institutional settings.[60] Additionally, some observers argue that lobbying in Brussels has gained an undeservedly negative, shadowy connotation: EU lobbying has been exclusively informational, especially before the internet era, where policy experts provided a needed resource to EU officials.[61]

European Interest Groups and EU Governing Capacity

How do European transnational interest groups impact the EU? The EU was designed as a club of sovereign nation states, not a separate or additional venue for absorbing organized interests across European society. This question has come full circle in fifty years: interest groups were central to the first neofunctional theories of European integration, but were absent from the next generation of intergovernmental theories explaining the lack of European integration. But interest groups were in Brussels even when they fell out of academic favor: while they didn't increase when neofunctionalists predicted they would, neither did they disappear when the EU was stagnant and IR theorists predicted that member-state interests would drive European integration. IR literature focuses on how collective action problems are overcome in international institutions, not how the content of policy or political outcomes is made or how international institutions interact with interest groups.[62] Attention to this question is growing, as the transnational mobilization of non-state actors is not just a European phenomenon. With increasing globalization, scholars have turned their attention to the intersection between international bureaucracies and non-state actors,[63] particularly the role

---

[60] See C. Mahoney, *Brussels versus the Beltway: Advocacy in the United States and the European Union* (Washington, DC: Georgetown University Press, 2008).

[61] D. Bilefsky, "Lobbying Brussels: It's Getting Crowded; Critics Urge Openness for Merchants of Influence," *International Herald Tribune*, October 29, 2005.

[62] As an international institution, it has been normal to view the EU through an intergovernmental lens: the study of issue formation in the politics of international institutions is often limited to structural or functional explanations. For realists or intergovernmentalists, it is the power dynamic and preferences of European member states that determine EU issues or agendas. The literature on international regimes offers more explanatory frameworks for explaining EU political outcomes. International regimes are often seen as functional outcomes of cooperation in response to international collective action problems (R. O. Keohane, *After Hegemony: Cooperation and Discord in the World Political Economy* [Princeton, NJ: Princeton University Press, 1984]; S. D. Krasner, "Structural Causes and Regime Consequences: Regimes as Intervening Variables," *International Organization* 36, no. 2 [1982]: 185–205).

[63] M. E. Keck and K. Sikkink, *Activists Beyond Borders. Advocacy Networks in International Politics* (Ithaca, NY: Cornell University Press, 1998).

of private authority over international public decision making.[64] This IR debate is evolving from "debates over *whether* non-state actors matter... [to an] analytical focus on *how* they matter."[65] In this environment, international bureaucrats face stark political dilemmas: a "choice between benefiting from efficiency gains that accompany the emergence of private authority or retaining sovereign authority at the cost of economic and technological marginalization."[66] EU studies now also take seriously the public policy of the EU as a comparative political system with agenda-setting processes, interest-group politics, and bureaucratic politics, and not just the as the international outcome of structural or functionalist conditions. Others see the EU as unique, deserving its own *sui generis* theories for explaining political outcomes.[67]

The grand theories of European integration elevated the role of organized interests in accelerating international cooperation. For

[64] See T. Büthe, "Governance through Private Authority: Non-State Actors in World Politics," *Journal of International Affairs* 58, no. 1 (2004): 281–91; A. C. Cutler, V. Haufler, and T. Porter, *Private Authority and International Affairs* (Albany: State University of New York Press, 1999); R. B. Hall and T. J. Biersteker, *The Emergence of Private Authority in Global Governance* (Cambridge: Cambridge University Press, 2002); W. Mattli and T. Büthe, "Accountability in Accounting? The Politics of Private Rule-Making in the Public Interest," *Governance: An International Journal of Policy, Administration, and Institutions* 18, no. 3 (2005): 399–429.

[65] Büthe, 281, italics in original. Tim Büthe has attempted to develop a research agenda for studying the relationship between international organizations and non-state actors, specifically: (1) does the source or type of private authority matter? (2) do different issue domains change power dynamics between public and private actors? and (3) in the nineteenth and twentieth centuries, the state had the most capacity for regulating and providing public goods such as market regulation, infrastructure, social insurance, education, and defense. Is there a shift away from the state as the most efficient provider of public authority and goods? Is there a reverse trend – at both the domestic and international levels – of capacity shifting from public authority to private authority? Is private governance even a good idea?

[66] Hall and Biersteker, 285.

[67] The academic literature on European interest groups is growing every year. From a bottom-up perspective, the EU is an emerging opportunity structure for social and economic interests, but it has no agency and is exogenous to any state–society interaction. At the domestic level of politics in nation states, the interaction between state and society happens at the organizational level: it develops between bureaucracies and interest groups (within administrations) or between legislative committees and interest groups (in legislatures). In the case of the EU, empirical accounts sometimes document that the heart of the interactions between the EU state apparatus and European society is occurring between supranational agencies or institutions and interest groups mobilized toward the activity in Brussels. This concentration of activity, however, and the effect it has on the emergence of policy domains, the content or agendas of those domains, and the institutionalization of these domains in EU politics, is unexplained. A key element of public policy analysis of the EU has focused on the explosion of interest organizations in Brussels. In the past decade, this body of literature has successfully addressed questions of mobilization and collective action, such as why national interest groups might open Brussels lobbying offices and what choices they have of interest representation strategies.

neofunctionalists,[68] business associations and trade unions were a core element to their theories of how power and authority would be transferred to the European level through social demand and spillover. However, the postwar process of European integration did not match these linear expectations, and Ernst Haas retracted his original theoretical expectation.[69] The role of nation states in the integration process continued to be important, and their preferences remained powerful and immovable to any bottom-up social demand. From this empirical record, Stanley Hoffmann[70] and others developed an intergovernmental account of European integration, allowing transnational interest groups a limited explanatory role. When the integration process moved forward again in the 1980s, scholars turned toward other theories to help explain why. A new generation of scholars focusing on EU institutions[71] argued that organized business interests had a large role in European integration.[72] In the 1970s, scholars in comparative politics began to study interest groups in the European Community.[73] They observed that European "pressure groups" formed in response to a new opportunity structure for power, decision making, and potential advantages from regulation or distribution.[74] Pressure groups responded to increases in EC authority, with real consequences for society and the market.[75]

There are many parallels between patterns of EU interest-group activity and those inside nation states. At times, fragmented and multilevel

---

[68] Haas; L. N. Lindberg, *The Political Dynamics of European Economic Integration* (Stanford, CA: Stanford University Press, 1963).

[69] Haas, 318–59.

[70] S. Hoffmann, "Obstinate or Obsolete? The Fate of the Nation-State and the Case of Western Europe," *Daedalus* 95, no. 3 (1966): 862–915.

[71] W. Sandholtz and J. Zysman, "1992: Recasting the European Bargain," *World Politics: A Quarterly Journal of International Relations* 42, no. 1 (1989): 95–128.

[72] M. G. Green Cowles, "Organizing Industrial Coalitions: A Challenge for the Future?," in *Participation and Policymaking in the European Union*, edited by H. Wallace and A. Young, 116–40 (Oxford: Clarendon Press, 1997). These claims are contested by liberal intergovermentalists (A. Moravcsik, *The Choice for Europe: Social Purpose and State Power from Messina to Maastricht* [Ithaca, NY: Cornell University Press, 1998]), who provide theoretical arguments and empirical evidence that any further integration processes can be tied directly to member state interests and bargaining outcomes among powerful member states. In these accounts, interest groups have a limited role to play in European integration or policymaking beyond their lobbying their national capitals.

[73] D. Sidjanski, "Pressure Groups and the European Economic Community," in *The New International Actors: The United Nations and the European Economic Community*, edited by C. Cosgrove and K. Twitchett, 222–48 (London, UK: Macmillan, 1970); J. Meynaud and D. Sidjanski, *Les groupes de pression dans la Communauté européenne, 1958–1968: Structure et action des organisations professionnelles* [Brussels: Éditions de l'Institut de sociologie [de l'Université libre de Bruxelles], 1971); Emil J. Kirchner, "International Trade Union Collaboration and the Prospects for European Industrial Relations," *West European Politics* 3, no. 1 (1980): 124–38.

[74] Kirchner, 96–7.   [75] Sidjanski, 402.

EU institutions have promoted pluralist patterns of interest intermediation, rather than permanent corporatist partnerships with powerful
interests.[76] Some argue that the EU is a pluralist arrangement, or some
form of elite pluralist, compared to more corporatist continental European nation states.[77] But the EU's interactions with society can also look
corporatist, where there are dense networks with social and business
interest groups.[78] These governance structures vary and coexist across
EU institutions: some policy domains might be more corporatist or
statist (monetary policy, agriculture), while other policy domains (market integration, environmental policy) might be more pluralist.[79]

The structure of EU social relations also spurs a normative debate.
Underlying the question of whether the EU has a democratic deficit is
the degree to which it is opaque or accessible to European society.[80]
From this perspective, European interest groups are an improvement in
social legitimacy and voice.[81] Scholars of the EU have taken a sociological approach to theorizing the growth of interest groups in Brussels,
characterizing the structure of relations as "multi-level governance,"[82]

[76] W. Streeck and P. C. Schmitter, "From National Corporatism to Transnational Pluralism," *Politics and Society* 19, no. 2 (1991): 133–65.
[77] D. Coen, "The European Business Interest and the Nation State: Large-Firm Lobbying
in the European Union and Member States," *Journal of Public Policy* 18, no. 1 (1998):
75–100; Maria Green Cowles, "The Transatlantic Business Dialogue and Domestic
Business-Government Relations," in *Transforming Europe: Europeanization and Domestic Change*, edited by Maria Green Cowles, James A. Caporaso, and Thomas Risse-
Kappen, 159–79 (Ithaca, NY: Cornell University Press, 2001); Vivien A. Schmidt, *The
EU and Its Member-States: Institutional Contrasts and Their Consequences*. Working Paper
No. 99/7 (Köln, Germany: Max Planck Institute for the Study of Societies, 1999).
[78] Svein S. Andersen and Kjell A. Eliassen, "European Community Lobbying," *European
Journal of Political Research* 20, no. 2 (1991): 173–87; Mazey and Richardson 2001,
124; C. Mahoney, "The Power of Institutions. State and Interest Group Activity in the
European Union," *European Union Politics* 5, no. 4 (2004): 441–66.
[79] R. Eising and B. Kohler-Koch, *The Transformation of Governance in the European Union*
(London, UK: Routledge, 1999); J. Richardson, "Policy-Making in the EU: Interests,
Ideas and Garbage Cans of Primeval Soup," in *European Union, Power and Policy-
Making*, edited by J. Richardson, 3–26 (New York, NY: Routledge, 1996/2001/2006);
A. S. Yee, "Cross-National Concepts in Supranational Governance: State-Society Rela-
tions and EU Policy Making," *Governance* 174 (2004): 487–524.
[80] Giandomenico Majone, "Europe's 'Democratic Deficit': The Question of Standards,"
European Law Journal 4, no. 1 (1998): 5–28; A. Moravcsik, "In Defence of the 'Demo-
cratic Deficit': Reassessing Legitimacy in the European Union," *Journal of Common
Market Studies* 40, no. 4 (2002): 603–24.
[81] D. Imig and S. Tarrow, *Contentious Europeans: Protest and Politics in an Emerging Polity*
(Oxford, UK: Rowman & Littlefield, 2001).
[82] G. Marks, L. Hooghe, and K. Blank, "European Integration from the 1980s: State-
Centric v. Multi-level Governance," *JCMS: Journal of Common Market Studies* 34, no.
3 (1996): 341–78; I. Bache and M. Flinders, "Themes and Issues in Multi-Level Governance," *Multi-Level Governance* (2004): 1–11.

"soft law,"[83] "shared authority,"[84] and "networked governance."[85] In labeling interest mobilization as a phenomenon of increasing transparency, democracy, access, and equality, these approaches bypass the usual questions about public–private interaction in most political systems: to what degree is there tension or an imbalance in power and resources between public and private interests?

If You Build It (EU), They (Interest Groups) Will Come

The ongoing normative debate about influence is premature, as there is little academic work establishing to what degree the presence and concentration of private activity affects EU political outcomes. State-based explanations of European integration marginalize interest groups as having little or no effect on EU outcomes because policy outcomes are determined by national power or EU decision rules. More sociological explanations of European integration give causal importance to the role of interest groups but are dependent on the degree of authority granted from member states to the EU. This means lobbying and advocacy affects the EU, but the amount of lobbying and advocacy is dependent on how much authority the EU has over a policy. I call this the "Field of Dreams" argument about the relationship between the EU and groups: where "if you build it, they will come." The converse is also supposed to be true: if there is no EU authority over a policy, there should not be any advocacy activity. In an area of high politics such as foreign policy or defense – with very little EU authority and some intergovernmental policy – there should be very little interest-group activity and, therefore, no interest group impact on EU outcomes.

This is not sufficient for explaining the variation of interest group trajectories and EU political outcomes. Sometimes – as this book demonstrates – the "Field of Dreams" argument is true: after member states create EU treaty authority, more groups mobilize to the EU. But in some policy domains, when the EU does get more authority, no interest groups mobilize to lobby it. This is the "you build it, and nobody comes" pattern. This is what the EU policy domain of JHA (over police cooperation, border security, and immigration policy) looks like. States gave the EU partial supranational authority over immigration policy in 1997,

---

[83] U. Mörth, *Soft Law in Governance and Regulation: An Interdisciplinary Analysis* (Cheltenham, UK: Edward Elgar, 2004).

[84] U. Mörth, *Organizing European Cooperation: The Case of Armaments* (Lanham, MD: Rowman & Littlefield, 2005).

[85] J. Torfing and E. Sorenson, "Network Politics, Political Capital and Democracy," *International Journal of Public Administration* 26 (2002): 609–34.

but there was little constructive response from society or the market for nearly a decade.

A third pattern of mobilization is "first they (interest groups) arrived, and then it (the EU) was built." We can see this in the case of defense and security industry actors. They mobilized to lobby Brussels more than a decade before the first institutional or treaty developments in defense in the late 1990s, and two decades before the Lisbon Treaty. Interest groups have been active in promoting the creation of European defense policy since the 1980s and have since been attempting to influence the creation of EU institutions, markets, and agendas.

Supply and Demand for EU Authority

Interest groups in Brussels lobby to influence policy and to monitor and advise EU institutions. But there are three distinct patterns of interest-group mobilization and density over time. How do these varying patterns change the outcomes of European integration and EU policy?[86] First I look at whether interest-group mobilization is linked to more EU legislation.[87] The presence or absence of interest groups somehow impacts the success or failure of EU policies and institutions, but why is that the case? I argue that the relative quality of EU institutions – or how Weberian they are – also explains EU political development. And institutional quality appears to vary with the presence or absence of mobilized interests in Brussels. Bureaucratic quality often depends on capacity. Capacity is the qualitative element of internal resources and external connections, allowing a bureaucracy to maximize effective policy outcomes. This capacity can come from traditional Weberian sources – such as meritocratic recruitment, resources, and staff size – but it can also come from outside of a bureaucracy, when its embeddedness with powerful interest groups allows it to do more than it would have otherwise with its internal resources. This is particularly true in the developing world.

---

[86] In asking this question, I am looking at the emergence of a structure of state–society relations at the European level, beyond individual policy outcomes and influence. Political outcomes can mean many things, but here they mean the volume of political activity (as reflected in EU legislation), the success of political activity (as reflected in the degree of successful legislation), and the content of the EU policy agenda.

[87] Recall that EU political outcomes are supposed to be influenced by the member states of the EU: either by their collective or majority interests or by the degree of supranational authority they have granted EU institutions, and should have no direct connection to the mobilization of interest groups. If interest groups mobilize, it is supposed to be after the EU gets a policy authority, not before.

The earlier interest groups mobilize in the life of an issue area, the more likely they are to establish close, informal relationships with EU bureaucracies. When organized interests mobilize in advance of EU treaty authority, the EU institutions in the policy domain are more likely to have increased capacity, leading to a greater ability to enact effective legislation. This may be the case whether or not the organized interests support or oppose EU authority over them or any specific EU policy proposals. The mobilization of organized interests makes an EU policy domain move faster than expected, because external support and expertise enhance the capacity of new EU bureaucracies. Conversely, when organized interests mobilize after EU treaty authority is established, EU institutions in that policy domain will have lower capacity and a comparatively reduced ability to enact effective legislation, regardless of the authority they have been granted to do so from member states. The EU will underperform expectations in that policy domain.

There are trade-offs and repercussions from the EU's capacity being enhanced from the outside in. When organized interests anticipate and mobilize in advance of EU authority, new EU institutions will enjoy capacity outperforming their authority, but their autonomy for setting agendas without private influence will be constrained. Ideally, the EU bureaucracies are autonomous enough to craft agendas relevant to social and market actors and enable effective implementation. The outcomes, however, vary across EU policy domains. Some domains are more autonomous than others, some are more embedded than others, and few are both embedded and autonomous.

Other patterns of interest-group activity also intersect with EU institutions. Sometimes social and market actors do not lobby the EU until after member states grant supranational authority or intergovernmental cooperation over their policy area. European integration proceeds here because of the interests of member states – and the resulting EU institutions first develop their Weberian features such as meritocracy and bureaucratic autonomy – and then those EU institutions interact with mobilized social and market actors. In this scenario, nascent EU institutions enjoy the benefits of enhanced external capacity in the form of expertise, information, coordination, and implementation. And because their organizational features were formed before a transnational demand for their existence, their policy agendas are enhanced by this interaction, but there is less risk of capture and corruption.

There is a last scenario. Sometimes – even after member states give the EU policy authority – there is little to no response from European markets and societies. In the case of this pattern, member states create additional European integration by creating EU treaty authority and

EU institutions. These new institutions are created with a clear mandate from member states giving them legal authority and legitimacy over a particular public policy area. They also enjoy a great deal of autonomy from private influence, as there is little to no private actor attention or particular demands on the EU agenda. In this situation, EU institutions have sufficient authority and autonomy for setting agendas and crafting legislation, but – until interest groups mobilize toward Brussels – political outcomes will suffer and the legislative agenda will stagnate. EU institutions – when new, weak, and facing herculean tasks of regulatory reform – can maintain purely public policy ideals and can develop an agenda untainted by any claims of private capture, but they will not have enough capacity to push that agenda forward. This is because the EU agenda is lacking social partners to provide the extra boost of capacity needed for nascent, developing bureaucracies in a policy environment dominated by national authorities. Eventually, social and market actors mobilize to lobby the EU in the policy domain. But when they get there, they find a less Weberian bureaucracy stymied in its attempts to get European legislation off the ground.

The previous scenarios have an important implication: there are windows of opportunity in the life of an EU policy domain. Different timing presents different constraints and opportunities for forging links between public and private actors. If interest groups do not mobilize, the public bureaucracy might lack transformative capacity for enacting and regulating its policy agenda burden with limited resources. Even when states delegate more authority to the EU and more groups mobilize in response to this authority, there might be too much pluralism for growing these intimate partnerships. Policymaking then happens in a vacuum, or in a cacophonous and weak network. When interest groups mobilize after the EU's authority increases, EU bureaucracies have the opportunity to access the external resources of interest groups after first establishing their own Weberian institutional features. And when interest groups are the first movers in a policy domain – when they are the ones setting a private agenda or private regulatory policy in advance of EU authority – there are two implications: the new EU institutions will be deeply embedded with interest groups upon their institutional creation, and they will have a difficult time insulating their public agenda from private capture.[88]

---

[88] This framing begins to touch on the most challenging element of studying public–private interactions: how to identify, understand, or trace influence in policymaking. Influence is a difficult concept, difficult enough even in the U.S. context, where there is readily accessible historical and contemporary data on interest groups and

The two cases of security represent extremes in their patterns of private interest mobilization. In contrast to the "Field of Dreams" argument (interest groups follow authority: the more EU authority, the more interest groups will mobilize to Brussels), EU–society relations cannot be sufficiently explained by delegated authority in a given policy domain. The hardest (least likely) case for testing this is CSDP. Defense is a classic case of high politics, where changes in authority are not supposed to attract the attention of organized interests. If there is any state–society interaction, it is not supposed to drive policy outcomes, as national (or EU) interests are supposed to be driven by the structure of the international system, not interest groups. A more likely case for interest-group mobilization should be JHA (borders and migration) policy domain, as interest-group activity in the domain is historically intense in national politics. Within conventional wisdom, there should be little to no private actor activity or influence in the CSDP domain because it is intergovernmental, but there should be a growing policy community of interest groups in migration policy because it is increasingly supranational. But neither case fits the idea of interest groups mobilizing in response to institutional authority: in the case of CSDP, the mobilization of interest groups predates the creation of EU-level competencies by almost a decade. In the case of migration and border security, the mobilization of interest groups lagged almost a decade behind the transfer of greater authority to EU institutions.

Scholars have turned their attention to interest groups in Brussels and the interaction between international bureaucracies and interest groups. Few hypotheses, however, link bottom-up interest mobilization to policy outcomes and agendas at the EU or international level. This book traces the role of interest groups in EU agenda setting and connects interest-group mobilization in Brussels to policy outcomes. Whereas this chapter links these broad structural phenomena to each other, the next chapter hones in on the ideas of bureaucratic quality, capacity, embeddedness, and corruption. Capacity cannot be captured by material proxies alone and is a relational concept measured in subjective and context-specific ways. Chapter 3 reviews the results of a survey about the subjective features of particular EU organizations, including quality, leadership, expertise, agenda control, and meritocracy. It also assesses the linkages between public and private actors, specifically their frequency of contact, density of organization, collaboration or conflict, and career paths between public and private channels. Chapters 4, 5, and 6 trace the

outcomes. This research design is an attempt to identify influence over EU political outcomes at a number of different levels.

influence of interest groups on the political developments of EU external and internal security.

Interest Groups and EU Authority: Which Comes First?

The conventional ("field of dreams") wisdom is that interest groups mobilize to Brussels in response to more EU formal treaty authority. Indeed, this is also the case in domestic politics, where interest-group formation happens in response to changes in the allocation of authority.[89] Wessels argued that the EU is the same, where interest groups either respond to changes in EU authority or anticipate it while treaty change is already in the air. He analyzed the formation of major industry groups, seeing whether they formed before or after major treaty dates granting the EC/EU greater authority. His data shows an overall increase of groups following treaties and no evidence for groups mobilizing in anticipation of changes in the regional allocation of authority.

Anecdotal and case evidence, however, point to interest-group mobilization in Brussels long before the EU has any say over a given policy domain. The goal of these early-mover organized interests seems to be to influence the nature of the future EU institution itself, rather than a particular policy outcome. Sometimes the EU gets more authority, which begets more groups. Sometimes the groups are present before the EU gets more authority. But in order to understand the dynamic of supply and demand in EU–society relations, we have to ask under what conditions these different patterns occur.

A new generation of scholars answers this question by resuscitating the tenets of neofunctionalism to provide a "systematic, full-fledged neo-functionalist argument on European integration."[90] This theory puts "transnational private actors," or organized interest groups, front and center as the bottom-up spark in the causal process. The causal logic is as follows: First, there is transnational or globalized pressure on their markets or interests; then interest groups mobilize to demand more EU regulation because it makes their transnational exchanges more efficient; then this "transnational exchange trigger[s] processes that generate movement toward increased supranational governance."[91] This

---

[89] B. Wessels, "Contestation Potential of Interest Groups in the EU: Emergence, Structure, and Political Alliances," in *European Integration and Political Conflict*, edited by G. Marks and M. Steenbergen, 199 (Cambridge, UK: Cambridge University Press, 2004).
[90] Sandholtz and Stone Sweet, 3.   [91] Ibid., 2.

contributes to "the dynamic nature of integration over time across different policy domains."[92] While national governments and their elites are an elemental part of European integration and EU politics, they argue that bargaining in the EU is "more often than not...responsive to the interests of a nascent, always developing, transnational society."[93] This is a "transaction-based" theory of EU integration: a one-way, bottom-up process toward supranational government, where technological changes create globalization pressures, prompting society to organize across European borders to lobby for more EU, leading to greater EU authority. The driving causal factor is globalization, and the outcomes coalesce toward one functional end point.[94]

In this neofunctionalist volume, Fligstein and McNichol (1998) questioned how policy domains emerged over the course of EU integration: Did intergovernmental legislation come first in each domain, followed by treaty revisions increasing EU authority, creating an opportunity for transnational groups to lobby? Or did the presence of transnational groups lobbying the EU precede intergovernmental legislation and treaties allocating increasing competencies to the EU in the domain? Indeed, do transnational groups precede or follow the openings in the treaties? By correlating a one-time snapshot count of groups in each domain with the incidence of legislation coming from EU institutions, Fligstein and McNichol estimated that transnational groups and other interest organizations might have formed before treaties in the domain increased the competencies of the EU.

Their findings indicate the possibility of a correlation between the activities of "transnational pressure groups" and the "production of legislation" from EU institutions.[95] They found that EU legislation grew under a few necessary conditions: in areas where the authority of the EU was expanded, where voting rules were changed, but also where there was a greater presence of transnational pressure groups. More importantly, they hypothesize that the activity from the pressure groups within

---

[92] Ibid., 8.   [93] Ibid., 12.

[94] The logic at work is an attempt to rescue neofunctionalism. The neofunctional logic of Haas relied on a "spillover" mechanism to explain how successes in one policy domain energize domestic societies to push their politicians to expand international treaties of cooperation into other policy domains. This original formulation did not materialize and lacked microfoundations that would explain the coordination of collective action across European societies to demand the next regime. Sandholtz and Stone Sweet's version of functionalism refines the neofunctional logic. Although preferences and coordination of society remain exogenous to their framework, their argument remains functional: first, "the expansion of transnational society pushes for supranational governance," which is then subsequently "exercised to facilitate and regulate that society" (19).

[95] Fligstein and McNichol, 24.

each policy domain precedes any intergovernmental treaties and the formation of EU institutions. In the 1970s, "pressure groups and legislation grew . . . in domains where EU competencies would later be enhanced by Treaty revisions."[96] Overall, the production of policy domains might be affected by the growing presence of transnational pressure groups "who went to Brussels to express their opinions to their governments," not the other way around.[97] These hypotheses are powerful but have not yet been tested with any longitudinal data or mechanisms linking interest groups to EU policy output.

These neofunctional frameworks have the necessary explanatory power for demonstrating why certain policy domains become supranational. Unfortunately, these resource dependency frameworks are not sufficient for explaining much of the timing, sequence, and dynamics of political processes at the EU. According to these supply–demand theories, there is activity initially from the bottom up, which creates transnational exchange dynamics, leading to a spillover of demand for a policy solution at the EU level. Alternately, the EU's increasing policy authority in a particular domain provides an "arena of contestation"[98] and/or attracts the attention of interest groups lobbying for resources or political voice. In supranational or regulatory policy domains such as consumer rights or environmental policy, these predictions, and the functional, linear dynamics underlying them, may be sufficient.

However, in policy domains such as European external and internal security policies, a bottom-up, resource-based explanation is not sufficient because there is simply too much variation. For example, when the EU policy authority over immigration, border security, and other "justice and home affairs" expanded, it was not the result of a bottom-up societal demand. The agenda for the emergent policy domain was set from within the institutions of the EU and European member states, not from the mobilization, access, or influence of interest groups. Pro-migrant NGO groups eventually mobilized their lobbying efforts toward the EU, but these groups made limited use of the new opportunity structure early on.[99] Even more conspicuous is the absence of interests at the European level representing skilled labor, employers, and other traditional constituencies. Although the policy domain is partially supranational, the actors mobilizing first with the greatest agenda-setting influence have been bureaucrats from European member-state justice

---

[96] Ibid., 14.   [97] Ibid., 60.
[98] Imig and Tarrow, "The Europeanisation of Movements?"
[99] V. Guiraudon, "De-Nationalizing Control. Analyzing State Responses to Constraints on Migration Control," in *Controlling a New Migration World*, edited by Virginie Guiraudon and Christian Joppke, 31–64 (London, UK: Routledge, 2001).

ministries. They pushed the agenda from one of low politics to high politics, focusing on the security and border implications of migration over the labor and humanitarian implications of migration. In the domain of armaments policy, the timing, sequence, and relationship are the opposite. The mobilization of private and industry actors preceded the formation of the domain at the European level, and their increasing concentration influenced the direction and nature of the policy agenda of the emergent domains of external and internal EU security policies.

If You Build It, Will They Come?

The mobilization of interest groups helps explain the process of European integration and EU policy outcomes. The interaction between the EU and European society is steadily growing in intensity and scope. There is an intense, opaque, and informal relationship between the EU institutions and organized nongovernmental actors, which is often noted but undertheorized. Understanding this state–society relationship requires combining an analysis of state–society relations and the Weberian internal organization of bureaucracy in a comparative institutional framework: by framing the simultaneous covariation of state bureaucratic structures, state–society relations, and political outcomes.[100]

If all of these things are evolving and varying simultaneously, we have to pin them down one at a time.[101] First, do interest groups precede, correspond to, or follow the transfer of authority from member states to the EU? This question is a departure from the other puzzles in the book, but a necessary departure. Testing this question functions as a null hypothesis for the rest of the study. If formal EU treaty authority changes explain

[100] This study is inspired by the embedded autonomy framework developed by Peter Evans but departs from it, as well: Evans studied the variation in state structures and state–society relations to assess their impact on subsequent changes in society, specifically on industrial organization. I link variations in EU structures and EU–society relations to EU governing capacity. In order to do so, it is necessary to build an understanding of both EU structures and EU–society relations over time, and whether they vary. Chapter 3 measures the mechanisms of EU capacity and embeddedness; this chapter establishes whether there is any validity to linking transnational private interests to EU governing capacity over time.

[101] In the first analysis of the data, it is the dependent variable. In the regression analysis (Models 1 and 2), it is the independent variable. Other independent and/or control variables include measures of authority, EU activity, EU human and financial resources, and proxies for EU capacity. The mobilization of interest groups is measured as a simple count of offices in Brussels per year.

all mobilization of interest groups to the EU and subsequent state–society relations, then there is no possibility that bottom-up changes in EU governing capacity are coming from interest groups. Informal institutions are less likely to form when formal authority already exists within a policy domain. They often form before or in the absence of formal authority changes.

I propose that neither bottom-up nor top-down dynamics explain all EU policy domains: the results will be context-dependent and depend on the historical dynamics of the policy domain. But measuring interest-group mobilization both over time and by policy area establishes the degree to which the state–society relationship varies at the EU level. I find that there is too much variation in the configurations of interest-group mobilization and the timing of EU formal authority changes for there to be one definitive answer to the question: it requires additional mechanisms and process tracing within specific policy domains.

The second goal of this chapter is to create rough measures of EU governing capacity, captured here by the output and performance of EU institutions. I then link this proxy for governing capacity over time to developments in the mobilization and density of interest groups. This is done through a lagged multivariable model establishing whether changes in interest-group mobilization correlate with changes in EU governing capacity. I use legislative output as a proxy for policy performance and capacity and predict that changes in legislative output over time will correlate with changes in the structure of organized interests. I find that interest-group mobilization has a strong positive association with EU governing capacity over time. Within particular policy domains and at different stages in time, however, the relationship is mostly positive and significant, but also more mixed. This justifies further process tracing of the mechanisms and timing of formal and informal authority within policy domains and attempts to measure more relational and subjective elements of state–society interactions.

What Do We Know about Transnational Interest Groups in Brussels?

In 2009, the EU was undergoing significant institutional change with the implementation of the Lisbon Treaty. At the same time, the state of the research on the role of EU interest groups was also changing. While scholars in the previous decade evaluated cases of lobbying using frameworks of corporatism and comparisons to European domestic state–society relations,[102] the focus moved toward large-N analyses, EU policymaking, and applying broader theoretical concepts from domestic politics.[103] This shift parallels research in the United States toward systematic analysis of interest-group mobilization and policy agendas.[104] Researchers in the United States have an informational advantage, however, allowing them to identify actors, policy processes, and outcomes. Interest group researchers studying the EU are hampered by the lack of transparency of the topic.

[102]   See Aspinwall and Greenwood 1998; Green Cowles, "The Transatlantic Business Dialogue and Domestic Business-Government Relations"; J. Greenwood, *Representing Interests in the European Union* (Basingstoke: Palgrave, 1997/2003); Mazey and Richardson, *Lobbying in the European Community*; R. H. Pedler and M. Van Schendelen, *Lobbying the European Union: Companies, Trade Associations and Issue Groups* (Aldershot, UK: Dartmouth, 1994); W. Streeck and K. A. Thelen, *Beyond Continuity: Institutional Change in Advanced Political Economies* (New York, NY: Oxford University Press, 2005).

[103]   See J. Beyers, "Voice and Access: Political Practices of European Interest Associations," *European Union Politics* 5, no. 2 (2004): 211–40; Jan Beyers and Bart Kerremans, "Bureaucrats, Politicians, and Societal Interests: How Is European Policy Making Politicized?" *Comparative Political Studies* 37, no. 10 (2004): 1119–50; J. Beyers and B. Kerremans, "Critical Resource Dependencies and the Europeanization of Domestic Interest Groups," *Journal of European Public Policy* 14, no. 3 (2007): 460–81; P. Bouwen, "The Logic of Access to the European Parliament: Business Lobbying in the Committee on Economic and Monetary Affairs," *Journal of Common Market Studies* 42, no. 3 (2004): 473–95; A. Broscheid and D. Coen, "Lobbying Activity and for a Creation in the EU: Empirically Exploring the Nature of the Policy Good," *Journal of European Public Policy* 14, no. 3 (2007): 346–65; D. Coen, "Business Interests and Integration," in *Collective Action in the European Union*, edited by R. Bulme, D. Chambre and V. Wright, 225–72 (Paris, France: Science-Po Press, 2002); D. Coen, "Environmental and Business Lobbying Alliances in Europe: Learning from Washington?," in *Business in International Environmental Governance: A Political Economy Approach*, edited by D. Levy and P. Newell, 197–220 (Cambridge, MA: MIT Press, 2004); R. Eising, "Multilevel Governance and Business Interests in the European Union," *Governance* 17, no. 2 (2004): 211–46; Rainer Eising, *The Access of Business Interests to European Union Institutions: Notes Towards a Theory.* Working Paper No. 29. University of Oslo, Norway, ARENA Institute for European Studies, 2005; C. Lahusen, "Commercial Consultancies in the European Union: The Shape and Structure of Professional Interest Intermediation," *Journal of European Public Policy* 9, no. 5 (2002): 695–714; C. Lahusen, "Moving into the European Orbit: Commercial Consultancies in the European Union," *European Union Politics* 4, no. 2 (2003): 191–218; Mahoney, "The Power of Institutions"; Mahoney, "Networking vs. Allying"; Princen; B. Wessels, "European Parliament and Interest Group," in *The European Parliament, the National Parliaments, and European Integration*, edited by R. Katz and B. Wessels, 107–28 (Oxford: Oxford University Press, 1999); Wessels, "Contestation Potential of Interest Groups in the EU."

[104]   See Baumgartner and Jones; F. R. Baumgartner and B. L. Leech, "The Multiple Ambiguities of 'Counteractive Lobbying,'" *American Journal of Political Science* 40 (1996): 521–42; D. Lowery and V. Gray, "A Neopluralist Perspective on Research on Organized Interests," *Political Research Quarterly* 57, no. 1 (2004): 163–75.

EU interest-group research has three major trajectories. The first focus is descriptive; it is to rectify the absence of information about lobbyists and interest groups, to describe organized interests and advocacy in Brussels.[105] With a lack of mandatory interest-group registers or research projects with longevity, this is a necessary "population ecology" of interest organizations in Brussels.[106] The second and third areas of research reflect the supply and demand sides of organized interests in Brussels. Supply-side analyses focus on the factors mobilizing groups to participate in a public policy opportunity structure, such as Truman's (1951) concept of changes – or disturbances – in a social or economic order spurring latent ideas to become organized interests. It is the bottom-up element of interest-group activity: why do groups lobby in Brussels? What are their available collective action strategies and resources? Demand-side analyses focus on what the government or politicians do to attract organized interests and shape their behavior or message, and why they might need to do it. On the demand side, what does the EU do to form or influence interest groups? What do EU

---

[105] J. Berkhout and D. Lowery, "Counting Organized Interests in the European Union: A Comparison of Data Sources," *Journal of European Public Policy* 15, no. 4 (2008): 489–513.

[106] D. Lowery, C. Poppelaars, and J. Berkhout, "The European Union Interest System in Comparative Perspective: A Bridge Too Far?" *West European Politics* 31, no. 6 (2008): 1231–52; A. Wonka, F. R. Baumgartner, C. Mahoney, and J. Berkhout, "Measuring the Size and Scope of the EU Interest Group Population," *European Union Politics* 11, no. 3 (2010): 463–76. Given the absence of a mandatory lobby register, the "who" of lobbying and advocacy is an elusive target. A single researcher tracked interest groups in the EC throughout the 1980s into the early 1990s (A. Butt Philip, "Pressure Groups and Policy-Making in the European Community." In *Institutions and Policies of the European Union*, edited by Juliet Lodge, 21–6. [London, UK: Frances Pinter, 1983]; A. Butt Philip, "Pressure Groups in the European Community, Working Paper No. 2," University Association of Contemporary European Studies Working Groups, London, UK: UACES, 1985; A. Butt Philip, *Directory of Pressure Groups in the European Community* [London, UK: Longman, 1991]; A. Butt Philip and O. Gray, *Directory of Pressure Groups in the EU* [London, UK: Cartermill, 1994]). He estimated in 1985 that there were more than 500 industry associations active in Brussels, up from 300 in the 1960s. Other queries in the late 1990s estimated between 700 and 800 "Euro-associations," and one study argued that more than two thirds of these organizations were formed before 1980 (J. Greenwood, L. Strangward, and L. Stanich, "The Capacities of EuroGroups in the Integration Process." *Political Studies* 47 [1999]: 129). A handful of phonebook directories existed since the 1990s for businesses and associations themselves (Landmarks, Euroconfedentiel), and the European Commission and maintained partial surveys of lobbyists taken at a few points in time (CONNECS [Consultation, European Commission and Civil Society] and DG Trade). Directories also measured different things at different times: not all directories were annual, some only included membership associations, and most only incorporated groups with offices in Brussels. An early effort to map the interest group population combined these early membership directories with the lists maintained by the European institutions for one point in time (Aspinwall and Greenwood, 1998, 2–3).

officials need from interest groups? Do interest groups change anything about EU institutions or policies?

Interest Groups: Who, What, When, and Where

Who is organized to lobby the EU? What kinds of interests and advocacy do they represent? Are any social or market interests over- or underrepresented? How permanent are they in Brussels? Have they merged into larger associations or consortia? What policy areas are more active than others? By answering these questions, scholars are coalescing on a partial understanding of advocacy in Brussels. There have been two comprehensive resources for interest group research: the 2002 CONNECS database[107] and the partial listings of expert groups consulting the European Commission on policy issues.[108] There are different organizational

---

[107] CONNECS was a service that functioned as a networking tool maintained by the commission. The original website for the voluntary survey stated that CONNECS was intended to (1) make the Commission more transparent, (2) to help interest groups advertise themselves to the Commission, and (3) help EU officials find interest group partners. The CONNECS data set has been used extensively by researchers for data analysis to find correlations between patterns of interest-group activity and other variables. Unfortunately, causal conclusions from analyses of the CONNECS data set must be viewed as limited, given the recent comparisons between the data set and other sources, such as the Landmarks telephone directories (Berkhout and Lowery). CONNECS listed only lobbying associations with transnational memberships, leaving out regional/territorial interests, individual firms, think tanks, national associations, national NGOs, and other important advocacy actors. Indeed, CONNECS incorporates only 56 percent of the organizations listed in the 2002 Landmarks telephone book, itself an incomplete picture of the interest population in 2002 (ibid.). It must be emphasized how troubling this is, given the almost exclusive reliance on the CONNECS directory for data analysis on the interest-group population in the past decade. Most of the causal and correlative relationships that have been identified in EU state–society relations have been dependent on this singular resource.

[108] The other source for an attempt at systematic data analysis has been the expert group directory for the European Commission. Expert groups and committees are not interest groups in the classic understanding of the term; expert groups ar-e consultative committees comprised of public or private sector experts. They are one of three types of committees organized by EU institutions for policy advice and governance (J. Beyers and J. Trondal, "How Nation States 'Hit' Europe: Ambiguity and Representation in the European Union," *West European Politics* 27, no. 5 [2004]: 919–42; Eising and Kohler-Koch; Wolfgang Wessels, "An Ever Closer Fusion? A Dynamic Macropolitical View on Integration Processes," *JCMS: Journal of Common Market Studies* 35, no. 2 [1997]: 267–99). Specifically, expert groups help prepare legislation and policy initiatives and help monitor the enforcement and coordination of policy in member states. Because these committees are the explicit creations of EU officials to help them with policymaking, one would think that the existence, purpose, and membership of these groups would be easily identifiable. This is not the case. In fact, the Commission itself does not know what the scale and the activities of the groups are, because committees can be formed by lower level bureaucratic initiative (T. Larsson and J.

forms of lobbying, including individual firms from a single state, multinational firms, national associations or NGOs, European associations or NGOs, and third-party lobbyists organized at either the national or European level.[109] There is an overrepresentation of business interests over social interests.[110] This might be because access to the EU is costly and unequal, and there might be some sort of structural obstacle for more diffuse or social transnational interests.[111] But business interests might also be unevenly represented, with more third-party political consultancies than individual firms or associations.[112]

Given the lack of a standard annual lobbying register, it is difficult to assess interest-group behavior over time in the EU. But in order to make any significant connections between bottom-up interest-group activity and top-down EU politics, some sort of temporal analysis is necessary for understanding whether interest-group activity precedes or follows authority and institutions.[113] If we want to say something significant about the interaction of state and society at the EU, we also need to understand how interest groups and the EU interact within each EU policy domain, because different policies have been institutionalized at different points in time. A single study developed the heuristics for asking systematic questions about how the EU is affected by interest group interactions, but it could not access the granular annual data necessary for answering them.[114] Others have grappled with the problem, specifically that an

Trondal, "Agenda Setting in the European Commission," in *EU Administrative Governance*, edited by Herwig C. H. Hofmann and Alexander H. Türk, 11–43 [Cheltenham, UK: Elgar, 2006]). Scholars have been trying to grasp the ontology of these groups for the past few years, building an understanding of what groups have been formed, the extent of their activity, and their distribution across different policy fields. Scholars have estimated that there are between 800 and 1,300 groups (ibid.), more than 1,000 committees (M. P. C. M. van Schendelen, *EU Committees as Influential Policymakers* [London, UK: Ashgate, 1998]), or, in January 2007, 1,237 expert groups (A. Gornitzka and U. Sverdrup. "Who Consults? The Configuration of Expert Groups in the European Union." *West European Politics* 31, no. 4 [2008]: 725–50). Previous reports cite 537 groups in 1975, 602 groups In 1990, and 851 groups in 2000 (Wolfgang Wessels, "Comitology: Fusion in Action. Politico-Administrative Trends in the EU System." *Journal of European Public Policy* 5, no. 2 (1998): 209–34; T. Larsson, "Precooking in the European Union. The World of Expert Groups." *ESO*, 2003. www.grondweteuropa.nl/9310000/d/europa/zwedneso.pdf).

[109] P. Bouwen, "Corporate Lobbying in the European Union: The Logic of Access," *Journal of European Public Policy* 9, no. 3 (2002): 373.

[110] Sonia Mazey and Jeremy Richardson, "Interests," in *Developments in the European Union*, edited by Laura Cram, Desmond Dinan, and Neill Nugent (London, UK: St. Martin's Press, 1999), 121.

[111] Pollack; Greenwood; Hix, *The Political System of the European Union.*

[112] Bouwen, "Corporate Lobbying in the European Union."

[113] Mahoney, "The Power of Institutions," "Networking vs. Allying"; Dür, 2008.

[114] Fligstein and McNichol.

empirical analysis of the interaction of supply- and demand-side influences is admittedly difficult; it would require time series data at fine enough intervals to tease out the relationship between the two sets of variables. Time series data of this nature... are extremely difficult to acquire on the European Union, as group activity has not been consistently tracked, and the developing nature of the Union makes collecting indicators of government activity an arduous endeavor.[115]

Interest Groups: Theories of Supply and Demand

Although difficult to measure, there is a great deal of variation in the organizational form, mobilization, and strategies of interest groups in Brussels.[116] Researchers have therefore focused on the bottom-up incentives and trajectories of interest groups in the multilevel system of the EU,[117] with less emphasis on the governance outcomes of interest-group activity. Studies have established who the lobbyists target and with what resources and tactics.[118] One study examines why some interest groups choose to informally lobby bureaucrats while others choose to litigate their interests in the European courts.[119] Others have explained the variation in the number of interest groups in different domains as either a functional outcome of increasing micro-level international

---

[115] Mahoney, "The Power of Institutions."

[116] The number of actors and organizations varies across policy domains; the types of actors and organizations vary across domains (nonprofit, for-profit, international, or territorial interests); the aggregation of actors and organizations vary across domains (individual interests and firms or aggregated interest associations). Indeed, the relative density of organized interests is not uniform across the EU as a whole: the existence of organized groups is remarkably unevenly distributed among different policy domains and institutional access points around the EU. This variation has motivated most research in the field: theorizing and researching the bottom-up patterns of interest-group mobilization and interaction. The dependent variable of this research has been the opportunity structure available to interest groups at the European level.

[117] Justin Greenwood, Jürgen R. Grote, and Karsten Ronit, *Organized Interests and the European Community* (London, UK: Sage); D. Coen, "The Evolution of the Large Firm as a Political Actor in the European Union," *Journal of European Public Policy* 4, no. 1 (1997): 91–108.

[118] See Coen, "The Evolution of the Large Firm as a Political Actor in the European Union"; J. Beyers, "Gaining and Seeking Access: The European Adaptation of Domestic Interest Associations," *European Journal of Political Research* 41 (2002): 586–612; Bouwen, "Corporate Lobbying in the European Union," "The Logic of Access to the European Parliament"; Mahoney, "The Power of Institutions"; Rainer Eising and Beate Kohler-Koch. *Interessenpolitik in Europa*. (Baden-Baden, Germany: Nomos, 2005); Mazey and Richardson, *Lobbying in the European Community*, 1993.

[119] P. Bouwen and M. McCown, "Lobbying versus Litigation: Political and Legal Strategies of Interest Representation in the European Union," *Journal of European Public Policy* 14, no. 3 (2007): 422–43.

transactions,[120] a bottom-up strategy of putting resources in the most salient policy areas,[121] or increasing arenas of contestation,[122] or as a functional response to increasing constitutionalization and increasing supranational authority in a particular domain.[123]

A major avenue of research established which classic political strategies interest groups use: "access" or "voice."[124] Given the lack of a common media or channels to a pan-European audience, voice strategies are far less common in Brussels than in national polities; however, access strategies are frequent in Brussels. The EU as a bureaucracy is resource poor and relies on external dependencies to complete its policy and governance tasks. Reminding other scholars that lobbying is not a one-way street, Bouwen developed a theoretical concept of "access goods" explaining what EU officials need out of the private sector to help them with their public role. He deduced that access goods determine the type of access given: firms provide "expert knowledge" that helps officials with specific questions, while associations provide information about "encompassing interests," or the "word on the street," about different constituencies.[125] It is the interest groups' organizational form – whether it is a broad-based membership organization or an individual firm with in-depth technical knowledge of the market – that determines the pattern of interest representation.[126] Organizational form (that is, individual firms, national associations, European associations) determines how much capacity the interest groups have to supply access goods, making them more or less attractive to EU institutions.[127]

Here is what we know so far about interest groups in Brussels: they mobilize to Brussels for a number of reasons, but it is no longer puzzling why because of the growing power of the EU over everyday policy across Europe. When they are in Brussels, they employ different strategies and come in all organizational shapes and sizes. We also know that the interest groups' relationship to EU officials can be adversarial, collegial, or a combination of both. In many cases, EU officials have sought out the resources or expertise of powerful interest groups, or attempted to influence the creation of private organizations assisting in developing EU policy agendas from the outside. More recently, we know that some interest groups are granted more access to EU institutions than others. What we know about interest-group mobilization or access does not directly translate, however, into any knowledge about interest-group

---

[120] Sandholtz and Stone Sweet.   [121] Mazey and Richardson 1993.
[122] Imig and Tarrow, *Contentious Europeans*.   [123] Fligstein and McNichol.
[124] Bouwen, "Corporate Lobbying in the European Union"; Beyers, "Voice and Access."
[125] Bouwen, "Corporate Lobbying in the European Union," 369.
[126] Ibid., 372.   [127] Ibid., 375.

influence over EU policies. The measurement of influence is notoriously difficult, made even more so in a constantly changing EU policy environment with many levels and layers of formal input and unregulated informal relations.[128] We also know little about variations in the degree to which EU institutions want or need interest group input or expertise. More broadly speaking, however, we know less about the impact of interest groups on EU institutions, such as whether their relative presence or absence changes EU political outcomes. On this last point, "there seems to be hardly any research dealing specifically with the policy consequences of interest representation" in the EU.[129]

Which Comes First, Authority or Interest Groups?

European interest groups and EU institutions are coevolving. But do interest groups respond to or anticipate member states giving more authority to the EU? Is this simple supply and demand, where interest groups respond to changes in EU authority and opportunity structures? Or does bottom-up interest-group activity stir long before member states agree to cooperate? This is no trivial question: the "who comes first" dynamic is central to the grand theories of European integration: neofunctionalists claim transnational, nongovernmental demand from below drives the creation of EU institutions, while intergovernmentalists hold member state interests ontologically prior to EU activity and interest-group mobilization. Although the larger question of this study addresses variations in the structure of state–society relations, it is important to first address whether or not everything about EU governance stems from changes in formal authority. To address this, I have measured the Europeanization of interest groups over time and by policy domain. Using the Landmarks European Public Affairs directory (1990–), I capture when a corporation, trade association, NGO, law firm, think tank, consultancy, and media organization first established a Brussels-based office.[130] The Landmarks Directories provide a consistent over-time measure of the

---

[128] Dür, "Measuring Interest Group Influence in the EU."   [129] Lowery et al., 4.

[130] The categories have changed slightly over the past two decades, as now there are many different kinds of political consultancies, including management and PR consultants, whereas in 1990 there was only one category. Public affairs directories function as phonebooks for decision makers, lobbyists, and journalists within policy circles. Only one aspect of the Landmarks Directory is lacking: it has published only those organized interests that have opened permanent offices in Brussels. This underrepresents the larger population of interest organizations, because some groups lobby on a more ad hoc basis or simply lobby from home cities near Brussels. *Source:* Landmarks European Public Affairs Directory, http://www.landmarks-publishing.com/publieuro.asp

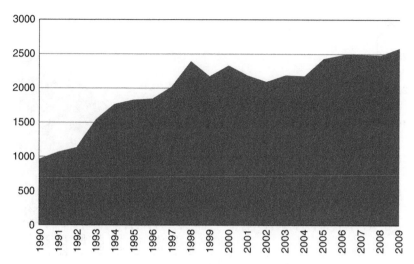

Figure 2.1 Total Organized Interests 1990–2009 (*Source: Landmarks Public Affairs Directories*)

landscape of organized interests in Brussels for almost twenty years (see Figure 2.1). In order to see the trend further back in time, Figure 2.2 includes estimates from earlier years.

Using a directory to understand the landscape of interest groups is helpful but far from perfect. Industry associations can merge, creating larger and more powerful actors, but then there are fewer organizations. In some markets such as health care or biotechnology policy, there could be thousands of small businesses lobbying Brussels. In contrast, only a handful of defense manufacturers exist across Europe, after decades of consolidation and mergers. It would be unhelpful to compare thousands of biotech companies to tens of defense contractors and conclude that the former are more important to public policy than the latter. There are better ways to capture and compare policy dynamics. The first is an *over-time* understanding of interest-group mobilization as a variable. This is interesting in the aggregate, but as EU policy areas have institutionalized and gained authority at different periods of time, the best mobilization data is disaggregated by policy domain and by types of organized interest.

The directory data allows us to analyze organized interests by type, including for-profit, nonprofit, and other forms, such as subnational government representatives or other international organizations. Figure 2.3

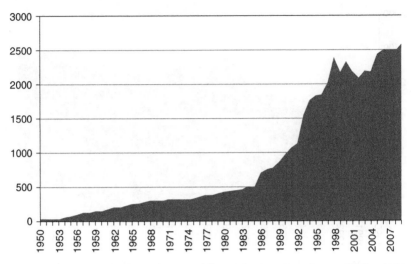

Figure 2.2 Total Organized Interests 1950–2009 (*Source: Philips 1989, 1992, 1996 and Landmarks Directories*)

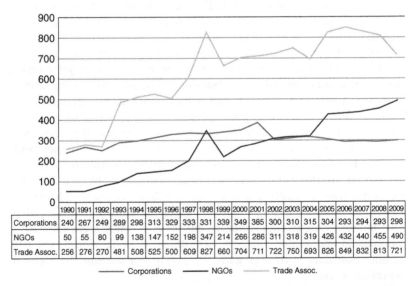

Figure 2.3 Organized Interests: For Profit and Nonprofit, 1990–2009 (*Source: Landmarks Public Affairs Directories*)

describes their different trajectories over the past few decades.[131] The number of individual firms in Brussels has remained somewhat constant and even declined in the past few years. The number of "peak" associations of industry or trade groups increased sharply over the 1990s but is also in recent decline. At the beginning of the EU in 1992, there were only eighty NGOs in Brussels. Their numbers have been increasing steadily every year and have started to outnumber individual corporations in Brussels. These descriptions are very similar to the research on the United States, where corporate interests are often better organized at the beginning of policymaking and institution building, but as policy domains and public institutions age, the policy environment becomes more pluralist as nonprofit groups mobilize in greater numbers. There are implications for this in agenda setting, where corporations are better able to act as external subgovernments earlier in this process and are unable to maintain this intimate relationship with public officials over time, due to the increasing complexity of actors and relationships. From the United States, we know policy domains start out corporatist and become more pluralist over time. Figure 2.4 describes the trajectories of other organizations in Brussels, including trade unions, think tanks, subnational regions, international organizations, law firms, and consultants. With the exception of labor unions, all of these groups have increased in numbers over time. The most rapid is the establishment of EU-level think tanks or outposts of national think tanks in Brussels.

Timeline of EU Policy Authority

Distinguishing actors and groups by policy domain is central to this research. Identifying overall EU trends is interesting but not as analytically helpful as individual policy domain dynamics. This is because the EU has institutionalized domain by domain with a series of treaties, so any meaningful questions of timing isolate one policy domain from another. The major treaties negotiating EU intergovernmental cooperation or supranational authority are the 1951 ECSC Treaty, the 1957 EEC Treaty, the 1985/86 Single European Act, the 1992 TEU (Maastricht), the 1997 Amsterdam Treaty, the 2001 Nice Treaty, and the 2007 Lisbon Treaty. Figures 2.1 and 2.2 demonstrated the estimated (1950–89) and precise (1990–2009) number of groups in Brussels for the first

---

[131] By using mobilization as a variable, I do not intend to make a causal assumption about access or interaction. It is an attempt to construct one aspect of the structure of organized interests in the EU by policy domain. Whether or not EU officials grant access or influence to mobilized interest groups is another story. These qualities are further explored in the case studies and survey analyses.

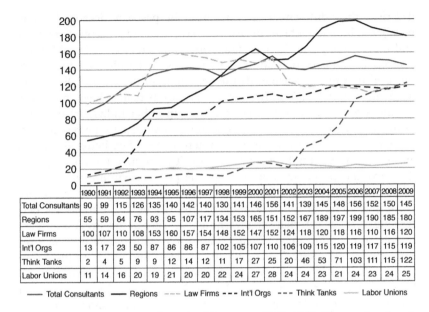

	1990	1991	1992	1993	1994	1995	1996	1997	1998	1999	2000	2001	2002	2003	2004	2005	2006	2007	2008	2009
Total Consultants	90	99	115	126	135	140	142	140	130	141	146	156	141	139	145	148	156	152	150	145
Regions	55	59	64	76	93	95	107	117	134	153	165	151	152	167	189	197	199	190	185	180
Law Firms	100	107	110	108	153	160	157	154	148	152	147	152	124	118	120	118	116	110	116	120
Int'l Orgs	13	17	23	50	87	86	86	87	102	105	107	110	106	109	115	120	119	117	115	119
Think Tanks	2	4	5	9	9	12	14	12	11	17	27	25	20	46	53	71	103	111	115	122
Labor Unions	11	14	16	20	19	21	20	20	22	24	27	28	24	24	23	21	24	23	24	25

—— Total Consultants   —— Regions   ---- Law Firms   --- Int'l Orgs   --- Think Tanks   —— Labor Unions

Figure 2.4 Other Organized Interests: 1990–2009 (*Source: Landmarks Public Affairs Directories*)

four decades of the European Community institutional structure. These years marked the successful negotiation of major EC/EU treaties advancing intergovernmental cooperation or supranational competencies. Prior to the 1992 creation of the EU, there is a steady and moderate growth of organized interests in Brussels over the four decades of the European Community. With the exception of the 1992 Maastricht Treaty, interest-group mobilization does not surge in response to EU treaty authority. But if the relevant institutional story of the EU happens within policy domains, we have to drill down one level and disaggregate the interest group patterns of mobilization.

EU Policy Domains

Over the past six decades, the EU has institutionalized policy domain by policy domain. At any given time, one domain might be institutionalizing rapidly, while other EU domains are stagnant, fully developed, or even in decline.[132] Looking at total EU activity is inadequate: If policy activity

---

[132] J. D. Donahue and M. A. Pollack, "Centralization and Its Discontents: The Rhythms of Federalism in the United States and the European Union," in *The Federal Vision:*

output surges in one domain, this might be washed out by a decline or stagnation of activity in another area. For example, fisheries policy was a big EC issue in the 1980s but faded in salience by the 1990s. But the 1990s was a time when other policy domains were debated and institutionalized as EU policy, and many interest groups mobilized to Brussels to participate.

I disaggregated the timeline by domains order to identify institution-alization patterns over the history of the EC/EU.[133] Because fifteen of the twenty current EU policy domains were established in 1957, there have been only modest changes in the boundaries of policy domains in the past twenty years. Indeed, the legal discussion of EU policy domains occurs long before actual policy activity commences or supra-national authority increases. Of the seventeen EU policy domains in 1990, thirteen had active interest groups.[134] Many of these older pol-icy domains (such as agriculture, competition policy, customs policy, competition policy, and transport policy) had the largest surge of docu-mented interest-group activity decades ago, with the founding of orga-nized interest groups in Brussels between 1958 and 1969.[135] These domains have had very few increases in interest-group activity in the ensuing decades. Policy activity is still high in these areas, and they have some of the largest constituencies of interest groups in Brussels, but there has been very little movement in their mobilization or overall numbers.[136]

Legitimacy and Levels of Governance in the United States and the European Union: Legit-imacy and Levels of Governance in the United States and the European Union, edited by Kalypso Nicolaidis and Robert Howse, 73–117 (Oxford: Oxford University Press, 2001).

[133] Policy domains in the EU effectively correspond to areas of EU treaties and functional sections of the European Commission bureaucracy. Parts Two, Three, and Five of the 1957 Treaty of Rome created a core of fifteen domains of legitimate policymak-ing. Additional treaties combined, added, and significantly expanded EU authority in more policy domains. When treaties expanded EU authority in policy domains, it usu-ally meant that voting rules changed from unanimous to majority voting, and policy competencies given to the European Commission to legislate under the community method.

[134] A. Butt Philip and O. Gray, *Directory of Pressure Groups in the EU*. London, UK: Carter-mill, 1994.

[135] Ibid.

[136] I subdivided the current domains into those created by the Treaty of Rome and those formed or substantially expanded after the Treaty of Rome. From this larger list of twenty policy domains, I have selected a subset of seven areas of policymaking that can be considered "new" policy domains of the EU. Though all relatively new, there is still variation in these policy domains: some of them are distributive in nature, some are regulatory, some are both. Some have had supranational authority for decades, others have very recent supranational mandates. I have selected this subsection for further analysis for two reasons: to have a manageable set of cases over time that can

Anecdotal evidence for the oldest, most established domains – where the EU has a great deal of authority, legitimacy, organizational resources, and capacity – demonstrates the state–society relationship grows more pluralist and stable after decades of institutionalized relationships with large interest-group constituencies. In newer domains, these relationships are less institutionalized, possibly with greater variation in mobilization and state–society interaction. The newest domains are listed below.

List of New Policy Domains: Created or Expanded after Treaty of Rome:

- Science, Education, Culture (1967–, **1973–**)
- Environment/Health/Consumer (1973–, 1986–, **1999–**)
- Regional policy (1973–, **1999–**, 2004–)
- Foreign and Security Policy/Security and Defence Policy (1992–, **1999–**, 2007–)
- Justice, freedom and security (1992–, **1997–**, 1999–, 2007–) (Justice and Home Affairs, judicial, police, border control, immigration, human rights, People's Europe)
- Energy (**1995–**)
- Humanitarian (**1992–**)

Experts in EU politics know that the creation of domain authority at the EU does not equal real authority or policy activity. For example, Table 2.1 indicates that the EU has had some treaty authority over energy policy since 1995, but policymakers complain about the lack of a strategic EU energy policy two decades later. There are other ways of categorizing the degree to which a policy domain is "Europeanized." Whether or not a treaty between EU member states mentions a policy domain is not the only dimension of authority. EU scholars, starting with Lindberg and Scheingold, Schmitter, and Hooghe and Marks, have attempted to measure the level of EU authority in different policy domains over time.[137] On a scale of 1–5, they demonstrated the degree to which policy

be studied for understanding the structure of EU–society relations, and for capturing the dynamics of institutionalization that happen in the earlier years of a policy domain, when there is a window of opportunity for mobilization and influence. The granular mobilization data provided by the Landmarks Directories covers only the years 1990–2009.

[137] L. N. Lindberg and S. A. Scheingold, *Europe's Would-Be Polity: Patterns of Change in the European Community* (Englewood Cliffs, NJ: Prentice Hall, 1970), 67–71; P. C. Schmitter, "Imagining the Future of the Euro-Polity with the Help of New Concepts," *Governance in the European Union* (1996): 125–6; L. Hooghe and G. Marks, "Optimality and Authority: A Critique of Neoclassical Theory," *JCMS: Journal of Common Market Studies* 38, no. 5 (2000): 795–816.

Table 2.1. *Schmitter's Measure of Degree of Authority*

Policy Domains and Levels of Authority in Europe: 1950–2001					
Issue arena	1950	1957	1968	1992	2000
ECONOMIC POLICY					
Goods/services	1	2	3	4	4
Agriculture	1	1	4	4	4
Capital flows	1	1	1	4	4
Persons/workers	1	1	2	3	4
Transportation	1	2	2	2	2
Energy	1	2	1	2	2
Communications	1	1	1	2	2
Environment	1	2	2	3	3
Regional development	1	1	1	3	3
Competition	1	2	2	3	3
Industry	1	2	2	2	2
Money/credit	1	1	2	2	5
Foreign exchange/loans	1	1	2	2	4
Revenue/taxes	1	1	2	2	2
Macroeconomic	1	1	2	2	3
SOCIAL/INDUSTRIAL POLICY					
Work conditions	1	1	2	2	3
Health	1	1	1	2	2
Social welfare	1	2	2	2	2
Education and research	1	1	2	2	2
Labor-management relations	1	1	1	1	2
LEGAL-CONSTITUTIONAL POLICY					
Justice and property rights	1	1	1	3	3
Citizenship	1	1	1	2	3
Participation	1	1	1	2	2
Police and public order	1	1	1	1	2
INTERNATIONAL RELATIONS/EXTERNAL SECURITY					
Commercial negotiations	1	1	3	5	5
Economic-military assistance	1	1	1	2	2
Diplomacy and membership of international organizations	1	1	1	2	3
Defence & war	1	1	1	1	2

Key:
1 = All policy decisions at national level
2 = Only some policy decisions at EC level
3 = Policy decisions at both national and EC level
4 = Mostly policy decisions at EC level
5 = All policy decisions at EC level.
Source: Schmitter 1996

Table 2.2. *New Policy Domains – Degree of EU Authority*

	New Policy Domains					
	1950	1957	1968	1992	2000	2007
Science, Education, Culture	1	1	2	2	2	2
Environment, Health, Consumer	1	1	1	2	2	3
Regional Policy	1	1	1	3	3	3
Development + Humanitarian	1	1	1	2	2	4
Foreign and Security Policy	1	1	1	1	2	3
Justice, Freedom, and Security	1	1	1	2	3	3
Energy	1	2	1	2	2	3

decisions were exclusively national level (1), exclusively EU level (5), or shared (2, 3, 4).[138]

The Schmitter scale describes the degree of EU level activity in each domain over time. I amended the table for the seven new policy domains by calculating new values for 2007, pre–Lisbon Treaty (Table 2.2).[139]

Does EU Authority Explain Interest-Group Mobilization?

Recall the conventional logic that interest groups follow authority, although there are exceptions documenting interest-group mobilization prior to EU treaties.[140] So we should see interest-group mobilization

---

[138] Schmitter made the original table in 1992 by querying EU experts such as Geoffrey Garrett, Peter Lange, Gary Marks, and David Soskice. The last update of the table was in 2001.

[139] Although the direction of this categorical variable will move in the same direction as the other categorical variables for treaty authority, it captures EU policy activity, not just the transfer of formal treaty authority. Also, the variation on this scale used to be greater at earlier points in time. By 2007, many policy domains settled into the category of shared competence between the EU and nation states. For the empirical analyses in this chapter, I use the treaty dates as independent categorical variables for an overall analysis of the mobilization of organized interests across the EU (eutreaty). For the specific domains, the EU treaty variable (eutreaty) is the first independent variable, then a domain-specific variable for the dates of increased authority (authdomain) and the Schmitter scale (authscale) to assess the correlations between the timing of interest-group mobilization and levels of EU authority in a given domain.

[140] For these models, the mobilization of interest groups (igmob) is the dependent variable. The EUTOTAL and EUDOMAINS data sets have different measures of authority: for EUTOTAL, the measure of authority is a categorical dummy variable (eutreaty) measuring the years of a major treaty negotiation, the two years before a major treaty

immediately after an increase in EU treaty authority.[141] But the alternate hypothesis, as elaborated by neofunctionalists, is that transnational social demand, or interest-group mobilization, precedes states granting the EU more authority.[142] I predict that overall, interest groups follow authority, but there will be variation and outliers in this dynamic across different policy domains, and regression analysis is by itself insufficient for clarifying the question.[143]

The first model and results (Table 2.3) indicate that an increase in EU treaty authority overall has a strong relationship to interest-group mobilization from 1950 to 2009. The next models document this relationship in the seven newest EU policy domains. In none of the new domains is the creation of major new EU treaties a significant predictor of a mobilization of interest groups. However, in most of the domains, an increase in policy-specific EU authority has a strong relationship to interest-group mobilization. The outliers are Defense and JHA, where there is a

negotiation, and the two years after a major treaty negotiation. Two categorical variables capture the effects of different periods of institutionalization. Dummy variables measure whether an observation occurred in the year that greater authority was granted to the EU through intergovernmental treaty. Coefficients from these dummy variables show the average difference between these years, the years before the treaty, and after the treaty.

[141] The null hypothesis is that interest groups (igmob) increase after the EU gets more authority through a treaty (EUTOTAL = eutreaty; EUDOMAINS = eutreaty, authdomain, authscale). The null hypothesis is the "if you build it, they will come" conventional wisdom of the EU as an opportunity structure.

[142] For the seven EUDOMAINS data sets, there are two variables measuring treaty authority: (1) a categorical dummy variable for each policy domain that marks a major shift in activity to the EU, essentially dividing the domain in to two time periods, before the increase in authority/activity and after (authdomain); and (2) the scale (0–5) of EU authority by domain developed by Schmitter (authscale). The model tested whether interest-group mobilization (igmob) over time (year) correlated with EU treaty authority increase (EUTOTAL = eutreaty; EUDOMAINS = eutreaty, authdomain, authscale). The other variables, including budget, staff, and legislative output, functioned as control variables in these regressions.

[143] An initial variant of this model with multivariable regression included the staff and budget variables as additional independent variables. I was particularly interested in the significance of the independent variables (staff) and (budget) on (igmob). The relationship between the staff and budget of the EU and interest groups was insignificant in single and multiple regressions but remained in the models as control variables. A null hypothesis was that when the resources of the EU or EU policy domains are greater, then interest-group mobilization will be subsequently greater (> staff and budget => igmob). I expect that low staff and budget values might have the opposite relationship with the mobilization of interest groups. It is possible that, in some domains, low staff and budget correlate with the mobilization of interest groups (< staff and/or budget => igmob). This is because resource-poor bureaucrats might need help with their tasks, and interest groups might subsequently mobilize, providing expertise and external capacity. None of the results were conclusive for hypothesis testing.

Table 2.3. *Does EU Authority Predict the Mobilization of Interest Groups?*

Independent Variables	B	Beta	R2	t	Lower Bound	Upper Bound	p
EU 1950–2009							
EU Treaty	293.59** (81.9)	0.426	0.426	3.59	129.73	457.47	0.001
Energy Policy 1990–2009							
eutreaty	4.6 (16.4)	0.065		0.278	− 29.9	39.1	0.784
authdomain	104.87** (36.8)	0.558	0.726	2.9	27.6	182.11	0.011
authscale	118.78*** (26.5)	0.726	0.527	4.5	63.1	174.48	<0.001.
Regional Policy 1990–2009							
eutreaty	0.265 (16.4)	0.004		0.016	− 34.3	34.8	0.987
authdomain	130.54*** (23.2)	0.798	0.637	5.623	81.8	179.33	<0.001.
authscale							
Environment, Health, Consumer Policy 1990–2009							
eutreaty	− 8.5 (44.4)	− 0.045		− 0.191	− 101.78	84.8	0.851
authdomain	341.91*** (66.1)	0.773	0.576	5.176	203.14	480.68	<0.001.
authscale	398.50*** (45.1)	0.901	0.813	8.833	303.71	493.30	<0.001
Science, Education, Culture Policy 1990–2009							
eutreaty	− 1.1 (32.3)	− 0.008		− 0.035	− 68.9	66.696	0.973
authdomain	248.30*** (47.4)	0.777	0.604	5.243	148.80	347.80	<0.001.
authscale							
Security and Defence Policy 1990–2009							
eutreaty	6.3 (5.5)	0.259		1.139	− 5.3	17.8	0.270
authdomain	39.2* (16.1)	0.497	0.247	2.428	5.3	73.0	0.026
authscale	34.4*** (4.5)	0.874	0.764	7.627	25.0	43.9	<0.001.
Immigration, Asylum and Border Security Policy (JHA) 1990–2009							
eutreaty	.8 (13.6)	0.014		0.058	− 27.8	29.4	0.954
authdomain	72.9* (28.5)	0.517	0.267	2.560	13.1	132.67	0.020
authscale	72.9* (28.5)	0.517	0.267	2.560	13.1	132.67	0.020
Humanitarian and Development Policy 1990–2009							
eutreaty	− 2.7 (8.2)	− 0.078		− 0.334	− 19.8	14.4	0.742
authdomain	46.1 (29.9)	0.342	0.068	1.544	− 16.6	108.87	0.140
authscale	70.6* (20.9)	0.623	0.388	3.379	26.7	114.47	0.020

*$p < 0.05$, **$p = 0.01$, ***$p < 0.01$; Standard deviation reported in parentheses below means.

Note: Controls are EU staff and EU budget (omitted from the table).

relationship between authority and mobilization, but it is significant at lower levels than the other domains.

EU treaty authority appears to be an important precondition to the overall degree of interest-group activity. Across the history of the EU in all domains, this correlation is positive and strongly statistically significant. However, this significance is much stronger in some domains than in others. Although the effect of major EU treaties had a strong correlation with mobilization over time, major EU treaties were not a factor in newer domains. With the exception of defense and JHA, a shift in authority or activity at the EU level has a strong correlation with interest-group mobilization.

Do Resources Explain Interest-Group Mobilization?

Do interest groups mobilize to the EU in response to an increase in budgetary resources? The EU budget is divided along the lines of policy domains.[144] Looking at the budget overall and by policy domain provides a description of the dynamics of EU authority and resources over time. Do interest groups mobilize in response to budget increases, for either redistributive resources or regulatory outcomes? This description of the EU budget and the mobilization of organized interests serves to clarify our understanding of the mobilization of transnational interest groups: whether or not they anticipate or respond to EU resources and authority. Figure 2.5 assesses two trends: the first is the EU total budget; the second is the mobilization of organized interests.[145] They closely track each other: both have been increasing over time, with some budget stagnation and dips. Although there is not enough here to determine whether mobilization follows or precedes EU budgetary changes, it is remarkable that more than half of the European interest groups were already present in 1992.

Figures 2.6 through 2.12 describe the relationship between the budget of the EU and the mobilization of organized interests in the seven

---

[144] EU appropriations are published in the Annual Budget (Volume II, Section III – European Commission). Since 2004, this section has been activity based (ABB short for "activity-based budgeting"); the budget is divided into some thirty policy areas, each of which described within a title. It is aggregated into smaller main policy domains in the financial framework, which contains a breakdown of the EU's budgetary expenditure in broad categories or headings.

[145] The budget axis on the left is measured by billions of euros (from 0 to 140), the mobilization axis on the right is the count of organized interests (with parameters from 0 to 3,000).

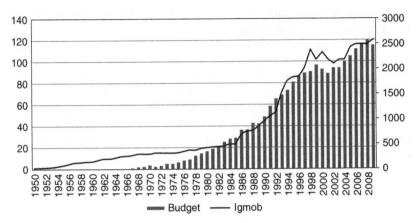

Figure 2.5 Overall Budget of EU and Mobilization of Interest Groups
(*Sources: EU Annual Budget and Landmarks Public Affairs Directories*)

new EU policy domains.[146] For most of the time, the domains follow a predictable, linear path. There are interesting anomalies, however. For example, in Figure 2.6, energy interest groups increase rapidly in 2000–3 and again in 2006–7 with no rise in the EU energy budget. In Figure 2.7, regional interest groups show no mobilization response to increasing budgets in the late 1990s but spike in anticipation of the Lisbon Treaty in 2009. Environmental and health interest groups (Figure 2.8) spike in 2001 immediately before a significant budget increase but then stagnate later in the decade, even with greater budget increases. Science, education, and culture interest groups increased threefold from 2002 to 2008, but there was almost no budgetary change in the EU (Figure 2.9). Security and defense policy stands out from all other domains (Figure 2.10) in that the interest-group population was mobilized long before any established EU budget spending and remained in Brussels even without major budgetary increases. The lack of additional mobilization in response to major budgetary increases after 2005 indicates that there may be no more latent interests to mobilize in this domain; they are already in Brussels. Immigration interest groups (Figure 2.11) have a unique pattern of mobilization: after a minor late-1990s mobilization, their numbers collapsed and did not increase again until after the EU budget in the

---

[146] The left axis represents the budget (in millions of euros) and the right axis represents the mobilization of organized interest groups.

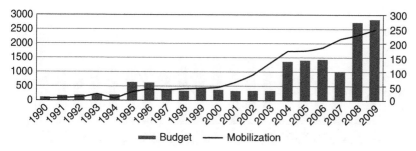

Figure 2.6 EU Budget and Interest Groups in Energy Policy (*Sources: EU Annual Budget and Landmarks Public Affairs Directories*)

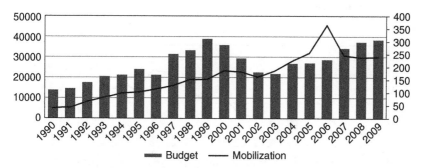

Figure 2.7 EU Budget and Interest Groups in Regional Policy (*Sources: EU Annual Budget and Landmarks Public Affairs Directories*)

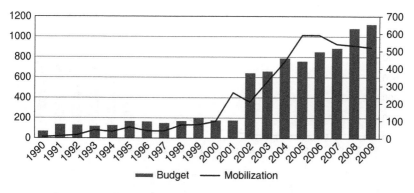

Figure 2.8 EU Budget and Interest Groups in Environment, Health, and Consumer Policy (*Sources: EU Annual Budget and Landmarks Public Affairs Directories*)

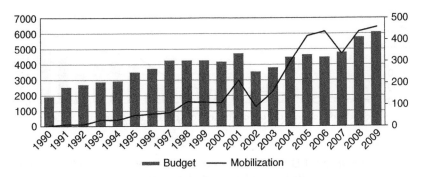

Figure 2.9 EU Budget and Interest Groups in Science, Education, and Culture Policy (*Sources: EU Annual Budget and Landmarks Public Affairs Directories*)

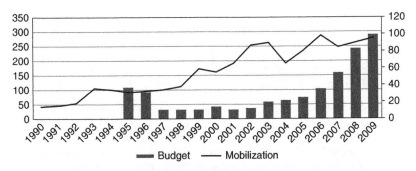

Figure 2.10 EU Budget and Interest Groups in Security and Defense Policy (*Sources: EU Annual Budget and Landmarks Public Affairs Directories*)

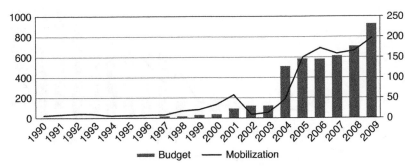

Figure 2.11 EU Budget and Interest Groups in Immigration, Asylum, and Border Security Policy (*Sources: EU Annual Budget and Landmarks Public Affairs Directories*)

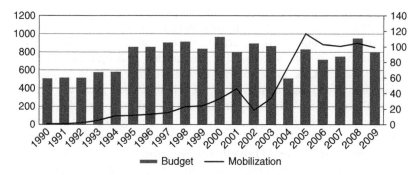

Figure 2.12 EU Budget and Interest Groups in Humanitarian and Development Policy (*Sources: EU Annual Budget and Landmarks Public Affairs Directories*)

domain tripled in 2004. In humanitarian policy (Figure 2.12), the EU budget has remained very stable over twenty years, and interest groups mobilized from 2002 to 2005 with no clear link to any changes in the EU resources in the domain. For these seven domains, the past two decades have been a time of change but with a great deal of variation across domains.[147] With so much variation, the conventional wisdom does not hold, and operational budget (as a proxy for either the authority or internal bureaucratic capacity of EU bureaucracies) does not explain why interest groups mobilize to Brussels. It appears that there is more to interest-group mobilization than a functional response to EU resources. It also appears that under some conditions, the EU budget rises after interest-group mobilization in the domain.

Does Interest-Group Mobilization Change EU Outcomes?

The models in this chapter explore the relationship between interest-group mobilization and proxies for governing capacity, in this case measured by legislative output and success.[148] The policy output of a

---

[147] In single and multiple regression analysis attempts, there was no instance in which the budget variable had a significant coefficient with any EU policy outcomes or mobilized interests, but it was used as a control variable in the multiple regressions detailed in the next section.

[148] Dependent variables include all of the legislative output of the EU in a domain (legisall), the legislation in force in a domain (legisforce), and the percentage of legislation passed in a domain (legispassed). This is done through a linear model with the independent and dependent variables, as well as a multiple regression with the treaty authority, treaty scale, staff, and budget variables included.

political institution may be the best indicator of how well it performs in its policy environment.[149] If governing capacity is the ability of an organization to effectively govern, a measure of it can be the amount of legislation it has successfully shepherded through all stages of the process.[150] One possible way to see whether interest groups are enhancing governing capacity is to see whether their presence – in the form of levels of mobilization – influences the output of legislation.

If the presence and embeddedness of interest groups enhances the governing capacity of the EU within a policy area, I expect that interest-group mobilization should broadly correlate with an increase in success-ful EU legislative output. One way of looking at interest group impacts on EU legislation is to calculate the ratio of legislative output and divide it by the number of interest groups in the policy domain. If the ratio is low, it could mean there is a great deal of legislation and a large num-ber of interest groups, creating a supranational and pluralist policy envi-ronment. A high ratio means there is a proportionally large degree of interest-group activity, where the interest groups are potentially domi-nating the policy and agenda processes. If the ratio is small, it could mean the policy domain is more supranational[151] or the domain is becoming more pluralist.

Figure 2.13 calculates the ratio of groups to legislation in each domain, revealing interesting patterns and variation. Some policies have had sta-ble ratios over time, but other policies have had windows of time where the ratios peak, such as security and defense policy in 1993–4, regional policy from 2003 to 2005, and other policies in the lead-up to the Lisbon Treaty. The ratio of interest groups to legislation in security and defense policy went from 18:0 in 1993 to 36:6 in 1994 to 34:24 in 1995. This

---

[149] This proxy is still flawed, as smaller, insignificant pieces of legislation are then method-ologically equal to the passage of significant legislation. Because I am trying to capture the effects of capacity, not political salience, I can justify that the amount of legislation generated does reflect overall bureaucratic activity in the area.

[150] In the EU, there are different categories of policy output: All Legislation and Legis-lation in Force. The latter is the legislation that is successfully enacted through the intergovernmental Council of Ministers and becomes EU Legislation in Force. It includes regulations and directives. The former is every recommendation, policy pro-posal, and formal legislation proposed by the European Commission and EU agencies and includes green papers, white papers, nonbinding policy recommendations, and policy guidelines. The other acts of legislation are a softer indicator of overall EU activ-ity in a domain but are not a precise reflection of capacity. These two indicators might not even be collinear with each other: the indicator of all legislation might contrast sig-nificantly with the proportion of actual policy in force in a domain. For example, there could be a large amount of soft legislative acts and very few actual in-force legislative acts. The unit of analysis is the number of legislative items within the particular policy domain in a given year.

[151] Fligstein and McNichol.

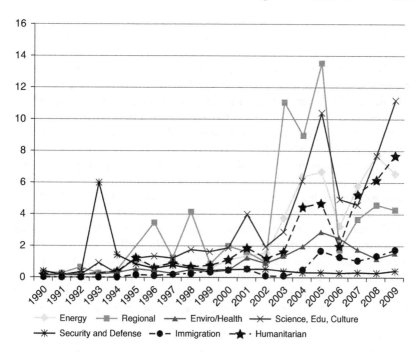

Figure 2.13 Ratio of Interest Groups to Legislation within EU Policy Domains (*Sources: EU Annual Report* and *Landmarks Public Affairs Directories*)

result refines our understanding of the relationship between European interest groups and EU outcomes: not all groups anticipate changes in EU authority, but some groups seem to be well positioned to influence outcomes at particular windows of opportunity in EU political development. This ratio calculation might also reveal the presence of informal institutions with agenda-setting windows of opportunity within policy domains over time.

The next step in testing this relationship is an empirical test to see whether the internal authority or resources of the EU or the mobilization of European interest groups helps explain the volume and success of EU policy outcomes within policy domains.[152] This is an evaluation of the

---

[152] The source of the numbers of overall legislation and legislation in force is the *Official Journal of the European Union* and the *Directory of Community Legislation in Force*. There are three variables from the journal: (1) All Legislation – a measure of the total activity within a policy domain; (2) Legislation in Force – a measure of all the successful legislation within a policy domain; and (3) Percent of Legislation in Force – a measure of how much legislation is successful out of all proposed legislative activity. I ran three separate

sources of EU governing authority, whether its sources are internal or external. Before reviewing the specific models,[153] Table 2.4 summarizes their variables and sources.[154]

The results indicate to what degree interest-group mobilization correlates to EU legislation across the entire EU for the years 1950–2009 (Table 2.5).[155] Interest-group mobilization is positive and significant for predicting the overall volume of EU legislative activity. The relationship is even stronger between interest-group mobilization and the implementation and success of EU legislation.

Within the specific policy domains, the relationship is positive but somewhat mixed. In some policy domains it is positive and significant with both legislative volume and legislative success, whereas in some domains (energy, regional) interest-group mobilization is not a significant predictor of legislative volume but does have a relationship with measures of legislative success. Again, the outliers are the security domains: the volume of external (security and defense) security policy has one of the strongest associations with interest-group mobilization but has mixed association with legislative success. Internal (immigration and border) security policy has a similar association at a lower significance level.

models with each of these as the dependent variable, exploring whether interest-group mobilization or authority has a more significant relationship with successful EU policy output. A fourth model uses these legislative variables as independent variables with the mobilization of interest groups as the dependent variable.

[153] There are two categories of models: the first assesses the relationship between degrees of EU authority and amount of interest-group mobilization, the second assesses the relationship between interest-group mobilization and EU legislation. There are two methods to analyze time series data. Some data contains cross sections over time (for example, domains over years). There are two potential problems that could lead to correlated errors. The use of time-series data means that if there are independent variables that are overlooked, there will be errors. Also, data used on the same units of analysis could also affect correlations. This can be addressed by estimating a random effects error components regression model (XTREG in Stata). Time-series data such as the data sets I use require measures to remove the trend effects of time interdependence from the independent and dependent variables. With the dependent variables, the problem posed by time-series analysis is autocorrelation. Errors from one time observation can be correlated with time adjacent observations. The test to address this issue is a Durbin-Watson test for evidence of autocorrelation. Where there was autocorrelation, I used procedure (ARIMA in Stata) to correct.

[154] I performed ANOVA and regression analysis with the authority proxies and mobilization variables in multiple dimensions. The first set of parameters for all domains in the EU from 1950 to 2009 (EUTOTAL data) identified patterns over a number of decades and through different phases of institutionalization. The second category of parameters looked at each of the seven policy domains (EUDOMAINS data) from 1990 to 2009.

[155] This data set was run as a multiple regression because the degrees of freedom (59) allow for multiple independent variables. The other variables included the authority measures, staff, and budget.

Table 2.4. *Description of Variables for Multivariable Model: 1950–2009*

Variable	Name	Data Source	Range	Comments
EU treaty time order indicator	Eutreaty	Documented EC/EU major negotiated treaties	0, 1, 2, 3 (indicating absence or time order of treaties)	Used in both Model 1 (all EU) and Model 2 (Specific Domains)
Major transfer of authority within domain	authdomain	Various documented sources for each domain.	0, 1	Dummy variable, used only on Model 2 (Specific Domains, 1990–2009). 0 = years before authority change, 1 = years of and after largest EU authority increase
Levels of EU activity/ authority by domain	Authscale	Schmitter 2001, own estimates for 2007.	0, 1, 2, 3, 4, 5	Categorical scaled variable, used only on Model 2 (Specific Domains, 1990–2009)
Mobilization of interest groups	Igmob	**1950–1989:** Phillips (1989, 1992, 1996). **1990–2009:** Landmarks Directories data set	25–2,580, but varies by domain	**1950–1989** Philips data are estimates. **1990–2009** my data are verifiable by year from the same directory source. **1950–2009** used in Model 1 (all EU) and **1990–2009** used in Model 2 (Specific Domains)
EU Staff size	Staff	Annual Report of the European Union	0–37,722, but varies by domain	For Model 1 (EU total, 1950–2009), all EU staff. For Model 2 (Specific domains, 1990–2009), EU staff within domain
EU Budget appropriations	Budget	Annual Budget of the European Union	0–1.1941E+11 euros, varies by domain	For Model 1 (EU total, 1950–2009), total EU budget. For Model 2 (Specific domains, 1990–2009), EU Budget for domain
EU legislation	Legisall	EU law online eur-lex. europa.eu	0–6,989, but varies by domain	Total EU legislation, including nonbinding
EU Legislation in Force	Legisforce	EU law online eur-lex. europa.eu	0–3,114, but varies by domain	EU legislation with legal force, including agreements, directives, regulations and decisions.
EU Legislation Passed	Legispassed	EU law online eur-lex. europa.eu	0%–92%	Percentage of legislation in force divided by all legislative output in domain.

Table 2.5. *Interest-Group Mobilization on EU Legislation*

Independent Variable	All Legislation B	Legislation in Force Beta	R2	B	Beta	R2	Legislative Success B	Beta	R2
EU 1950–2009									
Interest-Group Mobilization	2.378*** (0.160)	0.890	0.793	1.012*** (0.033)	0.970	**0.941**	0.000*** (0.000)	0.785	0.616
Energy Policy 1990–2009									
Interest-Group Mobilization	−0.062 (0.036)	−0.377		0.063* (0.027)	0.483	0.233	0.002*** (0.000)	0.834	0.695
Regional Policy 1990–2009									
Interest-Group Mobilization	−0.258 (0.223)	−0.263		0.008 (0.123)	0.015		0.002* (0.001)	0.529	0.28
Environment, Health, Consumer Policy 1990–2009									
Interest-Group Mobilization	0.325*** (0.057)	0.802	0.644	0.288*** (0.047)	0.823	0.678	0.048** (0.007)	0.840	0.704
Science, Education, Culture Policy 1990–2009									
Interest-Group Mobilization	−0.017 (0.028)	−0.140	0.482	0.046*** (0.009)	0.773	0.597	0.001** (0.000)	0.785	0.616
Security and Defense Policy 1990–2009									
Interest-Group Mobilization	3.897*** (0.038)	0.925	**0.856**	2.032*** (0.197)	0.925	**0.855**	0.003 (0.002)	0.271	
Immigration and Border Policy 1990–2009									
Interest-Group Mobilization	0.449** (0.110)	0.694	0.228	0.214* (0.067)	0.602	0.362	−0.001 (0.001)	−0.205	0.042
Humanitarian and Development Policy 1990–2009									
Interest-Group Mobilization	−0.749* (0.325)	−0.478		0.090** (0.024)	0.663	0.44	0.006*** (0.001)	0.821	0.673

$*p < 0.05$, $**p = 0.01$, $***p < 0.01$; Standard deviation reported in parentheses below means.
Note: Controls are EU staff and EU budget (omitted from the table).

Implications

There are two main sets of results. The first is the relationship between EU authority (in the form of treaties) or resources (in the form of operational budgets) and interest-group mobilization. The second results estimate the over-time relationship between interest-group mobilization and EU governing capacity (as volume or success of legislation).

There was no statistically significant relationship between existing EU resources and interest-group mobilization. Variations in the two trends over time prompt additional research questions, particularly in policy domains such as security and defense policy and immigration and border security policy. There was an association between existing EU authority and interest-group mobilization, but this was not uniform across all policy domains. In security and defense policy, there is a sustained interest-group presence long before any EU intergovernmental treaty agreement (in 1999) or EU supranational treaty authority (2007) in the domain. There is a level of interest-group presence unaffected by a lack of EU investment in the topic for over a decade. In immigration and border security policy, there is a puzzle about why there is no interest-group activity after EU intergovernmental cooperation in the area (1992) and the transfer of partial immigration and asylum policy authority to the supranational level (1997). However, when the interest-group mobilization line is contrasted to the budget expenditure line, it is less mysterious why there is a delay in interest-group mobilization: there was almost no EU operational budget in a domain in which the EU had supranational authority, even after 1997. There is a slight rise in interest-group mobilization from 1997 to 2001 in this domain, probably in response to this transfer of authority to the EU. It then dropped off to almost zero until a few years later, when both the budget and mobilization increased threefold.

Both analyses establish variation in interest-group mobilization over time and across policy domains. They also evaluate competing hypotheses regarding whether a transfer of authority is enough to explain the nature of changes in lobbying mobilization behavior. In the EU overall and in other policy domains, there is a linear relationship between budget, authority, and mobilization of interest groups. The time series results indicate that interest-group mobilization follows the establishment of greater intergovernmental cooperation or supranational authority. With an ANOVA analysis, however, the results are not indicated across the board: only 42.6 percent of variation is predicted by this relationship. It is not strong enough to validate or falsify either of the two extant hypotheses: interest groups precede or follow EU treaty authority.[156] In the domains of security and defense, immigration/border, and humanitarian/development policy, the model performed poorly.[157] In these domains, there is something nonlinear about the relationship between EU treaty authority and interest-group mobilization that begs for further explanation. The causal assumption that "if you build it, will they come" does not sufficiently explain EU political development. Europeanized interest groups are not simply responding to EU authority (in the form of formal treaty authority) or existing EU bureaucratic capacity (in the form of operational budgets). Their mobilization to Brussels follows a different path, including anticipating EU authority or creating informal political institutions to compete with or supplement EU formal institutions.

The purpose of the second model was to establish whether there is any correlation between interest-group mobilization and EU legislation, while holding constant the impact of other indicators such as staff, budget, and treaty authority. The results of this model suggest a very strong relationship between these two variables overall, and a variation in outcomes in the specific policy domains. Across all EU domains, interest-group mobilization is not only highly significant and positive, with increases in both legislation and legislation in force, but also accounted for 79.3 percent and 94.1 percent of the variation in all legislation and legislation in force, respectively. There is something structural in the relationship between interest-group mobilization and the volume and success of EU legislation. This state–society correlation opens up a range of questions involving which mechanisms are at work between mobilization and governing capacity, which are addressed in the rest of the book.

Within the specific domains, some domains had mixed or insignificant results from the model, including regional policy and science/education/culture policy. In humanitarian and development policy, the results were actually negative and slightly significant, but with weak prediction of variation. Domains such as energy policy and environmental/health policy had more positive and significant linkages between these

---

[156] Within the seven specific domains, EU treaty authority had no significant relationship with the mobilization of interest groups, although the relationship was more significant with the scaled authority (Schmitter authscale) and the measure of authority increase within the domain (authdomain). This was the case across all domains, although the variance predicted by this relationship varied greatly. In domains such as Energy, Regional, Environment/Health, and Science/Education/Culture, the variation explained was over 50 percent.

[157] ANOVA results predicting only 24.7 percent, 26.7 percent, and 6.8 percent variation, respectively.

variables. The most significant was in security and defense policy, where the results were not only positive and significant but predicted almost 86 percent of variation in all legislation and legislation in force. As noted elsewhere in this book, this relationship is outside expectations in a number of ways: there should be no organized interests in defense policy in Brussels because it is still a primarily intergovernmental policy domain, even with recent treaty changes. The fact that these organized interests have a marked structural relationship with EU policy outcomes defies the conventional wisdom, starting with assumptions that the politics of this domain happens exclusively in national capitals. It begs for more granular analysis and process tracing.

3   How Weberian Is the EU?

Although high quality bureaucratic institutions are critical to desired political outcomes such as economic growth, there are no widely accepted measures for comparing bureaucracies across countries, regions, and levels of politics.[1] We also do not systematically understand the role interest groups play in bureaucratic policy processes. Do denser interactions between bureaucrats and interest groups improve policy outcomes, or is it corruption, undermining bureaucracies and political outcomes?

This is already a murky question in the realm of national politics, but what about an international organization such as the EU? Political scientists generally treat the organizational features and performance of international organizations as exogenous to political outcomes in the contemporary study of international organizations. Although the EU literature has been more nuanced, it does not highlight bureaucratic quality. IR scholars have called for a research agenda promoting the ontology of international organizations, but such work is still relatively uncommon.[2]

We know from real life that bureaucracy matters in the EU and other international organizations; we also know public–private interactions have exploded in frequency between transnational society and international bureaucrats. Just as in nation states, these interactions can change political outcomes through policy agenda influence, regulatory capture, or a flow of resources from the private sector enabling bureaucracies to develop and pursue their missions. When bureaucrats interact with the private sector, the outcomes are context dependent and vary from improved policy implementation and policy design to incentive structures generating corruption.

---

[1] Steven Van de Walle, "Measuring Bureaucratic Quality in Governance Indicators." Paper presented at the 8th Public Management Research Conference, Los Angeles, CA, 2005.

[2] See Barnett and Finnemore, *Rules for the World*; D. L. Nielson and M. J Tierney, "Delegation to International Organizations: Agency Theory and World Bank Environmental Reform," *International Organization* 57, no. 2 (2003): 241–76; Haas.

This leaves two fundamental questions: (1) what explains variation in the performance and governing capacity of international institutions? and (2) how does this variation impact policy agendas and outcomes? In the previous chapter, I created proxies for internal bureaucratic capacity such as budget and staff resources. I also demonstrated how we can observe the effects of bureaucratic capacity through a number of different proxies: legislative output, amount of legislation passed and enforced, and percentage of legislation passed. But these measures do not precisely capture governing capacity because it is relational and context dependent. In order to capture governing capacity, I modified existing national governance-quality surveys to measure the organizational and relational features of international organizations.

This chapter has three goals. The first is to demonstrate variations in EU bureaucracy outcomes that do not align with EU treaty authority. Next, I theorize and measure the varying dimensions of international bureaucracies. Finally, I link the concepts of Weberian bureaucratic quality to the performance and governing capacity of international institutions.

International Organizations as Bureaucracies

International organizations have varying degrees of success in setting and implementing policies and policy agendas or varying governance capacity. Their success or failure is typically attributed to factors such as how much authority or organizational resources they have been granted by their member states. They are considered epiphenomenal institutions controlled by powerful states, empty arenas for international bargaining and negotiation, or mechanisms solving coordination and collective action problems for interested states.[3] In practice, however, international organizations are also bureaucracies that can be well or poorly organized, independently of their treaty-based authorities and resources.[4] While international policymakers intuitively understand this concept, it has been slow to establish in the field of international relations.

International organizations can also be bureaucracies with policy authority, which can become obsessed with their own rules, producing unresponsive, inefficient, and self-defeating outcomes.[5] Bureaucratic autonomy allows them to evolve and expand in ways unintended by their

---

[3] See D. A. Baldwin, "Neoliberalism, Neorealism, and World Politics," In *Neorealism and Neoliberalism: The Contemporary Debate*, edited by D. A. Baldwin, 3–25 (New York, NY: Columbia University Press, 1993); R. Gilpin, *The Political Economy of International Relations* (Princeton, NJ: Princeton University Press, 1987); Keohane.

[4] Nielson and Tierney; Barnett and Finnemore, *Rules for the World*.

[5] Barnett and Finnemore, *Rules for the World*.

creators. Autonomy can also lead to poor governing capacity outcomes because the internal resources of international bureaucracies might not be enough. And the governing capacity of international bureaucracies often does not match up with the formal authority delegated to them by states.

The EU "State" and European Society: Bureaucracy and Interest Groups

In the United States, lobbying activity of social and market interests is focused on legislative rather than regulatory or bureaucratic matters.[6] In contrast, EU lobbying is directed at bureaucrats such as executives in the Commission and other executive agencies.[7] European bureaucrats must seek out external resources and expertise in order to fulfill their policy tasks, but this dynamic has only been framed as dependent on the bottom-up supply of interest groups and their organizational forms.[8]

Ideally, any new bureaucracy might prefer complete autonomy and centralization in order to achieve policy goals. However, resource constraints and policy demands often necessitate innovative alignments of interests on the part of these bureaucrats in order to accomplish the tasks delegated from nation states. EU bureaucracies have constraints and tasks similar to those of state bureaucracies, but they share the burdens and dilemmas of organizations tasked with changing the political economy status quo, such as in developing states. This task is transformational in nature: some bureaucracies of the EU are attempting to reform the political economy between previous winners in society (that is, national champions, domestic monopolies, or existing corporatist arrangements) and their national governments.[9]

Theoretical Approach: International Bureaucratic Capacity

The ideas of bureaucratic quality, autonomy, and capacity as meaningful concepts evolved with the renewed importance of the state in

---

[6] Frank R. Baumgartner, Christoffer Green-Pedersen, and Bryan D. Jones, "Comparative Studies of Policy Agendas," *Journal of European Public Policy* 13, no. 7 (2006): 959–74.

[7] Mahoney, "Networking vs. Allying."

[8] Bouwen, "Corporate Lobbying in the European Union."

[9] For example, in characterizing the dilemma facing an EU agency such as the European Defence Agency, one official posited that transforming the existing relationships between winners and losers of the past is like being a lawyer helping out with a divorce, when one party wants out, but appearances must be kept up – it is a delicate situation of dependence and risk. In fact, some EU bureaucrats claimed that their task was more like the war on drugs, where you have suppliers, dealers, and addicts, and some authority is attempting to intervene.

promoting economic growth and development. Scholars in comparative politics argued that capacity was a feature of bureaucracies, including their ability to set quality agendas, craft effective issues and policies, and implement political solutions. Capacity (variously the ability to harness resources, make efficient decisions, and influence the policy agenda) as a variable has been theorized and measured by proxies, but usually only as a feature of the governance quality of developing states. State capacity and bureaucratic quality are considered a given in advanced industrialized states and international organizations, assumed by omission not to vary to any degree of significance.

As I argued in the previous chapter, the capacity of a state and its bureaucracies varies as a product of public–private interactions, rather than simply internal resources or authority. In many historical or ideal forms of bureaucracy, there was little room for direct interactions between bureaucrats and civil society, and public policy research focused solely on the delegation and interaction between the politicians and administrators. However, this ideal type has little to do to with the effectiveness of public administrations in non-Western countries, as delegation is not the sole product of power relations between branches of government.[10] Instead, relative state–society "embeddedness" is equally important to political outcomes. In the case of the EU, scholars have previously proposed a relationship between interest groups and the institutional capacity of the EU[11] or the supranationalization of the EU.[12]

Does a Weberian Political Authority Produce Better Political Outcomes?

Bureaucratic performance – and any resulting governing capacity – is at least partially dependent on the internal characteristics of a bureaucracy. It is necessary, within a Weberian state hypothesis, but it may not be sufficient, for an embeddedness hypothesis. But how to measure the Weberian characteristics of bureaucracies? Two proxies are frequently mentioned: budget and staff. But do budget and staff numbers correlate with greater authority (granted from member states to the EU) or greater capacity (generated by EU institutions themselves through internal or external resources)?

Internal Resources: Budget and Staff

Do the financial resources of a political institution equal its Weberianness? When a policy area is expanded in the EU, either through

---

[10] Moon and Ingraham.   [11] Fligstein and McNichol.
[12] Sandholtz and Stone Sweet, *European Integration and Supranational Governance*; Haas.

greater intergovernmental cooperation or supranationalization, the operating budget usually increases. Even when a policy area is regulatory and
not redistributive, its budget increases have a direct relationship with its
authority. It may be a good Weberian proxy for policy authority but is an
insufficient proxy for EU capacity.

A better proxy than budget for measuring the Weberianness of a political authority might be its human resources, as staff levels are necessary
for crafting and implementing policy outcomes. A large staff alone does
not make an institution Weberian – it could be poorly organized or have
perverse incentive structures. But the size of an institution can reflect
its internal resources, as bureaucracies with low staff might need external resources to enhance their capacity.[13] However, in regression analysis, both variables reflecting internal Weberian features of a political
authority – budgetary resources and staff size – had no statistical relationship with EU political outcomes (as measured by legislative output).
The Weberian features of EU institutions may vary, but they are not sufficient for explaining European political outcomes. There is something
else at work that cannot be measured by internal features such as staff
and budget. If the EU's capacity varies and has an impact on political
outcomes, such as developing states, it must come from other internal
characteristics (such as leadership, meritocracy, or common ideational
purpose) or from outside of EU institutions – a transformational capacity provided by its embeddedness with outside actors. Both concepts are
further elaborated below.

Bureaucrats and Interest Groups: Corruption or Embeddedness?

When we discuss interactions between state and society, it immediately
prompts normative questions about capture and corruption. Should
bureaucracies maintain firm boundaries with interest groups, seclud-
ing their officials against societal and economic interest groups intent
on capturing the public good with their private interests?[14] Are state

---

[13] Figures for the annual staff of the EU are published in the annual report. I have collected
these numbers for the entire EU from 1950 to 2009, and for the seven domains from
1990 to 2009. There were a few years missing from the domain staff numbers, but
I calculated staff figures from the budgetary figures on expenditures for staff salaries
by domain. Aligning these numbers with the expenditures per staff member for years
with accessible staff figures produced staff numbers with a high degree of confidence.
These parameters on staff figures had no significant coefficient with any EU policy
outcomes or mobilized interests, but they were used as a control variable in the time
series regressions.

[14] B. Geddes, *Politician's Dilemma: Building State Capacity in Latin America* (Berkeley:
University of California Press, 1994); O. E. Williamson, "Visible and Invisible Governance," *The American Economic Review* 842 (1994): 323–6.

and society inherently in opposition, necessitating the protection of new bureaucracies from diffuse social forces[15] and the protection of executives to concentrate their authority toward effective public policy?[16] Or is there more ambiguity in the state–society relationship? Perhaps bureaucrats need interest groups to help make informed decisions and implement effective policy. In the study of American politics, these questions drive the research agenda of interest-group politics and agenda setting; in comparative politics, these questions drive the developmentalist framework, where public–private linkages as "embedded autonomy,"[17] "governed interdependence,"[18] and "extended accountability"[19] describe successful state interventions into the economy or society as necessary preconditions to effective policymaking.[20] The concept of embeddedness is central: where a complex synergy between public and private actors improves policy outcomes, while blurring some institutional boundaries. But what about the international context, where we know public–private interaction is particularly intense, in a pluralist realm where the democratic oversight and constitutional boundaries of states are nonexistent?

Measuring Bureaucratic Quality and Capacity

At the domestic level of analysis, surveys measure state capacity and the "Weberianness" of national bureaucracies, including their governance quality and state–society embeddedness.[21] From 1995 to 1999, Peter Evans and James Rauch developed a survey measuring bureaucratic structure and bureaucratic performance. They sought empirical support for their hypotheses – derived from Max Weber – regarding the relationship between bureaucratic structure ("Weberianness")

---

[15] J. S. Migdal, *Strong Societies and Weak States: State–Society Relations and State Capabilities in the Third World* (Princeton, NJ: Princeton University Press, 1988).

[16] David Stark and Laszlo Bruszt, *Postsocialist Pathways: Transforming Politics and Property in East Central Europe* (Cambridge, UK: Cambridge University Press, 1998), 95.

[17] Evans, *Embedded Autonomy*; Weiss.

[18] L. Weiss and J. M. Hobson, *States and Economic Development: A Comparative Historical Analysis* (Cambridge, MA: Polity Press Cambridge, 1995).

[19] Stark and Bruszt.

[20] By extended accountability, Stark and Bruszt are referring to a process that "extends network ties beyond industrial elites and extend accountability beyond intrastate institutions" to include a broader range of interests and intelligence in decision-making centers (Stark and Bruszt, 101).

[21] This is done by asking a small sample of experts about the insulation, meritocracy, morale, relative influence, and public–private interconnectedness of their organizations. The best examples of these surveys are deployed by Evans and Rauch, the World Bank, and the European Central Bank.

and bureaucratic performance, and between these variables and economic growth and development. These hypotheses were first developed in Evans' 1995 work on the dialectic between the institutional embeddedness and bureaucratic autonomy of national states and their record on economic development. Although Evans' book was primarily theoretical, he and his collaborator, Rauch, subsequently investigated why some state bureaucracies appear more effective than others in supporting economic growth,[22] finding that variations in bureaucratic quality explained differences in national economic growth. The World Bank subsequently adopted their survey and concepts in order to measure governance quality across the developing world.

The key concept in measuring Weberianness is the professionalization of the bureaucracy. The institutional characteristics of a Weberian bureaucracy – as opposed to a corrupt and inefficient bureaucracy – include "meritocratic recruitment through genuinely competitive examinations, civil service procedures for hiring and firing rather than political appointments and dismissals, and filling higher levels of the hierarchy through internal promotion."[23] As to whether political appointees add to the capacity of an organization:

lengthen[ing] the period that public decision makers are willing to wait to realize the benefits of expenditures, leading to allocation of a greater proportion of government resources to long-gestation period projects such as infrastructure . . . this increased government investment in inputs complementary to private capital will increase the rate of economic growth.[24]

Evans and Rauch also attempted to build on Evans' hypotheses regarding embeddedness and measuring social ties and corruption. Before their study, there were few extant measurements of corruption for developing countries – privately produced risk analysis data such as the International Country Risk Guide (IRCG) and the Business and Environmental Risk Intelligence (BERI) – where corruption is used as an indicator of higher business risk and delayed economic growth.[25] By creating more subjective – yet comparable – indicators of governance variation, Evans and Rauch fundamentally questioned the methodological validity and reliability of these measures:

[22] Evans and Rauch, "Bureaucracy and Growth"; P. B. Evans and J. E. Rauch, "Bureaucratic Structure and Bureaucratic Performance in Less Developed Countries," *Journal of Public Economics* 75, no. 1 (2000): 49–71.

[23] Evans and Rauch, "Bureaucracy and Growth," 1.   [24] Ibid.

[25] S. Knack and P. Keefer, "Institutions and Economic Performance: Cross-Country Tests Using Alternative Institutional Measures," *Economics & Politics* 7, no. 3 (1995): 207–27; P. Mauro, "Corruption and Growth," *The Quarterly Journal of Economics* 110, no. 3 (1995): 681–712.

The rating services . . . offered little explanation of how their data were derived, or why they should be considered reliable. The data seemed to be based primarily on the assessment of consultants, but the basis on which these consultants were selected was not usually specified, and methodological issues were clearly not a primary concern.[26]

Although Evans and Rauch agreed that better bureaucracy and less corruption leads to economic growth and outcomes, their main critique of these country risk data sets was there were no indicators reflecting any institutional features of bureaucratic quality.

Corruption and Governance Quality

In the decades since Evans and Rauch published the results of their research, quantitative governance indicators for assessing the institutional quality of countries have proliferated.[27] Used to evaluate risk and conditional development aid, few are comparable across different levels of political authority.[28] Although cross-national, regional, or international comparisons of the public sector are rare, studies of public sector quality in industrialized, wealthy countries are rarer still.[29] Only the World Bank collects broad governance indicators evaluating developing

---

[26] Evans and Rauch, "Bureaucracy and Growth," 751.

[27] See, for example, the "public sector efficiency" indicators, including the European Central Bank's working paper "Public Sector Efficiency: An International Comparison," the World Bank's "Government Effectiveness" indicator, the "Public Institutions Index," part of the World Economic Forum's Growth Competitiveness Index, and the IMD's World Competitiveness Yearbook's Government Efficiency Ranking.

[28] See, for example, C. Rodrigues, *International management: A Cultural Approach* (Los Angeles, CA: South-Western, 2001); L. Peters and J. Verrinder, "The Size of the Government Sector from Different Perspectives," paper presented at The Size of the Government Sector: How to Measure: 24th The European Advisory Committee Information in the Economic and Social Spheres (CEIES) seminar, Vienna, Austria, October 23–24, 2003. A few studies contrast public sector quality across local municipalities, such as studies of tax administrations within Germany or fire services and local civil registries in Belgium (Van de Walle, "Measuring Bureaucratic Quality in Governance Indicators").

[29] The exceptions include a European Central Bank (ECB) study of OECD countries on "Public sector efficiency: An international comparison" (Antonio Afonso, Ludger Schuknecht, and Vito Tanzi, "Public Sector Efficiency: Evidence for New EU Member States and Emerging Markets," *Applied Economics* 42, no. 17 [2010]: 2147–64) and a follow-up study in the Netherlands attempting to focus on variations in EU countries. The ECB data set has four variables predicting administrative performance: corruption, red tape, quality of the judiciary, and extent of the shadow economy. Although it is the only one of its kind, scholars have criticized the variables for administrative performance as defective (Van de Walle, "Measuring Bureaucratic Quality in Governance Indicators," 5).

states along six criteria: voice and accountability, political stability, government effectiveness, regulatory quality, rule of law, and control of corruption. Of these, the government effectiveness metric is synonymous with the idea of bureaucratic capacity.[30]

There is still little agreement as to what is being measured when we discuss the variables of bureaucratic quality, performance, autonomy, or capacity (which are often used as synonyms). With the exception of comparative political scientists using the idea of embeddedness, however, there is a general reliance on defining bureaucratic quality as the absence of corruption. Not-corruption is an often-used proxy for bureaucratic quality. Many scholars call their dependent variables bureaucratic quality, but by quality they mean the inverse of corruption.[31] Even when corruption indicators directly measure corruption, it is an unresolved concept. Is corruption merely the buying of individual bureaucrats, the structural capture of policy agendas, or excessively revolving doors between public and private actors? Do these things all equally undermine governance, as the World Bank has concluded, or is it unclear whether bureaucratic quality is mutually exclusive with corruption, and even "possible that countries with high-quality institutions also have high corruption levels"?[32]

The relationship between corruption and bureaucratic quality is far from clear. In fact, if we accept the idea of embeddedness enhancing governance, there is a positive correlation between some form of corruption and bureaucratic quality. Particularly in new political institutions, ties between bureaucracies and the private sector can be beneficial in both the agenda-setting and the implementation stages of the policy-making process. The "Weberianness" of organizations often depends on whether the civil service emphasizes meritocratic recruitment and predictable, long-term careers. In developing countries, this concept captures the public sector's degree of independence from the influence of the entrenched and profitable private elite. In practice, the public sector is influenced by political interests and intervention (that is, political

---

[30] Within the United States, the Government Performance Project evaluates the bureaucratic quality of states and municipalities. It differs from many of the large-n efforts by focusing on "management capacity," itself as an outcome variable, rather than focusing on economic outcomes of different forms of governance as the key dependent variable (Ingraham et al., 2003).

[31] See Van de Walle, "Measuring Bureaucratic Quality in Governance Indicators"; Uslaner, E. M. 2005. "The Bulging Pocket and the Rule of Law: Corruption, Inequality, and Trust," Paper presented at "The Quality of Government: What It Is, How to Get It, Why It Matters" Conference, November 17–19, 2005, Göteborg University, Sweden; Mauro, "Corruption and Growth," for examples.

[32] V. K. Teles, "Institutional Quality and Endogenous Economic Growth," *Journal of Economic Studies* 34, no. 1 (2007): 2.

appointments) and thus can be affected by corruption and self-interest within the executive branch of government. For Evans and Rauch, this principal-agent problem is mitigated, in part, through an alternative form of bureaucratic control, where behavior is self-regulated by reinforcing the individual's sense of professionalism, while encouraging an *esprit de corps* and a sense of membership in a common set of goals and values; a socialization process shaped by meritocratic selection, promotion, and reward processes.

Economists adapted the Evans and Rauch survey as a tool for the Africa Economic Research Consortium and the World Bank.[33] It builds on the original, prompting descriptions of core agencies, the civil service, and the relationship between the bureaucracy and the private sector. The survey added temporal dimensions of change – such as "how often has the power of agencies changed over the last 20 years?" – and applied the concept of embeddedness and corruption from the individual career paths of bureaucrats to other dimensions of interaction, such as the general state of cooperation or conflict between the public and private sectors, the frequency of quid pro quos, the opportunities for private-sector input in the policy agenda-setting process, and the efficiency of the public sector.

Sociologists studying organizations have also developed techniques to map the networks and actors in policy domains by measuring variations in public–private embeddedness of one policy domain to another, comparing and measuring network density.[34] Density is the ratio of reciprocal direct ties between organizations to the total possible ties.[35] To identify how organizations aggregate into interest representation patters, researchers mine the public record of private efforts to influence public policies. The records of this influence can be found in witness lists before congressional committees, newspaper stories, lobbying registers, and court case participants, and the descriptions of journalists and academics.[36]

---

[33] "Survey for Analyzing the Bureaucracy," J. P. Court, P. Kristen, and B. Weder, "Bureaucratic Structure and Performance: First Africa Survey Results." United Nations University Tokyo, 1999. http://www.unu.edu/hq/academic/Pg_area4/pdf/unu-research .pdf

[34] See Laumann and Knoke, 94–108.

[35] See Knoke and Kuklinski, 45. In these studies, the U.S. energy and health domains had densities of 0.30, the U.S. labor domain 0.385, and German labor 0.20. The overall density is 0.038 of elites across many policy domains in the United States (Gwen Moore, "The Structure of a National Elite Network," *American Sociological Review* [1979]: 673– 92).

[36] The most important organizations are the ones that appear numerous (at least five or six) times, and generally amount to around 100 core organizations. Personal interviews

Survey Design

Existing surveys capture a concept of bureaucratic structure predicting bureaucratic performance and, in turn, economic performance. The variables measured personnel attributes such as internal promotion policies and individual career trajectories, and also tested the theory of embedded autonomy, such as estimating the degree of contact between bureaucracies and their external environments. These survey questions have three main aspects: (1) description of policy domain and environment, (2) Weberianness or bureaucratic structure, and (3) embeddedness. The World Bank governance surveys are the same, with minor adaptations. I modified these governance surveys of bureaucratic quality of the developing world – a product of capacity and embeddedness – in the context of international governance. There are three categories in this adapted questionnaire: (1) the institutional affiliation of the respondent; (2) key agencies, actors, boundaries, and characteristics of the respondent's primary policy domain; and (3) the scope, formality, intensity, and content of the relationship between the public and private sectors in the respondent's policy domain. The first two categories measure variation in organizational structure and quality, whereas the third category maps the policy network and the embeddedness or density of public and private actors.

Bureaucratic and Governing Capacity

Section 2 of the survey – Policy Domain and Key Organizations – captures a particular domain's (1) structure and dynamics of public institutions and (2) structure of state–society interaction. It measures the Weberian features of international organizations, such as the quality and training of civil servants (Q4–5).[37] Other questions (Q6–7) were adapted from the World Bank survey and capture the relative effectiveness of the bureaucracy in setting and implementing a policy agenda.

or surveys can then confirm the key actors, as well as information regarding interactions, resources, and event participation among the organizations in the domain. Additional sources of domain population can include participants at key conferences, public–private partnerships, and commissions, as well as criteria such as "being invited to two or more hearings on policies" (Thomas Koenig and Robert Gogel, "Interlocking Corporate Directorships as a Social Network," *American Journal of Economics and Sociology* 40, no. 1 [1981]: 37–50).

[37] Whereas Evans and the World Bank emphasized factors such as meritocracy and the socioeconomic compensation of bureaucrats vis-à-vis interest groups, these might not be as meaningful for measuring relative quality in more established bureaucracies. Weber's original concept of bureaucratic quality and effectiveness did not rest on the relative economic position of civil servants in their society, but it was an appropriate adaptation for evaluating the bureaucracies of less developed states.

The survey also measures variations in the general policy domain or environment (Q8–11) and the role of crises in policymaking (Q9–10). The impact of crises on institutions and policy agendas is complex: first, crises may affect one policy domain and not another, and second, the legitimacy of an organization or bureaucracy is likely to fluctuate with extreme and negatively judged events and processes. Further, the very existence (creation, rise, and fall) of international organizations is directly related to international crises. For example, European security and defense institutions were created in part as a response to crises such as the Balkan wars of the 1990s. Crises are also the source of opportunity structures, particularly when an organization does not have a great deal of power or autonomy; however, such crises also change the environment and the perception of the environment the organization is attempting to manage. If the organization is stuck in an environment perceived to be crisis ridden, this will impact individual perceptions of the stability or uncertainty of their policy environment. Questions 9 and 10 pinpoint the sources of uncertainty or crisis, both internal and external. Question 11 evaluates leadership meritocracy – whether key officials are recruited, appointed, or careerists – as explanatory sources of capacity and bureaucratic coherence. Career paths (for example, revolving door) of leaders after their tenure and the degree of policy agenda flux with leadership change are also possible indicators of capacity.

Bureaucratic Embeddedness

Section 3 – relationship between bureaucracy and the private sector – identifies the linkages between international civil servants and interest groups in their policymaking environments. With the exception of international development case studies, there are few systematic explanations of what happens when international bureaucrats and interest groups interact. Even at the level of domestic policymaking, the research agenda is stymied by an overwhelming emphasis on public–private linkages as either corruption or a pluralist outlet for private participation. The structural effects of this interaction on bureaucratic capacity and agenda setting are relatively unexamined. Evans and Rauch called this structural interaction embeddedness and theorized that the denser the linkages were between reformist public bureaucrats and interest groups, the more effective were the policy outcomes. This section of the survey resembles political domain analysis of policy network interactions in U.S. politics[38] but adapted to measure the structure of social actors and public–private

[38] Knoke and Kuklinski.

interactions in an international policymaking domain. Survey respondents listed the most influential or useful private actors – both for-profit and nonprofit – within their policy domain (Q12). Identifying the relative power and influence of private actors is particularly valuable in the realm of international policymaking, where advocacy and lobbying are opaque: a lack of democratic accountability usually shields the identities and activity of transnational private actors. The next questions (Q13–14) come from the World Bank survey, capturing the relationship between public and private actors: whether it was cooperative or antagonistic, and whether the dynamic was changing. This measure imports comparative politics questions of state–society relations into the study of international organizations. There is an unexamined normative bias in the existing literature on the interactions between international organizations and private actors: the literature on epistemic communities has a bias assuming benign public–private cooperation, and recent scholarship on NGO lobbying of international organizations implies an inclusive pluralism in an otherwise nondemocratic arena.[39] Question 14 actually tests this assumption, asking what opportunities international bureaucracies provide to interest groups for voicing their concerns or interests over policymaking.

The theory of embedded autonomy elevated the role of domestic bureaucracy to something varying in quality and structure and predicting policy outcomes. However, the "embeddedness" of the embedded autonomy measured the role of individual bureaucrats in their policy environment. Questions 15 and 16 replicate the Evans and Rauch questions exactly, asking about the frequency of public officials' time in the private sector and the occurrence of public officials' retirement into the private sector. These questions measure the degree to which public and private boundaries are blurred and the extent to which the state is embedded in society. Indeed, this revolving-door phenomenon is an important and undermeasured mechanism of state–society relations. But there are other important indicators beyond the revolving door reflecting informational flows and influence between the public and private divide. Policy agendas change over years or decades – time periods usually surpassing civil servant tenures – making the revolving door only one mechanism of many in public–private interactions. A series of new questions reflect other dimensions of public–private embeddedness: how

---

[39] Jonas Tallberg and Christer Jönsson, "Transnational Actor Participation in International Institutions: Where, Why, and with What Consequences?" In *Transnational actors in global governance*, edited by Christer Jönsson and Jonas Tallberg, 1–21 (London, UK: Palgrave Macmillan UK, 2010).

often individuals experienced interactions between the public and private sectors (Q18–19), whether it was formal (institutional partnerships, boards, or councils) or informal (phone calls, conferences, or outside interactions), and if this was increasing over time (Q17).

Survey Results

This survey was designed to analyze the EU across policy domains, but to be as flexible as possible to allow for future comparisons between EU bureaucracies or among international institutions, or multiple levels of governance. Although I collected responses across multiple EU policy domains, I focus here on reporting the comparisons between the two main case studies of the book, also reporting the averages across all EU policy areas.[40] The survey findings raise a number of interesting issues related to variation in EU bureaucracies, including aspects of bureaucratic capacity, agenda setting, and public–private relations.

Bureaucratic Quality and Governing Capacity

This book has accumulated evidence that bureaucratic quality varies among EU bureaucracies. In Chapter 2, I developed proxies for governing capacity by measuring the output of policies, successful policy implementation, and percentage of successful policies implemented. Specific questions in the survey are designed to measure bureaucratic quality in a more subjective manner. Two question results are highlighted here. The first, in Figure 3.1, demonstrates the differences between the two policy domains in an indicator of governing capacity – in this case framed as efficiency in implementing policy agendas – and notes their divergence over the past ten years. EU JHA/Immigration organizations have been viewed as having less governing capacity than the security and defense organizations. As new domains, bureaucracies in both areas have increased their governing capacity. In contrast to other EU domains, their trajectory is upward, while the overall EU trajectory of efficiency is downward. This might be representative of the increasing pluralist input and policy output demands on older EU bureaucracies, combined with relatively stagnant budgets and staff levels.

---

[40] For security and defense policy, there were 45 respondents to the survey (20 EU officials and 25 nongovernmental individuals, with a response rate of 23 percent). For immigration policy, there were 39 respondents, 28 EU officials and 11 nongovernmental individuals, with a response rate of 18 percent. For all EU domains, there were 420 survey respondents (13-percent response rate).

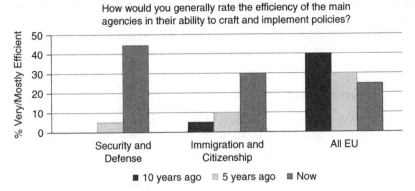

Figure 3.1 Efficiency of Main EU Agencies and Bureaucracies in Policy Domain

The variation between the two domains is consistent throughout the other results, including in Figure 3.2. Here, respondents were asked to rate the EU public officials themselves. Although opinions of bureaucrats in both domains have improved, the security and defense officials have been rising in esteem at a faster rate. Bureaucrats in both domains have a Weberianness level far below that of bureaucrats in other, more established EU domains.

Policy Agenda Dynamics

In Figure 3.3, respondents evaluated the agenda-setting role of EU bureaucracies. The differences between the two domains are not as

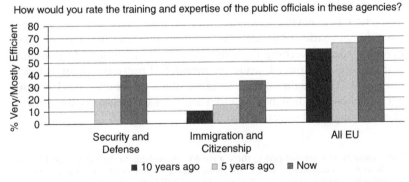

Figure 3.2 Expertise and Training of EU Bureaucrats by Policy Domain

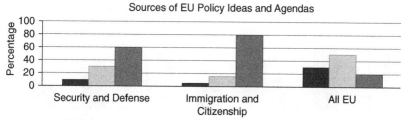

Figure 3.3 Sources of EU Policy Ideas and Agendas by Policy Domain

stark, as the majority of respondents identified these bureaucracies as less than dominant in formulating the original ideas for policy agenda. This question does not ask respondents where the ideas came from, if not from the main bureaucracies. For the EU, then, it is difficult to identify whether ideas and agendas came from another level of government, such as national parliaments or ministries, or from the private sector. The results advance a more refined interpretation of bureaucratic capacity, defined as the ability to set or formulate policy agendas.

A similar question is demonstrated in Figure 3.4. It reflects another concept of capacity, the ability to successfully implement policy agendas.

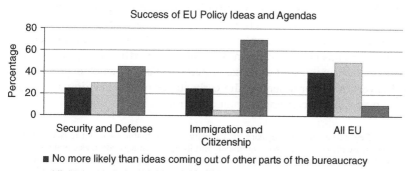

Figure 3.4 Success of Policy Agendas by Policy Domain

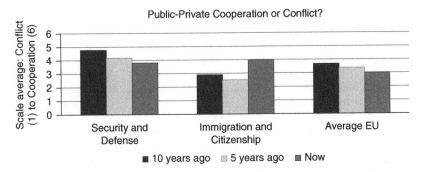

Figure 3.5 Degree of Cooperation or Conflict between Public and Private Actors by Domain

While the previous question reflects the origins of idea entrepreneurship, this reflects the actual success or failure of policy agendas.[41] Both domains have far less successful agenda outcomes than other EU domains.

Relationship with Interest Groups

The next four results reference the relationship between EU bureaucracies and the organized interests in their policy domains. Figure 3.5 reflects the subjective assessment on the part of respondents of how much cooperation there is between EU bureaucrats and nongovernmental actors in EU domains. The figures in the survey indicate bureaucrats and private sector or nonprofit actors believe their relationships have changed over time. Across all domains, respondents perceived increasing conflict and decreasing cooperation between public and private actors. Although there is not enough evidence to assert this point, this decreasing cooperation might simply be the result of increasing pluralism as policy domains get older and more established, attracting greater numbers of constituents and organized interests. The informal institutions or subgovernments prevalent in the early stages of a policy domain might fade over time, decreasing agenda cooperation.

[41] The Legislation in Force proxies for capacity are a valuable tool, but may be skewed slightly by the combination of significant and insignificant legislation as equal counts. A more subjective survey analysis allows for a result that appropriately weights significant legislation. On the other hand, bureaucrats trumpeting their own successes could also skew these results. There is still variation in the same direction, however, with EU Immigration ideas and agendas as far less successful than security and defense. This subjective result is stronger than as it was measured by an objective counting measure of Legislation in Force.

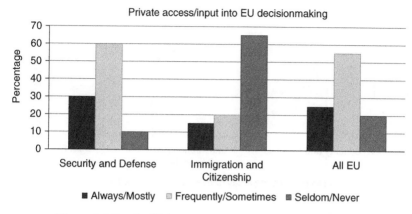

Figure 3.6 Level of Private Actor Access into EU Decisions by Policy Domain

While the security and defense domain has experienced a relatively high level of cooperation overall, experts perceive it as becoming slightly less cooperative in the past ten years. Given the early and intense presence of private organized interests in the early stages of this domain, they originally functioned as an informal institution. As interest groups have increasingly mobilized, this cooperation and consensus might have weakened. In the immigration domain, policymakers perceive more cooperation now than five to ten years ago.

Figure 3.6 is particularly telling for the core logic of this book. There has been far more perceived access in the security and defense domain than in the immigration domain. Security and defense has a higher level of access than the EU average. I do not know whether this is a function of the particular politics of defense markets, or whether this was because security and defense was a new, weak bureaucracy in particular need of information and expertise. In the JHA/immigration domain, EU organizations are also relatively new, but were initially granted more EU authority and resources than the security and defense institutions. Perhaps this is why there was less access granted to outside actors, as the need was not immediate for expertise and access goods.

The next two results are from the most important comparative measures in the Evans and Rauch survey. Two results document the frequency of interactions between public and private officials, both informal and formal in nature. Informal interactions could be cocktail parties, conference sessions, and other social events. Formal interactions are scheduled meetings, committees, conference calls, and other official

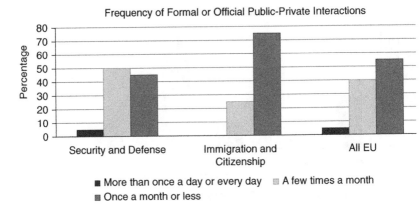

Figure 3.7 Frequency of Formal Interaction between Public and Private Actors

contacts. In Figure 3.7, respondents reported their formal interactions between the public and private sectors. Again, the security and defense domain is above the EU average for public–private interaction, and the immigration domain is below average. When it comes to informal public–private interactions (Figure 3.8), the differences are less stark, and both domains more closely resemble the average across EU domains.

An important variable for analyzing the structure of state–society relations at the EU level is also the density of interaction within a particular domain. Sociologists study policy domains along these lines, where the activity in one domain can be denser than that in another, meaning

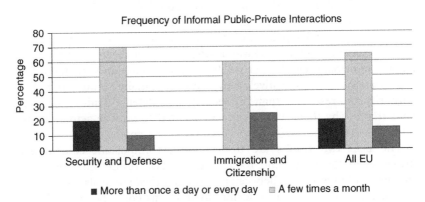

Figure 3.8 Frequency of Informal Interaction between Public and Private Actors

more overlap among the network of policymakers. This is measured by the degree of overlap there is in the subjective lists of key organizations. This measure has never been developed for the EU, where there is no information resource for this information. In the security and defense domain, the density of organized interests is 0.68. In the immigration domain, the density of organized interests is 0.37. This means nearly 75 percent of the reported lists of most influential private groups overlapped in the security and defense domain, while about 40 percent of the organizations overlapped in the immigration domain. The EU average across all domains was 0.26. This result suggests both domains have far denser policy domains than the EU average. This density could speak to the relative pluralism of established policy domains in the EU. The EU average suggests a degree of pluralism across multiple domains, while the newer defense and immigration domains might be experiencing the initial insular intensity of a domain with fewer influential actors and organizations. Given the more recent phenomenon of the mobilization of defense and security industry actors toward the internal and border security domain, I expect that this density has only intensified over the past decade, but will start to subside soon thereafter. In any case, EU border security is no longer the domain of "quiet" politics and has become quite salient in public discourses across Europe and beyond.

4   The Political Economy of European Defense

The restructuring of the European [defence and security] industry is far from being a simple pro rata adjustment of supply to changes in demands arising from objective changes in the security environment. It is inextricably bound up with the development of institutions, policy paradigms (in both the military and the industrial domains), business networks, and relationships between companies and governments.[1]

We absolutely need defence integration and to have common procurement in Europe... [w]e are asking for one customer.
– EADS Chairman Philippe Camus, 2001[2]

The story of EU CSDP began on December 4, 1998, in St. Malo, France. It was there that President Chirac and Prime Minister Blair agreed on a "Franco-British Summit Joint Declaration on European Defence." The St. Malo agreement made a plan for a common defense policy, including developing the capacity for autonomous action with credible military forces, developing intelligence and planning institutions, and strengthening armed forces with "a strong and competitive defence industry and technology."[3] The December 1999 EU Helsinki Summit committed to build a rapid response corps of 50,000 to 60,000 troops for deployment in humanitarian and peacekeeping tasks.[4] Other

---

[1] J. Lovering, "Which Way to Turn? The European Defence Industry after the Cold War," in *Arming the Future: A Defence Industry for the 21st Century*, edited by A. Markusen and S. Costigan, 342 (New York, NY: Council on Foreign Relations Press, 1999).

[2] D. Michaels, "European Defence: More Bang for Buck – Nations Begin to Pool Their Military Orders; Contractors, Likewise." *Wall Street Journal*, Eastern edition, March 9, 2001, A.11.

[3] For St. Malo text, see M. Rutten, ed., *From Saint-Malo to Nice. European Defence: Core Documents*. Paris, WEU-ISS, 2001 (Chaillot Paper No. 47), 8–9.

[4] At the 1999 Helsinki launch of the European Security and Defence Policy (ESDP), the EU adopted a policy target, the "Headline Goals." They were intended to increase the EU ability to carry out the "Petersburg tasks" of humanitarian and rescue missions, peacekeeping, and tasks of combat forces in crisis management, including peacemaking. Under this plan, the EU pledged by 2003 to deploy rapidly and then sustain forces capable of the full range of Petersburg tasks in operations up to corps level (up to fifteen brigades or 50,000 to 60,000 troops). The aim was to make those forces self-reliant from

130

CSDP institutions were created at the Thessaloniki Summit, such as a Political and Security Committee (PSC), EU Military Staff (EUMS), and a Military Committee. In 2003 the EU launched a European Security Strategy (ESS) identifying threats and challenges, as well as objectives and goals of the EU in defense and security. The St. Malo Summit was a direct response to the strategic failures of the EU to effectively respond to the Balkans crisis in the 1990s,[5] and European officials asserted that CSDP "has a shorter history than ten years ... compared to the UN and NATO, which have both existed for about sixty years."[6]

But the ideas behind CSDP are not new: European defense has a history almost as long as the EU project itself. Some defense integration projects have focused on coordinating common foreign or security polices, others have focused on coordinating European defense industry or markets. Most of these efforts were arranged between a handful of states and were outside the auspices of the EU. To say CSDP is simply a strategic response to failures in the Balkans begins the story in the 1990s; a longer view of the European integration project contains less-than-successful efforts to create defense integration well before St. Malo.

In this longer institutional history, multiple other factors explain the timing, institutional form, and agenda content of European defense. A political economy explanation of CSDP expands the logic of European defense beyond state actors to private actors, including armaments industry actors, who have been involved in attempting to influence the defense agenda for decades. Their mobilization and embeddedness with European officials explains the timing, content, and direction of defense agendas and institutions.

A Market Explanation for CSDP

The first effort to produce a common European defense policy was the 1948 *Brussels Treaty on Economic, Social and Cultural Collaboration and Collective Self-Defence*, signed by Belgium, France, Luxembourg, the Netherlands, and the United Kingdom – creating the *Western Union*, which became subsumed by NATO when the North Atlantic Treaty was signed in 1949. Under the *Paris Agreements of 1954*, West Germany and Italy (and later Greece, Spain, and Portugal) acceded to the

---

the U.S. or NATO, deployable within sixty days, and sustainable in the field for a year. In order to provide rotational support, the full troop level would have to be around 180,000.

[5] H. Bentegeat, "1998–2008: 10 Years of ESDP," *Impetus*, October 2008.

[6] H. Syren, "The European Security and Defence Policy – Great Challenges as Theory Is Turned into Practice." *defpro.news*, 2008. Accessed September 25, 2009. http://www.defpro.com/news/details/4536/

Brussels Treaty and the Western Union was renamed the *Western European Union* (WEU). For most of the Cold War period, the WEU provided an occasional forum for addressing European defense issues, and for a brief period in the 1990s assumed an independent military role, but was otherwise of marginal military and political significance. Alongside the ECSC in the 1950s, a *European Defence Community* (EDC) was proposed but failed after ratification in the face of French opposition.

For the rest of the cold war, NATO was the center of all strategic coordination for all European defense. Beginning in 1984, the WEU began to develop a "common European defence identity" in an attempt to boost the "European pillar" of NATO. From the mid-1980s to the 1990s, the WEU was the forum for proposing the interactions between NATO and the EU, and framing defense and security discussions relevant to Europe. The Maastricht Treaty of the EU referenced vague and basic defense language in 1991. In 1992, the WEU states agreed to common humanitarian and peacekeeping goals – later known as the Petersberg Tasks. These ideas became operational in 1996, when the Council of the EU asked the WEU for support on humanitarian operations in Africa. The first operations included mine clearance, refugee evacuation, and peacekeeping. These missions were supplanted by the concept of operational Rapid Reaction forces, or Battle Groups, to be operationally available for deployment in crisis management or other missions. The 2009 Lisbon Treaty established CSDP within the EU Treaties, expanding on the previous intergovernmental policies, creating a framework for Permanent Structured Cooperation (PESCO), adding a mutual assistance and solidarity clause, and creating an EEAS.

Why CSDP?

Particularly in the intergovernmental, high-politics areas of security and defense, the study of the EU has traditionally centered on the coordination of authority between nation states and the EU. But a state-based explanation is lacking for explaining the timing and content of CSDP. For example, there is no state, or coalition of states, whose preferences directly prescribed the creation of this domain. Currently, many observers cite France as the driving national power behind CSDP aspirations, but CSDP support in France has not been a consistent policy over the past three decades.

Interest groups must be accounted for in the emergence of CSDP. It should be a "least likely" case for interest-group involvement in any policy-timing, institution-building, or agenda-setting role. It is, and has always been, an intergovernmental policy domain, meaning there should be little independent supranational role for the EU to discount the interests of member states. There should also be no interest-group activity before the creation of EU cooperation in these domains, and even then, activity should be modest, matching the modest level of EU cooperation; however, this has not been the case. Interest groups have been active in supporting European defense policy since the 1980s and have constructed informal institutions for promoting security and defense agendas at the EU level for decades.

The mobilization and concentration of interest groups to Brussels – and the formation of informal defense institutions before the creation of CSDP institutions – help explain CSDP timing, agenda content and direction, and EU governing capacity in the domain. This explanation has three stages: (1) in the late 1980s and early 1990s there was an ad-hoc transnational lobbying attempt on behalf of national defense interest groups; (2) in the mid- to late 1990s, European industry associations and research institutes formed informal institutions in Brussels advocating for defense integration; and (3) after 2001, informal institutions supported formal CSDP institutions and accelerated defense integration. Once established, defense interest groups diversified their interest representation to include security and high-technology firms, associations, and expert groups at the European level.

CSDP: Rapid and Unlikely Progress?

The timing of CSDP is puzzling: why did the EU develop defense at a time when the EU was "most peaceful, prosperous, and secure," at the end of the 1990s?[7] Why did defense institutions accelerate and mature during the time of the greatest EU foreign policy rift, during the onset of the Iraq war in 2003–4? How were defense institutions, policies, and agendas developed in the absence of EU legal and constitutional authority prior to the 2009 Lisbon Treaty? As *Jane's Defence Weekly* noted in 2003 – in an article titled "EU Defence Surge Despite Constitutional Collapse" – new defense institutions were created without treaty authority, including the EU Military Operations Cell, the EDA, and the ESS.[8] These political milestones were achieved during the same year the EU constitutional process broke down and the EU

---

[7] "A Secure Europe in a Better World: European Security Strategy." *European Security Strategy*, 12 December 2003 Brussels, Belgium (2003), p. 1.

[8] L. Hill, "EU Defence Surge Despite Constitutional Collapse." *Jane's Defence Weekly*, 2003.

experienced open tensions in reaction to the invasion of Iraq.[9] This paradox was noted in 2004 by Javier Solana (former EU High Commissioner for Foreign and Security Policy): "of all the prerogatives of states, security and defence policy is probably the one which least lends itself to a collective European approach;... however, after the single currency, it is in this dimension that the Union has made the most rapid and spectacular progress of the last 5 years."[10]

While observers lament that CSDP has been neither an effective security framework for European interests, nor a mature tool for global expeditionary operations, the very development of defense institutions is notable, particularly during a time of low international threats to Europe.

Coordinating Armaments More Successful than Coordinating Operations?

Most CSDP observers focus on EU operations when assessing its impact over the past decade. While there is talk of coordinating the European defense and armaments market, it is usually cited as a milestone toward the ultimate goal of European military interoperability. A coordinated military operational policy has been a European policy goal since the inception of the Maastricht Treaty in 1992, and formalized in the St. Malo agreement in 1998, but has stagnated during much of the subsequent decade. A coordinated defense industrial base and common market was not even the formal EU agenda by 2003 but developed politically within a few years.

The European effort to coordinate the defense industrial base and security research and development has far to go but had relative early

---

[9] The delay in the constitutional treaty left three aspects of CSDP undecided: (1) "Mutual Defence Clause": designed to subsume the mutual defense clause of the former WEU (applying to 10 EU nations) while deferring to NATO as the supreme guarantor of security and defense and to the interests of neutral nations. The draft clause stated: "In the case where a member state is the object of armed aggression on its territory, other member states must provide assistance by all means possible, conforming to Article 51 of the United Nations Charter." (2) "Enhanced Co-operation on Defence," also known as "Permanent Structured Co-operation": open to all member states on a voluntary basis, but only if they comply with stringent requirements, including being able by 2007 to contribute forces for multinational combat operations within 5 to 30 days, supplying significant transport and logistics, sustainable for 30 days and prolonged to 120 days, in particular in response to a request by NATO. (3) Establishment of EU Foreign Minister: the matter most directly affecting operation of the EU's Common Foreign and Security Policy and CSDP Secretariats in Brussels.

[10] J. Solana, "Preface," in *EU Security and Defence Policy–The First Five Years (1999–2004)*, edited by N. Gnesotto (Paris, France: Institute for Security Studies, European Union, 2004), 5.

successes. This is unexpected because the conventional wisdom asserts that it is more difficult to establish cooperation in the most sensitive market of armaments than it is to coordinate singular multinational operations. In 2003, *Jane's Defence Weekly* quoted defense analysts predicting that the "EU could play [a] role in streamlining and integrating European defence industry; EU officials believe member states should take further steps toward establishing integrated defence market; analysts see need to resolve national differences."[11] Less than a year later, the EDA was established, governed by a board of defense ministers reaching decisions by qualified majority – not unanimous – rules, an exception for an intergovernmental policy domain.

Existing Explanations for CSDP

Explanations for why CSDP rapidly institutionalized when it did can be categorized as (1) regional or international geostrategy, (2) changes in European public opinion, or (3) the natural maturation of the EU into an international actor. They are all necessary but insufficient for explaining the emergence of CSDP in the late 1990s and the content and direction of its agenda.

Regional Threats or International Geopolitics

The geostrategic narrative begins the story during the 1990s, when Europeans became frustrated at their lack of ability to act during the Balkan crises. The creation of the CSDP happened because the EU was either explicitly balancing U.S. power,[12] or soft regional balancing against the unipolarity of the United States.[13] The Kosovo crisis is cited as the critical CSDP juncture. The strategic project of European defense was on hold during the height of the Cold War, and the issue of armaments cooperation was dealt with outside of EU institutions. From a strategic perspective, the sudden impetus toward CSDP at the end of the

---

[11] D. Lake, "Brussels Looks for Role in Industry Consolidation," *Jane's Defence Weekly*, March 26, 2003.

[12] J. Howorth, *European Security and Defence Policy* (Basingstoke, UK: Palgrave, 2007); S. G. Jones, "The Rise of a European Defence," *Political Science Quarterly* 121, no. 2 (2006): 241–67.

[13] R. Art, "Europe Hedges Its Security Bets," in *Balance of Power Revisited: Theory and Practice in the 21st Century*, edited by Paul and Wirtz, 179–213 (Stanford, CA: Stanford University Press, 2004); S. Brooks and W. C. Wohlforth, "Hard Times for Soft Balancing," *International Security* 30, no. 1 (2005): 72–108; B. R. Posen, "European Union Security and Defence Policy: Response to Unipolarity?," *Security Studies* 15, no. 2 (2006): 149–86; T. V. Paul et al., *Balance of Power: Theory and Practice in the 21st Century* (Stanford, CA: Stanford University Press, 2004).

1990s is either puzzling (issue of balancing) or obvious (Kosovo coordination failure). If the problem was a lack of operational coordination in Kosovo, and CSDP is the answer, one would expect to see more momentum toward operational cooperation. However, the issue of defense cooperation was gaining momentum since the 1980s but as a market issue, not a strategic opportunity. The core ideas behind the current policy agenda of CSDP were gaining traction – and spurring interest group formation – in the late 1980s, not the late 1990s. This is during the height of NATO and an era of bipolarity, alliance, and Europe–U.S. security cooperation.

The creation of CSDP after 1998 also defies a geostrategic explanation: it was a time of relatively harmonious transatlantic relations, and any evidence to support "soft balancing" only begins after 2003 and the policy differences that emerged over the Iraq war. Realist scholars argue that the powers of Europe such as France and the UK initiated CSDP as a way to bind Germany into soft balancing against the United States[14] or as a path to separating from NATO when interests diverge from the United States.[15] However, little evidence exists for this, further weakened by France reintegrating with the NATO command structure. If France used CSDP to soft balance against the United States while simultaneously rejoining NATO, this would be a costly set of contradictory decisions and redundant commitments. A French General argued NATO and CSDP are logically compatible:

I think that if France normalizes its relations with NATO, *European defence projects will become easier to move forward* . . . with the current situation of "one foot in, one foot out," there is always a suspicion of France having a hidden agenda. If France takes a place on the same level as the others, several worries and prejudices will be defused . . . There are several possible modes of cooperation. Like in Afghanistan today, NATO could have a military responsibility and the EU a civil responsibility (police, justice missions and so on). But there is another possible way. In agreement with the US, during crises, we could choose the organization which is the best adapted to the mission at hand. Otherwise, there would be no point in giving the Union military capacities. The EU's strength is possessing tools allowing a global approach, as much military as civilian.[16]

The other geostrategic explanation is that the EU simply needs real capabilities to deal with regional stability, independently of NATO. This is

[14] S. Jones, *The Rise of European Security Cooperation* (Cambridge, UK: Cambridge University Press, 2007).
[15] Posen.
[16] M. Walker, "Walker's World: Sarko's price for NATO." *UPI.* 2007. Accessed February 24, 2009. http://www.upi.com/Emerging_Threats/2007/09/27/Walkers_World_Sarkos_price_for_NATO/UPI-33681190904917/

the conventional policymaker wisdom: the EU developed strategic goals based on real strategic threats and challenges, these goals required the development of independent strategies and capabilities, and therefore a more unified defense industrial base would have to be developed to coordinate the strategies and capabilities. However, operational CSDP capabilities have severely lagged. There have been more than thirty CSDP operations, but most have been modest or primarily symbolic. The operational side of CSDP has been marked by as many failures to deploy interoperable forces as it has successful operations. It has also slowed down significantly after its first five years.

In terms of creating a common defense industrial base and defense market, however, the EU has made relatively rapid progress in a short time period. At face value, this defies logic: it should be easier to cooperate in an ad hoc or temporary military operation than to coordinate long-term procurement and armaments. The former takes place relatively frequently – often with little notice – between allies, whereas the latter requires decades of planning and risk analysis, given the long lead times of defense economics.

European Public Opinion

Another explanation for the emergence of CSDP is that it reflects the common will of the European public, who support European defense policy and also partially identify increasingly with Europe.[17] While compelling, it does not explain the timing and agenda of defense cooperation. First, although identification with Europe has increased moderately over time, support for EU security and defense policies has remained high since at least 1990. The same year in the UK – allegedly the least friendly populace to CSDP policies – 57 percent of polled respondents wanted a "full European defence policy," while only 25 percent were against the idea.[18] These numbers have not varied much over time. Support for European defense has increased over the past two decades, but not significantly. The European populace supports CSDP, but it always has. The public opinion Eurobarometer Poll has asked about defense for at least a few decades, and the results are surprising.

Figure 4.1 describes the opinion of individuals across the EU with respect to CSDP, as well as the most supportive and least supportive national publics, France and the UK. Overall, there is not a large gap between the most anti-CSDP and pro-CSDP publics. Figure 4.1

---

[17] S. B. Anderson, *Crafting EU Security Policy* (Boulder: Lynne Rienner, 2008).
[18] A. Sage, "Poll Backs EC Role in Defence," *The Independent (London)*, 1990.

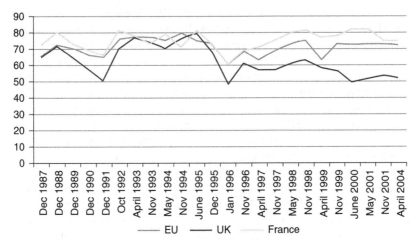

Figure 4.1 Common Defense and Security/Military Policy among the EU Member States (Percent Favor) (*Source: Eurobarometer*)

provides support for the underlying logic of CSDP but does not explain why it was created in 1999.

Secondly, changes in public opinion do not precede variations in the formation, success, or growth of the CSDP domain or its institutions. These numbers usually fluctuate during highly salient episodes, such as terror attacks, and cannot explain the emergence or growth of CSDP policies. There was no increase in support for CSDP after September 2001 or initiation of the Iraq War. Both of these events are theorized to be natural drivers of CSDP. 9/11 did not seem to change European opinion toward collective security. Similarly, the Iraq War seems to have had no demonstrable effect on public opinion, regardless of the diplomatic rift in Europe at the time.

Institutional Maturity or Development

A third explanation for the emergence of CSDP is that it is the final stage of the European integration project. Europeanization is federalization, and defense policy is its natural end point. Along these lines, the Portuguese Defence Minister argued

defence is a vital driver of European integration today. The EU must become a true defence community: Only then can it become a fully developed international actor ... Having a European defence system also means developing military capabilities ... we need to strengthen the rapid response capacity to deal with crisis situations ... this includes setting up battle groups covering land, air and sea; reinforcing planning and operations management capacities; and establishing a European industrial base, with a central role for the European Defence Agency. All this should complement NATO.[19]

Similarly, the U.S. Defense Department (DoD) called CSDP "a natural, even an inevitable, part of the broader development of European integration."[20]

European defense is not a new effort representing the final stage of integration. From the Pleven Plan for a European Defence Community in the 1950s, to the European Political Cooperation (EPC) initiative in 1970, there have been many defense cooperation efforts over the past sixty years, with little success until the last decade. The WEU, WEAG (Western European Armaments Group), OCCAR (Organisation Conjointe de Coopération en matière d'Armement), and the NATO-Independent European Program Group are also multilateral attempts to address European armament policy issues. None of these efforts had longevity, nor were they successful in building an institutional foundation for European defense or armaments cooperation. European defense institutions have been difficult to establish.

But the policy proposed at St. Malo has survived, and its logic formed institutions and agencies even before it gained legal authority from the 2009 Lisbon Treaty. When the Lisbon Treaty initially failed on the Irish "no" vote, the chairman of the EP Committee on Security and Defence argued that EU defense would continue to institutionalize "even without the Lisbon Treaty" through agencies such as the EDA.[21] When the Lisbon Treaty was ratified, "European defence [was] already a reality... [it will not be] a big bang... [it will just] give things momentum."[22] Similarly, "[t]here is little new about defence in the treaty. The provisions about the European Defence Agency are redundant, since that body was already created back in 2004."[23]

International security, soft balancing, common identity, and institutional maturation are all necessary explanations for CSDP, but they are not sufficient. Missing is the political economy of security, including the role of private industry groups and their preferences over defense procurement, acquisition, and technology. CSDP is not only about high

---

[19] Walker, "Walker's World: Sarko's price for NATO."   [20] Anderson, 32.
[21] V. Pop, "French EU Defence Plan is not Anti-NATO, Minister Says," *EU Observer*, April 11, 2008, http://EUObserver/9/27039
[22] "Ballot, Britain and Budget Dent France's EU Defence Hopes," *EUbusiness*, June 29, 2008, http://www.eubusiness.com/news-eu/1214708522.44
[23] N. Witney, "European Defence: How to Take 'No' for an Answer," *Financial Times*, July 28, 2008, http://www.ft.com/cms/s/0/0101fca0–5c98–11dd-8d38–000077b07658 .html

politics and strategy; it is also about low politics and economics. The economic rhetoric about CSDP – justifying a match of the supply of European armaments to a large home demand market – preceded the strategic development of CSDP by more than a decade. As Ernst and Young noted in 1994, there "is clearly an interrelationship between agreeing common defence operational requirements across Europe (i.e. customer driven) and defence industry itself rationalising (or 'supply side' rationalisation) [but] the reality is that both aspects are progressing, but with supply side rationalising more quickly than the customer side."[24] Defense industry groups wanted a unified EU defense market long before there was a political or strategic logic to do so.[25]

The Puzzle of CSDP

I focus on three puzzles over the next few chapters. First, what explains the stable emergence of CSDP in the late 1990s, when similar policies, forums, and institutions failed in the past sixty years? Second, what explains the rapid institutionalization since 1999, when there were minimal resource contributions or delegated authority from member states? Third, why has the main innovation of the CSDP agenda been to merge security and defense?

The following narrative first traces the mobilization and concentration of interest groups involved in defense at the European level of politics. Chapter 6 documents the same phenomenon in asylum, immigration, and border security interests. Introducing the history of industry mobilization and concentration in defense opens up a new avenue for evaluating the development of European defense: a political economy narrative. While some may argue that there are no political economy logics at work in areas of high politics – as they are public goods without private influence[26] – there is a subfield of international relations that specifically studies the political economy of security in various forms.[27] CSDP – as an intergovernmental policy in the realm of high politics – is a least-likely

---

[24] Ernst & Young, "The UK Defence Industry: Securing Its Future" Report, London, UK. May 1994, p. 9.

[25] The conventional wisdom of causality is that (1) there was an objective need to develop an autonomous capability for EU operations; (2) EU operations were unsustainable without a healthy and coordinated defense industrial base; and (3) both of these things needed further clarification, therefore the EU developed a security strategy in 2003.

[26] See Amy B. Zegart, *Flawed by Design: The Evolution of the CIA, JCS, and NSC* (Stanford University Press, 2000); Peter J. May, "Policy Design and Implementation," *Handbook of Public Administration* (2003): 223–33.

[27] Ethan B. Kapstein, *The Political Economy of National Security: A Global Perspective* (New York, NY: McGraw-Hill Humanities, Social Sciences & World Languages, 1992); Benjamin O. Fordham, *Building the Cold War Consensus: The Political Economy of U.S.*

case for the interaction of private actors in politics. Many argue that EU domains of high politics, like finance and defense, are most insulated against outside influence.[28] The opposite is also theoretically possible, however: that the most narrow, obscure policy domains are the most vulnerable to outside influence, particularly business interests.[29] Or perhaps all public policy domains – high and low – are equally vulnerable to external and private interests. Obscure and complex domains can be "unpacked into more manageable – and therefore bargainable – issues susceptible to group influence."[30]

The defense sector is a special category of the role of influence in supply and demand, unique in its public–private interactions in all states. In return for assured profits and guaranteed markets, defense industries are willing to accept an unnaturally high degree of government regulation.[31] A political authority can limit corporate autonomy by guaranteeing profits, even in the case of "enterprises producing for ordinary markets rather than for government contracts" where financial indulgence can be used to "offset regulatory severity."[32] The history of European defense is as much a story about industry regulatory issues as it is one of geostrategic necessity or institutional maturation. Since the 1980s, European defense industries have suffered from overcapacity, an

National Security Policy, 1949–51 (Ann Arbor: University of Michigan Press, 1998); Jean-Marc F. Blanchard, Edward D. Mansfield, and Norrin M. Ripsman, "The Political Economy of National Security: Economic Statecraft, Interdependence, and International Conflict," *Security Studies* 9, no. 1–2 (1999): 1–14; Gilpin; Jonathan Kirshner, "Political Economy in Security Studies after the Cold War," *Review of International Political Economy* 5, no. 1 (1998): 64–91; Michael Mastanduno, "Economics and Security in Statecraft and Scholarship," *International Organization* 52, no. 4 (1998): 825–54.

[28] Green Cowles, "Setting the Agenda for a New Europe"; Neil Fligstein, *Euroclash: The EU, European Identity, and the Future of Europe* (Oxford: Oxford University Press, 2008). Can be characterized by Green Cowles, who proposed that EU decision-making influence goes along a continuum of a two-level game, where some policy domains resemble a domestic federation and other domains resemble an international regime. In this model, nongovernmental groups will have the most influence in regulatory domains, moderate influence on distributive and redistributive policy, and little to no influence in security and defense issues.

[29] C. E. Lindblom, *Politics and Markets: The World Economic System* (New York, NY: Basic Books, 1977). See also M. A. Smith, *American Business and Political Power: Public Opinion, Elections, and Democracy* (Chicago, IL: University of Chicago Press, 2000). These narrow, obscure issues include defense, finance, taxation, regulation, trade, and appropriations.

[30] Mazey and Richardson, *Lobbying in the European Community*, 18. It is possible that the type of domain, or content of policy, does not determine openness to private interests. It is a matter of sequence and phase of institutionalization, where newer and weaker public institutions are more reliant on external groups to increase their capacity and legitimacy. Corporate interests are often the first actors in a domain, and when a domain is new and less salient, weak bureaucrats rely heavily on interest groups as a source of external capacity.

[31] Lindblom.   [32] Ibid.

imbalance in supply and demand. Regulatory measures were needed on a European scale in order to alleviate this oversupply. Industries also consolidated and merged in order to survive. But this was not enough: defense industries cannot simply be deregulated and merged across borders; they also require a certain amount of profit in the form of a guaranteed home market. Survival meant not just reform and consolidation but the promise of a large European market and a future common buyer, ideally one that could provide a safe haven from other business cycle fluctuations and the absorption of risk in long-term research and development of technology. The first challenge was defense industry executives realizing they needed an EU defense market and convincing other industry leaders of the need; the next challenge was lobbying for the creation of one, when NATO already existed for common defense.

Europeanizing the Defense Industrial Base: 1989–98

1980s: The Closure of the U.S. Market

In 1989, the Cold War was still a reality and the Berlin Wall divided Europe. Unforeseen political upheavals would soon change the European strategic balance, but the European defense industry was already dealing with changing market and government realities in the way defense equipment was marketed and sold. On the supply side, the European defense industry was becoming increasingly fragmented. On the demand side, the markets for defense acquisition were partitioned by national boundaries and redundant in spending and also penetrated by American industry.[33] The typical Cold War European defense industry was protected by its national ministry of defense customer and was oriented toward worldwide export sales.

Although the European defense industry was highly dependent on exports, it was becoming increasingly difficult to penetrate the unified, protectionist U.S. market. Protectionism became official with the U.S. Omnibus Trade and Competitiveness Act of 1988, which created a Committee on Foreign Direct Investment in the United States (CFIUS).[34] The CFIUS discourages foreign direct investment of

---

[33] European defense industries were limited because their home market demand was never great. In 1986, the year in which U.S. expenditures in the Reagan defense buildup peaked, the U.S. market was four times larger than Europe's, which consisted of separate and small national markets.

[34] The Secretary of the Treasury heads CFIUS with the participation of eleven other agencies, including the Departments of Defense, Justice, and Commerce. It is tasked to suspend or prohibit the foreign acquisition, merger, or takeover of a U.S. corporation due to U.S. national security.

European defense firms in the United States. The U.S. market became effectively closed to foreign firms, although some EU allies – such as the British – have been able to achieve a few partnerships through sub-contracting and partial direct investment in U.S. defense firms.[35] These challenges predated the end of the Cold War and anticipated the even greater challenges and downturn in demand that would follow.

In 1988, the WEU held a public–private conference titled "European Cooperation in Armaments Research and Development." The keynote speaker, British Defense Minister George Younger, predicted:

> after a period of very substantial growth in our defence budgets the prospect facing most of our countries now is of zero, or even negative, growth in the future . . . it is imperative that we find ways of making the limited resources available to us . . . in the era of post-INF (intermediate range nuclear forces treaty), Glasnost and the attractive new packaging of the Russian leadership it is more than ever important that we demonstrate the close cohesion of our own alliance.[36]

At the same 1988 conference, an industry leader called for a European Common Market for military equipment because "in this key sector of armaments, as elsewhere, it is only by acting in concert that Europeans will be able to maintain together their position at the forefront of tech-nological innovation and retain control of their destiny."[37]

A summer 1989 review by the European Defence Industry Study Group claimed Europe's defense industry was heading toward extinc-tion. This report predicted problems including duplication, overcapacity, non-standardization, political intervention, state control, fragmentation of market, and a diversity of requirements and procedures.[38] The report concluded that Europe had to create its own arms market, one producing

---

[35] The U.S. Department of Defense is relatively open to cooperation with European firms but has to go through the U.S. State Department's Office of Defense Trade Controls, which administers International Traffic in Arms Regulations (ITARs). With Congres-sional support, the State Department imposes difficult conditions on even favored allies in order to get an ITAR exemption. Although the Pentagon is open to international collaboration, it automatically requires contractors to have secret-level access, unless the government contracting authority determines that the result of an open contract advances U.S. national security interests. In addition, these legal requirements provide the material for inter-organizational power struggles because the ITARs are a valuable tool for the State Department to influence the otherwise vastly more powerful Depart-ment of Defense.

[36] "Younger Calls for Closer European Cooperation in Armaments Industry," *The Xinhua General Overseas News Service*, March 7, 1988.

[37] Ibid.

[38] "European Nations Attempt to Create Single, Competitive Arms Market, Unifying Europe's Markets," *Aviation Week & Space Technology* 130, no. 24 (June 12, 1989): 87.

economies of scale in a "home" market so Europe could be more competitive internationally. This market would also insulate aerospace, electronics, and other industries from commercial downturns in demand. If a continent-wide buyer enhanced demand for long-term defense contracts, there would be less uncertainty in commercial business cycles and fewer risks involved in planning research and development. In the absence of a common defense market, industry officials were concerned that intensified duplication in research and development and procurement would increasingly drag on their global competitiveness.[39]

When this industry study was published in 1989, the drafting of the 1992 Maastricht Treaty developing a single European market was underway. The 1992 Maastricht Treaty included a provision for common defense, creating the CFSP, and stipulating it "shall include all questions related to the security of the Union, including the eventual framing of a common defence policy, which might in turn lead to a common defence" (Article J.4.1). A common defense acquisitions market was excluded from these sweeping changes and remains formally exempt from the common market today. However, within CSDP, the acquisitions market agenda has outpaced the common operational goals, even though harmonizing a defense industrial base could be considered more difficult than coordinating common operational tasks. In 1995, Robin Beard, NATO's retiring armaments chief, announced that "any Europeans who think that there can be a truly integrated, independent European defence industrial base [are] deluding themselves."[40] Observers such as *The Economist* agreed: "the body best placed to encourage a North Atlantic armaments market is NATO."[41]

In this prehistory to the EU, however, there were already several industry-led national initiatives aimed at consolidating Europe's defense market and industrial base within the auspices of the EU. These included European national ministers' efforts to strengthen ties under the WEU, work by the Independent European Programme Group,[42] and an

---

[39] The study group proposed a series of changes to encourage more European cooperation, especially at the industrial and program level: (1) freedom for industry to acquire, merge, integrate, concentrate, and collaborate as necessary; (2) elimination of state controls and government intervention; (3) reformation and rationalization of the European defense base through industry initiatives, not political control; and (4) establishment of an open European market with freedom for industries to respond to market forces.

[40] "Markets and Maginot lines," *The Economist* (U.S. edition), October 28, 1995, 23.

[41] Ibid.

[42] Some early attempts by Europe to seek a larger share of the world defense market, begin a rationalization process, and raise its competitiveness came from the Independent European Programme Group. The goals of the group, which included all NATO

industry proposal for a European Defence Technology Initiative, a European equivalent of the U.S. Defense Advanced Research Projects Agency (DARPA). Future themes such as rising arms costs, the need to fund a growing portion of Europe's defense, and a declining Cold War threat all contributed to changing incentives in the defense market.

In the late 1980s, some sectors of the armaments industry anticipated changes from the 1992 Maastricht treaty by streamlining industry efforts to cooperate and facilitate mergers in the defense sector. The most internationalized sector was the aerospace industry, while shipbuilding and heavy industry remained tied to their national markets. In 1989, a senior European defense industry official said, "all of the major European programs for the next decade are already international, except for Rafale."[43] Another stated: "The single market does not necessarily mean a united Europe... the aeronautics industry is one of the most integrated already, but we collectively continue to suffer from individual solutions and nationalistic tendencies." These industry actors recognized, under duress, that the defense industry would either have to become internationally competitive or regionally competitive. Industry officials recall that although the Cold War threat was still real in the late 1980s and government demand was still high for armaments, they knew that their industry was unsustainable. A solution was a domestic market equaling that of the United States, where armaments firms could weather downturns in the commercial markets with military contracts and vice versa. However, they knew the tail could not wag the dog, and the EU could not be a market or the demand for their excess supply without a strategic purpose for their materiel. At the time, senior defense ministry and industry officials thought it would be impossible for Europe to carve out a separate strategic sphere from the United States and NATO.

Early 1990s: Industry Crisis and Consolidation

In the defense industry, the international environment of the 1990s was one of restructuring and rebuilding. The end of the Cold War caused sharp declines in defense budgets in the United States and Europe,

---

members except the United States, Canada, and Iceland, included establishing a European arms market, consolidating resources and funding for research, opening contracts and suppliers for more European-wide competition, and seeking cooperation with non-European countries that have developing defense industries.

[43] "Nations Attempt to Create Single, Competitive Arms Market, Unifying Europe's Markets," 87.

and the defense industries were forced to restructure. At the time, *The Economist* reflected:

the world's arms makers have suffered more than anybody except the world's apparatchiks from the end of the struggle against communism. Orders for weapons have plummeted. The American, British and French arms industries have lost some 1.5m jobs in the past five years. They cannot make up for lost orders at home by exports to the rest of the world, because except in East Asia everybody else is also spending less. At the same time, the weapons governments want get ever more sophisticated, and thus expensive to develop.[44]

According to several officials, the defense industry's downturn was so deep, many companies believed they could no longer preserve key research and development capabilities.[45]

With the demand for defense equipment collapsing in Europe, one of the first upheavals was the organized labor challenge of the armaments industry. In 1991, the Stockholm International Peace Research Institute (SIPRI) estimated that one in three defense jobs would be lost in European countries by the mid-1990s. In the UK, a political battle occurred between defense industry associations and unions and the UK government. After the government commissioned a Defence Costs Study, concluding the need for competitive defense contracts, reduce defense expenditure by 16 percent by 1996, and pursue off-the-shelf procurement outsourcing in the international marketplace, labor unions rebelled, taking their case to the attention of the European Parliament. The chairman of defense industrial unions proposed that the European Parliament should monitor the national mismanagement of the defense downturn of the 1990s:

Whole towns and regions depend upon defence expenditure . . . The MOD is the single biggest customer of British industry. Euro-candidates will be judged by defence workers on how they respond. The growing anger of an army who feel betrayed might well influence the outcome of the European Elections in marginal seats throughout Britain.[46]

---

[44] "Markets and Maginot Lines," 23.

[45] According to GICAT officials, French land defense industry's workforce decreased to 30,300, down from 41,600 in 1990. Sales decreased to $4.42 billion, down from $6.49 billion in 1990. Exports in 1993 plummeted to $1.73 billion, down from nearly $3 billion in 1990. The European defense industry had 660,000 employees in 1994. GRIP, a Brussels-based think tank, estimated that between 146,700 and 220,000 jobs would be lost in the industry by 1996.

[46] PR Newswire Europe, "Euro-Elections: Unions to Make Defence Cuts a Major Issue," *PR Newswire Europe*, May 23, 1994.

There was also a sudden downturn in demand in the United States, as Cold War weapons systems and platforms were reduced or eliminated.[47] In the three years between 1989 and 1992, the U.S. defense electronics market declined about 25 percent in real terms while Europe experienced a downturn of 15 percent. Between 1989 and 1994, defense exports declined by 70 percent worldwide. In 1993, Secretary of Defense Les Aspin called for the consolidation of American arms industries and provided transitional financial support for the restructuring.[48] In response, firms consolidated, merged, and established alliances with other companies in joint procurement bids in order to offset domestic sales losses with increased revenue from international sales.[49] By 1996, there were three near-monopolies: Boeing–Rockwell–McDonnell Douglas, Lockheed Martin–Northrop Grumman, and Raytheon–Hughes–Texas Instruments. These three firms accounted for 47 percent of worldwide defense profits.[50]

But consolidation was not enough for the U.S. firms to survive. As the only procurement authority, the U.S. Department of Defense absorbed a great deal of risk from the restructuring defense industry, encouraging industrial concentration and providing financial offsets for the social costs of restructuring in exchange for long-term savings.[51] Key policies allowing for a successful transition were the integrating of civilian and military markets through the use of technology transfer and commercial "off the shelf" technology. U.S. defense firms were also insulated from international pressures through regulations over dual-use production, export controls, and the protection of U.S. firms from foreign ownership or competition. European countries had no such policy to integrate their defense industries into a larger commercial market, and many industry actors grappled with this diminishing domestic market return.

From the European industry perspective, further reforms in technology policy and acquisition reform in the United States during the 1990s

---

[47] Between the end of the Cold War and fiscal year 2000, the U.S. government reduced the Department of Defense research and development and procurement annual budgets by about $60 billion.

[48] J. Dowdy, "Winners and Losers in the Arms Industry Downturn," *Foreign Policy* 107 (Summer 1997): 88–103.

[49] From 1990 to 2000, the U.S. defense industry went from thirty-three firms to five. See "Defence Trade: Contractors Engage in Varied International Alliances," United States General Accounting Office, 7 September 2000. Report to the Chairman and Ranking Minority Member, Subcommittee on Readiness and Management Support, Committee on Armed Services, U.S. Senate. GAO/NSIAD-00–213 Defence Trade.

[50] A. MacLeod, "Europe Seeks to Rival US Defence Giants," *The Christian Science Monitor*, December 16, 1997. http://www.cdi.org/ArmsTradeDatabase/

[51] See, for example, J. M. Deutch, "Consolidation of the U.S. Defence Industrial Base," *Defence Acquisition Review Journal* (Fall 2001): 137–52.

posed the greatest threats to their survival since the Trade Omnibus Bill of 1988. An industry study submitted to the European Commission claimed: "A new threat perception, arising not from the east but from the west, emerged in Europe during the...1990s. It was not a threat to national security and independence, but to European military-industrial survival and advanced technology competitiveness."[52] These threats from the "West" were the direct consequences of the Clinton administration's political linking of technology, defense, and economic security.[53] Some European analysts claimed the United States had been planning for decades to use the fusion of civilian and military high technology as an instrument to achieve economic and military dominance. There were claims the United States and its industries had launched a new "economic war" against Europe, which was fought through research and development budgets, particularly in the dual-use industrial sector.[54] Industry leaders such as Serge Dassault began promoting the idea of an EU rule of "*preference europeenne*" in armaments acquisitions to promote and shore up a pan-European defense industrial base. A Europe dependent on arms imports from America, he argued, would be a Europe dependent on America's foreign policy. At the time, French government policy was not in line with industry preferences, but President Jacques Chirac said he favored "a quite natural European preference."[55]

Under the umbrella of government reform, the Clinton administration created new organizations and policy agendas aimed at fusing the concepts of national security, civilian technology, and economic growth. In addition to the post–Cold War reductions in defense spending, President Clinton and Defense Secretary Perry implemented additional measures.[56] Key reforms informed directly by the Packard

---

[52] Science Policy Support Group, *Conclusions and Policy Implications* in "Management of European Technology: Defence and Competitiveness Issues," as set out in the Final Report to the European Commission, 31 Jan 2001, London, 91–106.

[53] Christopher, W. U.S. Secretary of State, "The Strategic Priorities of American Foreign Policy," Statement before the Senate Foreign Relations Committee, Washington, DC, November 4, 1993, U.S. Department of State Dispatch, Vol. 4, No. 47, Washington, DC: State Department (22 November 1993), 797–802.

[54] Y. Boyer, "Technologies, défense et relations transatlantiques," *Politique étrangère* 59, no. 4 (Winter 1994/95): 1005–15.

[55] "Markets and Maginot Lines," 23.

[56] The U.S. military went through impressive transformations during the late 1990s, making it the most effective, efficient, and technologically sophisticated force in the world. These changes were driven by two main factors. The first was the mid-1980s institutional reforms resulting in the 1986 Goldwater-Nichols Act forcing the first joint procurement programs and interoperability at the Department of Defense – rather than the services – level. The Goldwater-Nichols reforms were initiated because of a series of operational failures in the field – Vietnam, the Iran hostage crisis rescue attempt, the Marine Corps bombings in Beirut, and logistical problems during the invasion of

Commission's recommendations to encourage and harness new technologies were the 1994 Federal Acquisition Streamlining Act, which exempted procurement of commercial items from existing laws and expanded the definition of "commercial product" to broaden its applicability, and the 1996 Clinger-Cohen Act, which eliminated cost accounting standards discouraging commercial companies from doing business with the federal government. Defense Secretary Perry's 1994 "Perry Memo" mandated that the armed services use commercial, not military, specifications and standards when contracting for goods and services. The 1997 Defense Reform Initiative continued applying Packard Commission recommendations, including increasing reliance on commercial technologies and an integrated civil-military industrial base.[57]

Organizationally, a National Economic Council was created in 1993 to coordinate industrial policy with the National Security Council.[58] A series of offices and organizations were created within the Office of the Secretary of Defense (OSD), starting in 1994 with an assistant secretary of defense for economic security,[59] later merged into the deputy under secretary of defense for acquisition reform (also created in 1994) and the other organizations involved in the "Revolution in Military Affairs."[60] The organizational changes reflected the larger shift in military acquisition policy toward the synergy of civilian and military research and

Grenada – deemed to have happened because of a lack of interoperability between the armed services. The parallel problem to interoperability was inefficiency in acquisition and procurement, where high-profile cases of fraud, inefficiency, and waste highlighted the need for reforms. In the four years of wrangling among Congress, the Department of Defense, and the Armed Services, there were a number of commissions and studies, the most influential being the Blue Ribbon Commission on Defense Management (Packard Commission), which produced recommendations within the "Packard Report." The key findings of the Packard Commission were that the real solutions to a more efficient and effective defense were not simply about improving interoperability and streamlining acquisition but encouraging commercial innovation and the transfer of transformative technologies from the private sector. Many of these findings became part of the Goldwater Nichols legislation, but other reform aspects were implemented separately over the next decade.

[57] J. Gansler, *The Road Ahead: Accelerating the Transformation of Department of Defense Acquisition and Logistics Processes and Practices* (Washington, DC: Department of Defense, 2000).

[58] Presidential Executive Order 12835 (January 25, 1993). http://clinton6.nara.gov/1993/01/1993-01-25-establishment-of-the-national-economic-council.html

[59] Functioning from 1994 to 1996, and "responsible for setting DoD policy in the areas of industrial affairs, dual-use technology, and international cooperation programs ... The ASD(ES) works with and provides guidance to the Military Services in these areas, and serves as a liaison to private industry, the White House National Economic Council, the Departments of Treasury and Commerce, and other economic agencies within the Executive Branch." In William Perry, Secretary of Defence, "Economic Security – New Ways at Doing Business at Defence," *Annual Report to the President and the Congress* (February 1995).

[60] In February 1994, the Secretary of Defence issued a paper entitled *Acquisition Reform: A Mandate for Change*, http://www.dod.mil/execsec/adr96/chapt_14.html

development and production for the benefit and exponential growth of both. There were a number of high-profile efforts to remove barriers to procuring civilian technology and subcontracting with firms (especially innovative small/medium-size enterprises [SMEs] and commercial-off-the-shelf [COTS] technology). The reverse was also incentivized: harnessing military technology for civilian and market applications. The initial OSD program signaling this change was the 1993 Technology Reinvestment Program, promoting the military and civilian development of dual-use technologies.[61]

Consolidation of the European Defense Industry

The dilemma over dual-use civilian and military technologies was a challenge faced in both Europe and the United States, as technology became more commercially viable and Revolution in Military Affairs (RMA) needs were changing, which altered the balance of private and public technology investment incentive structures. However, there was no centralized procurement authority in the European market addressing this crossover of commercial and military technology. Dual-use technology was a simultaneous source of threat and opportunity, as the equipment was unrestricted from military arms control or procurement policies but had the potential for profit through military contracts. A 1989 piece noted that

> European defence industries are caught up in the powerful dynamics surrounding the Single European Act, not least because most defence contractors are substantial players in civil high-technology markets and because boundaries between civil and military technology are becoming harder to draw. Although different, the regulatory structures of the two sectors cannot therefore be kept completely separate – which means that there is a potential serious clash of interests between the authorities concerned with civil and with military industrial activities.[62]

This concept of dual-use technology and the transfer of technology between civilian and military applications was initially the greatest impediment toward the political consolidation of the European defense market. However, the EU solution to dual-use technology concerns took

---

[61] Goals included transitioning defense technologies into commercial fields; lowering costs for new defense technologies; and developing militarily useful and commercially viable technology in order to improve the Department of Defense's access to affordable and advanced technology. J. Richardson, J. Bosma, S. Roosild, and D. Larriva, "A Review of the Technology Reinvestment Program, PIPS 99–1" (Arlington, VA: Potomac Institute for Policy Studies, January 30, 1999).

[62] W. Walker and P. Gummett, "Britain and the European Armaments Market," *International Affairs* 65, no. 3 (Summer 1989): 420.

a circuitous path, ultimately establishing the foundations of an entire security strategy and justification for the institutionalization of defense and security at the EU level.

Defense industry consolidation was the dominant trend of the mid and late 1990s. Companies were motivated to merge not only to survive but to make those mergers transnational to extend the defense industrial base to include more than one country and offset some of the effects of shrinking domestic markets.[63] However, this consolidation did not expand to transatlantic mergers. In the face of cross-border European industry consolidation, the United States further protected its domestic market, closing it to European investors during the U.S. defense industry's post–Cold War restructuring, creating a strategic strain on EU NATO members. By 1997, a senior NATO official stated that Europe's ability to develop an independent security capability within NATO and meet its fair share of alliance obligations was contingent on its ability to consolidate its defense industrial base.[64] This official indicated that if such a consolidation did not occur, then European governments might be unable and unwilling to meet their NATO obligations in the future.

Based on this global and transatlantic contraction of access and demand, European companies such as British Aerospace, GEC-Marconi, Aerospatiale, Thomson-CSF, and DASA found their competitiveness was seriously undermined even in their home markets. *The Economist* observed:

The problem is at its worst in Europe. Every large country has its national champions and, to a greater or lesser extent, arranges things to their benefit. Even in the free internal market of the EU, this is all perfectly legal. Article 223 of the Treaty of Rome lets any member exclude defence companies from EU law on competition, mergers and procurement: a champions' charter that has helped ensure that there are no pan-European defence giants. Europe's fragmented industry now has to face an ever greater threat of competition from abroad. America is just as nationalist and protectionist about defence as other countries, if not more so; but it is also very big. In America, contraction and consolidation

---

[63] Consolidation of defense industries, however, was a secular trend in the 1990s. Even with the pressures of reduced markets and industry downturn, European defense companies were consolidating at a slower pace than U.S. defense companies. The combined defense expenditures of Western Europe were about 60 percent of the U.S. defense budget, but Western Europe has two to three times more suppliers than the United States, according to a 1997 Merrill Lynch Study. For example, the United States consolidated into two major suppliers in the military aircraft sector, whereas in the 1990s, six European nations each had at least one major supplier of military combat aircraft. See U.S. General Accounting Office, "European Initiatives to Integrate the Defense Market," Report to the Secretary of Defense, October 1997, NSIAD-98–6.

[64] U.S. General Accounting Office, "European Initiatives to Integrate the Defense Market," Report to the Secretary of Defense, October 1997, NSIAD-98–6.

have produced true giants, such as Lockheed Martin. Big American companies are proving increasingly good at expanding their export markets, to the detriment of European rivals.[65]

The European defense industry had begun to consolidate around these national champions by the early 1990s. Not until the mid-1990s did European firms respond to the wave of U.S. mergers and acquisitions from the 1980s and early 1990s. Under the competitive pressure of U.S. industry changes, European defense industrial consolidation took a few different forms. Firms either globalized or merged with non-European or American firms, or consolidated across European borders to create European defense conglomerates.

In the late 1990s, the defense sector began to take desperate measures to consolidate itself in the absence of any definitive governmental action. Up to the end of 1997, collaboration almost exclusively took the form of intergovernmental programs, which were then handed over to the respective national industries. This approach was favored by the emergence of "national industrial champions," starting with Finmeccanica in Italy and DASA in Germany. During the period 1997–9, there were a number of significant mergers and acquisitions, including British Aerospace's 1999 acquisition of the General Electric Company-UK (GEC) grouped in Marconi Electronic Systems to form BAE Systems, and the 1998 state-led restructuring of the French aerospace sector around the Aerospatiale-Matra. The European response to the American challenge further crystallized in 1999 with the establishment of two large groups: BAE Systems described above and the merger of Aerospatiale-Matra and DASA to form European Aeronautic Defence and Space (EADS). EADS was formed by combining former national champions Aerospatiale-Matra of France, DASA of Germany, and Construcciones Aeronáuticas SA (CASA) of Spain.[66] EADS combined all aerospace production (including Airbus) and systems of defense and security electronics, missiles, systems, avionics, satellites, launchers, and space structures.

Some firms, such as BAE Systems, Thales, and Rolls-Royce, also enjoyed joint ventures in the United States. There were also strategic alliances between U.S. defense firms and European firms in

---

[65] "Markets and Maginot Lines," 23.
[66] To varying degrees, defense industry restructuring occurred inside states, not between them. In France, Thomson CSF and Aerospatiale formed a company, Sextant Avionique, merging avionics and flight electronics activities. In Germany, restructuring primarily occurred in the aerospace sector. In 1995, Deutsche Aerospace became Daimler-Benz Aerospace, to make up about 80 percent of German industrial capabilities in aerospace. In 1995, Finemeccanica became about three-quarters of the Italian defense industry. In the United Kingdom, a number of mergers and acquisitions occurred.

shipbuilding and land systems.[67] Most observers came to realize that supply consolidation was not enough to save the industry and protect its technology. Mergers only unified suppliers, and unless the demand side (national procurement policy) united, there would be no transformational effect on European industry. Additionally, any diversification into the U.S. market with joint ownership or stakeholding was usually limited to financial aspects of ownership. The U.S. government insisted foreign parent companies of U.S. subsidiaries should have limited access to latest technologies funded by the U.S. government; thus U.S. subsidiaries of European firms such as BAE Systems and Rolls-Royce tended to be technologically separate from other elements of their European parent.[68] Therefore none of the technology transfer innovations occurring in the United States in the 1990s could benefit any European stakeholders.

New Solutions for Industry Survival

Key European aerospace and armament manufacturers held a strategy meeting at the Le Bourget air show outside Paris in 1994, concluding that their regional cooperation and consolidation efforts would not be sufficient for the industry to survive the decade. In consensus, they agreed to lobby for the creation of a European armaments agency to establish a unified European defense market and eliminate duplication of research and development programs. At a similar gathering – the *Eurosatory Land Defence Equipment International Exhibition* – eleven European armament industry trade associations cosigned a declaration urging increased European industrial collaboration and additional political initiatives to pave the way for a unified European defense market. Emile Blanc, outgoing president of GICAT (Groupement des industries de défense et de sécurité terrestres et aéroterrestres), France's land defense industries association, said most European defense-related companies had concerns going beyond the development, marketing, and production of their products:

The [defence] companies are suffering from considerable excess capacity. We must jointly address the resulting difficulties and manage the transition toward

---

[67] Shipbuilding consolidated transatlantically through AFCON, a strategic alliance among Bazan (Spain), General Dynamics/Bath Iron Works, and Lockheed Martin. Some European land system industries consolidated on a transatlantic basis when American firms bought shares of German Krauss-Maffei Wegmann (KMW) and Rheinmetall.

[68] S. Markowski and P. Hall, "Models of Defence Procurement and Their Relation to Industry Development," report prepared for the Department of Industry, Tourism and Resources, Canberra, 2003.

a revised industrial forces balance. We will promote wide-ranging industrial collaboration that should give birth to a European 'domestic' market, based on the harmonization of operational needs and common specifications.[69]

A joint GICAT-Ernst & Young survey circulated at the Eurosatory meeting revealed that 59 percent of 400 top officials in Europe's defense-related industries were convinced that too many producers were competing in the international market. By 1994, a majority of industry officials believed mergers and consolidation would not be sufficient,[70] and a larger European home market would be the only long-term solution. Fifty-one percent of industry officials believed implementing a political consolidation move was the key to survival, convinced their governments should cede authority to the EU to create a common armaments agency. Again, industry officials cited U.S. market closure and government support for defense technology as the critical juncture, although 44 percent of the defense executives had already given up on penetrating the U.S. market because access had already become "extremely difficult" or "impossible."

The WEU, GICAT, and other organizations such as GIFAS (*Groupement des industries françaises aéronautiques et spatiales*), the French aerospace industries association, began suggesting that a European political authority should systematically procure European defense systems, in order to fairly compete with U.S. industry. The president of another industry association complained, "Europe nevertheless should have fair and balanced relations with the U.S. But it is extremely difficult, sometimes impossible, to establish partnership agreements with U.S. partners – 'collaboration' does not have the same meaning in French- and English-language dictionaries."[71] Officials denounced U.S. "discriminatory [business] practices" in the international defense market to promote and protect U.S. industry, at the same time it was becoming the only surviving major buyer of defense goods.[72]

Establishment of Defense Interest Groups in Brussels

During the early 1990s, most industries and firms simply lobbied their national governments for solutions to their market crises, but individual defense firms and national associations started to sporadically lobby EU institutions to create a more level playing field between Europe and

---

[69] P. Sparaco, "Europeans Advocate Unified Defence Market," *Aviation Week & Space Technology*, July 25, 1994: 54.

[70] Ernst & Young, Prospects for the European Land Arms Industry. 1994.

[71] Sparaco, "Europeans Advocate Unified Defence Market," 54.   [72] Ibid.

Figure 4.2 Defense Firms with Established Brussels Lobbying Offices 1989–2012 (*Source: Landmarks Directories, corporate websites*)

the United States. Figure 4.2 documents the growth of defense firms establishing Brussels lobbying offices. A few of the earliest European firms to establish offices were Dassault (France) in 1990 and BAE (UK) in 1993, with more following suit thereafter. Some defense firms have never established EU public affairs offices, including the German firms ThyssenKrupp and Krauss-Maffei Wegmann. The presence of NATO near Brussels explains the activity of firms in Brussels in the 1980s, as they were mostly American firms, including Hughes, Honeywell, Lockheed Martin, and Raytheon. This changed over the 1990s, peaking before the St. Malo decision to create ESDP in 1998. The presence of defense firms in Brussels actually declined after 1999, which could be due to multiple factors. Individual firms might have felt better represented by the security and defense industry associations that consolidated and flourished in the 2000s; their reduced numbers could reflect the consolidation of the defense industry itself over the decade, or – possibly – the most important public affairs goal was the creation of a security and defense institution itself, not any subsequent EU policies.

In 1995, chairman of the German firm DASA, Manfred Bischoff, addressed the European Parliament:

We cannot wait for full integration of the EU's single market . . . why are there no incentives to create optional restructuring in Europe? At least, we should duplicate the US government's "Buy American" policy . . . why not a European missile company? Why not common export rules in the defence sector? I don't care . . . as long as there's a harmonized approach. If we do not coordinate our industries and policies we will soon grow weaker, with no central defence buyer.[73]

A Thomson executive claimed the future role of industry would be to convince the EU "it is unbelievable to split the concept of military and defence industry into different authorities dealing with each site. *We have to have the political and industrial vision at the same time.*"[74] He added that the defense industry's responsibility would be to observe institutions and inject ideas into the agenda, so EU officials "don't develop the wrong ideas" about dividing up the security, military, and industrial aspects of military policy.

An industry group presented a study to the European Commission on External Political Relations in 1997, titled "The Role of the Armaments Industry in Supporting the Preparation and Conduct of Military Operations."[75] The report questioned the interdependence of European nations, CFSP, and the defense industry in the future. It argued that the technological (and American) trends toward defense transformation put even greater pressures on states at the same time defense budgets were decreasing. The authors warned that these trends would collide in the future, because Europe would have to

either buy less capable but national or European equipment with security of supply assured but military superiority undermined, or to buy highly capable US equipment providing military superiority over potential opponents but with security of supply dependent on US willingness and capability to support European forces in specific scenarios. If decision makers want to avoid this choice and thus improve the prospects of a globally competitive European DTIB (Defence Technological Industrial Base), European Arms and defence industrial cooperation has to be improved dramatically and quickly.[76]

This report was presented to the Commission, but at the time, the Commission did not have the

institutional and organizational capacity for dealing with issues related to defence. This situation created a political problem when the Commission brought the issue of armaments onto the EU's political agenda ... When the Commission presented its communication on the restructuring of the defence

---

[73] B. Tigner, "Transatlantic Harmony Faces Many Obstacles," *Defence News* 10, no. 21 (May 29, 1995): 16.

[74] T. Guay, *At Arm's Length: European Union and Europe's Defence Industry* (Basingstoke, UK: Palgrave Macmillan, 1998). Italics added.

[75] P. Taylor and P. Schmidt, "The Role of the Armaments Industry in Supporting the Preparation and Conduct of Military Operations," Ebenhausen: Stiftung Wissenshaft und Politik, March 1997.

[76] Taylor and Schmidt, 48–9. See also U. Mörth, *Organizing European Cooperation: The Case of Armaments* (Lanham, MD: Rowman & Littlefield, 2005).

industry in January 1996 the issue of the defence industry was formally a matter for the foreign ministers, but they did not find the time to discuss it and the defence ministers were not allowed to meet.[77]

At the same time, industry actors had begun to consolidate their operations significantly. Two industry associations had formed in Brussels, and a handful of think tanks had started to address European defense industry issues. A common message emerged: consolidation of defense industries (supply) transnationally was not going to be an adequate solution. The defense industry requires a large, common source of demand, and the largest global source of demand (the United States) was effectively closed to European industry. The idea to promote a common European market was forming, and the industry associations attempting to influence future EU institutions and policies were beginning to mobilize. At this critical juncture, one observer said: "In many respects, European defence contractors *are finding that they have got ahead of their customers.* The supply side may now be organised on a European, transatlantic or global scale but the demand side remained primarily national in organisation."[78]

Defense Industry Mobilization and Institutions

What interest groups formed with a stake in the outcome of EU policies of internal or external security and defense? Naturally, there is heterogeneity of interests and groups in this area. Groups in this area are mobilized to influence the EU for many reasons, including for more EU authority on defense issues, less authority and regulation, and regarding policy-specific outcomes. For-profit actors include individual firms (such as EADS, Finemeccanica, Daimler-Benz Aerospace), national industry associations (for example, German Aerospace Industries Association [BDLI], Federation of German Industries [BDI], GICAT), and European industry associations (European Defence Industries Group [EDIG], European Association of Aerospace Industries [AECMA], Aerospace and Defence Industrial Association of Europe [ASD]). There are divergent preferences among these industry actors, ranging from anti-EU regulation and the protection of national markets to lobbying for greater EU regulation and the creation of EU markets for defense and security. In addition to industry interests, there are also nonprofit groups

---

[77] Ibid., 43.

[78] A. D. James, "Comparing European Responses to Defence Industry Globalisation," *Defence and Security Analysis* 18, no. 2 (2002): 137.

lobbying for EU operational actions or foreign policy developments, labor unions, and regions with heavy defense contracting interests.

Private and industry defense groups operated in a disjointed and decentralized manner at the beginning of the 1990s. There were no Europe-wide industry associations, just individual defense firms and national defense industry associations. This began to change a few years later, when national firms and associations formed EU-level industry associations. Later, many of the firms and associations now operating under the "security" market of homeland and border security technologies were undeveloped or associated with the high-tech electronics industry. Although some individual defense firms preferred European-level regulation and market, there was a good deal of pro- and anti-EU variation diverging throughout the 1990s. Although there are six dominant arms-producing countries in Europe, the dominant firms in the industry were British, French, and German.

Surveys of defense firms in the 1990s indicated that their most pressing concern was the extreme uncertainty of the future of defense markets. With extremely long lead and development timelines, firms and associations had no idea how to proportion their research and development planning and restructure their lines of production. Each European country maintained its own strategic planning and industry outlook (most of them redundant). Defense firms and associations were aware of the limitations of their national defense markets: while European nations wanted to protect the security of their supply and their national champions, some firms could foresee their impending fate of shrinking budgets and market globalization. Industry executives bemoaned their lack of success in influencing European developments in the 1990s, with many blaming the lack of political power of their industry sector as a result of fragmentation.[79] The savviest executives also knew timing would be an issue in creating EU defense institutions: if the European defense market were liberalized before a common armaments agency was established, the U.S. companies would probably rush in and dominate the market.[80]

There is no consensus on whether industry efforts influenced EU policies, at least in the early stages of the effort.[81] Some observers claim the industry associations were successful in influencing the EU on small technical issues by 1997 but not on the development of major policies.

---

[79] Guay.
[80] Author interview with defense industry official. Brussels, Belgium. November 9, 2007.
[81] Jakob Edler and Andrew D. James, "Understanding the Emergence of New Science and Technology Policies: Policy Entrepreneurship, Agenda Setting and the Development of the European Framework Programme," *Research Policy* 44, no. 6 (2015): 1252–65.

At that point, the defense industry was well organized to lobby for a greater EU role in regulating or resolving the 1990s crisis in the industry. However, interest cleavages between international competitive and national champion industries remained strong through the 1990s and early 2000s. Executives claim one of the reasons for this collective action was because most defense firms in Europe were not dedicated to defense production because defense sales were a small (and shrinking) part of the overall sales of parent "civilian" companies (such as DASA, owned by Daimler-Benz in Germany). This fragmentation problem also plagued the main labor unions, such as the European Metalworkers' Federation (EMF), representing defense industry interests. Although it was never influential due to national disaggregation, the EMF was lobbying in Brussels as early as 1991, endorsing an industrial policy at the EC/EU to "halt the decline in the arms industry... and create a climate conducive to conversion and introduce measures to safeguard jobs."[82]

Starting in the mid-1990s, defense industry firms, labor, and employer interests began to organize themselves to influence the EU, opening offices in Brussels and taking seriously the future role of the EU in this domain. The primary industry associations were the EDIG, AECMA, and the Association of the European Space Industry (EUROSPACE). From the beginning of its existence, the EDIG was lobbying the EU to expand its civilian research and development programs to assist military projects.[83] The Union of Industrial and Employers' Confederations in Europe (UNICE) had been lobbying the EU/EC since 1991 to harmonize the regulations and exports of dual-use technology. One of the main concerns of this association was that SMEs were unable to deal with multiple and overlapping regulations and would prefer to have one set of European regulations. This group was allegedly highly influential in helping frame early EU agendas and directives.[84]

What is fascinating about the transnational industry mobilization in the 1990s is that executives recall their presence as one-sided: there was no audience for their lobbying, therefore few opportunities to influence policymaking. They were too early, in a sense.[85] In the mid-1990s, the

---

[82] European Metalworkers' Federation. "EMF Position Paper on Peace, Disarmament, Employment, and Alternative Production," April 4, 1991.

[83] Guay, 13.

[84] Union of Industrial and Employers' Confederations of Europe, "UNICE in Favour of a Single European Export Control System for Dual-Use Products and Technologies." UNICE Position Paper, May 29, 1992. See also L. Collie, "Business Lobbying in the European Community: The Union of Industrial and Employers' Federation of Europe," in *Lobbying in the European Community*, edited by S. Mazey and J. Richardson, 213–30 (New York, NY: Oxford University Press, 1993).

[85] Author interview with U.S. defense official. Brussels, Belgium. May 25, 2009.

only EU institutions available to "hear" them were the European Commission and the European Parliament, and industry officials dismissed the former as only able to produce ideas and the latter as not interested in long-range industrial transformation. They knew it had to be a bureaucracy, an armaments agency, which would be able to accomplish both. Early adopters such as the EDIG still worked to establish themselves as informal institutions for European defense.

By 1998, defense industry firms and national associations had managed to consolidate their activities into interest associations in Brussels, aggregating national industry associations into transnational, European organizations. This allowed more coordinated access and the expertise sought by EU officials on the topic of European defense. On June 4, 1998, the European Parliament Subcommittee on Security and Disarmament held a session to address the ongoing crisis in the defense industry. Executives from the EDIG and the AECMA claimed little or nothing had happened at national or EU levels to address the problems and restructuring of the industry. The executives testified that the current public procurement instruments were insufficient, instead proposing the EU consolidate and follow the lead of the protectionist U.S. market.[86] The discussion went further than this, however. Reform could not just be in the field of armaments: it had to be bigger. They suggested the EU begin to "think like the U.S." in terms of technology transfer, dual-use, and synergies between security and defense. Finally, they suggested the EU outdo the United States in this area: Why simply make defense and high technology compatible? Why not reform the entire strategic way of thinking – from the top – by making the EU the only political authority removing all barriers between security and defense?[87]

The European Parliament subsequently released the following statement:

As a matter of urgency, Europe needs to establish a real domestic defence equipment market, to provide the foundation upon which existing Community instruments in the defence field should be adopted, so that the EU domestic market could be firmly established.[88]

The industry representatives also supported the Commission's proposal for a common position in drawing up a European arms policy. Areas of interest included the intra-Community transfer of defense equipment,

---

[86] "Bid for EU Domestic Defence Market," *1998 European Report,* June 10, 1998.
[87] Author interview with defense industry officials, Brussels, Belgium, April 14, 2007 and August 28, 2007.
[88] "Bid for EU Domestic Defence Market."

external arms exports, research and technology, public procurement, and competition and market access.

Merger of European Defense Industry Associations

Europe's Aerospace and Defence Industry Association (ASD) was formed in 2004 from the mergers of EDIG, AECMA, and EUROSPACE. The ASD represents the interests of national member associations and more than 800 individual member firms, including leading European technology manufacturers, systems integrators, and suppliers in twenty countries. The ASD's role also includes promoting more integrated business and trade relations across the European defense, aeronautic, and space industries, with an emphasis on promoting procurement at the EU level. On occasion, the ASD has expressed concerns that "regulating the EU market in a non-regulated world market could cause competitive disadvantage, especially in a sector where political, military and diplomatic involvement is sometimes called upon to support sales to governments," but they have generally relinquished any opposition to greater European regulation of armaments, in exchange for the goal of a centralized armaments agency with potential to procure weapons systems at the EU level.[89] ASD President Charles Edelstenne was at the forefront of proposing UAVs for European military and civilian use: "the main problem for potential manufacturers is how to introduce UAVs into air traffic. We need regulations in Europe to fix the way we can use them in air traffic... They can be used not just for military but also civilian purposes."[90] ASD has been a key agenda-setting industry body for more EU regulation and market development in most areas of defense. In 2008 it called for "the emergence of a mature, integrated European defence market, as well as for a greater collective effort on defence R&D... [he] underlined that any further rationalisation of the European defence industry can only go hand in hand with a deeper integration of European defence policies."[91]

ASD had been involved in the Commission efforts to create a defense industrial base by ending national protections and arms export offsets. ASD, however, remained consistent in its efforts to promote a common market and buyer as a complete solution, saying it

---

[89] Author interviews with defense industry officials, Brussels, Belgium, November 13, 2007 and November 30, 2007.

[90] "Defence: Industry Wants EU-Wide Regulation on Drones, Uninhabited Aerial Vehicles," *European Report*, Monday, April 2, 2007.

[91] "ASD Calls for Further Integration of European Defence Policies at French EU Presidency Conference," Defenceworld.net, November 4, 2008.

welcomes the effort undertaken by EU member states participating in the "Regime on Defence Procurement" [launched in 2006] to bring more transparency to offset practices linked to their national defence procurements under article 296 of the EU Treaty ... but [it is] the general lack of coordinated investments in defence technology more than the practice of offsets that endangers the future of the European DTIB.

In 2009, ASD advertised it was "actively involved" in the French EU Presidency, the debate on the EU Defence Package of two directives, covering defense procurement, and intra-community transfers of defense goods. ASD "promoted a small set of improvements to the proposed legislation, to ensure that market peculiarities would be recognised by EU lawmakers. The final versions of both directives, recently adopted by the European Parliament, reflect many of the views expressed by the European defence industry." ASD promoted their role in the

creation of a European air transport fleet, the launch of a European initiative in the area of naval interoperability and the realisation of a future programme of space-based observation (MUSIS [Multinational Space-Based Imaging System]), the reinforce[ment of] the role of the European Defence Agency, which they entrusted with the task of preparing two joint equipment programmes, one in the area of maritime mine clearance and the other in the domain of Unmanned Surveillance Air Vehicles, as well as a research programme on military technologies of the future ... By accepting to bring together some of their military resources, the Member States involved have paved the way for a thorough rationalisation of Europe's defence capabilities.[92]

Conclusion

This chapter is a complementary political economy narrative that demonstrates the bottom-up mobilization of private defense actors at the European level. It documents the formation of European industry associations and informal agenda-setting institutions in EU defense, and the emerging public–private dynamic in the development of the European defense industrial base and European defense markets. It provides the origination story of the dynamics of supply and demand for political institutions and governance in EU defense: linking bottom-up social demand for EU institutions to their creation and growth is in the spirit of neo-functional frameworks on the EU, where "the expansion of transnational society pushes for supranational governance" is subsequently "exercised to facilitate and regulate that society."[93]

---

[92] AeroSpace & Defense Industries Association of Europe, *Europe's Defense Industry: Shaping The Future*, Brussels: Maxhill, 2008.
[93] Sandholtz and Stone Sweet, 19.

A political economy narrative also traces the demand for institutions, but it introduces intervening mechanisms allowing for variation in the creation and content of EU institutions, rather than transnational demand directly producing the supply of institutions. The next chapter documents the political development of European defense, and demonstrates that (1) the timing and mobilization of demand help explain the timing of supply when attempts to create institutions have failed in the past; (2) the creation of informal institutions is critical; (3) informal institutions help explain the political development of one element of CSDP (armaments procurement) over another (military operations); and (4) variation in informal institutions helps explain the degrees of private influence over the content of the public EU agenda.

This is an alternative way of understanding the emergence of European defense: states created CSDP as a regional strategic response to crises such as Kosovo, but it has survived and accelerated because of informal institutions. Industry actors created informal institutions before there were any formal institutions to lobby – to offer their resources and expertise to resolve their industry supply–demand problem. Informal institutions have supplemented nascent CSDP institutions, giving the EDA and the Commission an outsized capacity compared to their formal legal authority.

The history of CSDP is as much a story of the special regulatory issues of the defense industry as it is one of geostrategic necessity or institutional maturation. The defense industries in Europe have been suffering from overcapacity since the 1980s. This crisis was exacerbated by (1) the U.S. defense market shutting out foreign firms in 1988 and (2) the global defense industry downturn in the 1990s. The competitive pressure on European defense industries was amplified by the measures taken by the Clinton administration to revolutionize domestic linkages between civil and military technology. In order to alleviate this oversupply, the defense industry needed a lifeline: in the short run, consolidating their supply through mergers, and in the long run, seeking regulatory measures on a European scale. Throughout the 1990s, industry executives came to realize that survival meant more than deregulation and mergers: they also needed a long-term guarantee of profit and risk projection in the form of a home market. This is what distinguishes defense from other aspects of political economy: its market actors are more willing to be highly regulated in exchange for a monopsonistic political authority. In order for demand for armaments and technology to be consolidated, the industry message shifted to lobbying for a single European market and a common buyer. An ideal European buyer would provide a safe haven from other business-cycle fluctuations and absorb the risk of long-term research and development of technology.

The problem was, there was no strategic justification for a consolidated European market: no reason for the EU to be separate from NATO in terms of armaments and technology. An emergent solution began to take shape among private actors to fuse the rhetoric of EU civilian and military strategy. This would create a niche strategy separate from NATO and make for a unique selling point for creating an EU defense market and institutions by way of eliminating the historical distinction between defense and civil security policies and technologies.

In the next chapter, this market narrative of bottom-up demand helps explain the timing and political development of defense institutions and policy agendas. CSDP started out as an echo of the original EDC of the 1950s, an effort to create a defense community with common operational and strategic goals. Today, the focus of the CSDP policy agenda is on regulatory market issues: the overlapping areas of security and defense, the synergy of civilian and military technology, and technocratic armaments and technology. It has, in essence, migrated from the height of high politics to the details of low politics.

5   The Political Development of EU Defense

Political Solutions to the 1990s Defense Industry Crisis

While the European defense industry anticipated the tightening of budgets and strategic changes starting in the 1980s, it was not until the 1990s that real changes in European defense markets and procurement occurred. After 1989, the "context and premise of defense procurement changed substantively. Political support for high levels of defense spending was shrinking. The absence of the old power bloc logic meant that considerations of armament cost effectiveness had increasing importance. Military procurement became increasingly geared toward the maintenance of operational capacity."[1] The 1990s marked an era of political attempts to resolve the defense industry crisis. Most political efforts came in the form of consolidating the supply side of national defense industrial bases. A U.S. Government Accountability Office (GAO) report from 1991 reported that some European officials already recognized that a unified European defense market would eventually be necessary to ensure the survival of the European defense industrial base, and the ability to craft European foreign and security policy.[2] The agenda emanating from informal European defense industry institutions – that individual national markets were too small to support an efficient industry – began to filter out into European political agendas, particularly as the issue of declining defense budgets became increasingly salient in the 1990s. At the same time, the continuing mergers and consolidations of the U.S. defense industrial base continued to destabilize the long-term competitiveness of a smaller, fragmented European defense industry.

---

[1] Stockholm International Peace Research Institute, *SIPRI Yearbook 2011: Armaments, Disarmament and International Security* (Oxford: Oxford University Press, 2011), 76.

[2] U.S. General Accounting Office. "European Initiatives: Implications for US Defense Trade and Cooperation." *Report to the Chairman, Subcommittee on Investigations, Committee on Armed Services, House of Representatives.* April 1991. NSIAD-91-167.

In the 1992 Maastricht Treaty, the responsibility for developing European defense markets was tasked to the WEU, an intergovernmental military body.[3] Its first significant development was the creation in 1993 of WEAG,[4] a forum for intergovernmental consultation aimed at strengthening European armaments cooperation. One WEAG task was to explore whether an armaments agency for joint procurement on behalf of member nations could be developed, but the process deteriorated because of confusion over procurement rules and a lack of internal resources for working out such a complex task. The task was to find a balance between the institutionalization of defense procurement at the EU and sensitive security and defense issues. It eventually reached a dead end, as security and defense could not be justified at the EU level because of redundancy with NATO.[5] The Technology-Aerospace Committee of the WEU attempted to promote a European armaments agency, although they claimed "a common defense policy still is far into the future."[6] France and Germany led a 1994 effort to form a joint armament agency that could be extended to other European countries.[7] In

---

[3] The WEU was founded by the 1948 Brussels Treaty on Economic, Social and Cultural Collaboration and Collective Self-Defence.

[4] Originally it was the Independent European Programme Group (IEPG), an informal body set up in Rome in February 1976 on the basis of an agreement between certain European members of the NATO military structure (Denmark, Germany, Greece, Italy, Luxembourg, Norway, the Netherlands, the United Kingdom, and Turkey) and France. Portugal and Spain later joined, and it was then brought into the WEU as the WEAG in May 1993.

[5] The transatlantic debate over NATO and the development of EU capabilities in the 1990s is well documented elsewhere. The United States, aware of the existential crisis of purpose facing NATO, opposed the development of European autonomous capability as decoupling, duplicating, and discriminatory (Madeleine Albright's 3Ds). The conflicts in Bosnia and Kosovo introduced the concept of "non-Article 5 actions," which enabled NATO to take actions for peace activities including peace enforcement and humanitarian intervention outside the NATO area. This additional function of NATO still failed to justify the continued role of the United States in European security issues; however, from the U.S. perspective, the development of European capability would undermine the transatlantic alliance. The United States wanted to promote a division of labor where the EU was responsible for post-crisis management and eventually accepted a partial development of EU capabilities but in support of NATO operations. At the NATO council in 1999, immediately after the St. Malo initiative, the "Berlin Plus arrangement was created, allowing the EU to undertake military and humanitarian operations using NATO assets and command structures. From American point of view, this arrangement would discourage some NATO Member States from pushing for the development of European autonomous capability because NATO would provide for EU forces, saving the cost of development, while improved EU forces would strengthen the capability of NATO itself." P. Sparaco, "Europeans Advocate Unified Defence Market," *Aviation Week & Space Technology*, July 25, 1994, 54. Some European members, particularly France, Germany, Belgium, and Luxembourg, were not happy with complete dependence on NATO assets.

[6] Ibid.   [7] Sparaco, "Europeans Advocate Unified Defence Market," 54.

1996, the WEAG managed to establish a prototype armaments agency, the Western European Armaments Organisation (WEAO), to develop defense research and development, procurement rules, and studies relevant to security and defense.

Industry leaders worked to support the WEU/WEAG effort in the early 1990s as they mobilized to build informal EU-level defense industry institutions. They hoped the WEU would achieve a common market for defense procurement, create operational security and defense institutions, face new threats, and develop a real European "defense procurement agency." According to the chairman of Thomson-CSF in 1992,

> we only can hope that the WEU profits quickly from the experience of the Independent European Program Group (IEPG) . . . to move toward a single European defence market truly worthy of the name. How could Thomson-CSF believe in anything other than a single European defence market that is ready to promote reciprocity with our U.S. allies, and that enables the establishment of a competitive and equitable partnership?[8]

The crisis in the industry had only worsened by the mid-1990s, having already shed 47 percent of its 1.6 million jobs between 1984 and 1994. But an imbalance between supply and demand remained, with an excess of supply. While total military spending in Europe dropped by 5.3 percent in real terms between 1985 and 1994, procurement of major weapons fell by 28.5 percent. Imports of major weapon systems from non-EU nations did not decline at the same rate, and arms purchases among member states were still a fraction of overall imports from the United States. Intra-European community trade accounted for only 3 to 4 percent of member states' expenditure on conventional weapons between 1988 and 1992. Roughly 75 percent of all defense imports came from the United States, which produced twice as much as Europe with one-third of Europe's production facilities. At the same time, European companies were exporting less than half as much as U.S. industry.

With a lack of Europe-wide policy solutions, think tanks and industry associations began to publicly debate and promote ideas for resolving this imbalance. In April of 1995, the WEU's Institute of Security Studies and the European Commission held a joint seminar: "Defence Markets and Industries in Europe: Time for Political Decisions?" The purpose of the seminar was to discuss the results of a think tank (Group for Research and Information on Peace and Security [GRIP]) study of the main issues affecting the development of a more integrated European defense

---

[8] "European Defence Industry Seeks Balanced Role with U.S.," *Aviation Week & Space Technology*, December 14, 1992/December 21, 1992.

industrial base.[9] A reality began to sink in at this conference and in meetings of industry officials: an intergovernmental body for coordinating a defense industrial base and eliminating national barriers to a common defense market was insufficient. EU rules regulating the free movement of goods and services might work in another marketplace, but the defense market was different. It was not enough to remove barriers; there would eventually have to be a common buyer, a single source of procurement for constituting the market. A former executive complained:

> there is, in essence, no such thing as a European defence marketplace. Furthermore, intergovernmental and cooperative programs are no substitutes for a genuine marketplace. If many of the weapons designed by multinational committees have actually proven militarily to be racehorses rather than camels, they have also tended to be lumbered by inefficiencies in terms of time and treasure, exceeding those normally encountered in the defence industrial sector.[10]

This reform agenda also deteriorated because of the impossibility of creating a common procurement market in the absence of any strategic justification for an independent European operational force.[11]

In 1995, the European Council created the Working Party on a European Armaments Policy (POLARM), an ad hoc working group on the issue of armaments. The group discussed armaments policy in the EU, specifically exploring options for "making recommendations for further action and proposing specific measures within the EU's jurisdiction."[12] POLARM also made little progress, citing the complex nature of public–private ownership jigsaws across Europe in the defense industry and the lack of a common European security strategy justifying an EU defense market. By 1996, the European Commission, responding to the demands of failing defense industries across Europe, attempted to demand the opening of U.S. defense markets to European industries. In a January 1996 report, the EC argued that European governments should remove trade barriers among EU defense markets, but simultaneously limit U.S. access unless it agreed to reciprocal market access.[13] The EC noted five barriers to the transnational consolidation of

---

[9] GRIP Press Release and Transcript, April 25, 1995. Brussels, Belgium.

[10] F. Heisbourg, "From European Defence Industrial Restructuring to Transatlantic Deal?" CSIS: Working Paper Number 4. Washington, DC, 2001.

[11] Author interview with EU defense official, Brussels, Belgium. June 15, 2007.

[12] Center for European Policy Studies, "Future Cooperation among European Defence Industries in the Light of European Multinational Forces." Report of a CEPS Working Party, 1999.

[13] European Commission, "The Challenges Facing the European Defence-Related Industry, A Contribution for Action at European Level," COM (96) 10 final (Brussels, January 28, 1996).

European defense firms: member states' unwillingness to risk political capital in industrial restructuring; differences in state or private ownership structures; differences in arms exports policies; the lack of transnational legal structures; and variations in national defense equipment requirements. The report also threatened U.S. defense exports to Europe with tariff barriers as a result of a harmonization of European import duties. The language left little interpretation regarding the key motivations: "the survival of an independent industrial and technological base in Europe is now being put into question. The state of our armament industries is such that if nothing is done, there is a real danger that within five years or so they will fall under technological and financial sway of U.S. masters – or undergo a process of national retrenchment."[14]

Industry Commissioner Martin Bangemann said the extension of general EU rules on transparency and non-discrimination in public procurement to the defense sector was vital to the competitiveness of European industry in an era of shrinking spending: "Unless action is taken soon, whole branches of the industry could disappear in Europe with massive job losses . . . The figures show we are buying a lot of weapons from the U.S. but they are buying very little from us."[15] Bangemann also linked CSDP to procurement, arguing the EU had to have a common procurement policy in place before a common foreign and security policy. Commission officials recall they came to this conclusion in part based on the expertise of defense industry groups promoting this argument. The Commission report noted that common foreign and security policy would be a long-term process, but the European defense industrial base was of immediate importance: As the EU already possessed tools for promoting unified markets and competitive industries, they should be employed as a first step toward the process of building a European security and defense identity.

The European Commission sensed a political opportunity to take the lead in developing a political solution to the defense market problem.[16] The 1996 report urged EU-level linkages between civilian and military industries and markets. The Commission argued for technology flow from the military to the civilian markets, the "spin-off effect" of technology transfers, but also emphasized harnessing civilian technologies for military purposes, a "spin-in effect" where the defense markets

[14] B. Tigner, "EU Official's Fear US Threat to Aerospace, Defence Base," *Defence News*, November 11, 1996.
[15] A. MacKinnon, "Commission Calls for Opening of U.S. Defence Markets," *Agence France Presse*, January 25, 1996.
[16] Author interview with former EU Commission official. Brussels, Belgium, November 10, 2007.

would also integrate high tech civilian solutions and platforms.[17] This had already been recognized in the United States, and Europe was lagging behind, as the industry groups had earlier warned. The Commission argued:

technological areas of potential dual-use account for as much as one third of the overall Community research budget . . . a number of companies and research organizations known to be active in the defence sector participate in the Community programs . . . some of these companies are also being consulted in the Framework of the Commission's Task Forces to improve the links between research and industry (for example aeronautics).[18]

Two more reports immediately followed the 1996 report. The September 1997 report further linked the civil and defense sectors together. The message was clear:

The need for restructuring is clear and urgent, regardless of which scenario is deemed most appropriate . . . The extra difficulties of restructuring in the defence sector should not serve as a pretext for delaying restructuring in the civil sector. The need for Europe-wide consolidation in the field of aerospace and the reality that no Member State can any longer retain complete autonomy in its aerospace capability have to be acknowledged through the acceptance of true interdependence within Europe in the interest of the continued well-being of the European aerospace industry as a whole.[19]

In the third report, published in November 1997, the Commission elevated the defense industrial base to both "a major means of production and essential to foreign and security policy. Any action by the EU has to take this dual nature into account, if necessary by adapting the resources within the Community's jurisdiction."[20] The Commission reports were a turning point in EU efforts to frame common defense as a market issue, with the building blocks of this logic the decade-long effort on the part of informal defense industry institutions researching, analyzing, and promoting agenda-setting policy on the European defense industrial base.[21]

Member states were also attempting to create intergovernmental and ad-hoc solutions to the defense industry issue. Out of frustration

---

[17] European Commission, "The Challenges Facing the European Defence-Related Industry," COM (96) 10 final.

[18] Ibid., 20.

[19] European Commission, The European Aerospace Industry Meeting the Global Challenge, COM (97) 466 final (Brussels, September 24, 1997).

[20] European Commission, Implementing European Union Strategy on Defence-Related Industries, COM (97) 583 final (Brussels, November 12, 1997).

[21] Author interview with former EU Commission official. Brussels, Belgium, May 22, 2009.

with the lack of progress on armaments cooperation in the WEU, the UK, France, Germany, and Italy established OCCAR in 1998 to help coordinate industry cooperation on project such as the A400M transport plane.[22] The same year, the six European countries most involved in aerospace and defense production (France, Germany, Italy, Spain, Sweden, and the UK) signed a Letter of Intent (LOI) in an attempt to integrate domestic markets. OCCAR's mandate was broad, including procurement security, export procedures, protection of classified information, research and development, exchange of technical information, standardization of military requirements, and legal relations.[23] In the end, however, all initiatives failed to reform fragmented national defense markets. New reforms only created additional fragmentation of European efforts with competing, overlapping, and ineffective efforts. Dual-use products and security research eventually fell under the mandate of the Commission, military products within the six LOI countries, and common procurement programs within the four OCCAR countries. Real political conflict and competition stagnated reform efforts by the end of the 1990s, particularly between the EU Commissioner for External Affairs and other authorities.[24]

The French, German, and British prime ministers (later joined by Spain and Italy) issued a joint declaration in December 1997, stating the urgent need for a reorganization of both the civilian and military branches. In 1997, the Amsterdam Treaty formalized defense cooperation by absorbing the WEU into the authority structure of the EU

---

[22] OCCAR was created as a result of French and German dissatisfaction with the lack of progress WEU was making in establishing a European armaments agency. Joined by Italy and the United Kingdom, the four nations agreed on November 12, 1996, to form OCCAR as a management organization for joint programs involving two or more member nations. OCCAR's goals were to create greater efficiency in program management and facilitate emergence of a more unified market. Although press accounts raised concerns that OCCAR member countries would give preference to European products, OCCAR never formalized any protectionist policies. Instead, it was agreed that an OCCAR member would give preference to procuring equipment that it helped to develop. In establishing OCCAR, the defense ministers of the member countries agreed that OCCAR was to have a competitive procurement policy. Competition was to be open to all thirteen member countries of the Western European Armaments Group.

[23] It was felt at the time that the initiative could "advance" integration in the EU's entire defense market by using as leverage the greater homogeneity of these countries in the sector and their interest in creating the conditions for guaranteeing a strengthening of the European industrial structure, above all with respect to the large-scale integration in the U.S. aerospace and defense industry in the first half of the previous decade. Indeed, there were serious doubts in 1998 regarding whether the EU 's ability could integrate the defense sector, as an equally ambitious 1997 policy agenda resulted in only a Code of Conduct for exports toward third countries.

[24] D. Zakheim, *Toward a Fortress Europe?* (Washington, DC: Center for Strategic and International Studies, November 2002), 23.

Council, specifically by framing it as armaments cooperation not operational cooperation. Article J7.1 of the Amsterdam Treaty states, "[t]he progressive framing of a common defence policy will be supported, as Member States consider appropriate, by cooperation between them in the field of armaments" (para. 4). The moment credited with the institutional birth of CSDP operations occurred a year later (December 1998) at St. Malo.

1999–2004: Emerging Defense Institutions and Agendas

EU defense policy developments increased rapidly in 1999. One MEP claimed:

The introduction of the single currency in January 1999, the entry into force of the Treaty of Amsterdam and its new provisions concerning the CFSP . . . the Kosovo war and finally, the fresh impetus given to its enlargement policy have completely changed the Union's self-image . . . the Union has reassessed its role, gained the self-confidence and determination it had previously lacked and decided to embark [on] what is, given the central importance for national sovereignty, the hardest part of the European integration process, i.e. security and defence.[25]

The initial focus of CSDP was operational: a plan for rapid reaction forces deployable in support of EU, NATO, or UN interests. In 1999, Commission President Romano Prodi claimed the "logical next step" in these developments would be the creation of an EU army, unless the EU wanted to be "marginalized in the new world history."[26] A number of ambitious operational goals were set forth but with little political or institutional development over the following decades.

After 2003, with the establishment of the EDA, the CSDP focus shifted from crisis management to defense industry and armaments. Without collaboration on procurement and improvements in European military hardware, attempts to cobble together operational units were increasingly implausible. The message emanating from defense industry groups in Brussels finally had its moment of opportunity: the cost of "non-Europe" in defense had reached a dangerous level, putting at risk Europe's contribution to NATO and harmony in transatlantic

---

[25] Lalumière C. (Rapporteur), "European Parliament Report on the Establishment of a Common European Security and Defence Policy after Cologne and Helsinki," European Parliament Report (2000/2005(INI)) Committee on Foreign Affairs, Human Rights, Common Security and Defence Policy, November 21, 2000.

[26] P. Norman and A. Parker, "Common EU Army the 'Logical Next Step,'" *Financial Times*, May 10, 1999. See also E. Bodino, "A Single European Army," *Financial Times*, May 10, 1999.

relations. While Europe spent significant resources on defense, its operational output steadily deteriorated as European states still defined their needs, planning, and expenditures on a national, rather than multinational, basis. The result has been a poor allocation of budgets, fragmentation and overlap, administrative overheads, and decreasing efficiency. Military leaders from the United States and EU began to conclude that increasing the output of military investments in Europe would require an overhaul of the entire process leading to defense integration.[27] The force planning structure inherited from the WEU had not fundamentally changed: it was simply an ad-hoc bottom-up process for setting up the Force Catalogue, itself only an inventory of national military capabilities earmarked for deployment in EU operation.

By the creation of the EDA in 2003, there was momentum behind the idea that the EU would eventually have to act collectively to create a European market to protect the future of the European Defence Technical Industrial Base (EDTIB). However, the narrative also included a causal logic in the reverse direction. In the keynote speech at the "Second EU Congress on European Defence" in Berlin in December 2003, Dr. Michael Rogowski, the president of BDI, argued:

High-performance defence companies secure our country a say in issues of future EU foreign policy, security policy and industrial policy. The rules of the game are: Only those industries with something to offer are admitted to the EU playing field! And especially industry in Germany, as the world leader in exports and the strongest EU economy, should have a voice in global politics on this matter![28]

By 2004, there were four dominant defense companies in Europe: BAE Systems, Thales, EADS, and Finmeccanica. These four were in the top ten defense companies worldwide, with combined revenues of about $40 billion in 2003 (the top four defense companies in the United States accounted for $93 billion). The consolidation trend of the 1990s slowed significantly, as firms had to adjust to the acquisitions of the late 1990s. The supply side of the market was complex in scale, but the mergers produced little cost savings. With the exception of EADS, the large firms remained national champions. In a 2004 *Financial Times* editorial, "Europe Must Set Its Defence Industry Free," the scenario was framed as grim:

---

[27] Joachim Hofbauer, Roy Levy, Gregory Sanders, Guy Ben-Ari, and David Berteau, *European Defense Trends: Budgets, Regulatory Frameworks, and the Industrial Base: A Report of the CSIS Defense-Industrial Initiatives Group*. Washington, DC: Center for Strategic and International Studies, 2010.

[28] M. Rogowski, President of the Federation of German Industries (BDI), "Speech on the Occasion of the Second Congress on European Defence," Berlin, Germany, December 9, 2003.

European governments are not likely to initiate joint procurement soon enough to provide a stable home market for the Big Four. Public funding of research and development is small compared with the U.S., and the order flow is inconsistent. Thus, new development projects based on multinational procurement are riskier than in the single-buyer U.S. market. European companies' operating performance is dismal. U.S. companies are much more profitable and have lower debt-to-equity ratios (at market value). European companies' weak performance constrains their ability to forge the large deals that would mark the next phase of consolidation. As a result, U.S. defence stocks have significantly outperformed European ones.[29]

The *Financial Times* article went on to frame three plausible future scenarios. In the first, the big four firms could consolidate further into two "mega-prime" contractors. The EU could spur this by developing more joint procurement based on a common security and defense policy, justifying a single buyer in the European home market. In the second, firms could de-merge, or break up into smaller firms. European firms would become subprimes for U.S. companies and would be strategically dependent on the United States for weapons systems and platforms. The third scenario was the continuation of the status quo, with consolidated firms as suppliers but limited joint European procurement. In this scenario, the "European technological capabilities would fall behind those of the U.S., and the European operational inferiority to U.S. forces would become more acute, making it tougher to mount joint operations."[30]

Coordinated Industry Agenda Setting

The aerospace industry was the first mover when it came to establishing EU offices and lobbying the EU, having a presence in Brussels since the early 1990s. By 2001, their message was clear:

Europe's defence ministers still work on the national level, but their suppliers think more broadly. The motivation is pure economics; big companies want big contracts . . . In the U.S., defence behemoths have one giant client: the Pentagon. Nothing comparable exists in Europe, so suppliers are attempting the next-best thing, offering lots of countries the same planes, helicopters and missiles. The strategy has scored some early hits.[31]

---

[29] K. Vlachos Dengler, "Europe Must Set Its Defence Industry Free," *Financial Times*, September 7, 2004.

[30] Ibid.

[31] D. Michaels, "European Defence: More Bang for Buck – Nations Begin to Pool Their Military Orders; Contractors, Likewise." *Wall Street Journal*, Eastern edition, March 9, 2001, A.11.

The chief executive of EADS also emphasized "[w]e absolutely need defence integration and to have common procurement in Europe ... [w]e are asking for one customer."[32]

In 2001, a public–private group called the European Advisory Group on Aerospace[33] formed to assess the adequacy of the existing political and regulatory framework for aerospace in Europe, and it produced a report to the European Commission in 2002. The report identified key areas of future competitiveness of the industry and its ability to contribute effectively to Europe's main policy goals. It argued:

the aerospace industry has to remain competitive while anticipating evolving foreign and security policies. Its well-being depends on both civil- and defence-related applications, complementary and mutually dependent areas. Operating within both markets means sharing skills and technologies and reaping economic benefits from a broad product range, but it also requires a coherent strategy and *single source of information and risk-hedging*.[34]

Conclusions: 1) Aerospace is vital to meeting Europe's objectives for economic growth, security and quality of life; 2) A strong industrial base provides Europe with choices and options with regard to its presence and influence on the world stage; 3) European aerospace must remain strong to be a full partner in the global marketplace; and 4) Europe must remain at the forefront of key technologies to have an innovative and competitive aerospace industry.[35]

Their policy recommendations urged the EU "to secure a level playing field, to develop a coordinated research strategy, to increase funding for R&D by €100 billion over 20 years, to develop tax incentives, and to develop a coherent EU security and defence structure with a common buyer and joint budgets."[36]

The report criticized European defense cooperation for being still too "governed by national policies" with traditional methods of industry cooperation "not providing the best value for money." It argued that the lack of EU investment and commitment would not only make Europe less competitive in twenty years but would also endanger the EU's ability to carry out CSDP tasks.[37] Jean-Paul Bechat, the president of AECMA, argued in the report the EU had to develop a "credible security and

---

[32] Ibid.
[33] The European Advisory Group on Aerospace membership included seven aerospace industry chairmen; five European Commissioners, including Research Commissioner Philippe Busquin, the EU High Representative for the Common Foreign and Security Policy; and two members of the European Parliament.
[34] European Commission, "Strategic Aerospace Review for the 21st Century," *Enterprise Publications*, July 2002. Available from www.europa.eu.int/comm/enterprise/aerospace
[35] STAR 21 European Advisory Group on Aerospace – Strategic Aerospace Review for the 21st Century, February 16, 2002.
[36] European Commission, "Strategic Aerospace Review for the 21st Century."
[37] H. Mahony, "EU Defence Paralysed by National Interests," *EU Observer*, July 16, 2002.

defence policy... [because] whereas European companies are expected to co-fund much of their military research and development, US industry R&D is fully supported," a situation that places "huge constraints" on EU efforts to remain competitive. Research funding had to be from one source, with one message for hedging future investment risk, and needed to be carried out "now to sow the seeds" for the next twenty years.[38]

National Resistance toward Armaments Cooperation

After 1999, defense industrial cooperation slowly shifted from exclusively national to partially European frameworks, but national defense ministries were still resistant to the idea of relinquishing control over this sensitive sector. National defense industry champions have been allowed to remain outside of EU common market policies. The 1992 Maastricht Treaty established this protection with Article 296 (formerly Art. 223), that

any Member State may take such measures as it considers necessary for the protection of the essential interests of its security which are connected with the production of or the trade in arms, munitions and war material; such measures shall not adversely affect the conditions of competition in the market regarding products which are not intended for specifically military purposes.[39]

Article 296 allowed member countries to protect any sensitive industries from competition pressures, which has led to a situation "where most defence contracts are awarded on the basis of national rules," resulting in "a lack of transparency and competition."[40]

However, defense economists and aerospace industries had long been arguing for the elimination of Article 296, combined with the creation of a subsidized and protected European defense market. Savings were estimated between 10 and 17 percent on collective defense spending, which was already shrinking and becoming unsustainable.[41] Javier Solana similarly argued, "none of us can any longer afford to sustain a healthy and comprehensive DTIB on a national basis. The future health, may be even

---

[38] STAR 21 European Advisory Group on Aerospace – Strategic Aerospace Review for the 21st Century.

[39] B. Schmitt, "The European Union and Armaments, Getting a Bigger Bang for the Euro," *Chaillot Paper 63* (Paris, France: European Union Institute for Security Studies, 2003), 9.

[40] European Parliament, Committee on Internal Market and Consumer Protection, Sub Committee on Security and Defence Report, June 23, 2005.

[41] K. Hartley, "The Future of European Defence Policy: An Economic Perspective," *Defence and Peace Economics* 14, no. 2 (January 2003): 107–15.

survival, of Europe's defence industry requires a European approach, and a European strategy ... We must develop greater mutual reliance on diverse centres of excellence, and less dependence on non-European sources for key defence technologies."[42]

There were a number of EU-level responses to this issue. In September 2004, the Commission published a "Green Paper" on defense procurement. The European Parliament also addressed the issue of defense procurement, calling it a "big black hole" of national favoritism, where national governments and defense ministers blocked EU defense procurement markets. The Commission also suggested it be given the right to participate in export control regimes and that a common defense equipment policy be drafted to push joint arms research and procurement.[43] Over the next decade, the Commission adopted a number of sweeping changes in defense procurement regulation, moving into security research that effectively merged market boundaries in civilian and military technologies as a way to work around Article 296 constraints on EU involvement in defense markets.[44] In creating a European homeland security market by subsuming the defense industrial base into the civilian security market, the Commission acted as a policy entrepreneur in merging security and defense technologies and industries without the buy-in or clear legal mandate from EU member states.[45] The idea to do this, however, stemmed from the agenda-setting efforts of informal industry institutions representing defense industry interests.

Defense Research and Development on the EU Agenda

The idea that the EU should move into defense research as a first step toward integrating defense markets also originally emerged from informal defense industry institutions. In 2002, senior executives within the European defense-aerospace giant EADS were actively lobbying Commission officials to model their defense and security research agenda

---

[42] "Solana, Verheugen, Svensson at EDA Conference – Radical change and true European market needed to secure future of European defence industry," European Defence Agency, Press Release, Brussels, February 1, 2007.

[43] "The European Commission," *Aviation Week & Space Technology*, March 17, 2003, 16.

[44] The EU took a step toward building a joint defense procurement market by introducing a "code of conduct" for advertising defense procurement contracts on an online bulletin board. Suppliers would then be able to tender for the projects in a more transparent manner, with more objective criteria being set for selecting bidders and awarding contracts. The Commission also sought to boost competition by tightening guidelines on the use of a special exemption from EU rules on competitive bidding for contracts.

[45] Edler and James.

on the U.S. DARPA model.[46] EADS Co-CEO Philippe Camus drafted an industry proposal for the establishment of such an agency. Industry leaders proposed the DARPA model within a larger package of reforms prepared by a task force headed by former French President Giscard d'Estaing, ahead of the EU Constitutional Convention. The original agenda proposed creating a European Security and Defence Research Agency (ESDRA) within a new European Defence Agency. Senior EADS officials viewed the ESDRA as a means toward securing key technological capabilities within Europe and combining two strategic areas of research: defense and security. A British industry analyst said, "the DARPA idea has been pushed onto the agenda for a new European convention, which has led to some initial confusion in certain quarters – it is, after all, extremely sectoral."[47] The industry proposal identified a "sustainable" European defense market as the primary goal, which would provide long-term support for the European defense industrial base. Camus argued that despite substantial budget increases, France's new multiyear spending plan failed to establish a coherent loop between observation, command, precision weapons, satellite, and UAV/Unmanned Combat Aerial Vehicle (UCAV) systems to permit operations such as the United States in the Afghan campaign. UAV programs presented in the plan were "insufficient and behind the times." EADS officials argued that "financial burden sharing" needed to be addressed through mechanisms such as determining a baseline percentage of national gross domestic product to be allocated to European research and procurement.

In response, the Commission immediately created a public–private forum for civilian research and development in security, run by "The Advisory Council for Aeronautics Research," citing "fragmented and uncoordinated" research and development efforts as a major obstacle to the competitiveness of the European aerospace industry. EC President Romano Prodi said reduced research spending in many countries was now a serious problem, and one far worse in the defense industry: "The defence industry is still very fragmented and there are still lots of economies of scale that are exploited in research in the USA which are not yet being exploited in Europe . . . If we are not careful, then the defence industry could slip through our hands."[48] The Commission

---

[46] Douglas Barrie and Mike Taverna, "EADS advocating EU DARPA," *Aviation Week & Space Technology*, Vol. 157, No. 22, November 25, 2002, 32.
[47] Ibid.
[48] Flight International, "Fragmented R&D Holds Industry Back, says EC," January 28, 2003, 14.

tasked the forum to reform the status quo of EU defense as an "incomplete internal market" where "fragmentation remains the rule as a result of incompatible national requirements."[49] The forum agenda included updating the 1997 action plan on implementing a European strategy on defense-related industries, which had stagnated due to a "lack of commitment by member states." The Commission recommended creating a defense-related advisory group, similar to the aerospace working group that led to formation of the European Aviation Safety Agency. The forum concluded that further military integration was necessary to further defense market integration but that bottom-up reforms could fuel the political development of markets, including personnel reforms such as engineer mobility and technology transfer rules: "The Brussels culture is focused too little on achieving results, and change, in the real world outside ... To this general friction, defence adds its own massive inertia. It is a hugely complicated business, operating to some necessarily long lead times, where the supply side needs a demand side to insulate it from risk and uncertainty."[50]

CSDP Agency: European Defence Agency

A significant EU-level political development in CSDP was the 2004 establishment of the European Defence Agency.[51] Intended as "a European Agency for Armaments Research and Military Capabilities," its purpose is fourfold: to "develop European defence capabilities; promote armaments co-operation in the EU; improve the European defence industrial and technological base; and promote collaborative defence research across the Union."[52] First proposed at the 2002 Convention on the Future of Europe, it was part of the legal mandate of the Constitutional Treaty, but the UK and France launched it extralegally at the Le Touquet defence summit in February 2003.[53]

The UK and France led the creation of the EDA, but based on divergent ideas about its proper role and purpose. Historically, the UK had opposed an armaments agency on the grounds it would "benefit

---

[49] Ibid.

[50] European Union Institute for Security Studies, "ESDP Newsletter: European Security and Defense Policy Issue #5 'Africa-EU,'" Brussels: General Secretariat of the Council of the European Union, December 2007, p. 22.

[51] Council Joint Action 2004/551/CFSP of 12 July 2004 on the establishment of the European Defence Agency. EDA is called the "Agency in the field of defence capabilities development, research, acquisition and armaments."

[52] EDA Background, Brussels, European Defence Agency, January 1, 2005.

[53] *House of Lords Report on the European Defence Agency* (London, UK: The Stationery Office, 2005), 2.

industry without regard to proper defence needs."[54] The UK backed the EDA to improve interoperability and defense capabilities but not to promote common armaments procurement.[55] France saw the EDA as "a platform to create a European defence manufacturing base, supported by more spending on research and development and with contract preferences for European firms."[56] The resulting agreement fused these agendas, creating an "amalgam of a capabilities-led agency which nonetheless has a very clear license to interest itself in the health of the technological and industrial base."[57] In December 2003, the EU began drafting plans for the agency, and in June 2004, other member states in the Council (with the exception of Denmark) authorized the creation of the agency as part of the final text of the Constitutional Treaty, in Articles I-41 and III-311. Although the Constitutional Treaty was derailed by referenda in the Netherlands and France, the development and establishment of the EDA moved forward as planned. Javier Solana, the EU High Representative for Foreign and Security Policy responsible for overseeing the agency, emphasized that the EDA had the advantage of being established before the setbacks of national constitutional referenda and was therefore able to work without constraint.[58]

The EDA is an intergovernmental agency reporting to the European Council, not the supranational Commission. The Council provides general guidelines and controls the overall budget framework, but the EDA Steering Board, made up of national defense ministers, sets the work agenda and the budget specifics. Projects require approval from the steering board members meeting twice a year, but voting is by qualified majority, not unanimity. Projects can also move forward based on groups of cooperating countries, and not all countries need to participate in order for agendas to move forward.

The initial 2005 operational budget of the EDA was €20 million, with a staff of seventy-seven. The proposed agenda of complete market transformation put forth by the European Council, however, was highly ambitious, provoking concern that the EDA would not be able to fulfill its mission. By design, the agency was small and not a threat to national defense ministry authority, and it was tasked to "prove its worth" before

---

[54] Ibid., 54.
[55] K. Eliassen and N. Sitter, *Arms Procurement in the European Union: Achieving Mission Impossible?*, REPORT 4/2006 (Oslo: The Centre for European and Asian Studies at Norwegian School of Management, 3006), 16
[56] T. Guay, *The Transatlantic Defence Industrial Base: Restructuring Scenarios and their Implications*, Monograph (Carlisle, PA: Strategic Studies Institute, 2005), 13.
[57] *House of Lords Report on the European Defence Agency* (London, UK: The Stationery Office, 2005), 54.
[58] Ibid., 4.

being awarded more resources.[59] It also did not require a large initial budget, as it was "intended to coordinate, rather than control, budgets for large scale research projects."[60]

EDA Mandate

When the EDA was launched in July 2004, it was tasked to carry out the ESS the EU had adopted the year before. In addition to capability coordination, it was tasked to create joint investment solutions to capability shortfalls (such as heavy lift equipment and helicopters) that would boost the EU's strategic autonomy and reduce its dependency on American resources and technologies. It was also tasked to coordinate with the Commission to develop technology and markets at the boundary of civilian and military applications, including civilian crisis management solutions such as UAVs, WMD defense, and software defined radio.

While the EDA's founding mission was to support member state capabilities, in practice, it mission was also to

help the EU develop credible, coherent and effective military forces, with the new EU Battlegroups a key element of the EU's rapid response capabilities. These autonomous forces should, of course, be able to respond quickly and decisively in a whole spectrum of crisis management missions, including humanitarian and rescue operations, peacekeeping tasks and possibly disarmament operations, while also providing support for third countries in combating terrorism and undertaking security sector reforms.[61]

This mandate incorporated a great deal of uncertainty. As Nick Witney, the first director of the EDA recalled, "where the mandate was no more precise than the European Council's call for 'an Agency in the field of defence capabilities, development, research, acquisition and armaments,' the opportunity was a strikingly wide one."[62] The EDA developed a Long-Term Vision Statement[63] in 2006, marking an important departure from the traditional concepts of European warfare. Witney echoed much of the rhetoric-building in Brussels for the previous decade when he argued the EDA vision

concludes that we must decisively break with the old concepts of warfare which obtained in the last century, which were all about unloading as much ordnance as possible on conventional opponents. It underlines that application of force

---

[59] Ibid., 3.   [60] Ibid.   [61] Ibid.
[62] European Union Institute for Security Studies, "ESDP Newsletter: European Security and Defense Policy Issue #5 'Africa-EU,'" 22.
[63] "An Initial Long-term Vision for European Defence Capability and Capacity Needs" (Brussels: European Defence Agency, October 3, 2006).

will have to be increasingly modulated with what is happening in the political arena; that operations will likely take place in constrained and ambiguous circumstances, under tight rules of engagement and 24/7 media scrutiny. It emphasises that the decisive capabilities of the future will be less heavy metal and high explosive, and more the capabilities that provide situational awareness, and allow rapid communication and decision-taking. Operations will be expeditionary, and multinational, placing a premium on interoperability, deployability and sustainability.[64]

This mandate included restructuring the European defense industrial base. Although during the Cold War markets remained relatively closed and governments tended to depend on domestic manufactures to supply arsenals, "this is no longer economically sustainable…Europe needs to move to more open markets."[65] In order to open markets within Europe, the markets also had to become more concentrated, protected, and rich with research and technology at the EU level: "Closing the gap with the U.S. in terms of arms technology is not about spending more, but spending more efficiently…European companies are up against big American groups with colossal budgets. Compared to the Americans, the Europeans are underweight. They need a market and buyer on a Continental scale to be profitable."[66]

EDA Policy Outcomes

Although limited by its intergovernmental status, the EDA launched several significant reforms. During the first few years of its existence, it introduced a voluntary code of conduct among EU states to promote transparency and cross-border competition in defense procurement; a 2006 Long-Term Vision report projected the risks and threats facing the EU and the military capabilities required in the future; a strategy to strengthen, deregulate, and reregulate EDTIB; and a centralized Joint Investment Program for strategic investment in defense research and development.[67] The latter program was initially the smallest but the most significant step, as the first EDA director affirmed:

---

[64] N. Witney, "Re-energising Europe's Security and Defence Policy." Policy Paper. European Council on Foreign Relations, 2008, 5–6. Available at www.ecfr.eu

[65] Ibid.

[66] R. Carter, "Europe's Armies 'Still in Cold War' Warns EU Arms Chief," *EU Observer*, September 29, 2004.

[67] The agency also played a leading role in the elaboration of the "Military Long Term Vision," which translates the European Security Strategy into a projection of security threats and challenges for the decennia to come. This is not a document that has caught the eye of the public. Its impact, however, could be significant: the ensuing Capability Development Plan, laying the ground for a new common definition of needs and a new planning cycle, which, in turn, would allow states to step in together from the outset and design acquisition programs to be implemented collectively.

There is a broad consensus that we can't have all procurement programs formulated on a solely national basis anymore...national market[s] [are] no longer sustainable in a globalised world economy. The demand side (governments) needs to increasingly come together on a continental scale for the supply side to respond to that demand in a continental scale of market. Despite all the political difficulties, there is a strong political will to get there together.[68]

In early 2007, the EDA developed its first three joint research and development contracts (funded by twenty member states for €55 million) in the Joint Investment Programme on Force Protection (JIP-FP), including technologies against snipers, booby traps, and robotized detection of chemical, biological, radiological/nuclear and explosive devices.[69] The program was "a prototype for the EDA's much wider 'Research & Technology' (R&T) ambitions, including the promotion of joint R&T to meet future defence requirements, but also the managing of defence R&T contracts and liaising with the European Commission to achieve as much synergy as possible with EU-sponsored R&T conducted in the context of security."[70] Unlike "previous cooperative projects on European defence R&T, which involved governments negotiating financial and industrial shares for each individual project, the JIP sets up a common EU budget to fund the whole programme."[71]

Subsequent policies included additional joint investment initiatives. In September 2007, the EDA negotiated a joint technology project for Britain, France, and Sweden for a compact, lightweight radar for UAVs.[72] An industry consortium (led by Thales) provided €21 million, with states matching funds and the EDA providing the legal oversight and management toward delivering a military technology foundation for 2020. That fall, the EDA also negotiated a joint project between Britain, France, and Spain to develop common technology in tactical missiles. In addition to these projects, the EDA developed a common procurement plan to develop helicopters and observation satellites with

---

[68] "Witney: On a Mission to Stop Defence 'Business as Usual,'" *Euractiv Newsletter*, March 27, 2007. Euractiv.com

[69] Leander Schaerlaeckens, "Analysis: European defence contracts." *UPI*, 2007, accessed September 26, 2009. http://www.upi.com/Security_Industry/2007/12/24/Analysis-European-defence-contracts/UPI-49431198507495/

[70] J. Lok, "European Defence Agency awards First R&T Contracts." *Aviation Week & Space Technology* 2008, accessed September 26, 2009.

[71] "European Defence Agency awards EUR 13.1 million to three research projects," *EDA Press Release*, 2007, accessed September 26, 2009. http://cordis.europa.eu/fetch?CALLER=EN_NEWS&ACTION=D&SESSION=&RCN=28874

[72] P. Tran, "France, U.K., Sweden Sign UAV Radar Study." *Defence News*, 2007, accessed September 26, 2009. http://www.defencenews.com/story.php?i=3774501&c=EUR&s=TOP

only EU defense contractors. Former EDA director Alexander Weis stated, "both programmes would allow the EU to close very critical capability gaps," which would be vital for accelerating "the political decision-making process . . . and allow the EU to consolidate our own position before we can move to a genuine transatlantic co-operation."[73]

In April 2008, the Council asked the EDA to produce "an Armaments Strategy to help meet future military needs, ensure interoperability and standardization, and share the ever-increasing costs of developing and procuring high technology defence equipment."[74] In December 2008, the Council officially highlighted the importance of the EDA in leading the process of creating a robust defense industry and fulfilling the 2003 ESS, in that, "Experience has shown the need to do more, particularly over key capabilities such as strategic airlift, helicopters, space assets, and maritime surveillance . . . These efforts must be supported by a competitive and robust defence industry across Europe, with greater investment in research and development. Since 2004, the EDA has successfully led this process, and should continue to do so."[75]

In addition to these policy initiatives and successes, the EDA has increasingly legitimized by external actors, including NATO and the U.S. Department of Defense. NATO and the EDA increasingly coordinate efforts to enhance Europe's in-theatre lift capability by pooling national helicopter fleets.[76] Arguably, the EDA has been more effective than its NATO counterpart in developing a defense industrial base, as

In its 60-year history, the alliance has failed to achieve much in the way of harmonization and integration of the defence industries . . . or streamlining research and technology spending by becoming the hub of cooperative armaments projects. Improving the alliance's overall defence capabilities through greater spending on cooperative armaments programmes and on joint projects across the Atlantic has quite simply proved to be out of NATO's reach . . . And despite the absence of the United States from the EDA's programmes, most EU member states regard the EDA as a more effective framework than NATO for mobilizing political

---

[73] D. Gow, "NGOs accuse miffed Mandy of neo-imperialism." *The Guardian*, 2007, accessed September 26, 2009. http://www.guardian.co.uk/business/2007/oct/24/davidgowoneurope.europe.

[74] European Defence Agency, "EU Governments ask EDA for Armaments Strategy, Agree Steps for More Defence collaboration," EDA Press Release, September 4, 2008.

[75] European Council. *Report on the Implementation of the European Security Strategy – Providing Security in a Changing World*, Brussels, December 11, 2008, p. 10.

[76] B. Tigner, "NATO, EDA Launch Plan to Boost European Lift Capability," *Jane's Air Forces News*. 2008, accessed September 26, 2009. http://www.janes.com/news/defence/air/idr/idr080220_1_n.shtml

will and marshalling the greater resources needed to improve Europe's defence capabilities.[77]

In the case of the U.S. Department of Defense, the EDA has been increasingly taken seriously as a transnational cooperation partner. In September 2009, EDA leadership met with DoD officials to discuss the development of a new heavylift transport helicopter, a resource both parties lack, but more seriously in Europe. The DoD director of international programs proposed "a transatlantic dialogue" on acquisition and procurement. This dialogue was in an effort to repair relations after the DoD cancelled the winning bid for the U.S. Air Force KC-X tanker contest by transatlantic team EADS/Northrop Grumman, instead retroactively awarding it to Boeing. The 2008 U.S. presidential election was cited as the official reason for the cancellation, although Europeans alleged that domestic lobbying dynamics influenced the decision.[78] By 2009, a number of key political developments occurred. In May 2009, the EDA was granted the authority to establish a European Framework Cooperation for Security and Defence together with the European Commission with the aim of "maximising complementarity and synergy between defence and civil security-related research activities."[79]

EDA Governing Capacity

Observers have often noted how small the EDA is as measured by personnel and resources. The leadership of the EDA has embraced this smallness and weakness as an opportunity to prove it can transform aspects of the defense landscape across Europe with minimal resources. They view their position of little regulatory authority and minimal direct procurement activity as a necessary, incubation-like phase of political development.[80] While defense industry associations were lobbying for more EU-level joint programs and the acceleration of the EDA as an EU-level "demand-side buyer," the EDA has resisted explicit movement in this direction. The acceleration of centralized procurement would bring a dangerous level of scrutiny to the process, threatening

---

[77] V. Parkanova, "In Some Ways, the European Defence Agency Is Stronger Than NATO," *Europe's World*, Spring 2009, accessed March 28, 2009. http://www.europesworld.org/NewEnglish/Home/Article/tabid/191/ArticleType/articleview/ArticleID/21340/Default.aspx

[78] B. Tigner, "EDA to Explore Heavylift Helo Collaboration with U.S.," *Jane's Defence Weekly*, August 6, 2009.

[79] Council of the European Union, 2943rd External Relations Council meeting, Conclusion on European Security and Defence Policy (ESDP), Brussels, May 18, 2009.

[80] Author interviews with EDA officials, May–June 2007.

the reforms toward an EU defense market and industrial base. This is somewhat counterintuitive to the conventional assumption that bureaucrats or organizations always seek more resources or authority over their domain. A common sentiment has been: "why ask for more resources or contracts, when that would create popular publicity and potential blowback?"[81] Instead, the EDA organizational strategy has been to build as much quiet institutional capacity as possible within these existing constraints so the organization would be effective, consolidated, and legitimate to its policy constituents in the long run.

At the beginning of its organizational life, the EDA characterized itself as:

an "outward-facing" organisation, constantly interacting with a wide range of stakeholders ... Internally, it works on a "matrix" principle, with multi-disciplinary teams forming and re-forming to pursue different elements of its work programme. Its business processes are flexible, oriented towards achieving results rather than following rigid procedures. Staff at all levels need to demonstrate the corresponding qualities of flexibility, innovation, and team-working; to work effectively with stakeholder groups, formal and informal; and to operate without the need of detailed direction.[82]

Officials and bureaucrats at the EDA promoted these organizational weaknesses as sources of organizational strength, features that forced EDA personnel to be particularly creative in how they solve problems and use resources. This aligned with their outlook that they did not necessarily need more direct resources or authority because the burden of resources could doom the organization to the fate of the stodgy, hierarchical national ministries that created defense duplication and redundancy across Europe. According to an EDA official,

Additional authority would give us resources to grow the bureaucracy, become more hierarchical and routine, but we like our role as under the radar facilitators. We want to be the Google Corporation, not the AOL-Time Warner Corporation. Some globally dominant organizations only have 300 employees. But a flexible, small organizational structure allows for operational efficiency and coordination with an informal policymaking network without building them into the core management function.[83]

This language of bureaucratic capacity is one built on meritocracy and flexibility and also with informal coordination with external actors. This

---

[81] Author interview with EDA official, November 13, 2007.
[82] EDA Industry and Market Directorate Assistant | Jobs.euractiv.com | The EU-Brussels Job website. Available at: http://jobs.euractiv.com/job/industry-and-market-directorate-assistant-4689 [Accessed September 23, 2009].
[83] Author interview with EDA Official, June 13, 2007.

capacity is not built on a material idea of resources but one of relational flexibility and coordination, aligning with the framework of embedded autonomy and transformational capacity. For early EDA leadership, policy outcomes had nothing to do with authority or resources, but everything to do with internal bureaucratic capacity and skillful coordination with outside actors.

Relationship with Industry

EDA officials have described the agency as "well-placed to identify links and synergies" between different stakeholders in member states, EU institutions, and industry.[84] Despite initial skepticism that the EDA would be a tepid and ineffective institution like its predecessors, informal defense-industry institutions have embraced it as evidence of real progress. In fact, the day after the EDA was authorized, the CEOs of EADS, BAE Systems, and Thales bought a full-page advertisement in European newspapers, accompanied by an open letter urging the EU to seize the day and boost its military spending:

Industry in Europe is under enormous competitive pressure from the United States with . . . around eight times that of Europe's fragmented total and with substantial growth in the Pentagon's vast procurement budget in a heavily protected national market, American industries are reaching new heights. While it is not the wish of Europe's elected governments or of industry to develop a Fortress Europe, it is equally not their wish to see indigenous defence technology overtaken or dependence on foreign technologies become a necessity, especially where technology transfer terms are very restrictive. Again . . . the Agency has a vital role to play.[85]

When the EDA logistics were first established in 2004, the small EDA budget "elicited a damning reaction . . . from the defence industry giant EADS," in the form of dismissing the EDA as "small staff, small start budget and a missed opportunity."[86] This initial disappointment soon turned into enthusiasm for the EDA project, where the defense trade association presidents and CEOs of firms such as Finmeccanica would

---

[84] U. Hammerstrom, "EDA Mission and Organization." Speech to European defense industry. European Defence Agency, Brussels, Belgium, 2007, p. 6.

[85] "The New European Defence Agency: Getting Above the Clouds," advertisement signed by Dennis Ranque (Thales), Philippe Camus (EADS), Rainer Hertrich (EADS) and Mike Turner (BAE Systems), June 15, 2004.

[86] *House of Lords Report on the European Defence Agency* (London, UK: The Stationery Office, 2005), 48.

"[pop] in to make sure we were getting on with it."[87] Industry leaders signaled their approval and made public their offers of support.[88]

Ongoing industry concerns included the limitations of the EDA budget and the lack of EDA direct authority over directing industrial policy. In lieu of a single EU buyer, industry placed their hopes on transformational changes via incremental centralization of future R&T investment, Commission efforts to fund basic research in civilian dual-use security technologies, and efforts to open up the EU defense market to regional competition. More than anything, industry needed the EDA to act as a shepherd for signaling and addressing the risks involved in forecasting and directing long-term investment strategies.

EDA officials have been acutely aware of how well organized the defense industry is in Brussels. Their strategies have been evolving for dealing with powerful interest groups, while their organization has been new, resource-poor, and operating under an uncertain mandate. External industry associations such as ASD are relied on heavily for expertise and general resources, although officials also have wished there were more neutral European institutes or alternate sources of expertise and resources.[89] At one point in time, ASD officials even complained of overwork on behalf of the EDA over its first decade of existence.[90] The ASD newsletter affirmed that

the ASD is an important permanent partner of the EDA and cooperates on resolving numerous problems. Topics such as stakeholders, long-term development of the Agency and re-formulation of R&T policy are being worked on with the help of the ASD. On the part of the ASD, these tasks are mainly undertaken by the Secretary General, the Director of Defence, the Technical Committee, members of the EU Working Group and individuals of ASD member companies.[91]

The EDA's job was to be "a conscience and a provocateur ... It's our job to produce good analysis and present the facts to defence ministers, and then make proposals."[92] This role, however, relies heavily on

[87] Ibid.
[88] Federation of German Industries, "Position Paper of the German Security and Defence Industry Regarding the European Defence Agency," *BDI Positionspapier* Document Number D 0037-E. Berlin, Germany, August 2006.
[89] Author interview with former EDA official, Brussels, Belgium, November 2007.
[90] Author interview with former Defense Industry Association representative, December 2014.
[91] Federation of German Industries, BDI Newsletter. Berlin, Germany, May 2006.
[92] "Witney: On a Mission to Stop Defence 'Business as Usual,'" *Euractiv .com*, 2005, accessed December 30, 2008. http://www.euractiv.com/en/security/witney-mission-defence-business-usual/article-134460

outside expertise about industries, markets, national politics, and technologies. Industry leaders have not been entirely satisfied with their privileged position of expertise, however, claiming their specific policy ideas have been "absorbed, diluted, erased and distorted by the intra-EU governmental politics and Brussels bureaucratic processes."[93] The former director of the EDA viewed any industry dissatisfaction as evidence of the bureaucratic capacity of the agency: that it has filtered industry ideas, but retained the public interest autonomy of the ESS and avoided industry capture. Industry provided the expertise, but the EDA had to translate expertise into strategy in the

long-term vision report, which describes the possible framework within which ESDP [European Security and Defence Policy] crisis-management operations could take place in the future and the sort of military capabilities which would be needed. That analysis is more concrete and more practical in the comprehensive Capabilities Development Plan, in which governments are sharing their thinking about what Europe is going to need in the medium term and how we can deliver it most efficiently.[94]

Although there have been consistent industry calls for a European demand-side buyer of equipment to consolidate the defense market, the EDA has had limited direct procurement and research and development authority. The direct procurement relationship between the EDA and industry has so far been in the form of outsourcing studies and policy analysis. For example, the German firm Elektroniksystem- und Logistik-GmbH (ESG) has advertised its role in helping the "European Union . . . carry out operations in areas of conflict more effectively in the future."[95] The outsourced project includes analyzing

the entire flow of information which is required for such missions to be carried out [and] developing future mission concepts and designing new control systems can be obtained from the results . . . [and] an analysis of the actual situation of the total exchange of information for military and civilian EU operations. All levels will be investigated, from the political, strategic and operative through to specific decisions during missions. Here, ESG is able to draw on two past projects it managed and implemented for . . . the EDA [where] the requirements of the exchange

[93] House Of Lords European Union Committee, 1st Report of Session 2006–07 "Current Developments in European Defence Policy: Report with Evidence," January 12, 2007, London, UK: The Stationery Office.

[94] European Union Institute for Security Studies, "ESDP Newsletter: European Security and Defense Policy Issue #5 'Africa-EU,'" Brussels: General Secretariat of the Council of the European Union, December 2007, p. 24.

[95] "ESG Supports the EU with Planning and Executing Overseas Operations," *Digital Battlespace*, 2008, accessed September 26, 2009. http://www.digital-battlespace.com/2008/07/esg-supports-the-eu-with-planning-and-executing-overseas-operations/

of information and the processing and decision patterns of various organisations and nations on a military level were analysed.[96]

An agency such as the EDA remains primarily regulatory and advisory in nature; its relationship with industry is still as a coordinator and facilitator of the European defense industrial base. As participants and observers have noted, the EDA cannot dictate or punish with resources and contracts; it can only nag and shame the national defense ministries and defense industries and associations to comply with its mission. Any direct contracting authority the EDA has is limited to operational concerns such as funding studies, conferences, and other non-material projects; however, the EDA is increasingly positioned to eventually transition from a coordination agency to a hybridized procurement agency. In its 2011 EU presidency, Poland proposed increasing the direct procurement role of the EDA. In order to strengthen CSDP, Poland is proposing that EDA capabilities include "directly purchas[ing] the most technically advanced weapons."[97]

In a similar vein, the leadership of the EDA has argued that "our focus must increasingly be on 'delivering the goods'... my objective for the Agency is that it should increasingly take the leading role in coordinating multinational armaments projects in Europe and should become the natural home for all joint development and procurement initiatives of that kind."[98] The justification for coordinating the defense industry through an EU body, rather than simply through the extant market forces of defense industry consolidation, is that Europe as a future procurement and strategic actor has to "consolidate our own position before we can move to a genuine transatlantic [market] co-operation."[99]

The first direct EDA procurement of defense technology was approved in April 2010 for a mobile forensics laboratory for "post-event analysis of improvised explosive devices (IEDs) in theatre, the weapons that have produced so many fatalities in Afghanistan and Iraq."[100] The decision to procure IED technology directly was the recommendation of a study commissioned by the EDA in 2008, after "European military

---

[96] Ibid.

[97] "Poland EU Agenda for 2011." *Polski Radio*, 2009, accessed September 23, 2009. http://www.polskieradio.pl/thenews/press/artykul116457_poland_eu_agenda_for_2011.html.

[98] European Union Institute for Security Studies, "ESDP Newsletter: European Security and Defense Policy Issue #5 'Africa-EU,'" 24.

[99] D. Gow, "NGOs Accuse Miffed Mandy of Neo-Imperialism," *The Guardian*, October 24, 2007.

[100] B. Tigner, "EDA Requests Purchase of Mobile IED Forensics Laboratory." *Jane's Defence Weekly*, April 26, 2010, accessed May 16, 2010. http://www.janes.com/news/defence/jdw/jdw100426_1_n.shtml

planners experienced with operations in Afghanistan and Iraq [became] concerned that the improvised explosive device (IED) threat may evolve to encompass chemical, biological, radiological and nuclear (CBRN) payloads."[101]

The EDA, with the external capacity of its network of informal industry institutions, has been slowly establishing transformational policy reforms and building linkages and legitimacy with the relevant national and industry actors over time. This slow, quiet pace has been necessary because of the continued resistance of domestic defense constituencies opposing the formation of an EU defense market. Some in the EDA leadership explicitly cited the relative strength and bargaining power of EU states and their national industry champions as a reason for remaining under the radar and promoting reform from a position of weakness: "we don't want to be the centralized procurement body just yet" because of experiences in defense contracting in states like Sweden, Italy, or Germany, where "the supply side (industry) is strong but the demand side (defense ministry and strategic needs) is weak," which leads to a locked-in imbalance of power between the supply side and the demand side.[102] Officials have worked to maintain strong industry ties but to keep these ties informal.

At an extremely informal level, actors in an agency like the EDA rely on external actors to manage the demands and constraints placed on them. There are many examples of this, but two are about hedging future risk: how will the EDA and its board of defense ministers forecast which technologies, industries, and projects the EU should promote over the next few decades, and how will this forecast be communicated to industry without any centralized R&T or procurement in place? With the latter concern, there are extremely informal arrangements for communicating intent about future strategic and technological direction to the industry. In the political economy of defense, who absorbs the R&T risk of gambling on the future is a key issue. The EDA and its steering board are trying to navigate the balance between their limited authority and their need to project the direction of future industry investments, which has to be communicated to industry to reduce future uncertainty.

In order to communicate over risk and market information, the EDA is in daily consultation with key industry players such as the ASD. The argument for leaning heavily on industry input is "they know the market," and there is no way that the EDA could generate the sort of

---

[101] B. Tigner, "Urgent EDA study investigates CBRN IED responses," *Jane's Defence Systems News*, 2008, accessed September 24, 2009. http://www.janes.com/news/defence/systems/idr/idr081223_1_n.shtml

[102] Author interview with EDA official, November 6, 2007.

bottom-up information about European markets and industry the industry associations can produce. Relying on the decision-making input of interest groups is a risky strategy in the long term. The EDA is a bureaucracy in the public interest, tasked with producing the best value for European defense and security in the future, not the best value for EADS or Honeywell, but it has not developed enough internal capacity to generate this intelligence on its own. The mobilized industry organizations know this; in fact, when asked to provide the EU with a recommendation for the EDA budget at the agency's founding, ASD and other industry representatives proposed a €200 million operational budget for the EDA. The justification for this budget was that the EDA would need to sponsor studies authored by ASD and others to help judge the future of the EU strategic markets and make the correct judgments about risk, investment, and reward. The European Council rejected this budget proposal and gave the EDA an initial operational budget of €6 million. This paltry budget was defended EDA official as a form of informal risk outsourcing:

The defence industry wants us to have a €200 million budget, but that would mean we would just pay them that to plan for the future and their R&T. When our budget is just €6 million, we can't pay anyone anything, and companies who want a piece of the pie in the future have to help us on their own resources, and they have to absorb the planning risks for the eventual EU market on their own, which makes them more invested in the long-term project, and it signals to us then what direction to lead the EU's defence technology and investment. If we formally paid them to tell us what to do, we might not get the right answer. This way we informally farm out long term planning, which we would have to formally contract or – impossibly – build it internally, if we had more resources.[103]

EU officials acknowledge three problems with this strategy. Most importantly, they are aware of the biased, private interests of outside industry actors. However, the key actors believe this boundary can be managed and defended in the future, if necessary: "We will need clearer roles and boundaries within our agencies when we accrete more authority, but until then, an undefined horizontal and vertical power structure with permeable social boundaries will help us build up to that point . . . and all of the formal processes will slow down our institutionalization and rapid capability-building."[104]

Second, the stated role of the EDA is not to simply aggregate capabilities where Europe has existing advantages or shortfalls in the defense industry but to guide the development of European security hardware in long-term planning. This involves absorbing risk from the private sector,

---

[103] Author interview with EDA official, June 2007.
[104] Author interview with EDA official, June 2007.

just as the U.S. Department of Defense had to do as it encouraged the restructuring of the U.S. industry. This means being a developmental or transformational bureaucracy, not simply a regulatory bureaucracy. The organization has to lead a strategy of taking advantage of areas of defense and security innovation that others, including the United States, are too bogged down to exploit. An example of this is the development of UAV technology as a European strategic resource. The development of UAVs as a key area of market development has been promoted by industry associations.

Third, little corporate knowledge accumulates within EU institutions when future risk decisions are informally outsourced. EU bureaucrats are already frustrated by the lack of independent and neutral knowledge and resources at the European level.[105] They have lobbyists and associations clamoring to help them, but the only source of neutral expertise has been organizations or think tanks at the national level. However, these experts do not necessarily know the EU.

The real experts on Europe, possessing far greater corporate knowledge than the bureaucrats, are the industry representatives. In response, EU officials have been actively promoting a think tank culture in Brussels, for sources of high-quality information and post-EU career prospects.[106] Frustrated by the slow, intergovernmental speed of EU defense, some officials argue that if member states discourage an open debate over defense collaboration, then innovative ideas will have to be formulated and vetted outside of the EU – through informal institutions. These can play a crucial role in sparking ideas and in providing solutions to policymakers: informal institutions "become idea brokers to government institutions by providing short and long-term policy studies and seminars."[107]

Nick Witney, the former EDA director, acknowledged that the aggressive, direct tactics of supranational integration pursued by the Commission in the past were often counterproductive to furthering cooperation and integration in the long run:

a change of the overall situation for European defence procurement can [not] be achieved with "dirigiste" measures from Brussels that members states are not

---

[105] In contrast, the perception of industry representatives is that the EU Commissioners and agencies are quick to come to industry for all of their needs, material resources, and policy development but that they are resistant to forging formal partnerships with industry because they know they do not have the comparative advantage (author interview with industry representative, November 2007).

[106] Author interview with EU Commission official, November 2007.

[107] House of Lords European Union Committee, 1st Report of Session 2006–07 "Current Developments in European Defence Policy: Report with Evidence," January 12, 2007.

comfortable with ... the EDA is designed to avoid rivalry and will work toward shared objectives with the Commission in a spirit of partnership ... In the creation of any competitive regime, you would have to be careful to handle the role of governments ... But I also think that there is pretty widespread realisation that actually no national defence market in the EU is any longer sufficient to sustain a national champion ... there is not a single European country that is not in trouble with defence budgets. Whether budgets are increasing or decreasing, they are all faced with the sense that there is not enough money to do what we want to do. The imperative to get greater efficiency is pretty absolute.[108]

While the EDA has been careful not to tread on the sovereignty of national governments and defense ministries to procure a secure defense supply chain, they also see their mission as breaking up the relationship between defense ministries and their national industry champions, whom they see as the ones holding up the integration process. These industries are the less competitive industries protected by the special historical relationship they have to the history of their country's statebuilding. Insiders even refer to this as "facilitating the divorce," which the member states would like to initiate but is politically infeasible at the domestic level. They see themselves as a new institution trying to co-opt and harness all of the existing authorities throughout Europe, but their goal is to minimize any direct threats or turf wars from these authorities.

Industry support has been crucial to the political development of the EDA and to its transformational task of reforming government-market defense relations across Europe by breaking down nationally protected markets. By nature of its task of enhancing defense capabilities and growing the EU defense market, the EDA has had a close and collaborative relationship with defense, aerospace, and electronics industries since its inception. Industry representatives were present before and during the creation of the EDA, eager to begin partnering with the agency and promoting its role and pushing for more agency resources. They created informal institutions before the EU created defense institutions, and the agendas of these formal and informal institutions aligned. While the EDA was created in 2004, a further policy breakthrough happened in the 2009 "defence market package," which was "steered by the defence industry and supported by the rulings of the European Court of Justice."[109] Defense markets are the critical domain of political development and transformational policymaking, rather than the politics of EU

---

[108] "Witney: On a Mission to Stop Defence 'Business as Usual.'"
[109] Mark Bromley, *The EU Defence Market: Balancing Effectiveness with Responsibility*, edited by Alyson J. K. Bailes and Sara Depauw (Brussels: Flemish Peace Institute, 2011), 68.

defense operations. EU defense operations have been relatively insignificant and declining since their inception in the early 2000s. On the
other hand, European defense market issues had informal institutions of
industry actors driving and accelerating EU policies. In the next chapter,
I trace how defense market issues later became intertwined with informal
institutions and interest groups in the immigration and security policy
domain of JHA. And in the concluding chapter, I discuss the blurring of
security and defense agendas as an outcome and implication of the politics of these informal institutions. As the late British diplomat Alyson
Bailes once said, "The real issue is not so much about 'militarization'
of the Union as about an increasingly salient securitization of its entire
identity and image, which the EU as a conscious organism is not yet
equipped to recognize, let alone to handle maturely, and from which the
(C)SDP's small do-gooding adventures can come almost as a relief."[110]

---

[110] Alyson J. K. Bailes, "The EU and a 'Better World': What Role for the European
Security and Defence Policy?," *International Affairs* 84, no. 1 (2008): 119.

6   The Political Development of EU Security

Political Economy and Political Development of JHA

The core of the EU is the common market, now known as the internal market. Its purpose is to eliminate barriers and simplify laws across the EU's four freedoms – the free movement of people, goods, services, and capital. Freedom of movement was codified in a number of treaties, culminating in the transfer of the issue area to EU authority in 1997. In the case of within-Europe migration, the issue of the free movement of people has grown to encompass nearly the entire EU from the small group of Schengen countries that initially established a borderless zone. On the other hand, de facto authority over migration and the legal status of people and workers from outside the EU remains firmly under the control of member states.

The European Commission and institutions such as the Court of Justice have consistently attempted to act on their legal mandate with a liberalizing policy agenda in immigration and asylum policies.[1] EU officials have promoted greater coordination and coherence of all aspects of immigration laws for decades, but very little policy output of any consequence has resulted. The only exceptions to this are minimal progress in asylum policy and more rapid progress in the effort to secure the external physical borders of the EU. The latter accelerated as a response to heightened security concerns after September 2001, as the successful parts of the policy agenda shifted toward tightened border security and increasing restrictions on non-EU citizens and asylum seekers.

Immigration and asylum policy is a controversial and high-profile public policy issue. The borderless flow of people within EU boundaries has exacerbated this problem because any migrant who arrives in any European port of entry may establish residency in other member

---

[1] Since 1958, there has been a directorate in the European Commission Directorate for Employment and Social Affairs called the Free Movement of Workers, Migrant Integration, and Anti-Racism.

states. Although there were fears that the expansion of the EU to East-ern Europe would prompt a massive influx of internal immigration from the East to the West, this has not materialized to the degree feared by policymakers. Instead, there was a massive influx of economic migrants from North Africa, as hundreds of thousands of undocumented refugees fled Afghanistan, Iraq, Sri Lanka, and other war-torn regions.[2] These migrants have settled disproportionately in a few states, such as Italy or Germany, and have led those countries to call for greater burden sharing in the EU over migrant policy. High-profile refugee crises in Mediter-ranean states such as Spain, Malta, and Greece have also raised the pro-file of illegal immigration across the EU and calls for common solutions. Millions of third-country nationals reside across Europe, and the issue of external immigration and border control is an explosive domestic issue within member states.

This free flow of people within Europe effectively externalized the problem of migration to the boundary of the EU. Despite these pres-sures, and despite immigration reform being pushed to the top of the political agenda by the European Commission, there has been little actual harmonization of EU immigration policy. The Commission has generated a number of policy proposals, although all but a handful of these policies have died in the intergovernmental European Council.[3] Of the policies that have been implemented, few have seen success in either legal interpretation or implementation.

The exception is border control policy, where the EU created a supranational agency – Frontex – in 2005 to coordinate the monitor-ing of external EU borders and manage the extradition and return of refugees. Although the EU has failed to implement any effective poli-cies dealing with common third-country national immigration issues, more restrictive policies have succeeded in creating an EU border con-trol policy domain.[4] While the EU has lacked a common migration or immigration policy for attracting skilled workers, establishing quotas, or remittances of asylum seekers, from a very early stage it has devel-oped a "securitized" border policy for criminalizing immigration, which

---

[2] Trauner 2007, 1.

[3] A. Caviedes, "The Open Method of Coordination in Immigration Policy: A Tool for Pry-ing Open Fortress Europe?" *Journal of European Public Policy* 11, no. 2 (2004): 289–310; A. Geddes, "Lobbying for Migrant Inclusion in the European Union: New Opportu-nities for Transnational Advocacy?" *Journal of European Public Policy* 7, no. 4 (2000): 632–49.

[4] T. Givens and A. Luedtke, "The Politics of European Union Immigration Policy: Insti-tutions, Salience, and Harmonization," *The Policy Studies Journal*, 32, no. 1 (2004): 145–65; C. Moraes, "The Politics of European Union Migration Policy," *Political Quarterly* 74, no. 4 (2003): 116–31.

deepened after high-profile terrorist attacks in New York, Madrid, and London.[5]

The relatively new policy issues of asylum, immigration, and border control are part of a broader policy field of EU JHA. The original 1957 Treaty of Rome did not include any language or authority on the coordination of these policies. JHA was launched as an intergovernmental domain in the 1992 Maastricht treaty. The 1997 Treaty of Amsterdam emphasized the need to abolish obstacles to the free movement of people while making internal security an EU objective. Under the Amsterdam Treaty, a large part of cooperation in the field of JHA was subsumed under the Community (supranational) method of decision making and governance. These competencies include areas such as border security, immigration and visa policy, asylum procedures, and rules for judicial cooperation in civil matters. Afterward, the intergovernmental third pillar of JHA covered only police and judicial cooperation in criminal matters. The 2003 Treaty of Nice further Europeanized the policy domain of immigration, asylum, and border security with additional majoritarian decision voting rules. The 2009 Lisbon Treaty substantially supranationalized decision rules by implementing the community method of decision making in many aspects of visa and asylum policy.

According to this timeline of authority in immigration policy from 1992 to 1997, there should have been little private-actor activity when JHA was an intergovernmental policy domain. After 1997, there should have been a subsequent growth of interest groups, when a large part of the agenda-setting power of the domain became supranational in scope. This would mean interest groups, such as immigration rights groups, employers and unions, homeland security industry interests, and other actors with a stake in EU policy outcomes, should have mobilized at the European level in response to the transfer of authority. This did not occur.

Instead of mobilizing, the unions, employers' associations, and business interests effectively ignored the first decade of EU political development, taking seriously only the immigration politics in national capitals. Pro-migrant NGOs mobilized to Brussels but had little interaction with JHA EU officials and agencies. Although it is not puzzling that interest groups sensed the lack of de facto EU authority in immigration affairs (even after 1997), it is notable they maintained their distance and skepticism toward EU institutions, with a more antagonistic than collaborative relationship. As a result, JHA institutions had an initially weak

---

[5] Jef Huysmans, *The Politics of Insecurity: Fear, Migration and Asylum in the EU* (London, UK: Routledge, 2006), 64.

state–society relationship. Although there are many elements to the dynamics of policymaking in EU immigration policy, the weakness of the state–society relationship led to delayed informal institutions in the policy domain, which initially contributed toward low governing capacity in these EU institutions.

This has been rapidly changing. Since 2001, defense interest groups began positioning themselves to take advantage of future EU civilian security markets. The creation of informal security institutions at the EU level has subsequently accelerated EU governing capacity. In the JHA case, the EU already had some formal authority before the industry creation of informal security institutions, but this development accelerated EU governing capacity in JHA institutions, increasing the EU's legitimacy and stature. This has led to major changes in JHA political authority and agendas.

Overview

This chapter traces three phenomena: The first is the development of EU authority in the policy areas of immigration, asylum, and security policy within the justice and home affairs policy domain[6]; the second is the actual policy output and governing capacity of JHA institutions; and the third is an account of the development and mobilization of interest groups in the JHA domain and their relative influence on agenda setting at the EU level.[7]

This analysis represents an unusual line of inquiry, rare in social science case research. It is initially a negative case – one in which standard theories predict a phenomenon should be happening, but the phenomenon is not happening. The EU had some formal authority over immigration policy, but it did not have much governing capacity over immigration policy. The case is an outlier because there was an initial absence and delay of key independent and dependent variables in this case, specifically two phenomena: (1) the development of EU immigration capacity (DV) after the transfer of formal supranational authority to

---

[6] The policy area is called "Freedom, Security, and Justice."

[7] The chapter builds on the insights of a few groundbreaking academic studies, including those of Caviedes ("The Open Method of Coordination in Immigration Policy"); Geddes ("Lobbying for Migrant Inclusion in the European Union"); Virginie Guiraudon, "European Integration and Migration Policy: Vertical Policy-Making as Venue Shopping," *JCMS: Journal of Common Market Studies* 38, no. 2 (2000): 251–71; and Adam Luedtke, "European Integration, Public Opinion and Immigration Policy Testing the Impact of National Identity," *European Union Politics* 6, no. 1 (2005): 83–112. In addition to these analyses of components of the immigration domain, I have used primary sources from EU documents, media reports, NGO and think-tank studies, personal interviews, and open-format survey responses to supplement the analysis.

the EU; and (2) mobilization (IV) and lobbying over issues of immigration, human rights, labor, citizenship, and security policies. Only recently has EU governing capacity been increasing in the domain, and I argue that this occurs only after the mobilization of interest groups toward the domain (laterally, from the defense domain) and the subsequent development of informal institutions in internal civilian security.

The domain of immigration, asylum, and border security policy is a puzzle for scholars and policymakers alike. Specifically, for the first few years of supranational JHA policy (1999–2004), there was very little output, and policy success scholars began to hypothesize why.[8] By 2002, the European Commission had proposed sweeping policy agendas for harmonizing national legislation on legal migration and creating a common European framework for legal migration. The policies included the immigration of reunited family members, a uniform application procedure for migrants seeking employment, a common student and other visa system, and a framework for coordinating the status and responsibility over long-term residents. Many of these policy agendas languished at the European Council and were never discussed or passed.[9]

It would be easy to dismiss this lack of policy success as lack of a mandate in an area fraught with concerns over national sovereignty and control. However, there are other areas of EU policymaking – potentially even more sensitive to national sovereignty concerns, such as monetary policy – where successful EU legislation commenced after the Europeanization of authority. The puzzle is "not simply the languid pace of policy development, but the absence of genuine pressure from below."[10] There was a decade-long delay in mobilization, informal institutional creation, or EU–society interaction after the initial political development of EU immigration policy.

The chapter is organized as follows. First, I introduce the background of the justice and home affairs policy domain, and more specifically immigration, asylum, and border security policy. I then review the history of EU intergovernmental cooperation and supranational authority in the area. Next, I assess the actual policy output, governing capacity, and content of agenda from EU institutions in immigration, asylum, and border control, including the Frontex agency. Finally, I trace interest group preferences first over EU immigration policy, then over EU security policy, including the creation of informal security institutions.

---

[8] See Givens and Luedtke; Luedtke, "European Integration, Public Opinion and Immigration Policy Testing the Impact of National Identity."

[9] Givens and Luedtke.

[10] A. Caviedes, "The Difficult Transition to Transnational Interest Representation: The Case of Immigration Policy," EUSA Conference, March 31–April 2, 2005, 13.

Section 5 identifies the later critical junctures allowing for the deepening of EU authority and JHA institutionalization.

History of Immigration, Asylum, and Border Security as an EU Policy Domain

In the twenty-first century, the EU is a destination for migrants. Before the 1970s, however, Europe was a place people left to seek opportunity and employment elsewhere. Within the course of a few decades, the European continent went from an outward flow of emigrants to an inward flow of immigrants when migrants first moved from the poorer countries of southern Europe to wealthier northern Europe, and individuals from former colonies sought work in Europe. European states had to quickly adapt to these changes, and at the same time began working toward the establishment of a borderless and liberalizing European economic community.

Ad Hoc International Cooperation

The late twentieth-century challenge of the influx of guest workers and migrants motivated European states to cooperate across borders to find solutions, first informally and then increasingly through intergovernmental and supranational EU institutions. States first created ad hoc diplomatic groups to deal with immigration and asylum issues, and also increased informational exchange between police and security forces. The first mention of transnational immigration issues was in the Tindemans Report in 1975, and the first EU-level intergovernmental effort was the Trevi Group formed in 1975 to coordinate state responses to terrorism.[11]

The themes emphasized by European states in the 1980s focused on reducing barriers to migration within Europe, while at the same time managing or restricting immigration from outside Europe. The

---

[11] V. Mitsilegas, J. Monar, and W. Rees, *The European Union and Internal Security: Guardian of the People?* (Basingstoke, UK: Palgrave/Macmillan, 2003), 25. Terrorism in Europe during the 1970s was mostly separatist or ethno-nationalist, but European states were also challenged by international threats from Palestinian hostage and hijacking crises, as well as domestic security crises from domestic terror groups such as the Red Army Faction in Germany and the Red Brigades in Italy. In 1985, the Trevi Group's competencies were extended to illegal immigration and the fight against organized crime. The TREVI Group was the institutional foundation for JHA policy, particularly in matters of counterterrorism (TREVI I), police cooperation (TREVI II), the fight against international crime (TREVI III), and the abolition of borders (TREVI 1992).

first real discussions over the elimination of internal border controls occurred at the European Council meeting in Fontainebleau in June 1984.[12] In 1985, West Germany, France, Belgium, Luxembourg, and the Netherlands created the Schengen Agreement to allow for free movement within internal borders, create common external borders, coordinate immigration issues, harmonize visa policies, and help control immigration in Europe after internal borders came down, and the Schengen partners agreed on the long-term objective of harmonizing visa policies. Intergovernmental groups such as Schengen facilitated voluntary cooperation on immigration and border control, but outside formal EC/EU channels.

With the intergovernmental implementation of the Schengen Agreement, the European Commission initiated its first attempt to frame immigration policy across Europe, issuing a guideline and official decision on liberalizing immigration and access for non-EU migrants.[13] Five member states brought their opposition to the case before the ECJ, and it annulled the decision in 1987. This effectively constrained the Commission's competence to the free movement of EU citizens within EU borders. The Single European Act of 1986 mandated the creation of an internal market without internal frontiers and included a political declaration of intent on the immigration of third-country nationals.[14]

In the 1980s, much of the activity regarding abolishing border controls across Europe took place in the Ad Hoc Group on Immigration (1986), where national representatives negotiated the terms of the 1990 Dublin Convention.[15] In the face of post–Cold War immigration flows, the European Council attempted to harmonize European asylum policy by creating a single adjudication mechanism. The Dublin Convention provided a legal framework for identifying which member state was responsible for being the first to admit an immigrant, as they are the ones responsible for processing a migrant's first asylum claim and future

---

[12] Ariane Chebel d'Appollonia, *Frontiers of Fear: Immigration and Insecurity in the United States and Europe* (Ithaca, NY: Cornell University Press, 2012).

[13] Commission of the European Communities (1985). *Orientations pour une politique communautaire des migrations*, COM(85) 48 def. Brussels: CEC.

[14] K. Nanz, "The Harmonisation of Asylum and Immigration Legislation within the Third Pillar of the Union Treaty – a Stocktaking," in *The Third Pillar of the European Union: Co-operation in the Field of Justice and Home Affairs*, edited by J. Monar and R. Morgan, 123–33 (Bruges: European Interuniversity Press and College of Europe, 1994).

[15] According to the Dublin Convention, a state assumes first asylum status based on the following criteria: (a) if the asylum applicant has a family member who has been recognized as a refugee in that state and is a legal resident there, (b) if the applicant has a valid residence permit in that state, (c) if the applicant has a current or expired visa in that state, and (d) if the applicant crossed the border of that state before entering another state that is a signatory to the Dublin Convention.

claims should the migrant move to another member state. The Dublin Convention took seven years to finally implement in 1997 because of concerns over state sovereignty in immigration and asylum. Dublin was eventually integrated into Title VI – which outlined JHA provisions – of the 1992 Maastricht Treaty.

1992 Maastricht Treaty: Justice and Home Affairs Policy Domain

The 1992 Maastricht Treaty marked the first time JHA policy was an official EU policy area. In Title VI of the Treaty of Maastricht, JHA cooperation is based on nine matters of common interest: asylum, crossing of external borders, immigration, policy relating to nationals of third countries, the fight against drugs and drug addiction, the fight against fraud on an international scale, judicial cooperation in civil matters, judicial cooperation in criminal matters, and customs and police cooperation, including the creation of the EU's law enforcement agency, the European Police Office (Europol).[16] There is also an explicit mention of EU citizenship linked to common rights.

Maastricht mandated the free movement of workers within the EU borders as part of the four freedoms of the EU, mandating the free movement of goods, capital, services, people, and labor within the internal market of the EU. This created a problem, however, regarding the status of legal worker or asylum-seeking third-party nationals within the EU. Once someone was admitted to one state, he or she could now travel to any other country in the EU. Having asylum and immigration policy decentralized was problematic, but Maastricht left this authority with member states, requiring constant ad hoc solutions.[17] JHA immigration policy was limited to unanimous intergovernmental cooperation in the areas of asylum and reciprocal recognition of transit visas.

In the early 1990s, the European Commission had no supranational agenda-setting authority over immigration policy – it was still firmly entrenched in the Pillar III area of intergovernmental politics – but that did not stop European Commission officials from attempting to frame a policy agenda in the area. In 1994, Immigration Commissioner Padraig Flynn presented a report chastising national governments for not harmonizing or accelerating their immigration processes, concluding that the 10 million legal residents of the EU should enjoy the same

---

[16] N. Nugent, *The Government and Politics of the European Union*, 4th ed. (Basingstoke, UK: Palgrave, 2003), 68.

[17] T. Kostakopoulou, "The 'Protective Union': Change and Continuity in Migration Law and Policy in Post-Amsterdam Europe," *Journal of Common Market Studies* 38, no. 3 (2000): 497–518.

rights, freedoms, and benefits as citizens of member states. The report also addressed the issue of asylum policy for the additional 10 million refugees across Europe. The commissioner rationalized that such as policy would "benefit the Union... and deal with all of the asylum applications that are being made – half a million of them – and the 10 million legally resident third-country legals that are living here and do not have, in my opinion, the sufficiently wide range of rights that we should give them."[18] In addition to the efficiency rationale, the Commission report also underscored the demographic rationale to immigration policy, that smart and coordinated immigration could be an important source of economic growth for an aging European population.

Transnational NGOs applauded the 1994 report, but saw it as an impossible goal. The spokesman of the NGO Caritas said:

there is not much hope that (the proposals) will go anywhere as long as this is a matter for the council of ministers to decide... they are motivated by public opinion and re-election concerns... but without a clear European immigration policy we won't be able to fight xenophobia, which is rooted in ignorance, fear and the impression that the government doesn't control the phenomena.[19]

The Commission's proposal died in the Council of Ministers under the opposition of national justice ministers. Observers cited the role of Germany in the deterioration of the proposal, after two German commissioners delayed the report and their ministers voted against it due to German laws limiting citizenship to individuals with German ancestry.

With few exceptions, this is the story of EU immigration policy agendas, particularly policy over non-EU citizens or third country nationals. Even after surprising and significant transfers of formal treaty authority to the EU in the late 1990s and after, this is still the norm. The intergovernmental Council of Ministers repeatedly failed to consider endless Commission initiatives of policy directives and legislation. The Commission has had little agenda-setting success in this area, even though it has had significant formal authority in the area. I propose that this has to do with the lack of social partners, informal institutions, and state–society relations in the domain.

From the beginning, an interest group community of pro-migrant NGOs was active in Brussels but acted as an observer and distant critic for years. This distance and antagonism has only increased with the more

---

[18] M. Evans, "EU Offers Immigrants Glimmer of Hope Report Urges Granting Legal Residents Same Rights and Freedoms as Citizens," *The Globe and Mail (Canada)*, February 24, 1994.

[19] Ibid.

recent (2005–) intensive activity of the EU in the operations of enforc-
ing and coordinating border security. More NGOs have mobilized post
2005, but in opposition and protest to EU immigration policy agendas. Other organized interests, such as employers' associations and labor
unions, have been conspicuously absent or silent over EU immigration
policy. These are the very actors that have been powerful social partners mobilized to assist EU officials in framing, legislating, and implementing policy in other key policies relevant to labor or capital interests. Some of the most influential non-EU actors in Brussels have been
national bureaucrats, representatives of national justice ministries promoting restrictionist policies in Brussels that would not survive domestic
democratic scrutiny. They have created expert groups closely advising
EU officials as their mandate and resources have grown. Most recently,
the armaments and security industry has crossed over to support the
development of EU border security policy, developing informal institutions and policy expertise that has not existed before.

Whereas the narrative on the legal immigration and asylum of non-
EU citizens stagnated for two decades at the EU level, the history of EU
external border security policy has been very different. Observers recall
an acceleration of the border security policy agenda as a response to the
September 2001 terrorist attacks, as a "securitization" of immigration
policy in the EU.[20] EU border security policy accelerated after September 11, 2001, but it was not the cause of the shift in agenda.[21] Ever since
ideas of an internal border-free Europe were formed, many observers
anticipated that the consequence of greater internal freedom would be
starker external border security.

Observers since the early 1990s predicted that internal liberalization would externalize the security issue to the EU border. In particular, NGOs such as Amnesty International and the European Citizen
Action Service (ECAS) sounded an early alarm about the future implications of the 1995 Schengen Convention,[22] predicting the implementation of the Schengen agreement would inevitably clamp down on asylum

---

[20] J. Huysmans, "The EU and the Securitization of Migration," *Journal of Common Market Studies* 38, no. 5 (2000): 751–78.
[21] d'Appollonia.
[22] The Treaty of Rome (1957) committed member states to allow freedom of movement for citizens across internal borders. However, the European Community made only limited progress on this policy in the first thirty-five years of its history. As a result, governments in France, West Germany, Belgium, Luxembourg, and the Netherlands decided to pursue the policy separately, resulting in the 1985 Schengen Agreement. Schengen became an EU Convention in 1995 and then expanded to include all original EU member states (except the UK and Ireland), plus Norway, Iceland, and Switzerland as signatories.

seekers, making it more difficult to request asylum because third-country nationals would need valid documents to enter the boundaries of Schengen territory.[23] This automatically removed any mechanism for refugees seeking asylum relief through approaching an embassy inside an EU Schengen state. Additional security measures such as the computerized Schengen Information System (SIS) on undesirable asylum seekers or countries were indications of the restrictive direction EU policy cooperation that followed in the next decade.

Almost immediately after the implementation of the Schengen Convention, pro-migrant groups such as the European Council on Refugees and Exiles (ECRE) began documenting how EU law accelerated asylum deportation. Because of the lack of a centralized asylum application or humane deportation mechanism, ECRE argued the EU was in violation of the 1951 Geneva Convention principle of "non refoulement" (anti-exclusion) entitling refugees to "fair and efficient refugee status determination procedure."[24]

Treaty of Amsterdam: Formal EU Authority over Asylum and Immigration

The Treaty of Amsterdam marked a turning point in the political development of JHA policy. It was negotiated in 1997 and implemented in 1999. The Amsterdam Treaty transferred the matters of immigration and asylum from the third intergovernmental pillar (JHA) to the Community pillar, subordinated to the supranational principle. These decisions would not continue to be made by nation states beyond 2004. Supranational policies included illegal immigration and illegal residence, rights and conditions under which nationals of third countries may reside in other member states, standards on procedures for issuing long-term visas and residence permits, and conditions of entry and residence within the EU.[25] Amsterdam also incorporated the 1985 Schengen Agreement into the EU Treaty, meaning the border-free Schengen zone was no longer intergovernmental but a supranational EU institution.

Although EU immigration law was binding after Amsterdam, there was still a degree of national control where member states had unanimous voting procedures in the European Council and the European

---

[23] B. Borst and D. Percival, "Europe-Immigration: Schengen Accord Is Bad News for Asylum Seekers," *IPS-Inter Press Service*, March 24, 1995.

[24] D. Percival, "Refugees: Report Exposes Myth of Europe as a Safe Place for Asylum," *IPS-Inter Press Service*, February 22, 1995.

[25] T. Palomar, "Migration Policies of the European Union," in *The Politics of Immigration in the EU*, edited by Jochen Blaschke (Berlin: Parabolis, 2004), 4.

Parliament did not have veto over immigration policy.[26] The Amsterdam Treaty outcome was a surprising turn of events, given the previous reluctance of member states to relinquish any control over immigration policy. At least one analysis of the negotiation claimed the radical changes to JHA features were snuck past national officials by Commission negotiators confusing them with 3,000 pages of regulations over the incorporation of the Schengen Convention, with the rest of the dramatic changes to JHA policy embedded within the technicalities.[27]

The Commission immediately interpreted its first pillar right of initiative under Amsterdam on asylum policy and began proposing major policy initiatives. In 1998, it created proposals for joint actions on the temporary protection of displaced persons, the integration of refugees into the EU, and burden sharing of refugee costs between member states.[28] In 1999, the Commission adopted a European refugee fund from its own budget to support and encourage member states to receive refugees. The fund covers reception, integration, and voluntary repatriation measures, divided across member states by the number of refugees accommodated.[29]

At the 1999 special European Council in Tampere, Finland, member states agreed to create a common EU migration policy agenda in line with the Geneva Convention by May 2004.[30] The five-year agenda became known as the area of freedom, security, and justice (AFSJ). The short-term goals were a clear designation of the state responsible for examining an asylum application, common standards for fair and efficient asylum procedures, and common minimum conditions of reception. The long-term goals were to create a common asylum system and legal status for refugees throughout the EU.[31] The European Commission introduced an institutional mechanism in the form of a six-month scoreboard of policy progress in the domain.

[26] Geddes, "Lobbying for Migrant Inclusion in the European Union."
[27] V. Guiraudon, "The Constitution of a European Immigration Policy Domain: A Political Sociology Approach," *Journal of European Public Policy* 10, no. 2 (2003): 270.
[28] European Council on Refugees and Exiles, September 1, 1998; Bulletin of the European Communities, December 1998, 1.4.4; Bulletin of the European Communities, December 1998, 1.2.25.
[29] Bulletin of the European Communities, December 1999, 1.5.8.
[30] Paragraph 21 of the Presidency Conclusions of the Tampere European Council, October 15–16, 1999, SN 200/99: "A person who has resided legally in a Member State for a period of time to be determined and who holds a long-term residence permit, should be granted in that Member State a set of uniform rights which are as near as possible to those enjoyed by EU citizens."
[31] Bulletin of the European Communities, October 1999, I.4; Bulletin of the European Communities, October 1999, I.1.

In the years 1999 to 2004, the Commission responded to this increased authority by generating a thorough policy agenda for creating a common legal immigration framework and EU citizenship and integration rights, complete with a number of policy proposals over these issues. These included directives over the status and rights of long-term resident migrants, issues of reunification of family members inside and outside the EU, and the centralization of visa and asylum applications. After 2000, the EU initiatives on migration pursued three main directions: broadening the rights provided for third-country nationals, urging on the adoption of integration policies for migrants, and undertaking long-term measures on migration.

Of all these Commission initiatives, only one became EU legislation: the European Directive on the Right of Family Return. It specified the right of residence – but not citizenship – for family members of resident third-country nationals in cases of family reunification. This policy also marked the beginning of more open and intense relations between the Commission's DG (JHA, now DG Justice, Freedom, and Security) and civil society or nongovernmental organizations. In the early agenda-setting stage of the treaty negotiations, NGOs such as the Migration Policy Group drafted proposals for directives in family reunification; consequently, they were invited to help draft directive outlines in public–private meetings and were generally considered valuable experts and partners.[32] After negotiations with the Council significantly watered down the original ideas, the proposal stalled anyway, and the Commission had to draft two new proposals over the next two years. The final adopted proposal in 2002 abandoned the idea of the harmonization of national laws and instead adopted a minimum standards approach, generally a lower degree of regulation than what most member states already had as law. NGOs were incensed that nearly all of their input had been abandoned in favor of the lowest common denominator, in this case, by defining the family as only heterosexual marriage and not children, parents, or siblings. NGOs battled to annul the law, but in 2006, the ECJ ruled that any appeals of the law were unfounded.

The Commission continued to promote a common immigration framework, proposing a proactive rather than restrictive immigration policy for streamlining legal immigration across Europe and coordinating labor market needs through immigration.[33] Similarly, the

---

[32] J. Niessen, "Overlapping Interests and Conflicting Agendas: The Knocking into Shape of EU Immigration Policies," *European Journal of Migration and Law* 3, no. 3 (2001): 422.

[33] Caviedes, "The Open Method of Communication in Immigration Policy."

Commission proposed that immigration policy be more holistic, taking into account issues of "employment, economic participation, education, language training, health, and social services, housing, town planning, culture and involvement in social life."[34] Although none of these proposals were successfully legislated, in 2004, the Council adopted a directive defining the conditions for recognition of refugee status and establishing refugee rights, and the Council agreed to a list of "safe transit countries" and "safe countries of origin" to which asylum seekers could be returned pending examination of their application.[35]

Agenda Post-2001: Emphasis on Security?

Apart from the 2002 Family Return and 2004 Asylum Directives, the majority of the legislation successfully implemented by the Council increasingly fell under the area of protectionist border security and anti–illegal immigration measures. To harmonize asylum policy, the Council initiated an automated European Data Archive Collection (EURODAC) for fingerprinting refugees, to be centralized and administered by the Commission and not member states.[36] Another EU measure was an image archiving system for centralizing electronic citizenship and identity papers to avoid immigration fraud.[37] Overall, the measures actually adopted were regarding further restrictions or surveillance of immigration policy, and the rest of the initiatives and legislation were ignored in the Council.[38]

In December 2003, the EU adopted the ESS – intended to address external security and defence – with a number of implications for the JHA domain. Mass terrorism and organized crime were among the threats explicitly mentioned in the first ESS. Part of the way the EU interpreted

safeguard[ing] its internal security [was] based on a comprehensive approach that included: closer police cooperation at European level, centralized collection of data by means of the Schengen Information System, a transversal policy

---

[34] J. Apap and S. Carrera, "Towards a proactive immigration policy for the EU." *CEPS Working Document*, 2003, 3.
[35] Council of the European Union, "Living in an Area of Freedom, Security and Justice," January 1, 2005, 27.
[36] Bulletin of the European Communities, January–February 1998.
[37] Bulletin of the European Communities, December 1998, 1.4.8.
[38] Communication from the Commission to the Council and the European Parliament, Biannual Update of the Scoreboard to review progress on the creation of an area of "Freedom, Security and Justice" in the European Union, first half of 2003, Brussels, 22.5.2003, COM(2003) 291 final.

to combat drugs, a global policy against trafficking in human beings and illegal immigration, integrated management of EU external borders, a strong fight against international terrorism, and close cooperation with third countries.[39]

The domain of immigration and asylum became increasingly subsumed by policies addressing internal security and the control of threats across borders. The progressive, human rights aspects of immigration policy had not been successful EU policies, but the regressive, threat control aspects were passing through the Council and Parliament successfully.

These developments have led scholars and analysts to claim that EU legislation – instead of liberalizing immigration and asylum law – has actually strengthened external border control, restricted immigration rights to the lowest common member-state denominator, and promoted the securitization of immigration policy overall.[40] Scholars and policymakers alike have claimed that the EU started down a path of liberalizing migrant policy and then shifted after 2001 to a more restrictive common policy emphasizing the security threats and criminality of migrants, with an emphasis on border security and crime. They have differentiated positive from negative immigration legislation, where positive legislation focuses on a common framework for legal immigrants and refugees, while negative legislation emphasizes migration restrictions. Policymakers claim the EU would have been on a path toward a rational immigration policy incorporating negative controls with positive incentives had the focus not changed so overwhelmingly to security. A think-tank expert recalled taking part in an EU committee reviewing the harmonization of EU rules, including the possibility of immigrants being allowed to move around the Union. She claimed, "the focus was on aging in Europe and how Europe would need specialized labor . . . then September 11 struck. We were told funding would be cut and that we would now be having a conference on security. The need for immigration went on the back burner."[41]

This narrative about the critical juncture of September 11 contrasts with prescient but sensational media accounts from as early as 1993, with titles such as *"Secret plans for brave new world of EU security; New intelligence networks will be well beyond the reach of elected officials."*[42] The

---

[39] Council of the European Union, "Living in an Area of Freedom, Security and Justice," January 1, 2005, 28.

[40] D. Bigo, *Polices en reseaux: l'experience européenne* (Paris, France: Presses de Sciences Politique, 1996); Huysmans, "The EU and the Securitization of Migration."

[41] T. Fuller, "Foreign Workers Face Turning Tide; Backlash in Europe," *The International Herald Tribune*, December 25, 2002, 1.

[42] L. Doyle, "Secret Plans for Brave New World of EU Security; New Intelligence Networks Will Be Well Beyond the Reach of Elected Officials," *The Independent (London)*, November 12, 1993, 12.

article described the meeting of the K4 Committee – a group of national security and interior ministers – two days after the Maastricht Treaty took effect, to "inaugurate an era of unprecedented inter-governmental co-operation on security matters in the new EU."[43] The committee was described as outside the democratic control of the European Parliament and national parliaments but with broad agenda-setting powers to coordinate the fight against drug trafficking, money laundering, illegal immigration, and asylum. The committee's agenda included preventing additional refugee migration from Bosnia, coordinating migrant expulsions, EURODAC, and an immigration database (European Information Service). The reporter claimed the committee's agenda was "to be rubberstamped by justice ministers at the end of the month," and, in retrospect, much of what was on the agenda of the committee became EU policy.[44]

A pre–September 11 securitization narrative can be found as early as 1991, when the Trevi Group held a special meeting to brainstorm and demonstrate resolve "due to the terrorist threats caused recently by Iraqi leader Saddam Hussein, of terrorist actions in the Western Europe in coming days."[45] The Minister of Justice from Luxemburg, Marc Fischbach, presided over an emergency meeting of EC justice ministers to order tightened security at "airports, seaports, border check points, especially on foreigners from non-EC countries. The European community nations are reinforcing their security control on their common borders against increasing threats of terrorism, radicalism, extremism and international violence."[46] The idea of a boundary between Europe and non-Europe within a framework of security and threat is nothing new: it existed before the EU was even founded in 1992.

The EU accelerated this negative legislation over positive legislation at the Seville (2002) and Thessaloniki (2003) summits. At the Thessaloniki summit, ministers adopted a Commission proposal to locate asylum detention centers outside the EU's borders, in places such as Albania, Libya, or elsewhere in Northern Africa.[47] At the Seville summit, immigration was high on the agenda and national leaders "invoked populist electoral breakthroughs in various European elections to step up the fight against illegal migration."[48] At Seville, the UK and Spain proposed EU legislation linking punitive measures such as trade sanctions or aid

---

[43] Ibid.   [44] Ibid.
[45] "EC Nations Strengthening Border Security Control," *Central News Agency – Taiwan*, January 24, 1991, accessed May 6, 2010.
[46] Ibid.
[47] "'Balkan Summit' Agenda Set," *EU Observer*, accessed May 5, 2010. http://EUObserver/?aid=11666
[48] Guiraudon, "The Constitution of a European Immigration Policy Domain," 264.

reductions to foreign refusal to accept rejected asylum-seekers.[49] Sweden and France opposed the plan to link development aid to immigration, which was also contested by the Commission, arguing that economically punishing states that created migrant crises might only exacerbate such crises in the future.[50] Less punitive measures were adopted, but the policies still involved aid incentives for non-EU states to stem the flow of immigrants to the EU.

In November 2003, the Council decided to create an external borders agency charged with helping member states harmonize external borders and operations. At the Thessaloniki summit, EU states agreed to establish the Frontex agency to coordinate and police the external borders of the EU. Frontex became operational in 2005. In 2007, the EU formed a border guard corps called Rapid Border Intervention Teams (RABITs) and a European training institute for border guards. The RABIT mechanism "aims to provide rapid operational assistance for a limited period of time to a requesting Member State facing a situation of urgent and exceptional pressure at points of the external borders."[51] This pool of border guards consists of 600 officers. Frontex and RABIT have been used by critics as further evidence that EU immigration policy shifted toward a "fortress Europe" mentality after the terrorist attacks in New York, London, and Madrid in the early 2000s, but others argued Frontex is "a logical continuation of the integration process and the principle of free internal movement in the EU, although this does not completely discount the security dimension."[52]

In 2004, the EU member states agreed to increase the role of the EU in immigration policy with the negotiation of the Hague Treaty. Hague included a timeline for meeting legislative and operational objectives on migration for the next five years (until 2009) in order to strengthen freedom, security, and justice in the EU. It again mandated the creation of a common asylum system and status based on common asylum procedures, internal and external borders of the EU, and more efficient migration management through strengthening the fight against illegal migration and human trafficking. Since May 2004, the European

---

[49] "EU Plans to Sanction Countries over Immigration," *EU Observer*, accessed May 5, 2010. http://EUObserver/?aid=6623

[50] "Immigration and EU Reforms to Top Seville Agenda," *EU Observer*, accessed May 5, 2010. http://EUObserver/?aid=6596

[51] Commission of the European Communities, Third annual report on the development of a common policy on illegal immigration, smuggling and trafficking of human beings, external borders, and the return of illegal residents, Brussels, 9.3.2009 SEC(2009)320 final. p. 4.

[52] A. W. Neal, "Securitization and Risk at the EU Border: The Origins of FRONTEX," *Journal of Common Market Studies* 47, no. 2 (2009): 333–56.

Commission has had an exclusive right of legislative initiative in matters of JHA under the community pillar. It introduced qualified majority voting in the intergovernmental European Council, effectively eliminating any member-state vetoes over illegal immigration and border control policy. It also gave the European Parliament codecision power with the European Commission, meaning Parliament could propose policy amendments and veto Commission legislation. Although Hague de facto supranationalized all aspects of asylum policy to the EU level, legal migration policy, including the status of legal resident third-country nationals, family reunification, and economic or skilled labor migration, remained at the national level of authority.

The Commission did not stop trying to promote its positive immigration agenda, including the attempt to centralize legal immigration in the EU, particularly of talented international labor. In January 2005, the European Commission issued the *Green Paper on Managed Migration* at the EU level. This policy proposal was meant to address labor or skills gaps in member states and streamline the process of employer access to skilled labor from abroad. It also addressed whether economic and social rights should be granted to migrant workers according to their length of stay and on what basis should they be issued a green card (similar to the American system): whether immediately on fulfillment of certain criteria or only to the renewal of an existing long-term permission. The Commission's attempt to seize the policy agenda on the legal migration of economic migrants was justified by the demographic crisis of the EU labor market, where Europe's workforce was projected to decline by 20 million between 2010 and 2030.[53]

Although the Green Paper policy proposal also stagnated, the Commission proposed a Blue Card legislation modeled after the U.S. Green Card in 2009,[54] allowing third-country nationals to have mobility within the EU and apply for permanent residence after five years in the EU. The proposal successfully passed through the Parliament and the Council, but the end legislation was highly restrictive, allowing national quotas, denying benefits under labor market scarcity, requiring permanent residents to wait eighteen months before moving within the EU, and requiring that they hold an employment contract for a minimum salary of 1.5 times the national average.

National politicians were growing aware of the unintended consequences of their lack of an EU mechanism for attracting skilled foreign labor. An opinion piece on this issue complained that "the lack of

---

[53] The European Commission, 2005. Green Paper on Managing Economic Migration.
[54] Council of European Communities, 2009.

attractive legal migration options to Europe has ensured that 85 percent of the world's best brains go to America and Australia, put off by Europe's bureaucracy and inflexibility, while most migrants who actually reach our shores have few, if any, qualifications."[55] Observers noted a severe lack of visible interest-group activity over these policies. The only forms of input were protest statements from international human rights NGOs, with little expert advice from the industries that would benefit from better international talent, such as the electronics, health, or pharmaceuticals industries.[56] The source of the EU immigration agenda is unclear: some think tanks suspect that the Commission has been generating empty proposals, designed to fail and embarrass national governments on immigration policy. Other NGOs allege that the Commission might be influenced by industry actors benefiting from keeping the dysfunctional EU immigration as it stands (in violation of the Geneva Convention), such as the agricultural and hospitality industries depending on the cheapest forms of labor.

The 2009 Lisbon Treaty eliminated the pillar system of EU decision making and legally incorporated all areas of migration policy – both legal immigration and asylum – to qualified majority voting rules and codecision procedures. It strengthened JHA agencies such as Frontex and Europol, the police cooperation body. It mandated an EU-wide "internal security strategy," focusing on the division of labor between Brussels and national capitals in counterterrorism, border management, civil protection, and judicial cooperation in criminal matters, with the "internal security" body (the Standing Committee on Internal Security [COSI]) within the Council of the EU for implementation and coordination.[57] It also included a Charter of Fundamental Rights of Citizens, which had been proposed by the French presidency in December 2000.[58]

Organized Interest Groups and Immigration Policy

What has been the interest group response to EU JHA policies of immigration, asylum, and border security? Have they mobilized to Brussels with each increase in EU treaty authority? What is the public–private relationship in European immigration policy, including the creation of

---

[55] "It's Time Europe Joined the Dots on Migration," *EU Observer*, accessed April 4, 2010. http://EUObserver/?aid=25937

[56] Author interviews with migration and humanitarian NGOs, May–June 2008.

[57] V. Pop, "Europe Moves toward Single Area on Justice and Home Affairs," *EU Observer*, December 12, 2009, accessed May 5, 2010. http://EUObserver/?aid=29139

[58] Council of the European Union, Living in an Area of Freedom, Security and Justice, January 1, 2005.

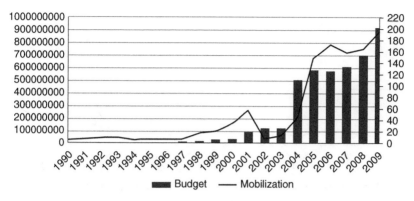

Figure 6.1 Organized Interests and EU Appropriations in Immigration, Asylum, and Border Security Policy Domain (*Sources: EU Annual Report and Landmarks Public Affairs Directories*)

informal institutions? The next few sections describe the mobilization, policy preferences, access, and influence of the various interest groups, including pro-migrant NGOs, labor unions and employer associations, bureaucrats and experts from national interior and justice ministries, and industries and associations from the electronics and border security industry.

Figure 6.1 depicts the overall mobilization of organized interests in the domain, juxtaposed with the appropriations in the areas of immigration, asylum, and border control. On the right axis is the number of organized interests; on the left axis is the budget in euros. With the background information on the history of the domain, the figure tells an interesting story. Although there were a few high-profile organized interests in Brussels in the early and mid-1990s, particularly international pro-migrant NGOs, there was almost no advocacy in the domain, with fewer than ten groups involved in the area. Organized interest groups also did not mobilize in anticipation of the 1997 Amsterdam Treaty. This is logical, as this historical record indicated that the developments in JHA policy came as a surprise to many actors, including the national officials negotiating the treaty. Pro-migrant NGOs, as detailed in the next section, were aware that there was a window of opportunity for change but became disillusioned with the Commission's intentions and abilities to promote their preferences. After 1997, the interest group population increased in response to greater EU authority fivefold, in a classic "if you build it, they will come" scenario. This was in lieu of the EU acquiring any substantial resources in the domain, indicating that the authority of Amsterdam

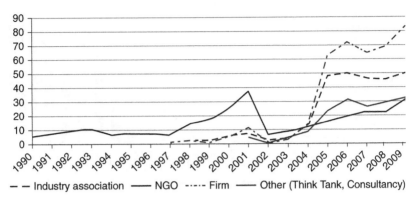

Figure 6.2 Immigration Domain Mobilization by Organization Type (*Source: Landmarks Public Affairs Directories*)

was empty, as became clear in the next few years. This scenario would have been a great opportunity for collaboration between the European Commission and organized interests, with the Commission possessing treaty authority but insufficient internal resources and capacity. Social partners and advocates could have helped craft better policies, read the political environment better than EU bureaucrats, and play two-level games between national capitals and Brussels in negotiations. Instead, there have been minimal interactions between the EU and these groups, as documented in this section. Figure 6.1 indicates an actual demobilization of organized interests as the EU proved ineffective in harnessing its authority into policy outcomes.

The jump in resources from 2003 to 2004 is an indication of the additional resources spent on the creation of Frontex and border security measures. Organized interests have responded to this shift in resources, but the interest groups are different: they are representatives of the security industry that is an important partner of the EU in developing border and internal security measures. This can be seen in Figure 6.2, where the distribution of organized interests is disaggregated into NGOs, industry associations, firms, and other groups such as consultancies or think tanks. NGOs are the first on the scene, and they mobilized and demobilized in response to the increase in EU authority after 1997. The large mobilization after 2003 is in the form of firms, industry associations, and consultancies for the electronics and security industries. In 2004, there was still parity between nonprofit NGOs and for-profit firms and industry associations mobilized in the domain. The for-profit population increased sevenfold in two years and continues to rise dramatically. By

2009, there were three for-profit mobilized interest groups for every one NGO.

History of NGO Mobilization in EU Immigration Policy

Generally, NGOs with a stake in defending the rights of immigrants and refugees across Europe have placed a great deal of hope in the EU to legislate in support of the free movement of persons. They have lobbied the EU to liberalize migrant policy and create a strong counterweight to any anti-immigration sentiments or laws in member states.[59] NGOs cite the Bosnian War refugee crisis as the impetus leading them to seek EU-level solutions to immigration problems, although most of their lobbying over the issue was mobilized toward national capitals.[60] International NGOs such as Pax Christie, Amnesty International, and the International Red Cross were vocal in calling for a common EU asylum policy in the aftermath of the Balkan wars.[61] In addition to national, European, and international human rights groups, other groups campaigning for migrant rights include church groups and groups of immigrants themselves.[62] Their focus is on individuals immigrating from outside of the EU, specifically asylum seekers, refugees, detainees, and migrants.

One of the first migrant NGOs was the European Union Migrants Forum (EUMF), a forum for migrants themselves explicitly created by the European Commission in 1991 in response to a Parliament Committee of Inquiry into racism and xenophobia.[63] The main motivation for the Commission was to "increase Commission's legitimacy as spokesperson for civil society by engineering an official channel of interest representation."[64] The EUMF suffered from major internal divisions

---

[59] Patrick R. Ireland, "Asking for the Moon: The Political Participation of Immigrants in the European Union," in *The Impact of European Integration: Political, Sociological, and Economic Changes*, edited by George A. Kourvetaris and Andreas Moschonas, 131–50 (Westport, CT: Praeger, 1996); Adrian Favell, "Citizenship and Immigration: Pathologies of a Progressive Philosophy," *Journal of Ethnic and Migration Studies* 23, no. 2 (1997): 173–95; Jan Niessen, "The Amsterdam Treaty and NGO Responses," *European Journal of Migration and Law* 2, no. 2 (2000): 203–14.

[60] European Council on Refugees and Exiles, September 1, 1998.

[61] Agence France-Presse, September 1, 1992; European Council on Refugees and Exiles, March 1996; European Council on Refugees and Exiles, March 1, 1997; European Council on Refugees and Exiles, March 1997; Agence Europe, October 25, 1995.

[62] Geddes, "Lobbying for Migrant Inclusion in the European Union," 638; E. Gray and P. Statham, "Becoming European? The Transformation of the British Pro-Migrant NGO Sector in Response to Europeanization," *JCMS: Journal of Common Market Studies* 43, no. 4 (2005): 877–98.

[63] European Parliament, *Report of the Committee of Inquiry on Racism and Xenophobia* (Brussels: OOPEC, 1991).

[64] Guiraudon, "De-nationalizing Control," 8.

reflecting migrants' backgrounds, nationalities, and differences in the purpose of the forum. The EUMF's main lobbying goal has been to incorporate uniform citizenship rights for third-country nationals. In the lead-up to the Amsterdam Treaty, the EUMF drafted an amendment of Article 8a of the EU Treaty to read: "Citizenship of the Union is hereby established. Every person holding a nationality of a member state or who has been lawfully residing in the territory of a member state for five years shall be a citizen of the Union."[65] This was not considered in the negotiation. Instead, the treaty article asserted exclusive citizenship rights for member-state nationals, reading: "Citizenship of the Union is hereby established. Every person holding the nationality of a Member State shall be a citizen of the Union. Citizenship of the Union shall complement and not replace national citizenship."[66]

Since the late 1990s, the main pro-migrant lobby groups active at the EU level were the Starting Line Group, EUMF, and the ECRE.[67] Of these, the Starting Line Group was the largest lobbying umbrella for hundreds of smaller NGOs. These pro-migrant groups have been highly visible in Brussels for years but have had a less than effective record in gaining access or influence on major EU treaties or policy decisions.[68] The only NGO with a major agenda-setting victory is the Starting Line Group, in successfully drafting and lobbying for the incorporation of a race directive adopted by the European Council in 2000 into the EU Treaty.[69]

Similarly, the NGO/think tank Migration Policy Group influenced the EU over a few minor issues related to immigration policy, such as promoting the inclusion of an antidiscrimination clause in the Amsterdam Treaty. One of the reasons given for this success was that the Migration Policy Group only had established access and ties with the Social Affairs Directorate (DG V) of the Commission, and an antidiscrimination

---

[65] Geddes, "Lobbying for Inclusion in the European Union," 9.
[66] Article 8a [I], Amsterdam Treaty 1999
[67] Geddes, "Lobbying for Inclusion in the European Union."
[68] A. Favell and A. Geddes, "Immigration and European Integration: New Opportunities for Transnational Mobilization?," in *Challenging Immigration and Ethnic Relations Politics: Comparative European Perspectives*, edited by R. Koopmans and P. Statham, 407–28 (New York, NY: Oxford University Press, 2000); Guiraudon, "European Integration and Migration Policy."
[69] This was established by Chopin and Niessen, who conducted a content analysis comparison between the Commission's proposed directive with that of the Starting Line Group and demonstrated the strong similarities between the documents (I. Chopin and J. Niessen, "Combating Racism in the European Union with Legal Means: A Comparison of the Starting Line and the EU Commission's Proposal for a Race Directive" [Brussels: Migration Policy Group, 2000]).

policy agenda was the result of their collaborative public–private effort.[70] These cases of access and influence are the exception rather than the rule. Scholars puzzle over why pro-migrant groups have been relatively ineffective in projecting influence over the EU agenda, but it may be a combination of EU weakness and opacity in the policy domain combined with the fact that these groups are often underresourced and not products of their domestic lobbying establishments but are instead entirely transnational entities.

In the late 1990s, NGOs in favor of refugee rights had high expectations that the EU would legislate a more humanitarian asylum policy. The Tampere agreements of 1999 resulted in legally binding EU agreements on asylum policy, but there was little effect until after 2004, with the beginning of the harmonization of national laws. In the lead-up to the 1997 Amsterdam Treaty and 2003 Nice Treaty, interest groups generally failed to mobilize and put little pressure on member states and EU officials.[71] Pro-refugee NGOs were "skeptical of a Community competence in those areas for a long time, as member governments did for many years play a two level game, putting forward more restrictive policies, while putting the blame for such policies on Brussels."[72] Groups such as the ECRE attempted to monitor the negotiations leading up to the treaty but were unsuccessful in establishing any social ties with the negotiators or bureaucrats. They were also angry about the outcomes of the treaties, arguing the treaties simply made policymaking more opaque and removed from national checks and balances, without incorporating supranational checks and balances.[73]

Another reason for the distance between NGOs and European officials might have been due to the organizational restructuring of the Commission after the Maastricht Treaty. From 1958 to 1992, DG V had been responsible for policy regarding the free movement of labor within the EU (migrants, refugees, and racism). Because this DG had no authority over third-country national policy, a small and insulated task force was set up to deal with these policy issues and liaise with the Council.[74]

[70] Author interviews with representatives from the Migration Policy Group and former European Commission officials, May 2008.

[71] Arne Niemann, "Dynamics and Countervailing Pressures of Visa, Asylum and Immigration Policy Treaty Revision: Explaining Change and Stagnation from the Amsterdam IGC to the IGC of 2003–04," *JCMS: Journal of Common Market Studies* 46, no. 3 (2008): 559–91.

[72] Ibid.

[73] European Council on Refugees and Exiles, "Analysis of the Treaty of Amsterdam in so far as it Relates to Asylum Policy" (Brussels: ECRE, 1997).

[74] Guiraudon, "European Integration and Migration Policy," 13.

While the DG V had extensive contacts with NGOs, the task force had none. The task force director argued that interaction with NGOs was unnecessary because one needs to be a "realist, in the sense of international relations theory. One needs to talk to the big players, the ministers of interior of the Member States who usually are political heavyweights in their respective governments."[75]

Despite this lack of interaction, NGOs eventually came to believe the EU was their best partner in terms of liberalizing immigration laws, but they failed to organize and mobilize to lobby the EU until the 2000s. NGOs considered this delay a missed opportunity, but in retrospect, they give a number of reasons for this delay. First, they argued there was no real indication from member states or the EU that these major changes in JHA policy and voting procedures would be on the agenda at the intergovernmental conference leading up to the Amsterdam Treaty. NGOs also perceived that the process was closed to civil society and the debate over JHA was not about specific policies but about larger changes in the supranationalization of rules.[76]

Since the adoption of the Hague Program in 2004, EU officials began to work more closely with NGOs.[77] EU officials seem to have realized that NGOs were potentially valuable partners in preventing illegal immigration through relief work outside the EU at the source of migration problems.[78] In the lead-up to the Lisbon Treaty, organized interest groups were better mobilized, better established, and better connected in Brussels. In stark contrast to the previous rounds of treaty negotiations, they perceived they had a prominent role in influencing the policy agenda of the Treaty through position papers and campaigns.[79] They consistently pushed for greater Europeanization of migration and asylum policy, including more powers of supervision for the ECJ over national disputes regarding immigration policy. On one hand, the relationship between relief NGOs and European institutions became closer, with NGO officials indicating more frequent interactions with JHA officials in both informal and formal settings and perceived input into EU policy

[75] Ibid.   [76] Niemann.
[77] International Association for the Study of Forced Migration, IASFM Newa 1, no. 2, Fall 2004.
[78] Ibid.
[79] See Deirdre Curtin and Steve Peers, "Joint Submission by the Standing Committee of Experts on International Migration, Refugee and Criminal Law, the Immigration and Law Practitioners Association, Statewatch, and the European Council of Refugees and Exiles to Working Group X (Freedom, Security, Justice) of the Convention on the Future of Europe," *Utrecht, London* (2002); Amnesty International Public Report, "UK/EU/UNHCR: Unlawful and Unworkable – Extra-Territorial Processing of Asylum Claims," 17 June 2003, Amnesty International.

agendas.[80] On the other hand, free-form survey reporting (in 2007–9) indicated a lingering dissatisfaction and distance between public officials and NGOs in the domain. Respondents perceived that EU agencies and bureaucrats were distant and did not take into account the views of civil society.[81] Pro-migrant NGOs were frustrated by disappointing EU asylum policy harmonization efforts and claim that political factors have resulted in lowest-common-denominator approaches to refugee protection, even with the policy of supranationalization under Amsterdam.[82] In a 2005 Oxfam report, the EU standards regarding refugees were lower than the existing minimum standards in many member states. Oxfam suggested that the main reason for closer integration on asylum has been member states' desire to keep as many asylum seekers off of their soil as possible and the belief that the EU – with its increasing control over borders – remains the best venue for achieving that goal.

NGOs Mobilized against JHA Policy

The relationship between the EU and pro-migrant NGOs was already relatively distant, but those NGOs were interested in being social partners with the EU and helping the EU frame policy agendas. With the increasing salience of EU border protection through Frontex since 2005, a new generation of activist NGOs mobilized against the EU. These NGOs (such as No Border, Statewatch, and Pro Asyl) accused the EU of a "fortress Europe" mentality and a militarization of the EU border,[83] and protested the Lisbon Treaty language and the Stockholm JHA Program for 2009–14, specifically the strongly worded text: "In order to maintain credible and sustainable immigration and asylum systems in the EU, it is necessary to prevent, control and combat illegal migration as the EU faces an increasing pressure from illegal migration flows and particularly the member states at its external borders, including at its southern borders."[84] The European Civil Liberties Network called on NGOs to boycott the Stockholm Program, citing the

---

[80] International Association for the Study of Forced Migration; European Migration Network, "Policy Analysis Report on Asylum and Migration: July 2004 to December 2005." Brussels, Belgium, March 2006.

[81] Survey free form responses. See Chapter 6 for survey results and appendix for survey design.

[82] Oxfam, *Foreign Territory: The Internationalisation of EU Asylum Policy* (London, UK: Oxfam, 2005).

[83] See, for example, http://www.noborder.org/news_index.php

[84] Valentina Pop, "Europe Moves toward Single Area on Justice and Home Affairs," *EU Observer*, December 12, 2009, accessed May 5, 2010. http://EUObserver/?aid=29139

electronic measures employed by the EU as "worse than the Patriot Act."[85]

Organizations working with asylum seekers were against Frontex acquiring greater resources and responsibility without being required to safeguard fundamental human rights.[86] Because of Frontex actions in the Mediterranean, the number of expulsions of migrants tripled from 428 in 2007 to 1,570 in 2009.[87] A Human Rights Watch report, titled "Pushed Back, Pushed Around," highlighted how Frontex helped the Italian authorities expel migrants to Libya without the opportunity to apply for asylum. In June of 2009, Frontex coordinated Operation Nautilus, where helicopters successfully pushed a boat of seventy-five migrants from the middle of the Mediterranean back to Libya.[88] Other groups campaigned against profiling methods such as those used by Frontex to train officers to "recognize the facial features of different ethnic groups and to quiz the arrivals on their purported country of origin."[89]

In 2008, a coalition of NGOs complained to the UN High Commissioner for Refugees (UNHCR) that Frontex actions constituted a broad and indiscriminate deterrent depriving migrants of their Geneva rights. In written evidence submitted to the UK House of Lords inquiry from the ECRE and British Refugee Council, Frontex failed to demonstrate adequate consideration of international and European asylum and human rights law in respect of access to asylum and the prohibition of refoulement.[90] ECRE has questioned the EU's immigration and asylum agenda, with a spokesman stating, "the pact may be tipping the balance further towards the security approach, which to date has not provided solutions to Europe's migration challenges, and away from the necessary actions to ensure human rights safeguards."[91] ECRE demanded increased democratic scrutiny over Frontex to ensure that its operations

---

[85] "Assinemos a Declaração contra o Programa de Estocolmo," *Blogo Social Português*, accessed September 24, 2009. http://blogosociaportugues.blogspot.com/2009/04/para-nao-dizermos-que-nao-sabiamos.html

[86] J. Pollak and P. Slominski, "Experimentalist but Not Accountable Governance? The Role of Frontex in Managing the EU's External Borders," *West European Politics* 32, no. 5 (2009): 904.

[87] D. Cronin, "RIGHTS: Expulsions from EU Rise Sharply," *Terraviva Europe*, 2010, accessed March 30, 2010. http://ipsterraviva.org/Europe/article.aspx?id=8256

[88] Ibid.

[89] "Greek Islands Struggle with Daily Arrival of Illegal Migrants," *Telegraph*. http://www.telegraph.co.uk/news/worldnews/europe/greece/6147032/Greek-islands-struggle-with-daily-arrival-of-illegal-migrants.html

[90] House of Lords, *Frontex: The EU External Borders Agency, 9th Report of Session 2007–08, Report with Evidence* (London, UK: The Stationery Office, 2008).

[91] "EU to Rubber-Stamp Common Immigration and Asylum Rules," *EU Observer*, accessed May 5, 2010. http://EUObserver/?aid=26924

were respectful of human rights because it had been "unable or unwilling to report on how many asylum seekers are impacted by its operations and what happens to them if they are pushed back to countries [beyond the EU]."[92]

Business, Labor, Industry Interest Groups

In contrast to the delayed but increasingly contentious role of NGOs lobbying the EU on immigration policy, there was a conspicuous absence of business lobby activity, at least in the beginning of the policy domain. Immigration policies are usually salient for labor and capital interests. At the national level, trade unions and employer associations in Spain, Italy, France, and Germany have created coalitions to lobby for liberalizing immigration policy.[93] At the EU level, however, these groups have had a minimal presence over the last two decades. Comparative research on the preferences of these actors over immigration policy is limited but indicates that employer and industry groups are in favor of liberalizing immigration policy across Europe and coordinating EU policy on attracting quality migrants.[94] The major social partners operating in Brussels with natural interests in the EU and its immigration policy are the European Trade Union Confederation (ETUC) and UNICE. However, the ETUC and UNICE, who act as active agenda-setting partners of EU policy in other social and industry areas, have demonstrated no interest in getting involved in EU immigration policy in the absence of effective EU or Commission authority in the area.[95]

The preferences of the EU labor and employer associations are divided along the lines of within-EU migration and migration of third-country nationals. In particular, UNICE has supported advances in internal EU migration and liberalization through expanding the Schengen zone into Eastern Europe, arguing that enlargement is beneficial for employers seeking affordable, quality labor across Europe.[96] Similarly, they have argued that the free movement of labor stimulates the economy and fills gaps in various sectors of old EU states' industries, such as tourism, construction, and agriculture.[97]

---

[92] Ibid.

[93] Caviedes, "The Open Method of Coordination in Immigration Policy," 306.

[94] A. Caviedes, "The Difficult Transition to Transnational Interest Representation"; J. Watts, *Immigration Policy and the Challenge of Globalization: Unions and Employers in Unlikely Alliance* (Ithaca, NY: Cornell University Press, 2002).

[95] Watts.

[96] L. Kirk, "Brussels Business Summit to Demystify Bureaucracy," *EU Observer*, May 6, 2002.

[97] *Polish News Bulletin*. September 2, 2006. "European Employers Back Opening of Old EU's Job Markets."

On the topic of third-party nationals, UNICE has criticized national immigration policies as "ineffective and overly restrictive," arguing that labor from outside Europe can "contribute to economic growth in the EU and can also help to mitigate the immense strain put onto social security systems of its member states."[98] This rationale has not necessarily translated into any lobbying strategies promoting EU-level solutions for third-party nationals, as UNICE has more often than not concluded "the solution to this problem will be up to the countries themselves."[99] Even after the transfer of formal authority to the EU, UNICE has maintained this distance and policy position. When the Commission attempted to propose the 2005 Green Card for attracting skilled labor migrants, UNICE responded by asserting that all aspects of immigration should remain at the discretion of member states, including total and per-country quotas and types of skills and labor sought.[100] UNICE acknowledged that a system to attract skilled labor was necessary, but unequivocally asserted that this was the purview of national states and the EU should not interpret its legal mandate to cover legal migration.[101] Instead, UNICE wanted the Commission to enable better access to the unskilled labor market for long-term foreign residents already inside the EU.

In contrast to UNICE, it has actually been the labor union association ETUC that has been more uniformly supportive of EU proposals over immigration policy. ETUC predicted excess illegal immigration would lead to labor tensions at the unskilled end of the labor market. ETUC was supportive of proposals such as the Green Card in 2005 and the more recent Blue Card but is generally skeptical of the Commission's focus on importing skilled labor from abroad without dealing with the existence of thousands of less skilled workers already in Europe.[102]

It is unclear why industry did not mobilize over immigration issues, usually a lobbying target for any industries seeking affordable or skilled

[98] "Slovenia: Employers Endorse Free Movement of Labour at a Meeting." *Eastbusiness .org*, November 16, 2006.

[99] "Slovenia: Employers Endorse Free Movement of Labour at a Meeting."

[100] Union of Industrial and Employers' Confederations of Europe, "Green Paper: Confronting Demographic Change: A New Solidarity between the Generations," July 5, 2005, Brussels.

[101] Union of Industrial and Employers' Confederations of Europe, 9.

[102] European Trade Union Confederation, "ETUC Response to the Commission's Green Paper on an EU Approach to Managing Economic Migration COM (2004) 811 final," March 2005, Brussels; European Trade Union Confederation, "ETUC Position Regarding European Commission's Proposals on Legal and 'Illegal' Migration," December 12, 2007, Brussels.

labor.[103] Some scholars have attributed this void to an economic slump and high unemployment, which demobilized business interests, which traditionally lobby for openness. These conjectural elements should not be neglected in understanding why migration became a security (as opposed to a labor market) issue in the 1990s.[104] Alex Caviedes has attempted to address why there is so little industry lobbying or support for EU-level immigration solutions, particularly because the EU has had formal legal precedence over member states in this area for years. In contrast to the small body of literature focusing on refugee and immigrant rights groups, he has focused on the relative apathy of employer and business interests toward the EU. His analysis rests on a lobbying Catch-22: although the EU has authority over the areas of immigration of interest to businesses (such as attracting highly skilled migrants), the national political arenas have remained the primary target of lobbying and mobilization because of an absence of legitimate policy activity or effective outcomes at the EU level.[105]

Immigration Interest Cleavages: NGOs, Security Industry, National Bureaucrats

Based on the landscape of immigration debates in national capitals, one would expect that the actors and interest groups in Brussels would be analogous. Instead, the structure of mobilized interests is very different. On the topic of the status of third-country nationals, there has been a highly contested political debate in Brussels, but the cleavages of opinion are different than they are in national capitals. Instead of business

---

[103] Gary P. Freeman, "Modes of Immigration Politics in Liberal Democratic States," *International Migration Review* (1995): 881–902.

[104] Guiraudon, "The Constitution of European Immigration Policy Domain."

[105] The incentives of business lobbies that are already fully locked in at the domestic level may be weak at the EU level. The very groups that should be offering advice and expertise at the EU level may be so entrenched in national labor politics that they see no point in entering an already pluralistic interest-group situation in Brussels when it comes to the domain of immigration (Caviedes, "The Open Method of Coordination in Immigration Policy"). In addition, there are sectoral and national cleavages within the EU-level associations themselves that have been too great to overcome for the sake of lobbying coherence. These cleavages have pitted associations from member states such as the UK and the Netherlands (in favor of liberalization) against associations with protectionist preferences from Austria or Germany, as well as sectoral and industry differences: "due to the general nature of the policy debate, the UNICE and ETUC become the most appropriate interlocutors, but their inability to reconcile sectoral or national differences renders their positions very tame and vague, which leaves most national social partners feeling inadequately represented" (Alexander Caviedes, *Prying Open Fortress Europe: The Turn to Sectoral Labor Migration* [Lanham, MD: Lexington Books, 2010], 25).

interests and refugee NGOs on different sides of the debate, they share the same side of the debate: in favor of more immigration liberalization and more Europeanization of immigration law. On the other side of the debate are representatives of national interior and justice ministries, who have mobilized to Brussels to lobby for greater EU political development but in favor of restrictive immigration and tightening border security policies.[106] This increasing securitization has been driving the content of the EU immigration policy agenda, leading to a "fortress Europe" outcome. Long established in Brussels, the representatives of national interior and justice ministries use their role in expert groups to push for EU legislation more restrictive than their domestic institutions allow.[107]

A Critical Juncture in JHA: The Lateral Mobilization of European Security Interest Groups

Over the course of the 2000s, the security industry also became increasingly active in JHA affairs. Tasked with providing high-technology solutions to the EU's border enforcement and controls, the security industry develops and implements solutions to monitor and data mine

---

[106] Guiraudon, "European Integration and Migration Policy"; A. Luedtke, "Uncovering EU Immigration Legislation: Policy Dynamics and Outcomes," EUSA Conference, May 17–19, 2007, Montreal, Canada.

[107] Guiraudon, "European Integration and Migration Policy." In immigration and migration control policies, Virginia Guiraudon has argued that only one of the many interests has successfully mobilized (or venue shopped their interests) to the EU. She traced the activities of national interior ministry bureaucrats and experts from the 1970s to the 1990s, finding that they were the first-movers in the advocacy of immigration and border control policy in Brussels (ibid.). Their model for action was the 1970s Trevi group that became a wining and dining "security club that discussed drugs or terrorism" (ibid., 10). These national bureaucrats were the first venue shoppers looking for another level of government through which to pursue their own policy agendas free from domestic adversaries. They resented the oversight of the national courts, parliaments, and social groups advocating more liberalization of immigration. Guiraudon claimed that it was in these nongovernmental – but European-level – forums that migration control officials made the first linkages between migration, asylum, crime, and security as one common policy agenda. These ad hoc forums were opaque, off the record, and freed interior ministry bureaucrats "from the national and/or political constraints which often make it difficult to deal with controversial matters which nonetheless have to be settled speedily" (D. Bigo, "The European Internal Security Field: Stakes and Rivalries in a Newly Developing Area of Police Intervention," in *Policing Across National Boundaries*, edited by Malcom Anderson and Monica Den Boer [London, UK: Pinter, 1994], 165). Not only did these justice ministers push for an accelerated timetable on programs such as Schengen and the new JHA domain of the Maastricht Treaty (Sandra Lavenex, *Safe Third Countries: Extending the EU Asylum and Immigration Policies to Central and Eastern Europe* [Budapest: Central European University Press, 1999], 114–5), they made themselves invaluable as technocratic experts on the topic for the nascent EU institutions.

information, uses biometrics and other technologies for identification, and develops methods for monitoring borders and territory. They include the manufacturers and systems integrators of coastal radar stations, surface ships, manned aircraft, satellites, and UAVs, with many industry crossovers to the traditional defense industry.[108] One association, called the European Biometrics Forum,

> has brought together key stakeholders including the finest experts from across the EU to determine how biometrics can most appropriately be applied in the context of the Charter of Fundamental Rights of the European Union . . . [we] will focus on promoting the development of new policy implementation schemes through working groups and workshops [in border control and immigration].[109]

During the late 1990s and 2000s, defense industries increasingly mobilized toward the EU. They formed informal institutions to first anticipate future policy, then interact with bureaucrats and parliamentarians, influence the outcome of EU policies (increase funding for civilian security technology, removing arms import barriers, increasing spending on homeland security technologies), and attempt to influence the future policy agenda of the EU. Their arrangements ranged from permanent and formal to temporary and informal, and included such influential task forces as The Group of Personalities, LeaderSHIP 2015, STAR 21, the European Security Research and Innovation Forum (ESRIF), and other groups sponsored by the European Commission. These have proliferated in the past decade, the most influential being the Security and Defence Agenda (SDA). The SDA has hosted a number of influential conferences, roundtables, and sponsored studies. The Kangaroo Group, a public–private expert group since 1978, created a 2004 working group on "The Economic Aspects of a Common European Defence Policy," urging the EU to create a common market for internal security, supported by a coherent homeland security and economic security strategy.[110]

Between 2001 and 2003, there was a shift in the landscape of lobbying in Brussels: where there had only been interested representatives of the traditional armaments, defense, and aerospace industries before, a number of interest groups proliferated in the domain of security, borders, and civilian protection. Much of this shift was driven by smaller defense suppliers looking to enter the security market, "driven by the belief that

---

[108] List generated from Frontex/Events. Accessed March 30, 2010. http://www.frontex .europa.eu/events/art15.html.

[109] European Biometrics Forum, accessed March 30, 2010. http://www.eubiometricsforum.com/index.php?option=com_content&task=view&id= 832&Itemid=95

[110] Kangaroo Group, Press Release, October 2004

there would be a new market with significant business opportunities."[111] As internal security became more salient post 9/11, defense suppliers began to see entry into the security market as necessary for future profits, and "consider[ed] it almost certain that there will be future public investments and procurement in this area. This is why some companies have re-organized themselves, adding a security dimension to former defence units and creating common 'security and defence' divisions."[112] Indeed, by 2014 the European homeland security market (including biometrics, screening, UAVs, Radio Frequency Identifications [RFIDs], and Closed Circuity Television Systems [CCTVs]) had a market in the billions of euros.[113] The EU Advisory Group on Aerospace argued in their 2004 STAR 21 report for the ultimate goal of a "harmonized security and European armaments policy to provide structure for the European defense and security equipment market."[114]

The European Organization for Security (EOS) was founded by the defense industry association ASD in 2007, with the mandate to promote industry initiatives in civilian security research.[115] The European Homeland Security Association (EHSA) was formed in 2004 and focuses on civil defense and protection. Operating as a nonprofit institute, the EHSA has partnered with other organizations such as SIPRI in Stockholm and CSIS in Washington, DC, and its corporate sponsors include Thales and EADS. Security and technology associations have been promoting a more comprehensive EU response to the development of a security market in Europe.[116]

Developing an advanced border control regime in the absence of unlimited financial resources or manpower requires industry partners with advanced sectoral expertise. Two recent examples are a computerized data-mining tool and a system of robotic border controls. The European Commission awarded the British defense contractor BAE systems

---

[111] European Commission (2010). *Study on the Industrial Implications in Europe of the Blurring of Dividing Lines between Security and Defence*. Contract no. SI2.516182, 141.

[112] Ibid.

[113] Prnewsire.co.uk, "New Aircraft Procurement Offers Sizeable Potential in the European Air ISR Command and Control Market, Says Frost & Sullivan," *SYS-CON MEDIA*, 2006, accessed September 23, 2009. Available at: http://www.sys-con.com/node/1096042

[114] European Advisory Group on Aerospace, "STAR21 – Strategic Aerospace Review for the 21st Century. Creating a coherent market and policy framework for a vital European industry," *EU Commission – Working Document*, 2002.

[115] AeroSpace and Defence Industries Association of Europe, "Annual Review 2007," Brussels, 2007.

[116] European Telecommunications Standards Institute, ETSI White Paper #1, Sophia Antipolis, France, 2003.

a contract to develop a "strategic crime and immigration information management system" for the EU, seeking

New capabilities [to] improve the ability to search, mine, and fuse information from National, trans-national, private and other sources, to discover trends and patterns for increasing shared situational awareness and improving decision making, within a secure infrastructure to facilitate the combating of organized crime and in particular people trafficking to enhance the security of citizens.[117]

In the 2000s, the EU began creating agreements with states such as Libya to limit migrant flows from sub-Saharan Africa. To help it enforce this deal, Libya spent €300 million on technology for a "large border security and control system," made by Selex Sistemi Integrati, part of Italian aerospace firm Finmeccanica.[118] The effort was part of the EU's Transportable Autonomous Patrol for Land Border Surveillance (TALOS) program, which developed border controls with human-sensing radars and aerial drones, based on "the need of an expanded 27-nation EU to guard its porous eastern border that it cannot afford to monitor conventionally."[119]

European Security Research Programme

In addition to existing security interest groups, the European Commission sponsored the creation of a number of interest and expert groups under its centrally funded research framework program. Coordinated under the "Framework Programmes" (FP), the seventh FP from 2007 to 2013 focused on security as the European Security Research Programme (ESRP). Because of restrictions on Commission involvement in defense procurement, these funds can be used for homeland security (or civilian) projects but not defense research and development. Dual-use technologies, a contentious topic since the 1990s, were initially excluded from the research program. The first security research program was the 2004 Preparatory Action in the field of Security Research, which required (PASR) consultation from both the academic and scientific community. Initial PASR project funds were awarded to industry and research institutions in various subjects, including space technology, 3D simulation technology for crisis management, geospatial data analysis, and network

---

[117] "BAE Systems Awarded EU Contract to Develop Organized Crime Database," 2010, accessed March 15, 2010. http://neoconopticon.wordpress.com/2010/03/02/bae-sciims-project/
[118] "Robot Border Guards to Patrol Future Frontiers," *New Scientist*, January 8, 2010, accessed June 8, 2010.
[119] Ibid.

security. Although civilian dual-use technologies, they form the building blocks of network-centric warfare and system of systems architecture that are the center of defense system integrator programs.

One public–private partnership under the FP 7 was a "Group of Personalities" in the field of security research, staffed by executives in the European defense, aerospace, and electronics industry. The group released a report in 2004 called "Research for a Secure Europe," echoing defense industry concerns. They argued the EU was falling behind the United States in technology and limiting its ability to fulfill a security strategy. Additionally, the 2007 ESRP was tasked to harness the duality of technologies and bridge the gap between civil and defense research, based heavily on U.S. government actions linking defense procurement with economic security in the 1990s. Their recommendations excluded the EU funding of offensive weapons development, but included crisis management, protection of vital public and private infrastructure, border and coastal surveillance, satellite intelligence capabilities, protection against incidents involving bio-chemical and other substances, and nonlethal means to counteract terrorist actions.

The report suggested:

an EU-funded ESRP that ensures the involvement of all Member States should be launched as early as 2007. Its minimum funding should be set at €1 billion per year in addition to existing funding. This spending level should be rapidly achieved, with the possibility to increase it further to bring the combined European security research investment level closer to that of the U.S.[120]

As a caveat, the report noted: "since the idea of matching the U.S. defence budget is unrealistic (and may not even be desirable), an ESRP should rather take the U.S. spending on Homeland Security Research as a reference."[121] In 2004, the initial security research budget was 65 million euros. When FP 7 began in 2007, it started with a 3.5 billion euro budget.[122]

The report also requested the EU fund research projects to boost Europe's security capability; close the gap between civil and defense research; maximize the benefits of different aspects of technology; stimulate synergies by encouraging transformation, integration of applications, and technology transfer between sectors; work out interoperability and

[120] Press Release, "European Industry Leaders and EU Policymakers Call for Budget Boost for Security Research," Brussels, March 15, 2004.

[121] Group of Personalities in the field of Security Research, "Research for a Secure Europe: Report of the Group of Personalities in the field of Security Research," Luxembourg: Office for Official Publications of the European Communities, 2004, 27.

[122] "EU Research – Building Knowledge Europe: The EU's new Research Framework Programme 2007–2013," memo 05/114, Brussels, April 7, 2005.

connectivity rules; develop the necessary rules for intellectual property rights (IPRs) and technology transfer in consultation with all relevant stakeholders; create new financing instruments to enable funding to be allocated, when appropriate, to cover 100 percent of costs of research; and develop a mechanism to identify future capability needs for internal security missions. Finally, the report suggested that:

A "Security Research Advisory Board" should be established to draw strategic guidelines to prepare the research agenda of an ESRP as well as to advise on the principles and mechanisms for its implementation. Moreover, it should identify critical technology areas where Europe should aim for an independent competitive capability. The Board should consist of high-level experts including public and private customers, industry, research organizations and any other relevant stakeholders.[123]

In 2005, the Commission adopted this recommendation and created ESRAB, consisting of fifty government and industry stakeholders. The ESRAB released its first report in 2006, making a number of specific policy recommendations regarding the capabilities and capacities of the EU. Their recommendation included a section on "security economics," stating:

Insecurity – and reactions to it – is mainly a matter of perception. There is significant evidence that the media, consumers and producers – and by extension policymakers – are poor judges of objective levels of insecurity, leading to imperfect security decisions. Furthermore, regulatory measures can initiate changes in market structures. Analogous to environmental regulation which enables firms to profitably contribute to "green growth," one can think of regulation that stimulates "secure growth" by enabling industries for security enhancing products or services. The European capacity for economic analysis and for policymaking in this field is weak, especially when compared to the United States ... To address these causes, it is recommended to establish a security economics network starting with a small kernel of known individuals or organisations and progressively widen the community through disseminating new research and policy insights emerging from European funded research activities.[124]

ESRAB also recommended the Commission create the public–private ESRIF to "foster greater dialogue and a shared view of European security needs."[125] In response, the Commission adopted the 2004 communication "Security Research: The Next Steps," "which subscribed

---

[123] Research for a Secure Europe: Report of the Group of Personalities in the field of Security Research. "Meeting the Challenge: The European Security Research Agenda." A report from the European Security Research Advisory Board September 2006.
[124] Ibid.   [125] Ibid.

to the main thrust of the recommendations of the group of personalities."[126]

European Security Research and Innovation Forum

In 2007, the European Commission declared that EU's homeland security research agenda would be coordinated through the public–private
ESRIF.[127] Funded by FP 7, its goal was allocating 1.4 billion euros
"to technology development projects aimed at protecting Europe's cit-
izenry, critical infrastructures and borders against attack."[128] Commissioner Gunter Verheugen argued, "we do not want the low level of effectiveness we see in defence spending brought into this field. We want value
for money," a framework where private sectors could work together easily. He continued: "a number of stakeholders think that a jointly drafted
strategic research agenda can be the central reference for work in this
field."[129]

The language surrounding this public–private partnership did not dis-
tinguish between the interests and preferences of the public and the private actors involved. This internal and border security partnership functioned as an informal institution in European security. ESRIF members
are "stakeholders" who "identify proposals for forming a strategic security research and innovation agenda," who "[lay] out a shared and clear
view of European security research needs and priorities . . . [s]hare ideas,
views and best practices in order to make better use of existing capabilities and enhance the use of technology in security-related domains."[130]
For the European Commission, this partnership was critical because of
the nature of the task at hand:

Public–private dialogue in the field of security research is important to increase
the security of infrastructures and utilities, fight organised crime and terrorism, help restore security in a crisis, analyse political, social and human
issues related to security research, and improve surveillance and border control.
Research and public–private partnerships have a role to play in protecting critical

---

[126] European Commission, "Press Release: FAQ on European Security Research and
Innovation Forum," IHS, September 12, 2007, http://aero-defence.ihs.com/news/
eu-en-security-forum-faq-9-07.htm. See also European Parliament Foreign Affairs
Committee (2005), Report on Security Research – The Next Steps, European Parliament, A6-0103/2005.
[127] Brooks Tigner, "Shaping EU Homeland Security," *ISN Security Watch*, Thursday,
March 29, 2007.
[128] Ibid.   [129] Ibid.
[130] European Commission, "Press Release: FAQ on European Security Research and
Innovation Forum," IHS, September 12, 2007, http://aero-defence.ihs.com/news/
eu-en-security-forum-faq-9-07.htm.

infrastructures such as airports, railway stations, roads, power stations, dams and bridges. They can also help make travel documents more secure and link reliably the document and its holder. Considering possible human rights implications of new technologies is also part of what public and private stakeholders need to do in partnership. By ensuring the connection between security research and security policy making, ESRIF will contribute to delivering more effective policies and, ultimately, better security to European Union (EU) citizens.[131]

In 2007, the Commission claimed, "ESRIF will present a joint security research agenda towards the end of 2009. This agenda will contain, where appropriate, recommendations to public authorities."[132] ESRIF also effectively linked EU institutions informally together, such as the Commission and the EDA. In 2009, it was touted as providing the "overarching structure for maximising complementarity and synergy between defence and civilian security-related research activities."[133]

European Organization for Security

In 2007, another private organization was formed to contribute to the emerging EU security and defense policy domain. The EOS was formed as an offshoot of the existing ASD. A press released said it was a framework for bringing together private, nongovernmental stakeholders such as security supply companies, and infrastructure operators and users to "provide support to the study, development and implementation of security solutions to the challenges faced by the European Union."[134] The goals of the EOS were (1) to promote a coherent EU security market and (2) to contribute to the definition of an all-encompassing, or holistic, European civil security policy. By linking the demand side with the supply chain, "it will act as a facilitator, thus contributing strongly to the creation of comprehensive and state-of-the-art civil security solutions for citizens, governments and the whole European economy... [and] further enhance the strong momentum in the European security sector."[135]

Markus Hellenthal, Senior Vice President of EADS, previous chair of ESRAB, and one of the main forces behind EOS, stated, "EOS will

---

[131] Ibid.   [132] Ibid.

[133] "EDA and EU Commission to Establish Framework Cooperation for Research," *Your Defence News*, May 20, 2009. http://www.yourdefencenews.com/eda+and+eu+commission+to+establish+framework+cooperation+for+research_32808.html

[134] Brooks Tigner, "Shaping EU Homeland Security," *ISN Security Watch*, Thursday, March 29, 2007.

[135] ERTICO News, "New European Organization for Security (EOS)." Press Release, July 24, 2007.

actively encourage the development and implementation of innovative security technologies, common procedures, systems and services. EOS will also contribute to the creation of a more homogenous European market for security solutions. Based on this, EOS will directly support European competitiveness in civil security solutions on a global scale."[136]

Overall, there was a significant shift in interest-group mobilization in EU security markets and policy over the 2000s. Defense firms anticipated future security funding opportunities and formed industry associations when there was no defined security market in Europe. Observers recall that defense firms were not forced to enter the security market but did so on their own terms.[137] When major security research funding programs began, this fueled additional interest-group mobilization, and the creation of informal security institutions that served to set agendas and advise the EU's investment decisions in the area. This defense industry effort has been broadly successful, as the firms have "played a key role in the definition of the orientation and priorities of the EU's research and development policy for security-related technical systems."[138] By 2009, the European Defence Agency established a common framework for security and defense, with the aim of "maximizing complementarity and synergy between defence and civil security-related research activities."[139] This was reflected at the strategic level, in the 2010 EU Internal Security Strategy declaration that "internal security cannot exist without an external dimension, since internal security increasingly depends to a large extent on external security."[140] In 2011, the Commission announced a defense policy task force with objectives of "exploiting synergies between security and defence industries,"[141] and in 2012, the Commission described security and defense markets as

---

[136] Ibid.

[137] J. Mawdsley, *A European Agenda for Security Technology: From Innovation Policy to Export Controls* (Brussels: Flemish Peace Institute, 2013), 31.

[138] Didier Bigo and Julien Jeandesboz, "The EU and the European Security Industry Questioning the 'Public-Private Dialogue,'" INEX Policy Brief no. 5, February 2010.

[139] May 2009: EDA/Commission est. Euro Framework Coop for Sec & Def, "maximising complementarity and synergy between defence and civil security-related research activities" (Council of the European Union, 2943rd External Relations Council meeting, Conclusion on European Security and Defence Policy [ESDP], Brussels, May 18, 2009).

[140] Council of the European Union, *Towards a European Internal Security Strategy for the European Union*, March 2010, 16.

[141] Julian Hale, "EU to Establish Defense Policy Task Force," *Defense News*, November 7, 2011. http://www.defensenews.com/article/20111107/DEFSECT04/111070302/EU-Establish-DefensePolicy-Task-Force

indistinguishable and stated that divisions between them reflected false policy and market fragmentation.[142]

Justice and Home Affairs Agency: Frontex

"Frontex is very conscious of the fact that it is a young agency and therefore it should learn to walk before starting to run. But, of course, we have no interest in seeing Frontex walk. We want it to run at great speed" (Simon Busuttil, Minister of European Parliament, Malta).[143]

On October 26, 2004, the Council of the EU established the EU border agency Frontex (from French: frontières extérieures for "external borders"). The Frontex mandate was to "Coordinat[e] [the] intelligence driven operational co-operation at the EU level to strengthen security at the external borders."[144] The borders of the EU include land borders 5,000 miles long (from the Finland–Russia border to the Black Sea) and 50,000 miles of maritime borders, including more than 3,000 Greek islands. Frontex was proposed on September 20, 2001, when the JHA Council asked the European Commission to immediately examine the "relationship between safeguarding internal security and complying with international protection obligations and instruments."[145] The Commission responded a few weeks later with a communication on illegal immigration, urgently calling for a border control policy to protect against crime and terrorism that would instill "mutual confidence between those Member States which have abandoned border controls at their internal frontiers."[146] At the December 2001 European Council of Laeken, the decision was formalized to establish "a mechanism or common services to control external borders."[147] The idea then languished for a few years.[148]

---

[142] European Commission (2012) Security Industrial Policy: Action Plan for an innovative and competitive Security Industry, COM (2012) 417 final, Brussels, July 26, 2012, p. 8.

[143] *House of Lords Report on Frontex* (London, UK: The Stationery Office, 2008), 24.

[144] "Frontex Mission Statement." http://www.Frontex.europa.eu/more_about_Frontex/

[145] European Council. JHA Council. "Conclusions adopted by the Council (Justice and Home Affairs)," SN 3926/6/01 – REV 6. Brussels, September 20, 2001.

[146] European Council, JHA Council, "Conclusions adopted by the Council (Justice and Home Affairs)."

[147] European Council, "Presidency Conclusions of the Laeken Meeting," December 14–15, 2001.

[148] The European Commission and a few EU states proceeded to sponsor feasibility studies to establish a European border guard or border policy, but this was dropped because of concerns that such a specific mechanism "did not appear in the mandate" of the European Council. In 2002 the Council promoted a more intergovernmental "Action Plan" that did not mandate member-state participation or financing but

The concrete plan for a border control agency was launched by the Greek presidency in the second half of 2003, and then operationalized by the Commission in November 2003.[149] Frontex was established by Council Regulation on October 26, 2004,[150] and opened its headquarters in Warsaw, Poland, on October 3, 2005.[151] Frontex was created as an agency under the policy authority of the supranational European Commission. With a somewhat hybridized authority structure, Frontex has a board with both Commission officials and member state border control directors.[152] Frontex is not financially dependent on member-state financial contributions; it receives financial and resource contributions from the Commission budget and from voluntary member-state contributions.

In July 2007, the Parliament and Council amended the regulation founding Frontex in order to facilitate the creation of RABITs.[153] The 2007 amendment expanded the authority of Frontex and suggested mandatory rather than voluntary resource contributions: "Member States shall make the border guards available for deployment at the request of the Agency, unless they are faced with an exceptional situation."[154] RABITs consist of EU-trained staff from national border guard agencies who can be deployed on the request of another member state in situations of "urgent and exceptional pressure."[155]

would instead initiate pilot projects under an "External Border Practitioners Common Unit," which consisted of the "Strategic Committee on Immigration, Frontiers and Asylum" (SCIFA) plus the heads of national border control services, which together became known as SCIFA+. See UK House of Lords (2005), The Hague Programme: A Five-year Agenda for EU Justice and Home Affairs, London, UK: Tenth Report of the House of Lord's Select Committee on the European Union, March 23, 2005.

[149] Commission of the European Communities, "Proposal for a Council Regulation Establishing a European Agency for the Management of Operational Co-operation at the External Borders." COM/2003/0687 final – CNS 2003/0273. Brussels, November 20, 2003. http://eurlex.europa.eu/LexUriServ/LexUriServ.do?uri=celex:52003pc0687:en:html

[150] Council Regulation (EC) 2007/2004/ (26.10.2004, OJ L3349/25.11.2004).

[151] Council Decision 2005/358/EC of 26 April 2005.

[152] Article 21, *Council Regulation (EC) No 2007/2004 establishing a European Agency for the Management of Operational Cooperation at the External Borders of the Member States of the European Union*. Brussels, 26 October, Official Journal of the European Communities L349.

[153] Art. 8, *Council Regulation (EC) No 2007/2004 establishing a European Agency for the Management of Operational Cooperation at the External Borders of the Member States of the European Union*. Brussels, 26 October, Official Journal of the European Communities L349.

[154] Art. 12: Art. 8(d)(8), ibid.

[155] Regulation (EC) 863/2007, Art.1; RABIT officials operate under the authority of the requesting state. The first RABIT training exercise took place on the Slovenian/Croatian border in April 2008, where twenty member-state border teams practiced surveillance and border control along the Balkan land borders of the EU.

Besides the joint security operations and joint asylum return operations, one of the key functions of Frontex is in short- and long-term risk assessment. These intelligence-driven studies create a common focal point for planning limited resources and operations. A 2010 assessment concluded:

With significantly lower number of migrants departing from Libya and a decreasing trend of arrivals in the Canary Islands, the relative importance of Algeria, Morocco, Tunisia and possibly Egypt as departure points is likely to grow throughout 2009 and 2010. Efforts by authorities there against illegal migration will be crucial for limiting the flow towards Italy and Spain. Gambia is expected to take over from Senegal the role of a major embarkation point on the West African coast. That said, in absolute numbers the Aegean Sea (at the border between Turkey and Greece) is expected to remain the main entry point at external sea borders in 2010 should cooperation with Turkey continue to be limited. With the strengthening of the southern EU maritime borders, migrants who initially considered sea crossing might opt for alternative way of entry. One of them might be the use of air borders, either with forged documents or after obtaining visa on false pretence. At the moment, such a shift has not yet been detected and the risk is considered rather low for 2010, but the situation at the air border should nevertheless continue to be monitored with vigilance.[156]

These risk assessments are based on internal Frontex work and aggregating the intelligence of member states. However, it is shifting to greater intelligence cooperation with third countries as the sources of migrants, in order to provide a "common pre-frontier intelligence picture."[157] Risk assessments also predict the coming points of vulnerability or increasing activity:

At the external sea borders, operational cooperation should continue to focus on the southern maritime areas where large number of illegal migrants have been detected and where migrants' life is most at risk, namely the maritime areas leading to: the Canary Islands, the Spanish south-eastern Mediterranean coast, the Island of Lampedusa, Malta – taking into account possible displacement to Sicily and/or Crete – Sardinia and the Greek Islands close to the Turkish coasts (Lesvos, Chios, Samos, Patmos, Leros and Kos).[158]

In 2010, the Commission proposed additional resources for Frontex in the form of legal guarantees on equipment or resources promised to

---

[156] Frontex Programme of Work 2010, September 30, 2009. Frontex: Warsaw, Poland, p. 18.
[157] European Commission, 2008. *Report on the Evaluation and Future Development of the Frontex Agency*. Brussels, COM(2008) 67 final, p. 9.
[158] Frontex Programme of Work 2010., p. 21

Frontex by member states.[159] While presently the member states contribute voluntarily with technical equipment to Frontex, these contributions would become compulsory. Frontex will decide on an annual basis a "minimum number per type of technical equipment" necessary to carry out joint operations, pilot projects, and return operations and the conditions for deployment and reimbursement of costs.[160]

The Commission – along with France, Italy, Spain, and Greece – proposed that Frontex should buy its own equipment without having to depend on member states but have its "own resources," human and material (ships and helicopters), to render it "more effective."[161] In January 2010, after nine immigrants drowned off the coast of Greece, the French minister for immigration, Eric Besson, announced he would demand that the Commission "ask that decisions taken by heads of state and government of European countries to strengthen Frontex be implemented without delay."[162] He argued the precedent was already in place: in October 2009, the European Council authorized direct cooperation between Frontex and the countries of origin and transit, notably Libya and Turkey, and the possibility of regularly co-chartering flights financed by Frontex for "grouped distancing operations at European level."[163]

EU Border Control Agencies

Commission officials such as the former Commissioner for Justice, Freedom and Security, Franco Frattini, believed Frontex exceeded all expectations in its first years. Frattini even boasted, "Frontex has already gained enough 'European medals' to qualify as one of the major achievements we are celebrating on the occasion of the 50th anniversary of the European Community... [it has] come a long way in a short time. We are a modern, dynamic European Agency that has had to become operationally effective in record fast time."[164]

A goal of the Frontex leadership has been that of "quiet politics," so as not to raise expectations for performance or incite backlash over border control politics. Frontex documents emphasize it has been only

[159] V. Pop, "Beefed Up Border Control Agency to Respect Rights," *EU Observer*, 2000, accessed May 5, 2010. http://EUObserver/?aid=29544

[160] "Frontex is Set to Gain More Powers," *Bill Cash's European Journal*, 2010, accessed April 30, 2010. http://europeanjournal.typepad.com/my_weblog/2010/03/frontex-is-set-to-gain-more-powers.html

[161] N. Vandystadt, "Commission Wants to Reinforce Frontex's Capacity for Action." *Europolitics*, 2010, accessed March 5, 2010. http://www.europolitics.info/commission-wants-to-reinforce-frontex-s-capacity-for-action-art263766-40.html

[162] Ibid.   [163] Ibid.

[164] "Frontex New Premises Just Opened," Press Release, 2007, accessed April 30, 2010. http://www.eu2007.bmi.bund.de/nn_1052590/EU2007/EN/ServiceNavigation/PressReleases/content__Pressemitteilungen/Frontex__Gebaeude__en.html

"an operational coordinator and contributor so as to avoid raising inaccurate or unrealistic public expectations,"[165] one operating "on the edge all the time when it comes to human resources."[166] Frontex grew significantly as an organization in its first few years, with budgetary increases more than tenfold in its first four years. It also had relatively little administrative oversight by the Commission or the Parliament. Although in 2009 the Parliament sought increased oversight over Frontex in the form of controlling one third of its budget, the director of Frontex argued, "it cannot be expected to operate according to the same rules and procedures as all other European Institutions. Even though Frontex was already effectively independent from the Commission, Mr. Laitinen asked for more flexibility and autonomy."[167] Frontex officials were concerned that additional oversight would "further bureaucratize" their organization and tie it down excessively.[168] Initially, Frontex possessed no permanent border control assets, maintaining that decentralized assets can work "if the Member States are willing to participate in these exercises and to deploy their assets . . . there is no need to have this kind of equipment itself."[169] In 2011, however, Frontex gained the operational authority to purchase and maintain its own dedicated border security equipment. One example is the European Border Surveillance System (EUROSUR), which focused initially on the southern and eastern external borders of the EU[170] but became a permanent Frontex program in 2013.[171] The 2016 launch of a new EU border security agency built on these developments, enabling it to procure its own equipment and have additional independent operational authority.[172]

Early Frontex Policies and Operations (2005–2009)

The activities of Frontex increased dramatically in its first few years. The number of pilot projects it has launched went from 522 in 2006 to 1,722 in 2010, and Joint Operations coordinated by Frontex went

---

[165] Frontex Vacancy Notice, Frontex/08/TA/AD7/03. Warsaw, Poland. 2007.

[166] *House of Lords Report on Frontex*, p. 58.

[167] *Frontex: The First Five Years*, "Border Security: Frontex is operational and steadily improving: interview with Ilkka Laitinen." (Warsaw: Frontex, 2009), 8–17.

[168] Ibid.

[169] Speech held at the Seminar on EU Policies and Inter-European Cooperation on Migration by Ilkka Laitinen in Maastricht, September 24, 2008.

[170] European Commission (2008), Communication from the Commission to the European Parliament, the Council, the European Economic and Social Committee and the Committee of the Regions, Examining the Creation of a European Border Surveillance System (EUROSUR). COM(2008) 68 final.

[171] J. Jeandesboz, "Reinforcing the Surveillance of EU Borders: The Future Development of Frontex and EUROSUR." CEPS Challenge Research Paper No. 11, 2008, retrieved October 22, 2008. http://shop.ceps.be/downfree.php?item_id=1693

[172] European Commission Press Release, IP/16/3281 Brussels, Belgium, October 6, 2016.

from 440 in 2006 to 4,564 in 2010. Frontex marks its own progress in metrics of illegal immigration, using decreasing figures of illegal immigrants as a measure of operational efficiency. In January 2008, Director Laitinen claimed that 70 percent fewer illegal immigrants arrived in the Canary Islands in 2007 than the previous year, due to the success of Frontex's Human Exploration Research Analog (HERA) mission.[173] On the other hand, "the Nautilus mission in the central Mediterranean area has not been effective since the number of arrivals has increased rather than decreased."[174] Overall, Frontex cited that – between 2008 and 2009 – illegal border crossings were down 22 percent and detections of illegal were down 30 percent.[175]

Independent observers told a different story about the effectiveness of the HERA and Nautilus operations. HERA was a Frontex–Spain effort to prevent migrants from reaching the Canary Islands from Mauritania, Senegal, and Cape Verde. It was broadly considered successful, as not one migrant boat landed in the Canary Islands during the mission. It remains unclear whether this was a result of European economic downturns attracting fewer migrants or Frontex's efforts. Frontex's other significant pre-2011 operation – Nautilus – centered on the island of Malta, coordinating the assistance of Italy and Malta. Launched in 2006, the goal of Nautilus was to stem sea-based immigration from Libya; however, by 2007, the operation was declared a failure due to a lack of ships, personnel, and helicopters promised by member states. Human traffickers had easily been able to choose other routes during the first Nautilus operation because they knew to avoid Frontex operations around Malta, instead traveling to the Italian island of Lampedusa.[176]

In 2008, the second Nautilus operation also failed. In September, Frontex declared the situation "increasingly alarming," and even saw itself as part of the problem rather than part of the solution: "This is the saddest part of the story. We have an increased level of operational activities which might be serving as a pull factor for traffickers." Operation HERA also shifted migration from the Atlantic to the Mediterranean: "Traffickers could be targeting Malta and Italy as an alternative

---

[173] "Frontex cree que el éxito de España avala la estrecha colaboración con los terceros países," *Diario Público*, January 30, 2008.
[174] Official Journal of the European Union, December 18, 2008. P6_TA(2008)0633 European Parliament resolution of 18 December 2008 on the evaluation and future development of the Frontex Agency and of the European Border Surveillance System (Eurosur) (2008/2157(INI)), p. 43.
[175] *Frontex General Report* (Warsaw: Frontex, 2009). http://frontex.europa.eu/assets/About_Frontex/Governance_documents/Annual_report/2009/gen_rep_2009_en.pdf
[176] "Frontex in the Mediterranean," August 16, 2009, accessed April 30, 2010. http://www.allincluded.nl/index.php/bajesboten-voor-criminelen-of-uitgeprocedeerden/199

to the Canary Islands. The number of clandestine immigrants reaching the Canaries has fallen considerably."[177] Arrivals on the Italian island of Lampedusa increased by 190 percent in the first six months of 2008. Frontex officials cited Libyan refusals to stem the flow of illegal departures and shifted focus to patrolling outside EU boundaries and closer to the Libyan coast.

In 2008, the Commission audited Frontex along the lines of its eight mandated areas of activity,[178] praising operational coordination: "more than 53,000 persons, for 2006 and 2007 together, have been apprehended or denied entry at the border during these operations. More than 2,900 false or falsified travel documents have been detected and 58 facilitators of illegal migration arrested."[179] Other areas of praise included Frontex's work in risk analysis and investment in new border management technologies (such as the Automated Biometric Border Crossings Systems for Registered Passengers at Four European Airports [BIOPASS] research project).[180] On the other hand, the Commission evaluated Frontex poorly in "joint return operations" (the deportation of asylum seekers en route), on the grounds that it had not done enough in this area, and "is lagging behind the progress made with regard to operation coordination."[181] The report concluded that EU resources spent on Frontex might not be of value because operations were unimpressive in results and cost the EU €455 per person denied entry across EU borders.[182] The Commission also warned that costs would inevitably rise because of future litigated personal injury or death claims from migrants handled during Frontex operations. In sum, the number of migrants decreased significantly over the first operational years of Frontex, but this cannot be attributed to any operational success on the part of the missions. Instead, other factors, such as offshoring immigration and border control to North African and other Mediterranean states, and an overall decrease in demand to immigrate to Europe – due to the economic crisis in Europe – may be more satisfactory explanations.

---

[177] I. Camilleri, "Frontex Chief Admits Failure," *Times of Malta*, September 21, 2008, accessed April 30, 2010. http://www.timesofmalta.com/articles/view/20080921/local/frontex-chief-admits-failure

[178] European Commission, 2008. Report on the Evaluation and Future Development of the Frontex Agency. Brussels, COM(2008) 67 final.

[179] Ibid., p. 3.

[180] Frontex, BIOPASS: Study on Automated Biometric Border Crossing Systems for Registered Passenger at Four European Airports. Warsaw, August 2007.

[181] European Commission, 2008. Report on the Evaluation and Future Development of the Frontex Agency, p. 7.

[182] Ibid.

The lack of overall impressiveness was also highlighted in a UK House of Lords EU Committee report: "We believe the increased resources may usefully lead to a modest increase in the number of operations in 2008, but should be concentrated on further increasing the quality of those operations."[183] The report recommended Frontex scale back its return operations, given the human rights discrepancies and uncertainties, specifically highlighting the NGO claims that Frontex operations have racially profiled migrants and screened out entire ethnic groups or nationalities, such as Iraqis.[184]

Frontex: Relationship with Interest Groups

NGOs and human rights campaigners have had an oppositional and negative relationship with Frontex, citing its operational independence and lack of transparency over human rights issues. Watchdog groups have been publicizing incidents since at least 2007, including women and children handcuffed on return charter flights and returned to cargo holds, hunger strikes in detention camps over abuse and conditions, and translators betraying asylum seekers by revealing their identities to authorities.[185] In a 2008 Statement on International Protection presented at the UNHCR Standing Committee, a broad coalition of NGOs expressed their concern that "much of the rescue work by Frontex is in fact incidental to a deterrence campaign so broad and, at times, so undiscriminating, that directly and through third countries – intentionally or not – asylum-seekers are being blocked from claiming protection under the 1951 Refugee Convention."[186] The ECRE and British Refugee Council claimed Frontex failed to demonstrate adequate consideration of international and European asylum and human rights law, including the 1951 Convention in respect of access to asylum and the prohibition of refoulement.[187]

The ECRE has been frustrated by the lack of access to Frontex information or operations: "There is a worrying lack of clarity regarding Frontex accountability for ensuring compliance with international and EC legal obligations by Member States involved in Frontex coordinated operations. This is compounded by the lack of transparency, and the

---

[183] *House of Lords Report on Frontex*, 29.   [184] Ibid., 270.

[185] David Cronin, "RIGHTS: Expulsions From EU Rise Sharply," *Terraviva Europe*, 2010, accessed April 30, 2010. http://ipsterraviva.org/Europe/article.aspx?id=8256

[186] "NGO Statement on International Protection: The High Commissioner's Dialogue on Protection Challenges." Accessed June 11, 2009. http://www.icmc.net/pdf/unhcr_stancom_08_ngo_stmt.pdf

[187] ECRE/BRC joint response to House of Lords inquiry on Frontex, May 10, 2007. http://www.ecre.org/resources/ecre_actions/955

absence of independent monitoring and democratic accountability of the Agency."[188] ECRE tried to propose that Frontex cooperate with the UNHCR and refugee NGOs to shift its agenda from security to protection and have Frontex actions monitored by an independent body, to ensure that the training of border guards and RABITs includes asylum and human rights law.[189]

EU responses to these criticisms have varied but have never aligned with NGO interests and agendas. JHA commissioner Malmstrom promised "explicit requirements for all border guards taking part in operations to have been trained in fundamental rights," so that migrants would not be deported before establishing their asylum claims, and return operations could have NGO observers to prevent human rights violations. However, Frontex dismissed NGO concerns as misplaced:

Human rights questions are present always where law enforcement authorities are involved. In order to avoid any misconduct, proper rules need to be introduced and people need to be trained. This is what we do everyday in our operational plans and training curricula. We also cooperate with different Government Organisations like UNHCR, IOM or EU Fundamental Rights Agency in this respect. I don't feel that people accusing Frontex of human rights' violations are really aiming at Frontex. They protest against the European migration policy, asylum policy or violations of human rights committed by people in different Member States. It is much easier to find one entity that could be blamed for everything. Attacking all law enforcement authorities in all Member States would not be so simple; therefore Frontex is an easy target. Frontex always takes seriously all allegations of human rights' violations committed during Frontex-coordinated operations. Every possible effort is always made during our activities to ensure that the fundamental rights are respected at all times by all national border services participating. However, it is worth to remember that Frontex powers are limited as the agency is neither a regulatory body nor an investigative one.[190]

Some NGOs concurred with this assessment, but deplored lack of accountability. According to the Meijers Committee and ECRE, Frontex is not the bad guy, but is "reinforcing the standards [of the lowest common denominator states] in terms of extraterritorial border controls" on the larger scale of the entire EU.[191]

---

[188] Refugee Council and the European Council on Refugees and Exiles (ECRE) joint response to Select Committee on the European Union Sub-Committee F (Home Affairs): Frontex Inquiry, Warsaw, Poland. September 24, 2007, p. 2.

[189] Sonia Sirtori and Patricia Coelho, "Defending Refugees' Access to Protection in Europe." *European Council on Refugees and Exiles (ECRE)*, December 2007.

[190] "Border Security: Frontex Is Operational and Steadily Improving." Interview with Ilkka Laitinen, 2009. *Independent Review on European Security & Defence* 2, p. 34.

[191] *House of Lords Report on Frontex*, 120.

In the spring of 2010, Frontex spokesperson Michal Parzyszek granted an interview with the ECRE NGO. In response to the question "Will there be more opportunities for civil society involvement in various aspects of Frontex's work?" Parzyszek responded,

Frontex is fully engaged in discussion with civil society. We talk to citizens through the media, receive their feedback, and reply to enquiries of private citizens, journalists and researchers. We actively participate in conferences and public debates. This interview is a good example of such a discussion, which we greatly appreciate. So far, the problem Frontex has faced has been the fact that Member States pledge to deliver equipment but they do not fulfill their pledge. The new (compulsory 2010) mandate obliges them to keep their pledges.[192]

He also argued that Frontex had a close relationship with UNHCR over refugee rights. However, the UNHCR liaison officer at Frontex complained in 2010 that

it remains difficult to evaluate the impact of [UNHCR's asylum and protection] training [of border officials] while information on operational activities at the borders, especially at sea, remains rather limited. Frontex operations should ensure disembarkation of those intercepted at sea to a place where they are not only safe physically, but where their basic rights – including the rights to seek asylum and receive protection – are respected. This is spelled out in the recently adopted European Union guidelines for maritime border operations. In any event, the operations should anticipate that some of those intercepted at sea will be particularly vulnerable, notably unaccompanied children, women, and torture victims. At this time, we believe there are not enough qualified staff at sea or land entry points to identify and support such vulnerable cases. To assist border guards in this identification process, UNHCR is currently discussing with Frontex the elaboration of ad hoc protection guidelines for some selected joint operations.[193]

In contrast to the Frontex–NGO relationship, the relationship between Frontex and informal internal security institutions grew closer and more productive. Many of the firms and industry associations maintaining relations with Frontex were the same as those with working relationships with the EDA and the European Commission in civilian security research. These public–private collaborations involve projects such

---

[192] ECRE Interview with Michal Parzyszek, Frontex Spokesperson. April 4, 2010. Available at: http://frontexplode.eu/2010/04/04/ecre-interview-with-michal-parzyszek-frontex-spokesperson/
[193] Q&A: Working for Refugees on Europe's Outer Borders, 2010. *UNHCR: The UN Refugee Agency*. UNHCR: Geneva. Available at: http://www.unhcr.org/4bf29c8b6.html [Accessed June 6, 2010].

as the development of a common European border surveillance system (EUROSUR); maritime surveillance solutions such as coastal radar stations, surface ships, manned aircraft, satellites, and UAVs. The Frontex research and development division promoted UAV land and maritime surveillance demonstrations,[194] involving firms involved in C4I, sensors, UAVs, radars, and system integrators to collaborate on security solutions. In 2010, the Frontex director made explicit that it would be the central buyer in a future European security market:

The Agency, if provided with an adequate budget and consistent powers, could become the catalyst for demand harmonisation in the European border surveillance security segment... The Agency could act by centralising procurement activity, commissioning significant R&D efforts and, potentially, also developing cooperation with defence actors also having responsibility in this area, in particular the surveillance of maritime borders. All these activities, however, would require a political decision to expand Frontex's remit.[195]

Over this time period, Frontex was increasingly able to procure its own border security and surveillance equipment. This procurement initially began with the procurement of services such as pilot projects in coordination with the European Union Satellite Centre, to use UAVs and satellite-based information to monitor areas outside of European borders, such as Libya, Syria, or Mali. The former Frontex director noted the growing importance of relationships with industry consortiums, as he saw "Frontex's job is to help steer the research and development of surveillance technologies by working with industry consortiums in areas such as remotely piloted aircraft systems (RPAS)"... "[o]ur experience with the co-operation with industry is very positive – they have a lot of good ideas and they brought many new innovations," because "Large firms in the EU aviation market, such as Dassault, Thales and BAE Systems, complain that member states' strict and fragmented laws on unmanned aircraft hamper development. They say that RPAS, which can serve dual military and civilian purposes, could generate €4.6 billion in profits annually."[196]

---

[194] Frontex/Events. Warsaw, Poland. Accessed April 30, 2010. http://www.frontex.europa.eu/events/art15.html

[195] European Commission (2010). Study on the industrial implications in Europe of the blurring of dividing lines between Security and Defence. Contract no. SI2.516182. pp. 112

[196] N. Nielsen, "Frontex Chief Looks beyond EU Borders," *euObserver*, January 14, 2013. https://euobserver.com/fortress-eu/118471

2009–11: Rapid Growth of EU Internal Security Governing Capacity

The period of 2009–11 represents a critical juncture in Frontex capacity, including the 2011 ability to purchase border security equipment[197] and negotiate agreements with countries outside Europe.[198] It also represents a major development in European Commission governance of civilian and border security markets, including the security research initiatives within "Framework Programme 7" (FP7) and Horizon 2020 (H2020). These developments cannot be explained by increases in migration flows: from 2008 to 2011, migration pressures on EU borders actually decreased.[199] For the most part, this shift started well before the Arab Spring in 2011, when increasing numbers of migrants and refugees began attempting to cross the Mediterranean. The timing and deepening of EU internal security governing capacity can be explained by changes to internal security governance as part of the 2009 Lisbon Treaty, but also by the mobilization of security interest groups and their informal institutions.

The first years of Frontex's existence were marked with a great deal of ambiguity over its authority and the scope of its tasks. This began to change in 2007 when Frontex gained the capacity to field Rapid Border Intervention Teams (RABITs), which would deploy officers to stop migrant arrivals.[200] While RABITs were authorized to bear arms and to use force (with member state consent), the legislation also insulated Frontex from future legal liability in operations outside of Europe, such as in the Mediterranean.[201] According to Frontex officials, human

---

[197] Regulation (EU) No 1168/2011 of the European Parliament and of the Council of 25 October 2011 amending Council Regulation (EC) No 2007/2004 establishing a European Agency for the Management of Operational Cooperation at the External Borders of the Member States of the European Union.

[198] Regulation (EC) No 863/2007 of the European Parliament and of the Council of 11 July 2007 establishing a mechanism for the creation of Rapid Border Intervention Teams and amending Council Regulation (EC) No 2007/2004 as regards that mechanism and regulating the tasks and powers of guest officers.

[199] "Frontex: Annual Risk Analyses 2008–2012," *Frontex.europa.eu*, 2016. http://frontex .europa.eu/publications/?c=risk-analysis

[200] Regulation (EC) No 863/2007 of the European Parliament and of the Council of 11 July 2007 establishing a mechanism for the creation of Rapid Border Intervention Teams and amending Council Regulation (EC) No 2007/2004 as regards that mechanism and regulating the tasks and powers of guest officers, at: http://eur-lex.europa.eu/ LexUriServ/LexUriServ.do?uri=OJ:L:2007:199:0030:0039:EN:PDF

[201] Regulation (EC) No 863/2007, July 11, 2007. Art 6(6). Accessed April 13, 2011. http://eur-lex.europa.eu/LexUriServ/LexUriServ.do?uri=CELEX:32007R0863:en: NOT

rights remained the responsibility of member states,[202] and Frontex was "not legally capable of violating human rights."[203] Capacity also grew significantly in 2010, when the Commission proposed that Frontex could "evaluate, approve and coordinate proposals for joint operations and pilot projects made by Member State"; "draw up" operational plans; "itself initiate joint operations and pilot projects" and "terminate" them; and "constitute a pool of border guards called Frontex Joint Support Teams."[204]

EU Internal Security: Delayed Governance Capacity

Scholars have puzzled over the paradox of EU immigration policy, and because of the free movement of people through the EU, the immigration issue is a shared social burden requiring a common solution. Terrorist attacks, social unrest, demographic challenges, recessions, and flows of weapons, people, drugs, and crime have made immigration and borders a high-profile policy area. While the EU created a liberal immigration policy within its borders, it has essentially failed to craft an effective policy agenda for dealing with the issue of outside immigration, with the exception of tightening asylum and border security. Scholars have concluded EU capacity in immigration has been constrained because of member state resistance to sensitive sovereignty concerns.[205]

This is an accurate assessment, but insufficient for explaining the delay of EU governance. It also fails to account for the more recent rapid development of EU governing capacity in internal security affairs, and dramatic leaps in the authority and resources of EU security bureaucracies. In other equally sensitive policy domains, such as defense politics or monetary politics,[206] European institutions have been able to

---

[202] European Parliament: Civil Liberties Committee (LIBE) Hearing: Interparliamentary Committee Meeting with National Parliaments on "Democratic accountability of the internal security strategy and the role of Europol, Eurojust and Frontex," Brussels, October 5–6, 2011, Session III: Director of Frontex, Ilkka Laitinen.

[203] Niels Frenzen, "Interview with Frontex Director Laitinen," *Migrants at Sea*, March 24, 2014; See also: European Ombudsman, "Full Summary on Frontex Inquiry," February 2014.

[204] COM (2010) 61 final "Proposal for a REGULATION OF THE EUROPEAN PARLIAMENT AND THE COUNCIL amending Council Regulation (EC) No 2007/2004 establishing a European Agency for the Management of Operational Cooperation at the External Borders of the Member States of the European Union (Frontex)."

[205] Andrew Geddes, *The Politics of Migration and Immigration in Europe* (London, UK: Sage, 2003); Givens and Luedtke.

[206] N. Jabko, *Playing the Market: A Political Strategy for Uniting Europe, 1985–2005* (Ithaca, NY: Cornell University Press, 2006).

circumvent national sovereignty concerns through effective framing and incremental policy change. National resistance to immigration reform stopped Commission legislation from passing through the European Council, but the Commission was particularly weak because of a lack of a constructive relationship with key social and market actors. This weakness meant there were fewer expert voices, external resources, and a network of constituents working to increase the legitimacy, legislation, and implementation of policies. Some NGOs mobilized early, but the relationship between informal and formal institutions remained antagonistic. Key industry actors such as sectors with a stake in attracting affordable or talented immigrants to resolve gaps in labor never mobilized to assist the EU in formulating agendas. National justice and interior ministers mobilized to form transnational advisory committees to influence the EU agenda toward more restrictive security policies. The Commission itself funded the creation of multiple informal institutions in internal security affairs.

The critical juncture in the EU's internal security governance came when the interest groups in the defense sector diversified – partially in response to the European Commission incentivizing civilian security research markets – creating informal security institutions. This surge of security industry interests has changed the structure of EU state–society relations in the domain of internal security and JHA. The presence and activities of security interest groups have provided the framework for emerging informal institutions for border and internal security. This external informal institution has had two major implications. The first is that the mobilization of private security actors moved the boundaries of the immigration and JHA policy domain away from a focus on immigration toward a focus on border security and population management. This has also driven the content of the JHA policy agenda toward more "product"-based border security solutions over other policy options. The second is that this informal institution has provided the EU with an external capacity that has recently enhanced its governing capacity in its border security and control efforts. While the EU has had formal authority over some JHA policy areas, it did not have governing capacity until the mobilization of security interest groups created informal institutions. This has accelerated the EU's JHA governing capacity over border security, in particular. It also appears that this governing capacity has preceded developments in formal EU security authority. Two key authority developments are Frontex's 2011 increase in independent operational authority and procurement authority, and the October 2016 creation of a European Border and Coast Guard Agency (replacing Frontex) with significantly increased independent and supranational authority over operations and procurement.

Compared to the case of EU defense, the JHA policy domain has had the opposite arc in both governing capacity and policy agenda setting. Immigration policy started out as low politics, where the policy issues were technocratic and legal. Over the course of the past few decades, coordinating immigration policy and securing external borders has become a top security concern of the EU, raising the issue to one of high politics. Internal security has been elevated to the highest of European interests, integral to its ESS and a foreign policy emphasizing a "comprehensive approach." Immigration and border security policy has been securitized, but it has also been pushed from low politics to high politics, based on the state–society interaction (and initial lack of interaction) of European political institutions and European interest groups.

Contrast this policy arc to CSDP: Defense started out as high diplomatic politics, where European states attempted to create a security community with the EDC and later projects such as the WEU. Today, EU defense has very little focus on actual deployable operations. Much of the activity in the domain is on cooperation of military acquisition and development of dual-use products across national borders. A focus on the economic logic of military cooperation has pushed EU defense from high politics down to the technicalities of low politics.

7 The Blurring of European Security and Defense

EU security and defense institutions accelerated in the 2000s. The conventional wisdom explaining why the EU needed security and defense is straightforward: the post-9/11 world necessitated additional policies and institutions to cope with the emerging transnational threats. A key development in the response to 9/11 has been to blur the areas of security and defense, and consider external and internal threats and responses along a single continuum.[1] The 2009 Defence Procurement Directive was framed as an explicit response to changes in the EU's strategic environment, where "[t]he emergence of asymmetrical transnational threats has increasingly blurred the boundary between the external and the internal and military and non-military security."[2] And the 2010 EU Internal Security Strategy argued that "internal security cannot exist without an external dimension, since internal security increasingly depends to a large extent on external security."[3] The 2003 European Security Strategy first identified a list of unconventional threats to European security, prescribing combined security and defense agendas and pre-emptive security before defense, and deploying joint civilian-military operations.

Although building EU security institutions in response to a changing security environment appears functional and straightforward, the timing, agenda, and structure of these responses were never predetermined, nor were they automatic. The existence of EU institutions and policies in security and defense, and the blurring of the boundaries between them, is a result of the particular path the development of the European

---

[1] See D. Bigo, "When Two Become One: Internal and External Securitizations in Europe," in *International Relations Theory and the Politics of the European Integration: Power, Security, and Community*, edited by M. Kelstrup and M. C. Williams (London, UK: Routledge, 2006).

[2] Defence Procurement Directive, EU Directive 2009/81/EC: http://eur-lex.europa.eu/legal-content/EN/TXT/?uri=celex:32009L0081

[3] Council of the European Union (2010). Internal Security Strategy for the European Union: Toward a European Security Model, Brussels, 23 February 2010, 5842/2/10, p. 16.

security state took in the decades prior to these developments. And it is as dependent on interest-group mobilization and the capacity of EU institutions as it is on critical security junctures such as 9/11. I argue that the core agenda-setting impetus behind the timing and blurring of EU security and defense was a bottom-up desire to create EU defense and security markets logic. This bottom-up mobilization first created informal industry institutions in defense; then the same defense actors created informal security institutions. These developments preceded and informed the creation of formal institutional developments in defense and then in security.

The origin of this industry mobilization was market competition with U.S. defense firms. The U.S. government first closed its doors to foreign defense contractors, and then it nurtured its own defense industrial base by supporting mergers and encouraging exports. Moreover, it incentivized technology transfer between civilian and defense technology and markets throughout the 1990s. This resulted in both technology improvements and access to new market sectors for U.S. defense firms. While the U.S. government fostered these linkages, EU states did not. The U.S. DoD encouraged and financially supported this industrial concentration, incentivizing these market reforms in return for the considerable fiscal savings achieved through streamlining economies of scale. European firms had no equivalent of this, as their home markets were not large enough to justify these reforms.

Increasing transatlantic and global pressures led to a second wave of interest-group mobilization on the part of market-seeking European security industry groups. The European Commission coordinated this effort to broaden its scope of influence over the emerging security domain in lieu of its lack of authority over national defense markets. By 2003, the Commission believed "Europe is paying a very high price for the artificial – and uniquely European – separation between civil and military research."[4] This separation might have been uniquely European, but so was the emerging political solution: the blurring of the historical separation between military and civilian agendas and institutions as a matter of EU policy. This blurring allowed for the Commission's mandate to regulate security industry and technology (including border security) to include the defense industry and defense technology, where the Commission had no legal mandate.[5]

---

[4] P. Sparaco and M. A. Taverna, "Propping Up R&D," *Aviation Week & Space Technology*, October 27, 2003.
[5] Edler and James, 2012.

Civilian-Military Fusion: Links between Security and Defense

A significant part of the ESS – and its emerging doctrine – involved the attempt to integrate the homeland security and external civilian crisis management mission with military force. In December 2004, the European Council launched the Civilian Headline Goal 2008 process,[6] which set out a number of ambitious goals, including a commitment to being able to act in six areas of activity (police, rule of law, civilian administration, civil protection, monitoring of various sorts, and other support functions). The Civilian Headline Goal 2008 was succeeded by the Civilian Headline Goal 2010.[7] The ESS promoted a Europe ready to

share in the responsibility for global security and in building a better world ... develop a strategic culture that fosters early, rapid and when necessary, robust intervention ... [and] be able to act before countries around [it] deteriorate, when signs of proliferation are detected, and before humanitarian emergencies arise.[8]

For domestic threats such as terrorism, weapons of mass destruction (WMD) proliferation, and organized crime, "the first line of defence now lies abroad."[9]

Two narratives explain the emergence of this strategic effort. The first is that civilian crisis management fused with military strength is required for dealing with an unstable world. By merging civilian expertise with a competent military force, the EU could accomplish foreign policy beyond its institutional limitations. As a foreign policy actor, EU specializes in police training, establishing judicial institutions, border controls, infrastructure creation, security sector reform, and nation building. Far from being a redundant and lesser version of NATO, the EU and its burgeoning CSDP provide a vital link between traditional military operations and more active peace enforcement styles of operations.

There is an alternate and complementary explanation for fusing of civilian–military, internal–external, and security–defense: that they are market-driven in their origins. Deploying civilian operations – with traditional military backup – was referenced as the "unique selling point" for

---

[6] Council of the European Union, "Civilian Headline Goal 2008," December 7, 2004, Brussels.

[7] Council of the European Union, "Civilian Headline Goal 2010," As approved by the ministerial Civilian Capabilities Improvement Conference and noted by the General Affairs and External Relations Council on 19 Nov 2007, Brussels.

[8] The Council of the European Union, A Secure Europe in a Better World, European Security Strategy, Brussels, December 12, 2003.

[9] Ibid.

the EU in differentiating itself from NATO.[10] After decades of attempts to create a real defense procurement market and research base, there was finally a strategic "in." Previous attempts always ran up against the reality that creating a European defense market could not be justified in parallel with the continuing existence of NATO. The informal institutions that helped set this agenda bypassed this problem by promoting an EU focused on "civilian and military technology, for internal and external security, and for joint civilian-military applications."[11]

The fusing of security and defense was primarily a bottom-up rather than a top-down phenomenon. The technology and markets came first, while the security policies and institutions came later. In the attempt to undo the traditional "historical distinctions between defence and civil security policies and technologies," former Commissioner Franco Frattini emphasized emulating the U.S. experience by eliminating the separation between "hard" (military) and "soft" (civilian) technologies: "We have to do the same in Europe, where government support efforts made by industry, and where the economy supports the role of governments in the fight against terrorism."[12] This distinction was first addressed in areas of security research and development, where the Commission and the EDA addressed defense-origin technology and equipment with dual-use applications toward internal and border security. These include satellite surveillance and communications, targeting technologies such as see-through-walls radar systems and detection of biological, chemical, and nuclear threats. These technologies have been increasingly developed via EU research programs and applied in civilian urban and maritime border settings.[13] The blurring also took place in market standards, where civilian market standards could be applied to the defense sector to increase competitiveness.

The primary agenda of informal defense institutions was to argue that distinctions between civilian and military technologies had been obsolete since the 1990s. As an EADS executive – speaking on behalf of the security industry group STAR 21 – said, "Industry cannot put forward institutional or policy changes, of course, but it can give EU . . . politicians new things to chew on," particularly in helping the EU define the boundaries (or integration) of defense procurement and industrial security

---

[10] Security and Defence Agenda Report, "Shaping Europe's Defence Debate," Brussels, Belgium, November 2007, p. 19.

[11] Author interview with EU official, Brussels, Belgium, November 9, 2007.

[12] "High-profile Frattini Keeps His Private Life from Public Scrutiny," *The Times (London)*, November 15, 2004, accessed October 29, 2016.

[13] B. Tigner, "EU Group to Discuss Unifying Defence Market," *Defence News*, July 16–22, 2001.

policy.[14] ASD programs, such as the Stakeholders Platform for Supply chain Mapping, Market Condition Analysis and Technologies Opportunities (Staccato), produced a study on how to build the European Security Market, framed as "pave[ing] the way for concrete European Cooperation between supply and demand in the domain of a defence and security market in Europe."[15] In 2004, the ASD Security Network for Technological Research in Europe (SeNTRE) program proposed a strategic research plan for European security by establishing and consulting a network of users and technology experts at national and European levels in support of, and to link with, the European Security Research Advisory Board (ESRAB). Coordinated by ASD, funded by the Commission, and with the participation of twenty-two private partners, SeNTRE produced "A strategic security research plan containing a list of prioritised short, medium and long term actions; A database of missions and technologies; An organized platform of users and technology experts for future consultation; A methodology to organise and analyse the security needs at the operational level."[16]

The idea of merging security and defense at the strategic level followed these low-politics market reforms. While by 2007, officials claimed that "the distinction between external defence and internal security exists only in cold war institutions and is an artificial dichotomy,"[17] this agenda had been worked out at the lower, technocratic level in previous years. Security industry interest groups stated it was their lobbying goal to have EU strategy and institutions reflect the military–civilian integration taking place in technology and industry.[18] At a 2004 agenda-setting conference over European defense, the director of an informal defense institution (Security Defence Agenda) urged defense industry executives to "Stop making macho ads with missiles and fighter planes" and start using "civil society language" so as to present the industry as "protecting civil society and the freedom of citizens."[19] And a Thales official observed "a shift in emphasis and an increasing balance between what we see as defence and homeland security. 'Security' is a more politically acceptable way of describing what was traditionally defence."[20]

---

[14] Ibid.
[15] "ASD – Staccato," ASD Report, Brussels, April 24, 2008. http://www.asd-europe.org/Content/Default.asp?PageID=34
[16] "ASD- SeNTRE," ASD Report, Brussels, December 2004, http://www.asd-europe.org/Content/Default.asp?PageID=23
[17] Author interview with EU official, Brussels, Belgium, November 6, 2007.
[18] Author interview with security industry representative, Brussels, Belgium, June 2, 2007.
[19] Corporate Europe Observatory, "Competing Ourselves to Death," April 2004, October 25, 2016. http://archive.corporateeurope.org/ebs2004.html
[20] Bromley, 16.

Public and Private Interests in a Developing "International" State

The boundary between the public agenda and myriad private interests is dynamic and contentious. This book has focused on one set of mechanisms at the boundary of public and private: those related to capacity, specifically the governing capacity of international bureaucracies maximizing their political capital through embedded public–private networks. Rather than ask what effect bureaucrats have on their environment, I have asked what effect interest groups and informal political institutions have had on EU defense and security outcomes. Capacity is a maddeningly fuzzy concept, but its effects can be seen in institutional outcomes, such as whether legislation and policy agendas are generated, well crafted, and successfully implemented. It is that extra factor producing outcomes that differ from functional or resource-based expectations. In a developing state, it is often interdependent with the mobilization, participation, and density of motivated interest groups and informal institutions.

Introducing the concept of capacity inevitably blurs into a discussion of power, legitimacy, and authority. Scholars often conflate the concepts of authority and capacity, assuming that they are equal, or that the formal authority or material resources of a state, government, or organization produce equal amounts of governing capacity, political capital, or organizational quality. One source defines authority as "the capacity, innate or acquired for exercising ascendancy over a group."[21] Weberian definitions of authority are also inseparable from capacity and legitimacy, when interpreted as "the normative belief by an actor that a rule or institution ought to be obeyed."[22] When power is exercised in high-capacity institutions, "the two concepts of power and legitimacy come together in the idea of authority."[23] Authority transforms "trust into a social relationship in order to introduce an additional pressure of conformity beyond that which the relationship itself can exert . . . if obedience is the counterpart of power, trust is the counterpart of authority."[24] The study of international organizations also intertwines delegated authority with the capacity of a bureaucracy to serve its constituents a valuable and legitimate social purpose.[25]

But authority and capacity are not the same and do not necessarily derive from the same source. Perhaps when tied to stable and legitimate

---

[21] Roberto Michels, "Authority," in *Encyclopedia of the Social Sciences, Vol. II* (New York, NY: Macmillan, 1930).
[22] Hall and Biersteker, 323.   [23] Ibid.   [24] Ibid., 330.
[25] Barnett and Finnemore, 21.

political authority, these concepts are inseparable. However, in newer bureaucracies or political authorities, the concepts of power, authority, legitimacy, and capacity are not so enmeshed. In the EU, only member states can give the EU more formal authority, but interest groups and informal institutions can give the EU more capacity through external expertise, policy development, and agenda setting. And this external capacity can enhance the legitimacy and effectiveness of new bureaucracies,[26] leading to greater autonomy vis-à-vis other political authorities, and even the development of more formal authority from informal authority networks. This is an alternative path to formal authority, where governing capacity – as a product of state–society interactions – precedes developments in formal authority.

A developing state can have large differentials between actual power and the ability to exercise power. Once authority and capacity are separated, it is possible to ask how developing political outcomes can differ from expectations based on formal authority and material resources. We can ask how increases or decreases in formal authority lead to increases or decreases in capacity. When separate, capacity can occur prior to authority: a bureaucracy maximizing its resources through its informal network – gaining increased legitimacy with its constituency – can prompt changes in its power and possibly its formal authority. When bureaucracies have a "degree of cultural support for an organization . . . to which the array of established cultural accounts provide explanations for its existence, functioning, and jurisdiction,"[27] then legitimacy and capacity can produce authority, not just the other way around.

This book has departed from traditional concepts of international organizations as entities with only member states as constituents. Understanding of power, authority, capacity, and legitimacy in international organizations requires a broader understanding of transnational interest groups and international public–private interactions. Framing a state–society dynamic at the international or regional arena of politics opens up even more questions about the role of private authority, particularly private international or transnational authority. We have begun to create a language for these interactions, where *private* is defined as "neither states, state-based, nor state-created" and *authority* is defined as "institutionalized forms or expressions of power" that are legitimate in the sense that "there is some form of normative, un-coerced consent or recognition of authority on the part of the regulated or governed."[28]

How should we conceptualize emerging public–private boundaries and dynamics when the interest groups are often well established and

[26] Carpenter.   [27] Meyer and Scott, 201.   [28] Büthe, 281–2.

resource rich and possess a wealth of expertise, when the public author-ities vary in their bureaucratic and governing capacity? International organizations are formed by client states to coordinate a larger pub-lic interest, but they are often constrained by limited budgets, legit-imacy issues, or convoluted decision rules that dilute coherent legal authority. In other cases, international organizations are well funded and resourced, with clear lines of legitimacy and authority over an issue area, but might fail to capture the attention of interest groups. When inter-national bureaucrats build networks with private actors and harness the resources or expertise of private authority, does this expand or constrain the limits of their organization? Are the causes and consequences of public–private relations at the international level comparable to public–private relations at the domestic level?

I have assumed there are more similarities than differences between domestic and international public–private relations. Whether interna-tional or domestic, government officials and interest groups have a nat-ural affinity to one another. Government officials are often overtasked or isolated and do not have access to all social or market information. Interest groups are attracted to the locus of decision making or regu-latory power for a number of reasons, including information gathering, the attempt to influence specific policies, or the attempt to influence the future of the public interest and policy agenda. Centers of power and policymaking are natural centers of interaction between state and society. In mature polities, these interactions become regular, taking the form of lobbying, commissions, task forces, public–private partnerships, outsourcing of government functions, privatization of government enti-ties, and individual career paths revolving between public service and private organizations.

We currently lack a common analytical language for discussing the interactions between public and private actors on the boundary of state and society. This is true when trying to compare national bureaucra-cies between the developed and developing world, let alone international organizations. The same type of activity – revolving-door career paths between public and private organizations – can be viewed as a benefi-cial public–private interaction or shameful corruption, depending on the place and time. Other loosely defined concepts of state–society bound-aries and interaction include influence, capture, autonomy, and insula-tion. These terms are subjective, are notoriously difficult to define and measure, and often are used loosely.

When discussing concepts such as influence, capture, autonomy, or insulation, it can be easier to deal in the subjective and normative than the comparative and analytical. Though the concepts are slippery, there are a number of recurring themes in the study of contemporary state–society boundaries and relations. First, what is the boundary between public or government interests and private or nongovernment interests? What is constant about these concepts, and what changes over time and across different polities? Have public–private boundaries fundamentally changed through the widespread trends of privatization and outsourcing to private authority? How is it different when a new public bureaucracy is institutionalizing in an era of increased private authority? Second, what is the effect of these interactions on government organizations and officials? What is the effect of these interactions on political outcomes, policies, laws, and political institutions? These are all questions at different orders of magnitude, ranging from the specific (a particular law) to the systemic (the political institutions). Third, what are "the causes and consequences of governance influence by private authority?"[29] Does the source of private authority change these dynamics, whether it is a corporation, business association, or NGO? Are there inherently different rules of the game between the national and international levels of politics, or between different policy issues areas?

A final concept in the discussion of public–private boundaries is "the normative assessment of a private provision of governance."[30] Do the benefits of private participation in governance – such as governing capacity increases – increase or narrow the general welfare of the polity? When interest groups are more involved in agenda setting at all stages of policy-making, where should the public look for accountability and the public interest? Within democratic theory, elected authority at the level of the nation state is the normative ideal. The involvement of interest groups and the increase of private authority through informal channels are complex and problematic for these normative ideals.

These questions are amplified when asking about the normative ideals of governance at the level of international organizations such as the EU. States designed international organizations as diplomatic arrangements, not institutions interacting with private social or market actors. In fact, the EU has long been accused of having a democratic deficit for these very reasons, as its role in citizens' lives has grown without a concomitant increase in formal channels of individual democratic participation. The increasing activity of interest groups through lobbying, committees, task forces, and other formal and informal means is a potential improvement on the democratic deficits of the EU institutional structure. It can increase the legitimacy of the EU among its constituents in a particular policy domain. In effect, it creates more EU, even when the final

---

[29] Ibid., 287.   [30] Ibid., 288.

product is to some degree the result of the activity and resources of interest groups. On the other hand, this private activity is unregulated and opaque, and it rewards the most motivated and earliest mobilized interest groups. This lack of transparency and accountability undermines the legitimacy of EU governance and, ultimately, undermines its power and authority.

Sorting through the complexities of international governance, Avant et al. identify a number of ways in which the traditional avenues of political accountability are being obscured by changes in global governance.[31] They argue that officials in international organizations sometimes seek more accountability as a means of increasing their authority and legitimacy. This dynamic of reintroducing accountability opens up a host of other questions, such as to whom, over what, and by what mechanism the global governors are accountable. On the first issue, the constituencies of international organizations have expanded to multiple kinds of public and private actors, away from the club of states models by design. On the latter issue, are public transparency and private participation normatively equivalent mechanisms for ensuring accountability of the public interest?[32]

Building EU Institutions in the Context of Public and Private Governance

Because of the history of the EU supranational integration process, scholars have primarily been concerned with the movement of formal legal authority between states and the EU over policy and governance. In contrast, at the nation-state level, where legal authority is comparably stable but political outcomes still vary, we ask questions about transformational capacity (that is, the ability to carry out the policies tasked to the organization, and the ability to survive and expand as a bureaucracy).[33] Few have assessed the strength and quality of EU political organizations, or the effect of this variation on EU political outcomes. As a developing state, the EU's governing capacity is at least partially the result of the timing and intensity of the relationship between EU bureaucracies and interest groups.

---

[31] Deborah D. Avant, Martha Finnemore, and Susan K. Sell, eds. *Who Governs the Globe?* Vol. 114. New York, NY: Cambridge University Press, 2010.

[32] A. Florini, *The Right to Know: Transparency for an Open World* (New York, NY: Columbia University Press, 2007).

[33] For example, see P. J. Katzenstein, *Between Power and Plenty: Foreign Economic Policies of Advanced Industrial States* (Madison: University of Wisconsin Press, 1978); Evans, *Embedded Autonomy;* Evans, Rueschemeyer, and Skocpol, *Bringing the State Back In.*

Although scholars have noted the overall "lack of a theoretical framework for linking social actors to the European political framework," the findings of this book deepen an agenda about interest groups and informal institutions in international security institutions.[34] Defense and security usually remain outside of discussions about interest groups and informal institutions, as they are high politics: sensitive policy areas where member states retain national sovereignty over decision making. When collective action problems or externalities force states to cooperate over security policy, they usually respond by creating small, understaffed EU bureaucracies with limited resources and mandates. Although states often design these institutions to minimally cooperate but ultimately fail in order to preserve their sovereignty, this opens the possibility of informal political institutions filling the void. The interest groups mobilized to lobby the EU are well organized, well funded, and well positioned to offer policy expertise and solutions. States may try to protect themselves from Europeanization by designing EU bureaucracies to fail, but this can lead to the accidental privatization of the policy agenda.

This book has produced results linking interest groups to political outcomes in EU governance, but its questions form a broad research agenda: What are the additional mechanisms at work between the mobilization of organized interests and international governance? Under what conditions does organized European society have more or less influence over EU policy agendas? This book began with political anecdotes about the presence and influence of organized European society in Brussels. There is evidence that some interest groups are active in Brussels before European leaders agree to greater European cooperation or authority. Observers have claimed that these interest groups have had a great deal of influence over EU policy agendas and political outcomes. However, there are also observations that organized interests have mobilized in response to greater EU political activity and authority over the past few decades.

The primary research question of the book asks what effect these variations in mobilization and state–society relations have had on EU political outcomes. I hypothesized that interest-group mobilization will be positively correlated with a greater volume of EU political activity and policy agenda success. When organized interests mobilize in advance of EU treaty authority, the EU institutions in that policy domain will have increased capacity, leading to more ability to enact effective legislation. Conversely, when the mobilization of organized interests is delayed until after EU treaty authority is established, the EU institutions in that policy

[34] Imig and Tarrow, *Contentions Europeans.*

domain will have lower capacity than other policy domains, leading to a reduced ability to enact effective legislation.

I also hypothesized that there would be unintended consequences of this increase or decrease in EU capacity. Specifically, when organized interests anticipate EU authority and mobilize early, EU institutions will enjoy increased capacity, but their public autonomy for setting policy agendas without private influence will be constrained. This lack of autonomy, however, is also a high degree of embeddedness, which makes policies more relevant to social and market actors and enables effective implementation.

Alternately, when there is a surfeit of organized interests in a policy domain, the EU institutions will have sufficient legal authority but relatively weak capacity, although they will have a great deal of autonomy from private influence. This protects their policies from accusations of corruption or cronyism, but the quality of the policy agenda will suffer from a lack of key social partners to provide information or assist with implementation. In other words, there is a window of opportunity early on in the life of an EU policy domain. This window allows for the forging of key partnerships between weak public and strong private actors. If interest groups are not mobilized, the public bureaucracy remains low in its transformative capacity. Even when states delegate more authority to the EU and more groups mobilize in response to this authority, there might be too much pluralism for growing these key partnerships. Policymaking then happens in a vacuum or in a cacophonous and weak network.

This argument aligns with the expectations of the agenda-setting literature from U.S. politics. When there is more conflict of interest among organized interests, the mobilized groups are less likely to influence the government. When there is less conflict, the group that is most enthusiastic and mobilizes first will likely define the policy issue area and agenda and act as a subgovernment.[35] When an issue area has more public exposure, there is less room for concentrated interest-group influence.[36] With less public exposure or in areas of low politics, there is potential for influence by concentrated groups.

This book has identified the EU governing capacity as the link between the structure of European society and the political development of the EU. Just as developing states attempt to transform economic linkages and manage risk, new EU bureaucracies can be relatively weak

---

[35] Baumgartner and Jones.
[36] R. D. Arnold, *The Logic of Congressional Action* (New Haven, CT: Yale University Press, 1990).

institutions sometimes reliant on external actors and organizations to promote effective political solutions and gain legitimacy. The ideal outcome of this interaction is enhanced governing capacity, often the product of informal political institutions, networks of public actors legislating and implementing policies, and interest groups with social or market expertise. When this relationship between public interests and private expertise is well balanced, it is called embedded autonomy, allowing for private input without policy capture. Even in less balanced outcomes, the governing capacity of a bureaucracy might be enhanced by its interactions with private interests. When private interests are stronger and better established than public bureaucracies, however, there might be a trade-off between increased capacity and the content or direction of the public agenda. Whether the agendas of interest groups and their informal institutions match public agendas also drives whether or not their interaction produces deeper formal authority for public bureaucracies.

Bibliography

Afonso, Antonio, Ludger Schuknecht, and Vito Tanzi. "Public Sector Efficiency: Evidence for new EU Member States and Emerging Markets." *Applied Economics* 42, no. 17 (2010): 2147–64.

Andersen, S., and K. Eliassen. "EU Lobbying: The New Research Agenda." *European Journal of Political Research* 27, no. 4 (1995): 427–41.

Andersen, Svein S., and Kjell A. Eliassen. "European Community Lobbying." *European Journal of Political Research* 20, no. 2 (1991): 173–87.

Anderson, S. B. *Crafting EU Security Policy: In Pursuit of a European Identity.* Boulder, CO: Lynne Rienner, 2008.

Arnold, R. D. *The Logic of Congressional Action.* New Haven, CT: Yale University Press, 1990.

Art, R. "Europe Hedges Its Security Bets." In *Balance of Power Revisited: Theory and Practice in the 21st Century*, edited by Robert Art, T. V. Paul, and James Wirtz. Stanford, CA: Stanford University Press, 2004: 179–213.

Aspinwall, Mark, and Justin Greenwood. "Conceptualising Collective Action in the European Union." In *Collective Action in the European Union: Interests and the New Politics of Associability.* London, UK: Routledge, 1998: 1–30.

Avant, Deborah D., Martha Finnemore, and Susan K. Sell, eds. *Who Governs the Globe?.* Vol. 114. New York, NY: Cambridge University Press, 2010.

Bache, I., and M. Flinders. "Themes and Issues in Multi-Level Governance." *Multi-Level Governance* (2004): 1–11.

Bailes, Alyson J. K. "The EU and a 'Better World': What Role for the European Security and Defence Policy?" *International Affairs* 84, no. 1 (2008): 115–30.

Baldwin, D. A. "Neoliberalism, Neorealism, and World Politics." In *Neorealism and Neoliberalism: The Contemporary Debate*, edited by D. A. Baldwin. New York, NY: Columbia University Press, 1993: 3–25.

Barnett, M., and M. Finnemore. *Rules for the World: International Organizations in Global Politics.* Ithaca, NY: Cornell University Press, 2004.

Barnett, Michael N., and Martha Finnemore. "The Politics, Power, and Pathologies of International Organizations," *International Organization* 53, no. 4 (1999): 699–732.

Baumgartner, Frank R. "EU Lobbying: a View from the US." *Journal of European Public Policy* 14, no. 3 (2007): 482–8.

Baumgartner, Frank, and B. Jones. *Agendas and Instability in American Politics.* Chicago, IL: Chicago University Press, 1993.

Baumgartner, Frank R., and B. L. Leech. "Interest Niches and Policy Bandwagons: Patterns of Interest Group Involvement in National Politics." *Journal of Politics* 64 (2001): 1191–213.

Baumgartner, Frank R., and B. L. Leech. "The Multiple Ambiguities of 'Counteractive Lobbying." *American Journal of Political Science* 40 (1996): 521–42.

Baumgartner, Frank R., and C. Mahoney. "Gaining Government Allies." Paper presented at the Midwest Political Science Association Annual Meeting, Chicago, IL, April 25–28, 2002.

Baumgartner, Frank R., Christoffer Green-Pedersen, and Bryan D. Jones. "Comparative Studies of Policy Agendas." *Journal of European Public Policy* 13, no. 7 (2006): 959–74.

Baumgartner, Frank R., Jeffrey M. Berry, Marie Hojnacki, David C. Kimball, and Beth L. Leech. *Lobbying and Policy Change: Who Wins, Who Loses, and Why*. Chicago, IL: University of Chicago Press, 2009.

Berkhout, J., and D. Lowery. "Counting Organized Interests in the European Union: A Comparison of Data Sources." *Journal of European Public Policy* 15, no. 4 (2008): 489–513.

Berry, J. *The Interest Group Society*, 2nd ed. New York, NY: HarperCollins, 1989.

Beyers, J. "Gaining and Seeking Access: The European Adaptation of Domestic Interest Associations." *European Journal of Political Research* 41 (2002): 586–612.

Beyers, J. "Voice and Access: Political Practices of European Interest Associations." *European Union Politics* 5, no. 2 (2004): 211–40.

Beyers, Jan, and Bart Kerremans. "Bureaucrats, Politicians, and Societal Interests: How Is European Policy Making Politicized?" *Comparative Political Studies* 37, no. 10 (2004): 1119–50.

Beyers, J., and B. Kerremans. "Critical Resource Dependencies and the Europeanization of Domestic Interest Groups." *Journal of European Public Policy* 14, no. 3 (2007): 460–81.

Beyers, J., and J. Trondal. "How Nation States 'Hit' Europe: Ambiguity and Representation in the European Union." *West European Politics* 27, no. 5 (2004): 919–42.

Bigo, D. "The European Internal Security Field: Stakes and Rivalries in a Newly Developing Area of Police Intervention." In *Policing Across National Boundaries*, edited by Malcom Anderson and Monica Den Boer. London, UK: Pinter, 1994: 161–73.

Bigo, D. *Polices en reseaux: l'experience européenne*. Paris, France: Presses de Sciences Politique, 1996.

Bigo, D. "When Two Become One: Internal and External Securitizations in Europe." In *International Relations Theory and the Politics of the European Integration: Power, Security, and Community*, edited by M. Kelstrup and M. C. Williams, 171–204. London, UK: Routledge, 2006.

Bigo, Didier, and Julien Jeandesboz, "The EU and the European Security Industry Questioning the 'Public-Private Dialogue.'" *INEX Policy Brief* no. 5, February 2010.

Blanchard, Jean-Marc F., Edward D. Mansfield, and Norrin M. Ripsman. "The Political Economy of National Security: Economic Statecraft, Interdependence, and International Conflict." *Security Studies* 9, no. 1–2 (1999): 1–14.

Bob, Clifford. *The Global Right Wing and the Clash of World Politics*. New York, NY: Cambridge University Press, 2012.

Börzel, T. A. "Mind the Gap! European Integration between Level and Scope." *Journal of European Public Policy* 12, no. 2 (2005): 217–36.

Börzel, T. A., and Risse, T. "Governance without a State: Can It Work?" *Regulation & Governance* 4 (2010): 113–34.

Bouwen, P. "Corporate Lobbying in the European Union: The Logic of Access." *Journal of European Public Policy* 9, no. 3 (2002): 365–90.

Bouwen, P. "Exchanging Access Goods for Access: A Comparative Study of Business Lobbying in the European Union Institutions." *European Journal of Political Research* 43, no. 3 (2004): 337–69.

Bouwen, P. "The Logic of Access to the European Parliament: Business Lobbying in the Committee on Economic and Monetary Affairs." *Journal of Common Market Studies* 42, no. 3 (2004): 473–95.

Bouwen, P., and M. McCown. "Lobbying versus Litigation: Political and Legal Strategies of Interest Representation in the European Union." *Journal of European Public Policy* 14, no. 3 (2007): 422–43.

Boyer, Y. "Technologies, défense et relations transatlantiques," *Politique étrangère* 59, no. 4 (Winter 1994/95): 1005–15.

Bromley, Mark. *The EU Defence Market: Balancing Effectiveness with Responsibility*, edited by Alyson J. K. Bailes and Sara Depauw. Brussels: Flemish Peace Institute, 2011.

Brooks, S., and W. C. Wohlforth. "Hard Times for Soft Balancing." *International Security* 30, no. 1 (2005): 72–108.

Broscheid, A., and D. Coen. "Insider and Outsider Lobbying of the European Commission: An Informational Model of Forum Politics." *European Union Politics* 4, no. 2 (2003): 165–91.

Broscheid, A., and D. Coen. "Lobbying Activity and for a Creation in the EU: Empirically Exploring the Nature of the Policy Good." *Journal of European Public Policy* 14, no. 3 (2007): 346–65.

Burley, A., and W. Mattli. "Europe before the Court: A Political Theory of Legal Integration." *International Organization* 47, no. 1 (1993): 41–76.

Burns, C. "Codecision and the European Commission: A Study of Declining Influence?" *Journal of European Public Policy* 11, no. 1 (2004): 1–18.

Burns, T. R., and M. Carson. "Actors, Paradigms, and Institutional Dynamics: The Theory of Social Rule Systems Applied to Radical Reforms." In *Advancing Socio-Economics: An Institutionalist Perspective*, edited by J. Rogers Hollingsworth, Karl H. Mueller, and Ellen Jane Hollingsworth, 109–47. Oxford, UK: Rowman & Littlefield, 2002.

Büthe, T. "Governance through Private Authority: Non-State Actors in World Politics." *Journal of International Affairs* 58, no. 1 (2004): 281–91.

Butt Philip, A. *Directory of Pressure Groups in the European Community*. London, UK: Longman, 1991.

Butt Philip, A. "Pressure Groups and Policy-Making in the European Community." In *Institutions and Policies of the European Union*, edited by Juliet Lodge, 21–26. London, UK: Frances Pinter, 1983.

Butt Phillip, A. "Pressure Groups in the European Community, Working Paper No. 2." University Association of Contemporary European Studies Working Groups, London, UK: UACES, 1985.

Butt Philip, A., and O. Gray. *Directory of Pressure Groups in the EU*. London, UK: Cartermill Publishing, 1994.

Butt Philip, A. "Business Alliances, Network Construction and Agenda Definition: Recent Development in Lobbying Activities in Brussels and Strasbourg." EUSA Conference, Seattle, WA, May 29–June 1, 1997.

Callaghy, T. M. *The State–Society Struggle: Zaire in Comparative Perspective*. New York, NY: Columbia University Press, 1984.

Carpenter, Daniel P. *The Forging of Bureaucratic Autonomy: Reputations, Networks, and Policy Innovation in Executive Agencies, 1862–1928*. Princeton, NJ: Princeton University Press, 2001.

Caviedes, A. "The Difficult Transition to Transnational Interest Representation: The Case of Immigration Policy." EUSA Conference, March 31–April 2, 2005.

Caviedes, A. "The Open Method of Coordination in Immigration Policy: A Tool for Prying Open Fortress Europe?" *Journal of European Public Policy* 11, no. 2 (2004): 289–310.

Caviedes, Alex. "Troubled Transnationalism. Diverging National and EU-Level Social Partner Preferences in Immigration Policy." Paper presented at a conference titled European Integration: Past, Present and Future, Kitchener, Ontario, pp. 1–33. 2010.

Caviedes, Alexander. *Prying Open Fortress Europe: The Turn to Sectoral Labor Migration*. Lanham, MD: Lexington Books, 2010.

Chopin, I., and J. Niessen. "Combating Racism in the European Union with Legal Means: A Comparison of the Starting Line and the EU Commission's Proposal for a Race Directive." Brussels: Migration Policy Group, 2000.

Christiansen, T. "The European Commission: Administration in Turbulent Times." In *European Union, Power and Policy-Making*, edited by Jeremy Richardson, 95–114. New York, NY: Routledge, 1996/2001.

Cobb, R. W., and C. D. Elder. *Participation in American Politics. The Dynamics of Agenda-Building*. Baltimore, MD: The Johns Hopkins University Press, 1972.

Coen, D. "Business Interests and Integration." In *Collective Action in the European Union*, edited by R. Bulme, D. Chambre, and V. Wright, 225–72. Paris, France: Science-Po Press, 2002.

Coen, D. "Environmental and Business Lobbying Alliances in Europe: Learning from Washington?" In *Business in International Environmental Governance: A Political Economy Approach*, edited by D. Levy and P. Newell, 197–220. Cambridge, MA: MIT Press, 2004.

Coen, D. "The Impact of US Lobbying Practice on the European Business–Government Relationship." *California Management Review* 41, no. 4 (1999): 27–44.

Coen, D. "The European Business Interest and the Nation State: Large-Firm Lobbying in the European Union and Member States." *Journal of Public Policy* 18, no. 1 (1998): 75–100.

Coen, D. "The Evolution of the Large Firm as a Political Actor in the European Union." *Journal of European Public Policy* 4, no. 1 (1997): 91–108.

Collie, L. "Business Lobbying in the European Community: The Union of Industrial and Employers' Federation of Europe." In *Lobbying in the European Community*, edited by S. Mazey and J. Richardson, 213–30. New York, NY: Oxford University Press, 1993.

Court, J., P. Kristen, and B. Weder. "Bureaucratic Structure and Performance: First Africa Survey Results." United Nations University Tokyo, 1999. http://www.unu.edu/hq/academic/Pg_area4/pdf/unu-research.pdf

Culpepper, Pepper D. *Quiet Politics and Business Power: Corporate Control in Europe and Japan.* New York, NY: Cambridge University Press, 2010.

Cutler, A. C., V. Haufler, and T. Porter. *Private Authority and International Affairs.* Albany: State University of New York Press, 1999.

d'Appollonia, Ariane Chebel. *Frontiers of Fear: Immigration and Insecurity in the United States and Europe.* Ithaca, NY: Cornell University Press, 2012.

Deutch, J. M. "Consolidation of the US Defence Industrial Base." *Defence Acquisition Review Journal* (Fall 2001): 137–152.

Dinan, D. *Ever Closer Union: An Introduction to European Integration.* Boulder, CO: Lynne Rienner, 1999.

Donahue, J. D., and M. A. Pollack. "Centralization and its discontents: the rhythms of federalism in the United States and the European Union." In *The Federal Vision: Legitimacy and Levels of Governance in the United States and the European Union: Legitimacy and Levels of Governance in the United States and the European Union*, edited by Kalypso Nicolaidis and Robert Howse, 73–117. Oxford: Oxford University Press, 2001.

Dostal, J. M. "Campaigning on Expertise: How the OECD Framed EU Welfare and Labour Market Policies – and Why Success Could Trigger Failure." *Journal of European Public Policy* 11, no. 3 (2004): 440–60.

Dowdy, J. "Winners and Losers in the Arms Industry Downturn." *Foreign Policy* 107 (Summer 1997): 88–103.

Downs, A. *Inside Bureaucracy.* Little, Brown Boston, 1967.

Dür, A. "Measuring Interest Group Influence in the EU: A Note on Methodology." *European Union Politics* 9, no. 4 (2008): 559–76.

Dür, A., and D. De Bievre. "Inclusion without Influence: NGOs in European Trade Policy," *Journal of Public Policy* 27, no. 1 (2007): 79–101.

Dür, A., and D. De Bievre. "The Question of Interest Group Influence," *Journal of Public Policy* 27, no. 1 (2007): 1–12.

Edler, Jakob, and Andrew D. James. "Understanding the Emergence of New Science and Technology Policies: Policy Entrepreneurship, Agenda Setting and the Development of the European Framework Programme." *Research Policy* 44, no. 6 (2015): 1252–65.

Eising, R. "Multilevel Governance and Business Interests in the European Union." *Governance* 17, no. 2 (2004): 211–46.

Eising, R. "The Access of Business Interests to EU Institutions: Toward Elite Pluralism?" *Journal of European Public Policy* 14, no. 3 (2007): 384–403.

Eising, Rainer. *The Access of Business Interests to European Union Institutions: Notes Toward a Theory*. Working Paper No. 29. University of Oslo, Norway, ARENA Institute for European Studies, 2005.

Eising, R., and B. Kohler-Koch. *The Transformation of Governance in the European Union*. London, UK: Routledge, 1999.

Eising, Rainer, and Beate Kohler-Koch. *Interessenpolitik in Europa*. Baden-Baden: Nomos, 2005.

Eliassen, Kjell A., and Nick Sitter. "Arms Procurement in the European Union: Achieving Mission Impossible." Oslo: Norwegian School of Management. *Report* 4 (2006).

Ernst & Young, "The UK Defence Industry: Securing Its Future" London, UK: Ernst & Young. May 1994, p. 9.

Ernst & Young, "Prospects for the European Land Arms Industry" London, UK: Ernst & Young. October 1994.

European Parliament. 2003. "Lobbying in the European Union: current rules and practice," Directorate for Research Working Paper AFCO 104, April 2003.

Evans, P. B. *Embedded Autonomy: States and Industrial Transformation*. Princeton, NJ: Princeton University Press, 1995.

Evans, Peter. "The State as Problem and Solution: Predation, Embedded Autonomy and Structural Change." In *The Politics of Economic Adjustment: International Constraints, Distributive Conflicts, and the State*, edited by Stephan Haggard and Robert R. Kaufman, 176–92. Princeton, NJ: Princeton University Press, 1992.

Evans, Peter B. "Predatory, Developmental, and Other Apparatuses: A Comparative Political Economy Perspective on the Third World State." *Sociological Forum* 4, no. 4 (1989): 561–87.

Evans, P. B., and J. E. Rauch. "Bureaucracy and Growth: A Cross-National Analysis of the Effects of 'Weberian' State Structures on Economic Growth." *American Sociological Review* (1999): 748–65.

Evans, P. B., and J. E. Rauch. "Bureaucratic Structure and Bureaucratic Performance in Less Developed Countries." *Journal of Public Economics* 75, no. 1 (2000): 49–71.

Evans, Peter B., Dietrich Rueschemeyer, and Theda Skocpol. *Bringing the State Back In*. New York, NY: Cambridge University Press, 1985.

Favell, A. "The European Union: Immigration, Asylum and Citizenship." *Journal of Ethnic and Migration Studies* 24, no. 4 (1998, Oct): 705–88.

Favell, Adrian. "Citizenship and Immigration: Pathologies of a Progressive Philosophy." *Journal of Ethnic and Migration Studies* 23, no. 2 (1997): 173–95.

Favell, A., and A. Geddes. "Immigration and European Integration: New Opportunities for Transnational Mobilization?" In *Challenging Immigration and Ethnic Relations Politics: Comparative European Perspectives*, edited by R. Koopmans and P. Statham, 407–28. New York, NY: Oxford University Press, 2000.

Fligstein, N. "Markets as Politics: A Political Cultural Approach to Market Institutions." *American Sociological Review* 61 (1996): 656–73.

Fligstein, N. "Social Skill and the Theory of Fields." *Sociological Theory* (2001): 105–25.

Fligstein, N. *The Transformation of Corporate Control.* Cambridge, MA: Harvard University Press, 1990.

Fligstein, Neil. *Euroclash: The EU, European Identity, and the Future of Europe.* Oxford: Oxford University Press, 2008.

Fligstein, N., and J. McNichol. "The Institutional Terrain of the EU." In *European Integration and Supranational Governance,* edited by A. Stone Sweet and H. Sandholtz, 59–91. Oxford: Oxford University Press, 1998.

Fligstein, N., and A. Stone Sweet. "Constructing Polities and Markets: An Institutionalist Account of European Integration." *American Journal of Sociology* 107 (2002): 1206–43.

Florini, A. *The Right to Know: Transparency for an Open World.* New York, NY: Columbia University Press, 2007.

Follesdal, A., and S. Hix. "Why There Is a Democratic Deficit in the EU: A Response to Majone and Moravcsik" *Journal of Common Market Studies* 44, no. 3 (2006): 533–62.

Fordham, Benjamin O. *Building the Cold War Consensus: The Political Economy of U.S. National Security Policy, 1949–51.* Ann Arbor: University of Michigan Press, 1998.

Freeman, Gary P. "Modes of Immigration Politics in Liberal Democratic States." *International Migration Review* (1995): 881–902.

Gansler, J. *The Road Ahead: Accelerating the Transformation of Department of Defense Acquisition and Logistics Processes and Practices.* Washington, DC: Department of Defense, 2000.

Geddes, A. *European Integration and Immigration.* Manchester, UK: Manchester University Press, 1999.

Geddes, A. "Lobbying for Migrant Inclusion in the European Union: New Opportunities for Transnational Advocacy?" *Journal of European Public Policy* 7, no. 4 (2000): 632–49.

Geddes, Andrew. "Immigrant and Ethnic Minorities and the EU's 'Democratic Deficit.'" *JCMS: Journal of Common Market Studies* 33, no. 2 (1995): 197–217.

Geddes, Andrew. *The Politics of Migration and Immigration in Europe.* London, UK: Sage, 2003.

Geddes, Andrew. "The Representation of Migrants' Interests in the European Union." *Journal of Ethnic and Migration Studies* 24, no. 4 (1998): 695–713.

Geddes, B. *Politician's Dilemma: Building State Capacity in Latin America.* Berkeley: University of California Press, 1994.

Gerschenkron, Alexander. *Economic Backwardness in Historical Perspective: A Book of Essays.* No. HC335 G386. Cambridge, MA: Belknap Press of Harvard University Press, 1962.

Gilpin, R. *The Political Economy of International Relations.* Princeton, NJ: Princeton University Press, 1987.

Givens, T., and A. Luedtke. "The Politics of European Union Immigration Policy: Institutions, Salience, and Harmonization." *The Policy Studies Journal*, 32, no. 1 (2004): 145–65.

Greif, Avner, and David D. Laitin. "A Theory of Endogenous Institutional Change." *American Political Science Review* 98, no. 4 (2004): 633–52.

Grindle, Merilee S. "Policy Content and Context in Implementation." In *Politics and Policy Implementation in the Third World*, edited by M. S. Grindle, 3–34. Princeton, NJ: Princeton University Press, 1980.

Goldthorpe, J. H. *Order and Conflict in Contemporary Capitalism.* Oxford: Clarendon Press, 1984.

Gornitzka, A., and U. Sverdrup. "Who Consults? The Configuration of Expert Groups in the European Union." *West European Politics* 31, no. 4 (2008): 725–50.

Gourevitch, Peter. "The Second Image Reversed: The International Sources of Domestic Politics." *International Organization* 32, no. 4 (1978): 881–912.

Grande, E. "The State and Interest Groups in a Framework of Multi-Level Decision-Making: The Case of the European Union." *Journal of European Public Policy* 3, no. 3 (1996): 318–38.

Gray, E., and P. Statham. "Becoming European? The Transformation of the British Pro-migrant NGO Sector in Response to Europeanization." *JCMS: Journal of Common Market Studies* 43, no. 4 (2005): 877–98.

Green Cowles, M. G. "Organizing Industrial Coalitions: A Challenge for the Future?" In *Participation and Policymaking in the European Union*, edited by H. Wallace and A. Young, 116–40. Oxford: Clarendon Press, 1997.

Green Cowles, M. G. "Setting the Agenda for a New Europe: The ERT and EC 1992." *Journal of Common Market Studies* 33, no. 4 (1995, December): 501–26.

Green Cowles, M. G. "The EU Committee of AmCham: The Powerful Voice of American Firms in Brussels." *Journal of European Public Policy* 3, no. 3 (1996, September): 339–58.

Green Cowles, Maria. "The Transatlantic Business Dialogue and Domestic Business-Government Relations." In *Transforming Europe: Europeanization and domestic change*, edited by Maria Green Cowles, James A. Caporaso, and Thomas Risse-Kappen, 159–79. Ithaca, NY: Cornell University Press, 2001.

Greenwood, J. *Representing Interests in the European Union.* Basingstoke: Palgrave, 1997, 2003.

Greenwood, Justin, Jürgen R. Grote, and Karsten Ronit. *Organized Interests and the European Community.* London, UK: Sage, 1992.

Greenwood, J., L. Strangward, and L. Stanich. "The Capacities of EuroGroups in the Integration Process." *Political Studies* 47 (1999): 127–38.

Grindle, M. S. *Politics and Policy Implementation in the Third World.* Princeton, NJ: Princeton University Press, 1980.

Guay, T. *At Arm's Length: European Union and Europe's Defence Industry.* Basingstoke, UK: Palgrave Macmillan, 1998.

Guay, T. *The Transatlantic Defence Industrial Base: Restructuring Scenarios and Their Implications*, Monograph. Carlisle, PA: Strategic Studies Institute, 2005.

Guild, E. "Competence, Discretion and Third Country Nationals: The European Union's Legal Struggle with Migration." *Journal of Ethnic and Migration Studies* 24, no. 4 (1998): 613–25.

Guild, E. *The Developing Immigration and Asylum Law of the EU.* Dordercht, the Netherlands: Kluwer, 1995.

Guiraudon, V. "De-Nationalizing Control. Analyzing State Responses to Constraints on Migration Control." In *Controlling a New Migration World*, edited by Virginie Guiraudon and Christian Joppke, 31–64. London, UK: Routledge, 2001.

Guiraudon, V. "Policy Change behind Gilded Doors: Explaining the Evolution of Aliens' Rights in Contemporary Western Europe." Doctoral dissertation, Harvard University, 1997.

Guiraudon, V. "The Constitution of a European Immigration Policy Domain: A Political Sociology Approach." *Journal of European Public Policy* 10, no. 2 (2003): 263–82.

Guiraudon, Virginie. "European Integration and Migration Policy: Vertical Policy-Making as Venue Shopping." *JCMS: Journal of Common Market Studies* 38, no. 2 (2000): 251–71.

Guiraudon, Virginie. "Third Country Nationals and European Law: Obstacles to Rights' Expansion." *Journal of Ethnic and Migration Studies* 24, no. 4 (1998): 657–74.

Haas, E. B. *The Uniting of Europe: Political, Social and Economic Forces, 1950–1957.* Stanford, CA: Stanford University Press, 1958.

Haggard, Stephan, and Chung-In Moon. "Institutions and Economic Policy: Theory and a Korean Case Study." *World Politics* 42, no. 2 (1990): 210–37.

Hall, Peter A. *Governing the Economy: The Politics of State Intervention in Britain and France.* Oxford: Oxford University Press, 1986.

Hall, Peter A., and R. C. R. Taylor. "Political Science and the Three New Institutionalisms." *Political Studies* 44, no. 5 (1996): 936–57.

Hall, R. B., and T. J. Biersteker. *The Emergence of Private Authority in Global Governance.* Cambridge, UK: Cambridge University Press, 2002.

Hartley, K., "The Future of European Defence Policy: An Economic Perspective," *Defence and Peace Economics* 14, no. 2 (January 2003): 107–15.

Haufler, V., and T. Porter. "The Contours and Significance of Private Authority in International Affairs." *Private Authority and International Affairs* (1999): 333–76.

Helmke, Gretchen, and Steven Levitsky. "Informal Institutions and Comparative Politics: A Research Agenda." *Perspectives on Politics* 2, no. 4 (2004): 725–40.

Hirschman, A. O. *Shifting Involvements: Private Interest and Public Action.* Princeton, NJ: Princeton University Press, 2002.

Hix, S. *The Political System of the European Union.* New York, NY: St. Martin's Press, 1999.

Hix, S. *What's Wrong with the European Union and How to Fix It.* Cambridge: Polity Press, 2008.

Hix, Simon. "The Study of the European Union II: The 'New Governance' Agenda and its Rival." *Journal of European Public Policy* 5, no. 1 (1998): 38–65.

Hobson, B. "Feminist Strategies and Gendered Discourses in Welfare States: Married Women's Right to Work in the United States and Sweden." In *Mothers of a New World: Maternalist Politics and the Origins of Welfare States,* edited by Seth Koven and Sonya Michel. 396–429. London, UK: Routledge, 1993.

Hofbauer, Joachim, Roy Levy, Gregory Sanders, Guy Ben-Ari, and David Berteau. *European Defense Trends: Budgets, Regulatory Frameworks, and the Industrial Base: A Report of the CSIS Defense-Industrial Initiatives Group.* Washington, DC: Center for Strategic and International Studies, 2010.

Hoffmann, S. "Obstinate or Obsolete? The Fate of the Nation-State and the Case of Western Europe." *Daedalus* 95, no. 3 (1966): 862–915.

Hooghe, L., and G. Marks. "Optimality and Authority: A Critique of Neoclassical Theory." *JCMS: Journal of Common Market Studies* 38, no. 5 (2000): 795–816.

Howorth, J. *European Security and Defence Policy.* Basingstoke, UK: Palgrave, 2007.

Huntington, Samuel P. *Political Order in Changing Societies.* New Haven, CT: Yale University Press, 1968.

Huysmans, J. "Migrants as a Security Problem: Dangers of 'Securitizing' Societal Issues." In *Migration and European Integration,* edited by R. Miles and D. Thränhardt, 53–72. London, UK: Pinter, 1995.

Huysmans, J. "The EU and the Securitization of Migration." *Journal of Common Market Studies* 38, no. 5 (2000): 751–78.

Huysmans, Jef. *The Politics of Insecurity: Fear, Migration and Asylum in the EU.* London, UK: Routledge, 2006.

Ikenberry, G. John. *Reasons of State: Oil Politics and the Capacities of American Government.* Ithaca, NY: Cornell University Press, 1988.

Imig, D., and S. Tarrow. *Contentious Europeans: Protest and Politics in an Emerging Polity.* Oxford, UK: Rowman & Littlefield, 2001.

Imig, D., and S. Tarrow. "The Europeanisation of Movements? A New Approach to Transnational Contention." In *Social Movements in a Globalizing World,* edited by D. della Porta, H. Kriesi, & D. Rucht, 112–33. London, UK: Macmillan, 1999.

Ingraham, Patricia W., Philip G. Joyce, and Amy Kneedler Donahue. *Government Performance: Why Management Matters.* New York, NY: Taylor & Francis, 2003.

Ireland, Patrick R. "Asking for the Moon: The Political Participation of Immigrants in the European Union." In *The Impact of European Integration: Political, Sociological, and Economic Changes,* edited by George A. Kourvetaris and Andreas Moschonas, 131–50. Westport, CT: Praeger, 1996.

Jabko, N. *Playing the Market: A Political Strategy for Uniting Europe, 1985–2005.* Ithaca, NY: Cornell University Press, 2006.

Jackman, R. W. *Power without Force: The Political Capacity of Nation-States.* Ann Arbor: University of Michigan Press, 1993.

James, A. D. "Comparing European Responses to Defence Industry Globalisation." *Defence and Security Analysis* 18, no. 2 (2002): 123–43.

Johnson, C. A. *MITI and the Japanese Miracle: The Growth of Industrial Policy, 1925–1975.* Stanford, CA: Stanford University Press, 1982.

Jones, S. *The Rise of European Security Cooperation.* Cambridge: Cambridge University Press, 2007.

Jones, S. G. "The Rise of a European Defence." *Political Science Quarterly* 121, no. 2 (2006): 241–67.

Kallas, S. "The Need for a European Transparency Initiative." Speech at the The European Foundation for Management, Nottingham Business School, March 3, 2005, Nottingham, UK.

Kapstein, Ethan B. *The Political Economy of National Security: A Global Perspective.* New York, NY: McGraw-Hill Humanities, Social Sciences & World Languages, 1992.

Katzenstein, P. J. *Between Power and Plenty: Foreign Economic Policies of Advanced Industrial States.* Madison: University of Wisconsin Press, 1978.

Katzenstein, P. J. *Small States in World Markets: Industrial Policy in Europe.* Ithaca, NY: Cornell University Press, 1985.

Keck, M. E., and K. Sikkink. *Activists Beyond Borders. Advocacy Networks in International Politics.* Ithaca, NY: Cornell University Press, 1998.

Kelemen, R. D. "Built to Last? The Durability of EU Federalism." In *Making History: European Integration and Institutional Change at Fifty,* edited by S. Meunier and K. R. McNamara, 51–66. New York, NY: Oxford University Press, 2007.

Keleman, R. D. "The Politics of 'Eurocratic' Structure and the New European Agencies." *West European Politics* 25, no. 4 (2002): 93–118.

Keohane, R. O. *After Hegemony: Cooperation and Discord in the World Political Economy.* Princeton, NJ: Princeton University Press, 1984.

Kingdon, J. W. *Agendas, Alternatives, and Public Policies,* 2nd ed. New York, NY: HarperCollins, 1995.

Kirchner, Emil J. "International Trade Union Collaboration and the Prospects for European Industrial Relations." *West European Politics* 3, no. 1 (1980): 124–38.

Kirshner, Jonathan. "Political Economy in Security Studies after the Cold War." *Review of International Political Economy* 5, no. 1 (1998): 64–91

Knack, S., and P. Keefer. "Institutions and Economic Performance: Cross-Country Tests Using Alternative Institutional Measures." *Economics & Politics* 7, no. 3 (1995): 207–27.

Knoke, D., and J. H Kuklinski. *Network Analysis.* London, UK: Sage, 1982.

Koenig, Thomas, and Robert Gogel. "Interlocking Corporate Directorships as a Social Network." *American Journal of Economics and Sociology* 40, no. 1 (1981): 37–50.

Kohler-Koch, B. "Changing Patterns of Interest Intermediation in the EU." *Government and Opposition* 29, no. 2 (1994): 166–83.

Kohler-Koch, B., and R. Eising. *The Transformation of Governance in the European Union*. London, UK: Routledge, 1999.

Kohler-Koch, Beate. "Catching Up with Change: The Transformation of Governance in the European Union." *Journal of European Public Policy* 3, no. 3 (1996): 359–80.

Kostakopoulou, T. "The 'Protective Union': Change and Continuity in Migration Law and Policy in Post-Amsterdam Europe." *Journal of Common Market Studies* 38, no. 3 (2000): 497–518.

Krasner, S. D. "Sovereignty: An Institutional Perspective." In *The Elusive State*, edited by J. Caporaso, 87–103. Beverly Hills, CA: Sage, 1989.

Krasner, S. D. "Structural Causes and Regime Consequences: Regimes as Intervening Variables." *International Organization* 36, no. 2 (1982): 185–205.

Krasner, Stephen D. *Defending the National Interest: Raw Materials Investments and U.S. Foreign Policy*. Princeton, NJ: Princeton University Press, 1978.

Krasner, Stephen D. "Sovereignty an Institutional Perspective." *Comparative Political Studies* 21, no. 1 (1988): 66–94.

Kugler, J., and W. Domke. "Comparing the Strength of Nations." *Comparative Political Studies* 19, no. 1 (1986): 39–69.

Lahav, Gallya. "Immigration and the State: The Devolution and Privatisation of Immigration Control in the EU." *Journal of Ethnic and Migration Studies* 24, no. 4 (1998): 675–94.

Lahusen, C. "Commercial Consultancies in the European Union: The Shape and Structure of Professional Interest Intermediation." *Journal of European Public Policy* 9, no. 5 (2002): 695–714.

Lahusen, C. "Moving into the European Orbit: Commercial Consultancies in the European Union." *European Union Politics* 4, no. 2 (2003): 191–218.

LaPira, Tim, and Herschel F. Thomas. "Congressional Analytic Capacity, Party Polarization, and the Political Economy of Revolving Door Lobbying." Paper Presented at the American Political Science Association Meeting, August 9, 2016, Philadelphia, PA.

Larsson, T. "Precooking in the European Union. The World of Expert Groups." *ESO*, 2003. www.grondweteuropa.nl/9310000/d/europa/zwedneso.pdf.

Larsson, T., and J. Trondal. "Agenda Setting in the European Commission." In *EU Administrative Governance*, edited by Herwig C. H. Hofmann and Alexander H. Türk, 11–43. Cheltenham, UK: Elgar, 2006.

Laumann, E. O., and D. Knoke. *The Organizational State: Social Choice in National Policy Domains*. Madison: University of Wisconsin Press, 1987.

Laumann, Edward O., and David Knoke. "Policy Networks of the Organizational State: Collective Action in the National Energy and Health Domains." 17–56. In *Networks of Power: Organizational Actors at the National, Corporate, and Community Levels*, edited by Robert Perrucci and Harry R. Potter. Livingston, NJ: Transaction, 1989.

Lavenex, S. "The Europeanization of Refugee Policies: Normative Challenges and Institutional Legacies." *JCMS: Journal of Common Market Studies* 39, no. 5 (2001): 851–74.

Lavenex, Sandra. *Safe Third Countries: Extending the EU Asylum and Immigration Policies to Central and Eastern Europe*. Budapest, Hungary: Central European University Press, 1999.

Levi, Margaret. *Of Rule and Revenue*. Berkeley: University of California Press, 1988.

Levi, Margaret. "The State of the Study of the State." In *Political Science: The State of the Discipline*, edited by Ira Katznelson and Helen V. Milner, 33–55. New York, NY: W. W. Norton, 2002.

Lindblom, C. E. *Politics and Markets: The World Economic System*. New York, NY: Basic Books, 1977.

Lindberg, L. N. *The Political Dynamics of European Economic Integration*. Stanford, CA: Stanford University Press, 1963.

Lindberg, L. N., and S. A. Scheingold. *Europe's Would-Be Polity: Patterns of Change in the European Community*. Englewood Cliffs, NJ: Prentice Hall, 1970.

Lovering, J. "Which Way to Turn? The European Defence Industry after the Cold War." In *Arming the Future: A Defence Industry for the 21st Century*, edited by A. Markusen and S. Costigan, 334–70. New York, NY: Council on Foreign Relations Press, 1999.

Lowery, D., and V. Gray. "A Neopluralist Perspective on Research on Organized Interests." *Political Research Quarterly* 57, no. 1 (2004): 163–75.

Lowery, David, and Virginia Gray. "How Some Rules Just Don't Matter: The Regulation of Lobbyists." *Public Choice* 91, no. 2 (1997): 139–47.

Lowery, D., C. Poppelaars, and J. Berkhout. "The European Union Interest System in Comparative Perspective: A Bridge Too Far?." *West European Politics* 31, no. 6 (2008): 1231–52.

Luedtke, A. "Uncovering EU immigration legislation: Policy Dynamics and Outcomes." EUSA Conference, May 17–19, 2007, Montreal, Canada.

Luedtke, Adam. "European Integration, Public Opinion and Immigration Policy Testing the Impact of National Identity." *European Union Politics* 6, no. 1 (2005): 83–112.

Mahoney, C. *Brussels versus the Beltway: Advocacy in the United States and the European Union*. Washington, DC: Georgetown University Press, 2008.

Mahoney, C. "Networking vs. Allying: The Decision of Interest Groups to Join Coalitions in the US and the EU." *Journal of European Public Policy* 14, no. 3 (2007): 366–83.

Mahoney, C. "The Power of Institutions. State and Interest Group Activity in the European Union." *European Union Politics* 5, no. 4 (2004): 441–66.

Majone, G. "A European Regulatory State?" In *European Union: Power and Policy-Making*, edited by J. Richardson, 263–77. London, UK: Routledge, 1996.

Majone, G. "Two Logics of Delegation. Agency and Fiduciary Relations in EU Governance." *European Union Politics* 2, no. 1 (2001): 103–22.

Majone, G. "The European Commission: The Limits of Centralization and the Perils of Parliamentarization." *Governance* 15, no. 3 (2002): 375–92.

Majone, Giandomenico. "Europe's 'Democratic Deficit': The Question of Standards." *European Law Journal* 4, no. 1 (1998): 5–28.

Mann, M. *The Sources of Social Power.* Cambridge: Cambridge University Press, 1984.

Marks, G., and D. McAdam. "Social Movements and the Changing Structure of Political Opportunity in the European Union." *West European Politics* 19, no. 2 (1996): 249–78.

Marks, G., L. Hooghe, and K. Blank. "European Integration from the 1980s: State-Centric v. Multi-level Governance." *JCMS: Journal of Common Market Studies* 34, no. 3 (1996): 341–78.

Marks, G., & M. Steenbergen. "Understanding Political Contestation in the European Union." *Comparative Political Studies,* 35 (2002): 879–92.

Mastanduno, Michael. "Economics and Security in Statecraft and Scholarship." *International Organization* 52, no. 4 (1998): 825–54.

Matthews, Felicity. "Governance and State Capacity." *The Oxford Handbook of Governance* (2012): 281–93.

Mattli, W. "Public and Private Governance in Setting International Standards." *Governance in a Global Economy: Political Authority in Transition* (2003): 199–225.

Mattli, W., and T. Büthe. "Accountability in Accounting? The Politics of Private Rule-Making in the Public Interest." *Governance: An International Journal of Policy, Administration, and Institutions* 18, no. 3 (2005): 399–429.

Mauro, P. "Corruption and Growth." *The Quarterly Journal of Economics* 110, no. 3 (1995): 681–712.

Mawdsley, J. *A European Agenda for Security Technology: From Innovation Policy to Export Controls.* Brussels: Flemish Peace Institute, 2013.

May, Peter J. "Policy Design and Implementation." *Handbook of Public Administration* (2003): 223–33.

Mazey, Sonia. "The European Union and Women's Rights: From the Europeanization of National Agendas to the Nationalization of a European Agenda?" *Journal of European Public Policy* 5, no. 1 (1998): 131–52.

Mazey, S., and J. Richardson (eds.). *Lobbying in the European Community.* Oxford: Oxford University Press, 1993.

Mazey, S., and J. Richardson. "Interest Groups and EU Policy-Making: Organizational Logic and Venue Shopping." In *European Union: Power and Policy-Making,* edited by J. Richardson, 247–65. London, UK: Routledge, 1996/2001/2006.

Mazey, Sonia, and Jeremy Richardson. "Interests." In *Developments in the European Union,* edited by Laura Cram, Desmond Dinan, and Neill Nugent, 105–29. London, UK: St. Martin's Press, 1999.

McCarthy, J. D., and M. Zald. "Resource Mobilization and Social Movements: A Partial Theory." *American Journal of Sociology* 82, no. 6 (1977): 1212–41.

Meier, K. J. *Regulation: Politics, Bureaucracy, and Economics.* London, UK: Palgrave Macmillan, 1985.

Meyer, J. W., and W. R. Scott. *Organizational Environments: Ritual and Rationality.* Beverly Hills, CA: Sage, 1983.

Meynaud, J., and D. Sidjanski. *Les groupes de pression dans la Communauté européenne, 1958–1968: Structure et action des organisations professionnelles.* Brussels: Éditions de l'Institut de sociologie (de l'Université libre de Bruxelles), 1971.

Michalowitz, I. "EU Lobbying: Chaos or Functional Divisions?" Paper presented at the European Consortium for Political Research, September 6–8, 2001, University of Kent at Canterbury, England.

Michalowitz, Irina. "What Determines Influence? Assessing Conditions for Decision-Making Influence of Interest Groups in the EU 1." *Journal of European Public Policy* 14, no. 1 (2007): 132–51.

Michels, Roberto. "Authority." In *Encyclopedia of the Social Sciences, Vol. II.* New York, NY: Macmillan, 1930.

Migdal, J. S. *Strong Societies and Weak States: State–Society Relations and State Capabilities in the Third World.* Princeton, NJ: Princeton University Press, 1988.

Mitsilegas, V., J. Monar, and W. Rees. *The European Union and Internal Security: Guardian of the People?* Basingstoke, UK: Palgrave/Macmillan, 2003.

Moon, Myung-Jae, and Patricia Ingraham. "Shaping Administrative Reform and Governance: An Examination of the Political Nexus Triads in Three Asian Countries." *Governance* 11, no. 1 (1998): 77–100.

Moore, Gwen. "The Structure of a National Elite Network." *American Sociological Review* (1979): 673–92.

Moraes, C. "The Politics of European Union Migration Policy." *Political Quarterly* 74, no. 4 (2003): 116–31.

Moravcsik, A. "In Defence of the 'Democratic Deficit': Reassessing Legitimacy in the European Union." *Journal of Common Market Studies* 40, no. 4 (2002): 603–24.

Moravcsik, A. "Preferences and Power in the European Community: A Liberal Intergovernmentalist Approach." *Journal of Common Market Studies* 31, no. 4 (1993): 473–524.

Moravcsik, A. *The Choice for Europe: Social Purpose and State Power from Messina to Maastricht.* Ithaca, NY: Cornell University Press, 1998.

Mörth, U. *European Public-Private Collaboration: A Choice between Efficiency and Democratic Accountability?* Cheltenham, UK: Edward Elgar, 2008.

Mörth, U. *Organizing European Cooperation: The Case of Armaments.* Lanham, MD: Rowman & Littlefield, 2005.

Mörth, U. *Soft Law in Governance and Regulation: An Interdisciplinary Analysis.* Cheltenham, UK: Edward Elgar, 2004.

Nanz, K. "The Harmonisation of Asylum and Immigration Legislation within the Third Pillar of the Union Treaty – A Stocktaking." In *The Third Pillar of the European Union: Co-operation in the Field of Justice and Home Affairs,* edited by J. Monar and R. Morgan, 123–33. Bruges, Belgium: European Interuniversity Press and College of Europe, 1994.

Neal, A. W. 2009. "Securitization and Risk at the EU Border: The Origins of FRONTEX." *Journal of Common Market Studies* 47, no. 2 (2009): 333–56.

Nielson, D. L., and M. J. Tierney. "Delegation to International Organizations: Agency Theory and World Bank Environmental Reform." *International Organization* 57, no. 2 (2003): 241–76.

Niemann, A. "Dynamics and Countervailing Pressures of Visa, Asylum and Immigration Policy Treaty Revision: Explaining Change and Inertia from the Amsterdam IGC to the Constitutional Treaty." In 9th Biennial EUSA Conference, Austin, 2005. Available at http://aei.pitt.edu/3079/01/EUSA2005_paper_A.Niemann_JHA-final.pdf

Niemann, Arne. "Dynamics and Countervailing Pressures of Visa, Asylum and Immigration Policy Treaty Revision: Explaining Change and Stagnation from the Amsterdam IGC to the IGC of 2003–04." *JCMS: Journal of Common Market Studies* 46, no. 3 (2008): 559–91.

Niessen, J. "Overlapping Interests and Conflicting Agendas: The Knocking into Shape of EU Immigration Policies." *European Journal of Migration and Law* 3, no. 3 (2001): 419–34.

Niessen, Jan. "The Amsterdam Treaty and NGO Responses." *European Journal of Migration and Law* 2, no. 2 (2000): 203–14.

North, D. C. *Institutions, Institutional Change, and Economic Performance.* Cambridge: Cambridge University Press, 1990.

North, D. C. *Understanding the Process of Economic Change.* Princeton, NJ: Princeton University Press, 2005.

North, Douglass Cecil. *Structure and Change in Economic History.* New York, NY: W. W. Norton, 1981.

Nugent, N. *The Government and Politics of the European Union,* 4th ed. Basingstoke, UK: Palgrave, 2003.

Oxfam. *Foreign Territory: The Internationalisation of EU Asylum Policy.* London, UK: Oxfam, 2005.

Painter, Martin, and Jon Pierre. "Unpacking Policy Capacity: Issues and Themes." In *Challenges to State Policy Capacity,* edited by Martin Painter and Jon Pierre, 1–18. London, UK: Palgrave Macmillan UK, 2005.

Palomar, T. "Migration Policies of the European Union." In *The Politics of Immigration in the EU,* edited by Jochen Blaschke, 88–92. Berlin, Germany: Parabolis, 2004.

Pappi, F. U., and C. H. C. A. Henning. "The Organisation of Influence on the EC's Common Agricultural Policy: A Network Approach." *European Journal of Political Research* 36 (1999): 257–81.

Paul, T. V., et al. *Balance of Power: Theory and Practice in the 21st Century.* Stanford, CA: Stanford University Press, 2004.

Pedler, R. H, and M. Van Schendelen. *Lobbying the European Union: Companies, Trade Associations and Issue Groups.* Aldershot, UK: Dartmouth, 1994.

Peters, L., and J. Verrinder. "The Size of the Government Sector from Different Perspectives." Paper presented at The Size of the Government Sector: How to Measure: 24th The European Advisory Committee Information in the Economic and Social Spheres (CEIES) seminar, Vienna, Austria, October 23–24, 2003.

Peterson, John. "The European Union: Pooled Sovereignty, Divided Accountability." *Political Studies* 45, no. 3 (1997): 559–78.

Pierson, Paul. "Increasing Returns, Path Dependence, and the Study of Politics." *American Political Science Review* 94, no. 2 (2000): 251–67.

Polanyi, K. *The Great Transformation: The Political and Economic Origins of our Time*. Boston, MA: Beacon Press, 1944.

Pollack, M. *Delegation, Agency, and Agenda Setting in the European Community*. Cambridge: Cambridge University Press, 2003.

Pollack, M. "Representing Diffuse Interests in EC Policy-Making." *Journal of European Public Policy* 4, no. 4 (1997): 572–90.

Pollak, J., and P. Slominski. "Experimentalist but Not Accountable Governance? The Role of Frontex in Managing the EU's External Borders." *West European Politics* 32, no. 5 (2009): 904–24.

Posen, B. R. "European Union Security and Defence Policy: Response to Unipolarity?" *Security Studies* 15, no. 2 (2006): 149–86.

Princen, S. "Agenda-Setting in the European Union: A Theoretical Exploration and Agenda for Research." *Journal of European Public Policy* 14, no. 1 (2007): 21–38.

Princen, S., and B. Kerremans. "Opportunity structures in the EU multi-level system." Paper presented at the CONNEX Research Group 4 Civil Society and Interest Representation in EU-Governance. Leiden, NL, April 14–16, 2005.

Princen, S., and M. Rhinard. "Crashing and Creeping: Agenda-Setting Dynamics in the European Union." *Journal of European Public Policy* 13, no. 7 (2006): 1119–32.

Richardson, J. "Policy-Making in the EU: Interests, Ideas and Garbage Cans of Primeval Soup." In *European Union, Power and Policy-Making*, edited by J. Richardson, 3–26. New York, NY: Routledge, 1996/2001/2006.

Riker, William H. *The Art of Political Manipulation*, Vol. 587. New Haven, CT: Yale University Press, 1986.

Rodrigues, C. *International Management: A Cultural Approach*. Los Angeles, CA: South-Western, 2001.

Rosamond, B. *Theories of European Integration*. New York, NY: St. Martin's Press, 2000.

Sabatier, P. A. "An Advocacy Coalition Framework of Policy Change and the Role of Policy-Oriented Learning Therein." *Policy Sciences* 21 (1988): 129–68.

Samuels, R. J. *The Business of the Japanese State: Energy Markets in Comparative and Historical Perspective*. Ithaca, NY: Cornell University Press, 1987.

Sandholtz, W., and A. Stone Sweet. *European Integration and Supranational Governance*. Oxford, UK: Oxford University Press, 1998.

Sandholtz, W., and J. Zysman. "1992: Recasting the European Bargain." *World Politics: A Quarterly Journal of International Relations* 42, no. 1 (1989): 95–128.

Scharpf, F. W. "Legitimacy in the Multi-Actor European Polity." In *Organizing Political Institutions. Essays for J. P. Olsen*, edited by M. Egeberg and P. Lægreid, 261–88. Oslo, Norway: Scandinavian University Press, 1999.

Scharpf, F. W. "Negative and Positive Integration in the Political Economy of European Welfare States." In *Governance in the European Union*, edited by

G. Marks, F. W. Scharpf, P. W. Schmitter, and W. Streeck, 15–39. London, UK: Sage, 1996.

Schattschneider, E. E. *The Semi-Sovereign People*. New York, NY: Harcourt Brace College, 1960/1975.

Schmidt, V. "Procedural Democracy in the EU: The Europeanization of National and Sectoral Policy-Making Processes." *Journal of European Public Policy* 13, no. 5 (2006): 670–91.

Schmidt, Vivien A. *The EU and Its Member-States: Institutional Contrasts and Their Consequences*. Working Paper No. 99/7. Köln, Germany: Max Planck Institute for the Study of Societies, 1999.

Schmitter, Philippe C. "Imagining the Future of the Euro-polity with the Help of New Concepts." In *Governance in the European Union*, edited by Gary Marks, Fritz W. Scharpf, Philippe C. Schmitter, and Wolfgang Streeck, 1–14. London, UK: Sage, 1996.

Schmitter, P. C., and G. Lehmbruch, eds. *Trends toward Corporatist Intermediation*. London, UK: Sage, 1979.

Schneider, G., and K. Baltz. "The Power of Specialization: How Interest Groups Influence EU Legislation." *Rivista di Politica Economica* 93, no. 1–2 (2003): 1–31.

Schneider, G., D. Finke, and K. Baltz. "With a Little Help from the State: Interest Intermediation in the Domestic Pre-negotiations of EU Legislations." *Journal of European Public Policy* 14, no. 3 (2007): 444–59.

Schuknecht, L., A. Afonso, and V. Tanzi. 2003. "Public Sector Efficiency: An International Comparison." Frankfurt: Germany, European Central Bank, ECB *Working Paper Series*.

Sidjanski, D. "Pressure Groups and the European Economic Community." In *The New International Actors: The United Nations and the European Economic Community*, edited by C. Cosgrove and K. Twitchett, 222–48. London, UK: Macmillan, 1970.

Skocpol, Theda. "Bringing the State Back In: Strategies and Analysis of Current Research." In *Bringing the State Back In*, edited by Peter B. Evans, Dietrich Rueschemeyer, and Theda Skocpol, 3–43. New York, NY: Cambridge University Press, 1985.

Skowronek, S. *Building a New American State: The Expansion of National Administrative Capacities, 1877–1920*. Cambridge: Cambridge University Press, 1982.

Slaughter, A. M., A. Stone Sweet, and J. Weiler. *The European Court and National Courts – Doctrine and Jurisprudence: Legal Change in Its Social Context*. New York, NY: Bloomsbury Press, 1998.

Smith, A. *Politics and the European Commission: Actors, Interdependence, Legitimacy*. London, UK: Routledge, 2004.

Smith M. A. *American Business and Political Power: Public Opinion, Elections, and Democracy*. Chicago, IL: University Chicago Press, 2000.

Smith, Mitchell P. "How Adaptable Is the European Commission? The Case of State Aid Regulation." *Journal of Public Policy* 21, no. 3 (2001): 219–38.

Smyrl, M. E. "When (and How) Do the Commission's Preferences Matter?" *JCMS: Journal of Common Market Studies* 36, no. 1 (1998): 79–100.

Soifer, Hillel, and Matthias vom Hau. "Unpacking the Strength of the State: The Utility of State Infrastructural Power." *Studies in Comparative International Development (SCID)* 43, no. 3 (2008): 219–30.

Solana, J. "Preface," *EU Security and Defence Policy – The First Five Years (1999–2004)*, edited by N. Gnesotto, 5–10. Paris, France: Institute for Security Studies, European Union, 2004.

Stark, David, and Laszlo Bruszt. *Postsocialist Pathways: Transforming Politics and Property in East Central Europe.* Cambridge: Cambridge University Press, 1998.

Stensöta, Helena Olofsdotter. "Impartiality and the Need for a Public Ethics of Care." In *Good Government: The Relevance of Political Science*, edited by Sören Holmberg & Bo Rothstein, 87–149. Cheltenham, UK: Edward Elgar, 2012.

Stockholm International Peace Research Institute. *SIPRI Yearbook 2011: Armaments, Disarmament and International Security.* Oxford: Oxford University Press, 2011.

Stone Sweet, A. *Governing with Judges: Constitutional Politics in Europe.* Oxford: Oxford University Press, 2000.

Stone Sweet, A., and T. L. Brunell. "Constructing a Supranational Constitution: Dispute Resolution and Governance in the European Community." *American Political Science Review* 92, no. 1 (1998): 63–81.

Strange, Susan. *The Retreat of the State: The Diffusion of Power in the World Economy.* Cambridge: Cambridge University Press, 1996.

Streeck, W., and K. A. Thelen. *Beyond Continuity: Institutional Change in Advanced Political Economies.* New York, NY: Oxford University Press, 2005.

Streeck, W., and P. C. Schmitter. "From National Corporatism to Transnational Pluralism." *Politics and Society* 19, no. 2 (1991): 133–65.

Tallberg, J. "The Agenda-Shaping Powers of EU Council Presidency." *Journal of European Public Policy* 10, no. 1 (2003): 1–19.

Tallberg, Jonas, and Christer Jönsson. "Transnational Actor Participation in International Institutions: Where, Why, and With What Consequences?" In *Transnational Actors in Global Governance*, edited by Christer Jönsson and Jonas Tallberg, 1–21. London, UK: Palgrave Macmillan UK, 2010.

Teles, V. K. "Institutional Quality and Endogenous Economic Growth." *Journal of Economic Studies* 34, no. 1 (2007): 29–41.

Thurber, J. A. "Representation, Accountability, and Efficiency in Divided Party Control of Government." *PS: Political Science and Politics* (1991): 653–57.

Tigner, B. "Transatlantic Harmony Faces Many Obstacles." *Defence News* 10, no. 21 (May 29, 1995)

Tillotson, Amanda R. "Open States and Open Economies: Denmark's Contribution to a Statist Theory of Development." *Comparative Politics* 21, no. 3 (1989): 339–54.

Tilly, Charles. *Coercion, Capital, and European states, AD 990–1992.* Hoboken, NJ: Wiley-Blackwell, 1992.

Torfing, J., and E. Sorenson. "Network Politics, Political Capital and Democracy." *International Journal of Public Administration* 26 (2002): 609–34.

Trauner, F. *EU Justice and Home Affairs Strategy in the Western Balkans: Conflicting Objectives in the Pre-Accession Strategy*. Brussels: Centre for European Policy Studies, 2007.

Truman, D. B. *The Governmental Process: Political Interests and Public Opinion*. New York, NY: Alfred A. Knopf, 1951.

Tsai, Kellee S. "Adaptive Informal Institutions and Endogenous Institutional Change in China." *World Politics* 59, no. 1 (2006): 116–41.

Tsebelis, G. "The Power of the European Parliament as a Conditional Agenda Setter." *American Political Science Review* 88, no. 1 (1994): 128–42.

Uslaner, E. M. 2005. "The Bulging Pocket and the Rule of Law: Corruption, Inequality, and Trust." Paper presented at "The Quality of Government: What It Is, How to Get It, Why It Matters" Conference, November 17–19, 2005, at the Quality of Government Institute, Göteborg University Sweden.

Van de Walle, S. "The State of the World's Bureaucracies." *Journal of Comparative Policy Analysis: Research and Practice* 8, no. 4 (2006): 437–48.

Van de Walle, Steven. "Measuring Bureaucratic Quality in Governance Indicators." Paper presented at the 8th Public Management Research Conference, Los Angeles, California, 2005.

van Schendelen, M. P. C. M. *EU Committees as Influential Policymakers*. London, UK: Ashgate, 1998.

van Schendelen, M. P. C. M. *Machiavelli in Brussels: The Art of Lobbying the EU*. Amsterdam: Amsterdam University Press, 2002.

Vogel, D. *Fluctuating Fortunes: The Political Power of Business in America*. New York, NY: Basic Books, 1989.

Walker, W. and P. Gummett, "Britain and the European Armaments Market." *International Affairs* 65, no. 3 (Summer 1989): 419–42.

Warleigh, A. "'Europeanizing' Civil Society: NGOs as Agents of Political Socialization." *Journal of Common Market Studies* 39, no. 4 (2001): 619–39.

Warleigh, A. "The Hustle: Citizenship Practice, NGOs and 'Policy Coalitions' in the European Union – The Cases of Auto Oil, Drinking Water and Unit Pricing." *Journal of European Public Policy* 7, no. 2 (2000): 229–43.

Watts, J. *Immigration Policy and the Challenge of Globalization: Unions and Employers in Unlikely Alliance*. Ithaca, NY: Cornell University Press, 2002.

Weber, M. *Economy and Society*, translated by Guenther Roth and Claus Wittich. New York, NY: Bedminster Press (Originally published 1922), 1968/1978.

Weiss, L. *The Myth of the Powerless State*. Ithaca, NY: Cornell University Press, 1998.

Weiss, L., and J. M. Hobson. *States and Economic Development: A Comparative Historical Analysis*. Cambridge, MA: Polity Press, 1995.

Wessels, B. "Contestation Potential of Interest Groups in the EU: Emergence, Structure, and Political Alliances." In *European Integration and Political Conflict*, edited by G. Marks and M. Steenbergen, 195–215. Cambridge: Cambridge University Press, 2004.

Wessels, B. "European Parliament and Interest Group." In *The European Parliament, the National Parliaments, and European Integration*, edited by R. Katz and B. Wessels, 107–28. Oxford: Oxford University Press, 1999.

Wessels, Wolfgang. "An Ever Closer Fusion? A Dynamic Macropolitical View on Integration Processes." *JCMS: Journal of Common Market Studies* 35, no. 2 (1997): 267–99.

Wessels, Wolfgang. "Comitology: Fusion in Action. Politico-Administrative Trends in the EU System." *Journal of European Public Policy* 5, no. 2 (1998): 209–34.

Williamson, O. E. "Visible and Invisible Governance." *The American Economic Review* 842 (1994): 323–26.

Woll, C. "Lobbying in the European Union: From Sui Generis to a Comparative Perspective." *Journal of European Public Policy* 133 (2006): 456–69.

Wonka, A., F. R. Baumgartner, C. Mahoney, and J. Berkhout. "Measuring the Size and Scope of the EU Interest Group Population." *European Union Politics* 11, no. 3 (2010): 463–76.

Yee, A. S. "Cross-National Concepts in Supranational Governance: State–Society Relations and EU Policy Making." *Governance* 174 (2004): 487–524.

Zakheim, D. *Toward a Fortress Europe?* Washington, DC: Center for Strategic and International Studies, Nov. 2002.

Zegart, Amy B. *Flawed by Design: The Evolution of the CIA, JCS, and NSC.* Stanford, CA: Stanford University Press, 2000.

Zysman, J. *Governments, Markets, and Growth: Financial Systems and the Politics of Industrial Change.* Ithaca, NY: Cornell University Press, 1983.

Index

Ad Hoc Group on Immigration, 202
Advisory Council for Aeronautics
    Research, 178
AECMA. *See* European Association of
    Aerospace Industries (AECMA)
Aerospace and Defence Industrial
    Association of Europe (ASD), 157,
    161, 162, 188, 191, 228, 233, 254
AFSJ. *See* Justice and Home Affairs (JHA)
ALTER-EU, 63
Amnesty International, 205, 217
Amsterdam Treaty, 1, 89, 171, 172, 198,
    206, 207, 215, 216, 218, 219, 220,
    221
ASD. *See* Aerospace and Defence
    Industrial Association of Europe
    (ASD)
Association of the European Space
    Industry (EUROSPACE), 159, 161
Asylum Directives, 209
authority, 7
    legitimacy, 7
    political, xi, 2, 3, 4, 5, 19–25, 28, 33,
        47, 50, 114, 117, 141, 160, 163, 199,
        256

BAE, 152, 155, 173, 187, 228, 245
Bringing the State Back In, 28
bureaucracy, 27
    autonomy, 3, 28, 35
    effectiveness, 36
    interest groups, 24
    international, 110, 260
    legitimacy, 28, 256
    quality, 110
    structure, 26
    uncertainty, 22–24
    Weberian, 116
Burson-Marsteller, 62

capacity, 43, 71, 255, 261
    bureaucratic, 2, 32, 40, 45, 118

coercive, 31
corporatist, 35
external, xi, 3
extractive, 31
governed interdependence, 47
governing, 2, 15, 17, 24, 28, 33, 46, 79,
    101
infrastructural, 32
legitimacy, 8
security, 248
state, 28, 113
transformational, 24, 34, 38
CFSP. *See* Common Foreign and Security
    Policy (CFSP)
Civilian Headline Goal, 252
Common Agricultural Policy (CAP), 59
Common Foreign and Security Policy
    (CFSP), 41, 144, 156, 172
Common Security and Defence Policy
    (CSDP), xii, 1, 14, 17, 74, 130–144,
    163, 164, 169, 172, 175, 179, 190,
    249, 252
corruption, 4, 15, 39, 47, 65, 114,
    118

DARPA. *See* Defense Advanced Research
    Projects Agency
Dassault, 155, 245
Defense Advanced Research Projects
    Agency (DARPA), 145, 178
defense industry, 17
    civil society, 254
    consolidation, 151
    European, 142, 152
    interest groups, 16, 140
DG V. *See* Social Affairs Directorate
    (DG V)
DTIB. *See* European Defence
    Technological Industrial Base
dual-use technology, 16, 150, 159, 160,
    170, 171, 188, 229, 230, 253
Dublin Convention, 202, 203